TABLE OF CONTENTS

Acknowledgments 13

Foreword 17

Prologue 27

Chapter One: Save Wilson! 41

Chapter Two: The Alumnae vs. The Board of Trustees 167

Chapter Three: The Aftermath and Perspectives 227

Chapter Four: Beginning Again 110 Years Later: 1979-1981 297

Chapter Five: Securing the Future: 1981-1989 359

Epilogue 425

SOURCES

1. The Wilson College Archives: Save Wilson
2. Wilson College Quarterlies
3. Wilson College Press Releases
4. Wilson College Alumnae Newsletters
5. Wilson College Annual Reports
6. Minutes of the Board of Trustees
7. Franklin County Court of Common Pleas, Orphans Court Division: Testimony Transcripts, Court Decision and Decree Nisi
8. The New York Times, New York, New York
9. The Public Opinion, Chambersburg PA
10. The Associated Press in Wilmington Delaware Journal
11. The Pittsburgh Post-Gazette, Pittsburgh, PA
12. The Tribune-Review, Greensburg, PA
13. News-Chronicle, Shippensburg, PA
14. The Chronicle of Higher Education
15. Journal of Fund-Raising Management (no longer in print)
16. Carlisle Evening Sentinel, Carlisle, PA
17. Lancaster New Era
18. Trustees, Trusteeship and the Public Good: Issues of Accountability for Hospitals, Museums, Universities and Libraries, Quorum Books
19. Telegram from the President of the United States
20. Alice L. Beeman Case Study
21. Boston Magazine
22. American Council on Education
23. Change Magazine

24. Association of Governing Board Reports
25. The Moon Report from the Academy of Educational Development
26. Report from the Middle States Accrediting Association
27. Personal Journal of Nan Hudnut Clarkson
28. Sermon by the Reverend Virginia Leopold '63
29. Writings from Nancy Adams Besch, Joan Foresman Edwards, Carol Ann Tschop from Archives
30. Writings submitted to the author for the book by Martha Baum Walker, Anne Pearce Lehman, Donald Bletz, Gwen Jensen, Lorna Edmundson and Barbara Mistick
31. Personal calls and emails to the author

IN HONOR OF THE SAVE WILSON LEADERSHIP VOLUNTEERS: ALUMNAE AND OTHERS

Carol Phillips Bauer '58
Nancy Adams Besch '48
Julia Billings Crothers '38
C. Elizabeth Boyd '32
Susan Breakfield-Fulton '61
Carolyn Smithson Burger '62
Joan Foresman Edwards '58
Jane Troutman Ensminger '52
Jane Taylor Fox '59
Phyllis Gansz-Green '50
Leslie J. Gottschalk '74
Marilyn R. Mumford '56

Joyce Morrison '70
Madelon Nordquist
Marcia Kirchoff Rodenhaver '49
Eudora R. Roseman '63
Carolyn Trembly Shaffer '50
Jane Sheller
Drew Steis
Dolly Swisher '73
Kathi Torpy '72
Carol Tschop '72
Gretchen Van Ness '80
Marie Williams '62

It is impossible to name everyone who helped—literally hundreds of alumnae and spouses and friends were a part of saving Wilson College. Those named above gave extraordinary effort and were at the center of the activity. Please consider this page in honor of every single person who took part in Save Wilson.

IN HONOR OF THE PETITIONERS AND THOSE WHO TESTIFIED FOR THE ALUMNAE AT THE TRIAL

PETITIONERS

Jean Colgan Zehner, trustee; David Platt, faculty; Isabel Fulton, Mrs. J. McLain King, Nancy Adams Besch, alumnae; Karen Devey, senior; Gretchen Van Ness, junior; Susan Nussbaum, sophomore; Laurel Bauer, freshman; Merry Hope Maloy, admitted students for fall, 1979.

TESTIFIED

FACULTY
James Applegate
Harry Buck
Jose Diaz
David Grove
David Platt

STAFF
Deborah Cramer
Kathryn Louise Haines
John Mason

STUDENTS
Laurel Bauer
Susan Nussbaum
Gretchen Van Ness

ALUMNAE
Nancy Besch
Susan Brooks
Susan Fulton
Leslie Gotschalk
Mary King
Janet Henry Riley
Carolyn Shaffer
Mary Stevens
Phoebe Tobin

Board of Trustees
Jean Zehner

Church
J. William Royer

Experts
David Ascell
Marjorie Bell Chambers
William F. Elliott
Dean Kelsey
Elizabeth Tidball

IN HONOR OF THE BOARD OF THE ALUMNAE ASSOCIATION
1979 and 1980

For their devoted and hard work towards keeping open and rebuilding their beloved college.

Joanne Sotzing Bast
Julia E. Billings
Carolyn Smithson Burger
Karen Ellensen Coulson
Elizabeth Ann Diely
Jane Troutman Ensminger
Jane Taylor Fox
Celeste Van Sickel Gallup
Phyllis R. Gansz
Leslie Gottschalk
Martha Sloan Greenawalt
Susan Hagerty
Kimberley L. Hurst
Cornelia Van Altena Lentz
Marilyn R. Mumford
Patricia Raff Riley
Eudora K. Roseman
Virginia Gehr Stackel
Jane Rambo Stewart
Carolyn Trembley Shaffer
Mary I. Stephens
Marguerite Kauffman Thomas
Nannette P. Willis

IN HONOR OF THE BOARD OF TRUSTEES 1979-1981

For the courage and passion to assume the legal and fiduciary responsibility of a college ordered by the court to remain open!

Nancy Adams Besch
Beatrice Fenner Blackadar
Susan Breakefield-Fulton
Robert W. Brown
Elethea Hitchens Caldwell
Elizabeth Hudnut Clarkson
Robert G. Crist
Jane Troutman Ensminger
Phyllis R. Gansz
Caryl Kline
Basil L. Livas
George C. Mason
Donald E. May
Jane Morris
John H. Myers
Sidney M. Palmer
Ella Dohrman Pethick
George H. Pike
Gloria Scott
Mary I. Stephens
Stanley Stillman
H. Woodruff Turner
Edgar A. Yale

IN HONOR OF FACULTY 1979-1981

These faculty deserve endless credit and gratitude for staying with the College when there was no certainty that the obstacles to its existence could be overcome. For some years after 1979- 80, they accepted the sad fact that there would be no increases in compensation. Low pay, increased workload, no leaves and countless challenges were just some of the ways the faculty made sacrifices contributing to the success of the college. Most stayed well into the 1980's and many beyond!

Nadine R. Anderson, Assistant Professor of Psychology
Raymond Kemp Anderson, Associate Professor of Religion Studies
Virginia R. Anderson-Stojanovic, Assistant Professor of Classics and Fine Arts
James Earl Applegate, Professor of English
Eugene L. Beecher, Assistant Professor of Elementary Education
Calvin Hobson Blair, Associate Professor of Economics
Florence Techer Bloom, Professor of History
Kip B. Branch, Assistant Professor of Fine Arts and Physical Education
Alice Martin Brumbaugh, Associate Professor of Sociology
Harry Merwyn Buck, Professor of Religion Studies
Vern Buckles, Associate Professor of German
Theony Condos, Associate Professor of Classics
Trina A. Collins, Assistant Professor of Fine Arts and Physical Education
Robert L. Coon, Associate Professor of Fine Arts
Robert Franklin Curtis, Professor of Political Science
Jose A. Diaz, Professor of Spanish
Joyce E. Donatelli, Assistant Professor of Physical Education
Kathy Loren Ermler, Assistant Professor of Physical Education
Charles Jacob Farris, Associate Professor of Music
Godfrey Leonard Gattiker, Associate Professor of English Suzanne Gilliotte-Blumenthal, Associate Professor of French
Karin Glassman, Director of Equitation and Instructor of Physical Education

Robert Glick, Assistant Professor of Biology
Davison Greenawalt Grove, Professor of Biology
Donald L. Henry, Associate Professor of Physics
Alice L. Ingraham, College Librarian
Joseph H. Mancuso, Assistant Professor of Fine Arts
Helen Adams Nutting, Professor of History
David Sellers Platt, Professor of Philosophy
Walter O. Portmann, Professor of Mathematics
Vasant H. Raval, Assistant Professor of Business Studies
Donald Ruch, Assistant Professor of Biology
Thankamma E. Varkey, Assistant Professor of Chemistry

IN HONOR OF THE CLASS OF 1979

To those in the Class of 1979 who worked diligently to engage the alumnae and joined them in the effort to Save Wilson!

Chandrani Amarasinghe
Martha McCurdy
Karen Lynn Arigot
Eleanor Philip McHugh
Cheryl Lynette Kathryn Bauman
Madlyn A. McPartland
Josephine Anne Beinincasa
Betty Ora Grace Mesler
Lisa Dawn Bivona
Kimberly Ann Minor
Michele Lynn Bredau
Leslie Kerry Murphy
Deborah Sue Brown
JoAnn Marie Murray
Gwen A. Cherry
Becky Ellen Myers
Elizabeth-Anne Clark
Duyen Thi Hong Nguyen
Cindy Joyce Comstock
Linda M. Peirce
Kathy Ann Corcelius
Janet Claire Serdy
Laurie Jean Covert
Audrey Merryn Sharp
Jaye Ann Cunningham
Stephanie Anne Shoemaker
Karen Lynne Devey
Gillian Linville Shuman
Colleen Driscoll
Linda M. Shuman
Lynda Carolyn Eggiman
Susan Lynette Snoberger
Cecelia Terese Elder
Margaret Marie Spede
Lynn Marie Feliziani
Jane Spicher
Carol Jane Gibson
Gretchen M. Thomson
Marjorie Ale Halpine
Waraphan Thoopthong
Janet Peters Hargrave
Wendy Louise Von Plinsky
Susan Gurney Hayward
Leslie Anita Walker
Mary Cathryn Hendricks
Susan Kay White
Elizabeth Hull
Linda Marie Whiteley
Tina M. Krauss
Sara Workeneh-Martin
Jeanne Kay Marshall
Barbara Diane Mattheu
Shirley A. Maxwell

IN HONOR OF THE CLASS OF 1980

We pay honor to those students who had no security—only faith—in the fact that the college would survive.

Melissa Ann Allen
Alicia Peyton Armstrong
Phyllis Jean Bard
Laura Sue Barrett
Louise Elizabeth Barsy
Susan Elizabeth Bryson
Lora G. Bucher
Mary Elizabeth Campbell
Susan Garle Czibik
Gail A. D'Avino
Arilda Elskus
Joan Elizabeth Geary
Sandra Jean Graffley
Kendal Leah Hopkins
Zahra Karbelay Seyed Hossein
Pamela Randi Johnson
Ingrid Klimanskis
Carol A. Kipe
Gwendolyn Shank McEntire
Kathryn Michele Safran
Cindy S. Sebastian
Kathyrn Frances Smith
Robin A. Smith
Karen Ann Steiner
Deirdre Cope Sutter
Lynn J. Torrey
Gretchen Marie Van Ness
Charlotte A. Wilt
Maria L. Zapp

IN HONOR OF THE STAFF 1979 and 1980

With very small budgets at their command and few, in any salary increases, the staff worked diligently, tirelessly and creatively to see that the students were served, that programs were created and that policies were followed.

Donald F. Bletz, President

Marilyn R. Mumford, Provost for External Affairs

Theony Condos, Dean of College Alice Ingraham, College Librarian
   Elizabeth Boyd, Library Director Alice L. Leighty, Registrar

Adeline Thompson, Assistant to Registrar

   Carman A. Jordan-Cox, Dean of Students

   Susan D. Waring, Director of Career Planning and Counseling

   Linda K. Byrnes, Coordinator of Counseling Services

   Herbert H. Nauss, Jr., Director of Student Services

   Marjorie Castro, College Nurse

   Dorothy L. Peters, College Nurse

   Frank J. Kamus, Director of Admissions

   Debbie Cramer, Admissions

   Kathryn Haines White, Director of Financial Aid

   Cheryl A. Wilhite, Assistant, Director of Admissions

   Gloria Weagley, System 6 Technology

   Annabelle Foster, Secretary, Admissions

Kathi A. Torpy, Director of Alumnae Affairs

Bonnie Rosenbaum, Assistant Director of Alumnae Office

Ethaline Cortelyou, Volunteer Coordinator

James R. Hyatt, Business Manager Alan D. Sheeley, Comptroller

Alan McKee, Head of Security

Carol A. Tschop, Director of Development

Jeannette B. Lehman, Assistant Director of Development

Jo-Ann E. Morisse, Contracts and Grants Officer

Margaret Taylor, Director of Public Affairs

Richard Brunner, Director of Information and Publications

Mary Emmons, Communications and Post Office

Shirley Moul, Bookstore

ACKNOWLEDGMENTS

Nancy Adams Besch, Class of 1948, was my collaborator throughout the entire process. She provided much of the material, guided my thinking, and read every word multiple times. Joan Foresman Edwards, '58, was also deeply involved until her death on August 25, 2019. Nancy Besch and I pay tribute to Joan Foresman Edwards, '58 and to Carol Tschop, '72. Joan served in so many volunteer capacities at the college—president of the Alumnae Association, member of the Board of Trustees, and all-around volunteer in whatever activity needed her! Carol deserves honor for her volunteerism and for her invaluable work as Director and then Vice President of College Advancement from 1979-1991. In later years she, with Joan and Nancy, organized and wrote some of the materials contained in this book.

> **I am most grateful for those who gave so generously and unstintingly of their time, talent, energy and support during the writing/compiling of this book:**
>
> **Dr. Donald Bletz, Dr. Gwen Jensen, Dr. Lorna Edmundson, and Dr. Barbara Mistick** all contributed to the book.
>
> **Nan Hudnut Clarkson**, '47, for her personal diaries written during the time of 1979- 1982. Nan served as Chairman of the Board of Trustees from June 1979 to June 1982 and took copious notes.
>
> **Drs. Patricia and Raymond Cormier, H. Woodruff Turner** and my dear husband, **Dr. Peter Armacost**, for the hours they

invested in reading and commenting with some superb ideas to improve the book.

Carla Dean Day, '63, a part-time copyeditor and a graduate of the College, who did much of the copy editing.

Lynne DiStasio, President of the Alumnae Association for writing letters to secure reprint permissions and with the **Board of the Alumnae Association** saw that the book was published. **Marybeth Famulare,** Director of Alumnae Relations, helped to gather information and keep the book moving forward.

Anne Pearce Lehman, '49 contributed some background found in the Prologue.

President Barbara Mistick and her staff followed by **Dr. Richard Kneedler**, Interim President who assured full access and support for this effort. **Amy Ensley** and **Kieran McGhee** worked overtime to get the necessary archival material.

Martha Walker, Chairman of the Board during the time of the crisis, contributed to this book and helped assure me that this is a fair representation of what happened.

I joyfully and gratefully chose to take on this assignment to honor the work of Nancy Adams Besch, '48, Joan Foresman Edwards, '58 and Carol Ann Tschop, '72 as well as the literally hundreds of alumnae who over this ten-year period of time shared their time, talent and treasure to keep the momentum of this College going. The vindication of their works lies, in no small part, with the presidencies following mine: Gwendolyn Jensen (1991-2001), Lorna Duphiney Edmundson (2001-2011), and Barbara K. Mistick (2011- 2019).

And, finally, on a personal note, Wilson was and remains the highlight of my professional life. I pay homage to my dear Mother, Madeleine Case Sorber (known in college as Casey), Class of 1930. Her father was "bull elder" in the First Presbyterian Church in Jeannette, Pennsylvania, and was an early advocate for women's education in general and Wilson College in particular. He died while Mother, age 19, was in college. Her love, guidance and influence on me cannot be over-estimated, both in pursuing an education and in my career. I cannot conceive of my ten years at Wilson without her constant prayers, guidance and support.

Mary-Linda Sorber Merriam Armacost
October 14, 2019

FOREWORD

Many original sources are quoted in full or in part in this book. The materials from various sources had been categorized and kept in the Wilson College Archives including the court transcripts. Nancy Adams Besch, Joan Foresman Edwards, and Carol Ann Tschop were responsible for categorizing the archival material in and around 2012. My job has been to draw from and, in many cases, quote from these and other sources. Some notes from which I have drawn had no named person; I could not properly attribute them although I use quotations. The attempt has been to tell the story in the words of those involved using their voices as written at the time or later as they reflected on the events. There were handwritten and some typed notes, one 20-page written account, an invaluable chronology of events of the Save Wilson effort, newspaper and journal articles, and four case studies, including one I had put together for my module on "Small Colleges," taught at the University of Pennsylvania periodically from 2005, with the years 2014-2017 centering on Wilson. For the years 1981-1990, I had many documents saved from my presidency from which I drew.

The chronology of the Save Wilson College Committee guides Chapter One of this book. Chapter Two summarizes the main themes with many quotations from the Court Proceedings, the transcripts of the testimony, and the Adjudication and *Decree Nisi*. Chapter Three recounts the aftermath of the Court decision taken from minutes of the Board of Trustees, articles and personal perspectives of key people involved in the court case. Chapter Four chronicles critical events in the reorganization led by Dr. Donald Bletz. Chapter Five focuses on key events and the results in the continuing building of the College which I had the privilege of leading. The Epilogue summarizes the major accomplishments of the three succeeding Presidents—Dr. Gwendolyn Jensen, Dr. Lorna Edmundson and Dr. Barbara Mistick—in the ongoing building and strengthening of the College as it continued to change throughout the years to keep pace with the times.

"A College on the Rise - Wilson continues to make strides" is the cover page of the Fall 2017 volume of the *Wilson Quarterly*. What greater testimony could there be to the remarkable and amazing work of Save Wilson than forty years later seeing continued growth. Such success is attributable to the capable and committed leadership of all constituencies and a willingness to change with the times. From the article in the Quarterly entitled *Wilson Recognized for Value, Quality* written by Cathy Mentzer:

> Wilson's programs, affordability and value, and overall quality are increasingly gaining recognition nationwide. In the 2018 *U.S. News and World Report* "Best Colleges" guide, released in September, Wilson College was ranked fifth in the "best value" category among regional colleges in the North and was rated 11th overall in the same classification. Wilson also was named a "best college for veterans," ranking sixth in the North region.
>
> In addition, Wilson was named one of the nation's Colleges of Distinction for its "commitment and proven achievement" in a variety of areas. According to Colleges of Distinction, the College has created a unique learning environment where students not only earn college degrees and valuable life experiences but also participate in character-building first-year seminars, spring break service programs, multidisciplinary study, service-learning programs, undergraduate research, study-abroad and internships in a collaborative academic environment. Colleges

of Distinction is a consortium of member institutions formed in 2000.

> "Colleges of Distinction applauds Wilson College for enriching the college experience with high-impact educational practices and providing every student with an education that stretches far beyond what's typically required from an academic major," said Tyson Schritter, chief operating officer for Colleges of Distinction.
>
> According to Schritter, Colleges of Distinction is more than an annual ranking. "Our goal is to select the best schools that are 100 percent focused on the student experience and on producing the most well-rounded graduates who are prepared for a global society and economy," he said.
>
> In addition to its *U.S. News* value ranking, Wilson remains a "Tuition Hero" for holding tuition without an increase over the past seven years, affirming the College's commitment to providing a high-quality, affordable education. **(end)**

What an accolade to the women and men who worked so hard to keep this College alive who, believing in its future, were certain that it still had much to contribute. I might note that Wilson appeared in *U.S. News and World Report* in 1989, fourth among the best regional colleges—ten years after Save Wilson. The college appeared again in 1990.

Our book begins in 1979 and ends in 1989 when over one thousand alumnae, friends, students, faculty and staff came together in Laird Hall to celebrate ten years of the revitalization of Wilson College after a near closing. It was quite a night!

This is a long overdue story told in numerous articles, court documents and in the words of those who actually lived the experience of those ten years. Please note that the ways in which alumnae are named vary—largely because I was true to the words of those I have quoted.

A fitting place to begin is with the words of Joan Foresman Edwards, '58, excerpted from notes she wrote on May 26, 1999, some 20 years ago. Her intention was to write a memoir and what follows is directly quoted from a hand-written rough draft of her first few pages.

Quoting from the writings of Joan Foresman Edwards, '58:

> For twenty years a voice within [me] and my friends and strangers urged me to write down the history of the 1979 Save Wilson Story. Various accounts have been published in the media, in Wilson documents written to celebrate anniversary events, and in at least one book. However, to my knowledge, never have the events been documented by those who were the participants. Although many of the principal players in that dramatic chapter of Wilson history threatened to and/or promised to write a book, we find the task never undertaken some twenty [now forty!] years later.
>
> I believe that there are two reasons for this: (1) those persons found themselves so involved in the aftermath (the real saving of the College) on the Board, or in other volunteer roles, that there was no real time to reflect on and write the history; (2) what is in modern lingo called "political correctness" was a huge factor. Understandably, post '79 college administrators faced with the challenges of recruiting students and raising funds wished that the story of Wilson's near closing would be forgotten, the sooner the better. Others argued that the dramatic intervention of the alumnae to save one of the endangered species of women's colleges was and is a story that should be remembered and celebrated because it was a testimonial to the liberally educated woman, in particular, the "Wilson Woman" of whom we are unabashedly proud. After all, was this not what 1979 was all about? Did not the alumnae insist that the mold not be broken? Not go out of existence?
>
> ... The day in May 1979, when the court decided that the demise

of tiny Wilson College was not to be allowed, most people were shocked by the outcome. We had learned respect, admiration and a certain "underdog" appeal of the community and some of the press and even the grudging admiration of a few of the adversaries. Around here Judge Keller [Judge of the Orphan Court who decided the case] was a hero, but ultimately, in the search for whom to credit, one of our young attorneys said it best: "A classy bunch of broads."

Now "classy" means "of superior quality, stylish." I'll accept that. The origin of the slang word "broad" I'd rather not get into, except that it does stand for woman, and who can argue that Wilson alums are that? When the dust settled, we were delighted with his compliment...

The other very female thing about the situation was the exuberant use of the telephone. My husband, with four women in the family, remarked early on that I was an expert in that area. The fact is that 90% of the planning was done on the phone—the housewives during the day, the career gals far into the night. You see, we lived all over the country, and many people have remarked, probably quite accurately, that AT&T profited highly from the threatened closing. The principal figures in Save Wilson actually compared phone bills in each of those months. It seemed a badge of commitment! When the bills went back to normal, we knew the crisis was over.

If you have never joined a cause, you won't believe this story. If you have, then you will empathize. It is not only my story—thousands of Wilson Alumnae shared it—the only difference being that you lived further away and perhaps felt you were doing too little.

For those of us in Chambersburg, "on the scene," it was a period of four months of intense emotion, frustration, excitement, fear and ultimately joy. There were so many moments I ached to share with all of you—the <u>pride</u> of being one of those remarkable Wilson women who were doing such a brave and wondrous thing! Those of us who were here received so much encouragement from the reporters who had become our friends, and we tried to tell them that we were only a miniscule part of a vast alumnae body; when the judge so compassionately refused to "take possession" of our pledge cards entered in evidence; ... the <u>pride</u> when Wilson students, faculty members and alumnae quietly spoke of their commitment to their beloved College. Those courtroom moments—indeed, five long days of testimony—the parade of 33 witnesses, all from academia— five college presidents, everyone except underclassmen, possessing 1, 2, or 3 degrees— perhaps none like it ever anywhere.

The word <u>dignity</u>—perhaps maligned early on, but a byword for Wilson women—still prevails in today's student world. The current students at Wilson: women. I was at first amazed at the way in which the current students conducted themselves, but like most truths, there was a very simple explanation for their dignity + maturity under intense emotional pressure: they <u>are</u>, after all, Wilson Women! They not only started the protest, but they also enlisted us immediately and were the first to return. ... I know only a few dozen by name, but their leadership has been the only factor to sustain me through many a dark moment. Apparently, Wilson, at half strength, has the same impact on her students as it has always had.

And the faculty—present, former and *emeriti*—what a role they played! Again, I was puzzled by this unusual commitment, until I fell upon the simple truth that most of them had more years at Wilson than any of us...

My involvement was perhaps accidental, perhaps providential, as was Sarah Wilson's on whose family lands I think I live. My credentials to dare to recount historical events are simply that I am a Wilson alumna who happened to live nearby, who like so many hundreds of her sisters, became a part of the Save Wilson effort. Like so many others, that involvement led to subsequent leadership opportunities. Mine were all volunteer activities with the Alumnae Association, the Board of Trustees and related committees too numerous to mention. Others were hired by the College.

In conclusion, … the success of the effort to Save Wilson College can be attributed to the dedicated effort of a coalition of hundreds if not thousands of individuals. **(end)**

Quoting from the writings in 2012 of Carol A. Tschop, '72, titled "Wilson Narrative."

By dawn, on Monday, February 19, 1979, south-central Pennsylvania, as well as much of the northeast United States, was blanketed with nearly two feet of heavy wet snow. Schools were closed, businesses shuttered, and traffic, with the exception of the occasional snowplow, was almost non-existent. The residents of Chambersburg, Pennsylvania, drank their coffee and prepared to spend the day shoveling their sidewalks and digging out their cars.

I had just come into the house after beginning this chore when the phone rang, about 12:30 pm. I assumed the call was from a friend, calling to commiserate about the weather and the labor ahead. Instead, the caller was a Wilson College student, a member of the Kittochtinny Players, the school's drama club, for whom I had just begun to direct their spring production, *The Last of the Red Hot Lovers*. The conversation went something like this:

"Carol, you won't believe what just happened! They voted to close the College!"

"What? Who voted to close the College? What are you saying?"

Tearfully, she replied, "the Board of Trustees voted to close Wilson at the end of this academic year and to create a foundation to supposedly support women's education. We have to do something! Can the alumnae help?"

Thus, began one of the most improbable odysseys in American higher education, one that even the most creative Hollywood screenwriter could hardly imagine. Wilson College, founded in 1869, was one of the oldest women's colleges in the United States. The next 100 days would witness the improvised formation of the "Save Wilson Committee," a group of alumnae whose primary bond was a fierce devotion to their *Alma Mater* and a deep skepticism toward the institution's current leadership and its lack of transparency in decision making.

Sub-committees on everything from curriculum to admissions to fund-raising to public relations made colleagues of alumnae across the decades and the country, women who were largely strangers but who shared the special memories of their Wilson experience. These women—community volunteers, business executives, homemakers and educators—came together to raise money, hire attorneys, bring a lawsuit against the Board of Trustees, and ultimately triumph in court to win a new life for their beloved *Alma Mater*. They accomplished this through tenacity, perseverance, focus, and a single-minded belief that they were in the right. And all of this began with the "Blizzard of '79," continued through the nuclear scare of Three Mile Island, and during the nation's preoccupation with the Iran Hostage situation. What this group of determined women accomplished was unprecedented.

I've often reflected on the serendipitous conditions that made this victory possible. To begin with, the snowstorm paralyzed much of the East Coast, where a sizable percentage of Wilson's 7,000 alumnae lived. Once the news became public, alumnae had plenty of time to call their fellow Wilsonites across the country to bemoan the decision and debate whether an alternative was possible. The news spread VERY fast.

Secondly, the Governing Board of the College had vastly underestimated the potential result of their secrecy and arrogant disregard in communicating the College's difficulties to its most loyal constituency. Most alumnae were not officially informed of the decision to close until a bulk-rate mailing reached them almost three weeks after the announcement to close. By then, alumnae were thoroughly disgusted with the Board and its decision and were already organizing in opposition.

Thirdly, because the College President had not petitioned Pennsylvania's Department of Education for permission to close the College as a teaching institution, the judge assigned to the case placed the burden of proof in the case on the Board of Trustees.

Instead of the Save Wilson Committee having to prove why the College should remain open, the Board of Trustees had to prove why it should close.

Finally, one can't disregard the presence of good luck. News of several significant bequests to the College buoyed the fundraising coffers and gave renewed energy to the quest for funds to support the effort going forward. An alumnae spouse, a journalist currently between assignments, was dispatched by his wife to head up the public relations effort of the committee, resulting in daily press releases and an interview on NPR for the Save Wilson Committee chairman. A difficult decision on what kind of attorney was most suitable to try the case in Franklin

County's Orphan's Court resulted in the choice of a pair of attorneys from neighboring counties who were familiar with the rulings of the judge assigned to the case. The committee's faith in their counsel was not misplaced.

As this book will illustrate, the events of the spring of 1979 were nerve-wracking, all-consuming and unprecedented. Thirty-three years later [this was written in 2012], Wilson College is alive and planning its next chapter. Being a part of the effort was one of the greatest privileges of my life. If anyone doubts what a group of highly motivated women can accomplish, read on.

Carol A. Tschop, '72 **(end)**

What follows is the book Nancy, Joan and Carol were determined to have written!

Joan Foresman Edwards '58, Carol Ann Tschop '72, Nancy Adams Besch '48

PROLOGUE

The 1970s were a challenging time for higher education. This was no less true for Wilson College. Dr. Paul Swain Havens retired in 1970 after 34 years in office. Following a long-time president is never an easy transition and particularly so when the culture is changing. In the late 1960s and early 1970s, the role of women was transforming as was the responsibility of the College to serve *in loco parentis*. Dr. Charles Cole followed Dr. Havens and served for five years; he was followed by Dr. Lawrence Dennis for five months as Interim President, and Dr. Margaret Waggoner for four years. Declining enrollment, use of unrestricted endowment to fund operating deficits, changing relationships between students and the College with the demise of *in loco parentis*, and the changes in the roles of women all influenced Wilson in the 1970s with its roots in the late 1960s.

For small colleges (under 1,000) in rural and semi-rural areas, survival has never come easily. Many private colleges in the early 1970s were experiencing declining enrollments and operating budget deficits. The number of women's colleges dropped dramatically, with some closing and some merging. A Ford Foundation study in 1974 declared that if enrollment was under one thousand, survival was severely in doubt. Wilson's highest enrollment was 723 in 1967 and over 900 (headcount) in 1989. In 2019 it is said that a college is in danger if under 2,500. Very few small colleges are sufficiently endowed to sustain themselves primarily from endowment income.

A 1979 study done by the National Association of Independent Colleges and Universities and the Western Interstate Commission on Higher Education indicated that in Pennsylvania the number of high school graduates would drop by 24% in 1987, another 20% in 1988, and 39% in 1994. This did not tell the whole story, however, since college-aged young people (18-21 years of age) accounted for less than half the total college population by 1980. Between 1970 and 1980, the growth rate for total enrollment was more than three times as large as that of first-time enrollment. After sharp drops in the early part of the 1970s, enrollments at women's colleges held steady but more older men and women were attending college, and there was definite growth in graduate and professional schools.

The availability of a variety of federal and state options for financial aid played no small part in enrollments in private higher education. In the early 1980s, disproportionate cuts were threatened in Pell grants (for those below the poverty line); work study; supplemental educational opportunity grants that went to institutions to help with financial aid; national direct student loans; and State Student Incentive grant funding. This had major repercussions for small colleges like Wilson, where 84-90% of our students required financial aid, generally from multiple sources.

The implications of these changes were that Wilson needed to do more to attract a population beyond the traditional age of 18-21, present more flexible opportunities for education on a part- time basis, and have well-functioning continuing education credit and non-credit programs. Dr. Havens' era really ended several years before he retired in 1970. Although Dr. Cole attempted to put in a new continuing education program to respond to some of the cultural changes, the resistance within the College was too great for him to succeed.

A BRIEF HISTORY OF THE COLLEGE

Prologue

On Friday, August 31, 1979, there was a Wilson College Special Section in the *Public Opinion*. Lorrie Brooks wrote an article entitled "Wilson Pioneer in Women's Education," which included interviews with Dr. Paul Swain Havens, a son of a Wilson graduate and President of Wilson from 1936-1970, and Dean Margaret Disert. For these reasons, I chose this article as the basis for the history which can be corroborated from a number of other sources. (Reprint permission granted)

"Anyone who wants to understand Wilson College must go right back to the beginning to a conversation between two clergymen who sat facing each other across a table," said Dr. Paul Swain Havens, President Emeritus, Wilson College.

In the summer of 1867, three years after the burning of Chambersburg, Dr. Tryon Edwards, pastor of the Presbyterian Church of Hagerstown, Maryland, asked his host, the Reverend James W. Wightman, pastor of the Presbyterian Church of Greencastle, if he would help him found a seminary for females in the Cumberland Valley.

Wightman said he would have nothing to do with the idea ... "but if you would like to join forces in founding a college for women that will give them as good an education as the best colleges for men offer men, I'm with you heart and soul."

"Colleges for women were not heard of in the 1800s," Dr. Havens said. "Parents didn't think girls were educable at that time, and the girls weren't too sure. Wilson was a pioneer college, the beginning of a great movement in the United States, and it has continued without a break since its founding."

The founders decided that the College should be nonsectarian, but predominantly Christian, should make ample provisions for physical as well as academic training and should be a first-class college. The Reverend Wightman insisted on receiving his students as adults, not as children or "pretty young things."

Securing a board of trustees was not difficult but raising money for the College was. The Board asked for subscriptions from Franklin County residents and offered to locate the College in the township offering the largest amount.

On Oct. 14, 1868, the Board met in Greencastle and announced that Chambersburg led with a pledge of $23,000. "Norland," the home of Col. A.K. McClure, who had moved to Philadelphia, was for sale for $45,000—more than the Board had.

Among the pledges was $10,000 from Sarah Wilson, a St. Thomas area farm girl who wore a black dress and white bonnet and was affectionately called "Aunt Sally." Her parents had been Edenville landowners. The Reverend Edwards and board members visited Sarah and secured an additional gift of $20,000 which enabled them to purchase the 52-acre estate, site of the present college.

A charter was granted by the legislature of the Commonwealth of Pennsylvania on March 24, 1869, and Wilson College, named in honor of Sarah Wilson, officially opened October 12, 1870.

The Reverend Edwards was President of the Board of Trustees and the College, but the actual administration of the College was in the hands of the Reverend Wightman, the Vice-President.

The new College had a faculty of eight; 23 of its students were residential and 42 were nonresidential. Annual tuition was $350.

Religious training was regarded as essential and Biblical instruction was insisted upon. The College President was required to be an ordained Presbyterian minister.

Sports and gymnastic drills were also required. A 40 x 70-foot gymnasium was built in 1877 featuring a skating floor and bowling alley.

On commencement day 1872, the Reverend Wightman resigned

and the Reverend Edwards relinquished the Presidency of the Board. The Reverend Dr. James F. Kennedy became Vice-President of the College. The Reverend Dr. George Archibald became President for one year—1873-1874.

The early years were not without problems. In 1875-76, enrollment dropped from 83 to 69. The College was new and the idea of higher education for women was new. Members of the faculty had their own ideas about both, and those ideas were not always in accordance with the policy of the Board and the administration.

In 1876, the President-elect, the Reverend W.T. Wylie. became Wilson's President and reorganized the College. He established two separate faculties for the College and the preparatory departments. He resigned in 1878 but left behind a curriculum to remain unchanged for many years.

For the next three years, the Reverend Dr. T.H. Robinson served as president *pro tem,* but the actual management was entrusted to "Lady Principal" Abby Goodsell.

In 1881, the Reverend Dr. J.C. Caldwell became president, and enrollment increased when he established a School of Music and special courses in the fine arts. Also in 1881, Jennie W. Criswell, music teacher, became the first of many Wilson students to return as faculty.

After the Reverend Caldwell's resignation in 1883, the board searched extensively for a new president. Morale was low and enrollment was dropping.

By 1883, Wilson's thirteenth year, there had been six presidents (although not all called by that name) with an average tenure of slightly more than two years.

After a long search, the Reverend Dr. John Edgar was elected president. According to Dr. Havens' *History of an Idea* (Wilson's history from 1869-1903), "at no time had the Board of Trustees made a more fortunate selection of the chief executive officer."

President Edgar established a master's degree program and dropped the tuition to $250 a year, "with no extras except laundry and pew rent." By 1885, growth began in every department, standards for graduation were raised, and an extension to Main Hall was built.

By 1887-88, enrollment was at 164 from 16 states and the District of Columbia. Two buildings near campus were rented as dormitories, and the third addition to Main Hall was completed in 1891.

Eleven years after becoming president, the Reverend Edgar died.

A disastrous fire struck the campus March 26, 1894, but it served to hasten the completion of Main Hall. The section on the north matched "Norland" on the south, and the building looked much as it does today.

The new president, in 1895, was the Reverend Dr. Samuel A. Martin. By the end of his fifth year, seven new buildings had been erected: President's Hall, Harmony Cottage, Science Hall, Latin School, South Hall, a new gymnasium, and a new dining hall. Later he added Frank Thomson Music Hall. He wrote in 1899 that "the equipment of Wilson College is unsurpassed in the country."

Hockey as a major sport and the May Day Fete as an annual event have been part of Wilson since the nineteenth century. The May fete included a Maypole dance and was highlighted with the Queen of May.

In 1912, Dr. Anna J. McKeag became Wilson's first woman president, succeeded by the Reverend Dr. Ethelbert D. Warfield in 1915. He retired in June 1936, a month before he died.

In the early part of the twentieth century, Wilson College—like Chambersburg and the rest of the country—struggled through hardships incurred by World War I, a major flu epidemic, and the Depression. Yet, two "Wilson girls" of that era who reside in Chambersburg now, have warm memories of those years.

The trolley system was a vital part of Wilson and Chambersburg, linking the College to all town points and surrounding communities for a nickel a ride. Jessie Gordy, a 1916 graduate, lived in the west end of town and rode the trolley to school each day with two transfers, one at the Western Maryland Railroad tracks and another at Memorial Square.

Dorothy Crider, a 1922 graduate, remembers riding the trolley to Caledonia each year for "Caledonia Day." But her fondest trolley memory—which has been mentioned by several other alumnae—goes like this: Students phoned orders for sundaes to Haller's Drug Store near the square. Mr. Haller sent an employee to the trolley with the order, and the students met the trolley at the College gate to get their ice cream.

"We had to do more on campus because we couldn't go off much," she said. She recalled that the campus clubhouses of the College's two literary societies—Chi Tau Pi and Phi Chi Si—were "lovely places to entertain," and said that the societies entertained each other often with plays.

College officials decided to quarantine rather than close the College during the 1918 flu epidemic. Morning classes were shortened, and outdoor military exercises, for the students to get fresh air and exercise, were held in the afternoons.

That year, when the armistice was signed to signal the end of World War I, the townspeople held a victory march. Wilson students participated, and to the applause of many, performed their military drills in Memorial Square.

Wilson College's aim was for excellence, not numbers. According to the Carnegie Study of Teacher Preparation of 1929, elementary and secondary teachers prepared at Wilson stood at the top of their profession, far ahead of teachers prepared by the state teachers colleges.

Margaret C. Disert has the rare distinction of having been a part of the three segments of Wilson—students, faculty and administration. "I've been around more than most," she said recently, "and remain in very close contact with alumnae. It was a privilege to work at Wilson. The quality of the people—faculty, students and administration—made it very exciting. Many alumnae tell me they learned the pleasure of learning."

A 1920 graduate, she was mathematics instructor at the College from 1924 to 1928, when she became Dean of Freshmen and Director of Admissions and served in that capacity during the Depression years. She became Dean of the College in 1938 and served until her retirement in 1964.

During World War II she was contacted by the U.S. Navy to help with its WAVES recruitment program. She was the first WAVE commissioned in Pennsylvania, and what was supposed to be a one-year enlistment lasted four years. After the war, she returned to her position at Wilson.

"Some people have the idea that Wilson has not made curriculum changes," she said. "The term 'liberal arts' is esoteric. It's more significant to use the term 'liberal education.'"

Dr. Havens, a 33-year-old professor of English at Scripps College, Calif., was elected President by the Board in 1936, and, in 1939, he launched a $1 million 70th anniversary campaign.

Men were accepted at Wilson in 1946 for the first time; however, they were accepted as non-residents only. Twenty men enrolled that term. *(author's note: men did live in McElwain – first floor)*

Although ground was broken for a new science center in June 1966, problems for Wilson started in the 1960s. The College experienced increasing enrollment, which reached more than 700 by 1966, but the percentage of undergraduates staying to graduate began a steady decline.

Dr. Havens retired in June 1970, and was succeeded by Dr. Charles C. Cole, Jr., the following month.

Despite decreasing enrollment in the early 1970s, the College acquired the adjoining 200-acre campus of the former Penn Hall Junior College, bringing the size of Wilson to 300 acres.

Enrollment dropped to 364 by the 1974-75 school year. "Action teams" began an intensive recruitment drive, and the board discussed enrollment and financial difficulties. Dr. Cole resigned as president.

On February 24, 1975, the Board appointed Dr. Lawrence E. Dennis acting president, and Dr. Margaret A. Waggoner was formally installed as president September 27, 1975.

In October 1976, the College sought $1.25 million in grants from corporations and businesses in an effort to balance its budget. An anonymous gift of $500,000 was received in February 1977, and two months later the College received $1 million from the estate of Emily Findlay Van Lear, daughter of an 1889 graduate.

For the 1976-77 fiscal year, Wilson reported a balanced budget for the first time in nine years, and freshmen enrollment numbered 61, up from the previous year's 39.

On February 19, 1979, the Board of Trustees announced that

Wilson College would cease operations at the end of the academic year. The decision was reversed by Judge John W. Keller, of the Franklin County Court, on May 25, 1979.

"The College, through the years, has served as a cultural and resource center for residents of Chambersburg and the surrounding area. Lectures, concerts, library facilities and a variety of courses are open to the public," Disert said. "Wilson can and should live to serve future generations of young women."

"Everyone who cherishes Wilson College is delighted by the new lease on life that has been granted her," said Dr. Havens. "I am confident that, with the continuing devotion of alumnae, Trustees, faculty and friends, the College will serve the future well as it has served the past." (pp. 14-15) **(end)**

A letter to Dr. Laura Bornholdt, Vice-President for Education for the Lilly Endowment, written on October 11, 1979, by Dr. Dorothy Weeks, a former professor at Wilson, found in the Wilson College Archives adds a few interesting historical points.

From 1911 to 1915, Anna J. McKeag was President of Wilson College. Miss McKeag's professional life was divided between Wilson College and Wellesley College. Earlier she taught at Wilson. Then she returned to Wilson from Wellesley to become Wilson's first woman president. She was chosen President to effect a very important change in Wilson's curriculum. Prior to 1911, Wilson's most outstanding department was music. It attracted many students, young women from well-established families. One such student was the future Mrs. Newton Baker, wife of the Secretary of War during part of President Wilson's administration. Miss McKeag was to establish a curriculum at Wilson that would provide a high academic liberal arts college for women. Four years later, in 1915, Miss McKeag returned to Wellesley. ... Miss McKeag had established the desired curriculum.

In 1915, Ethelbert D. Warfield, former President of Lafayette College, became Wilson's president. Dr. Warfield was a younger brother of the President of the Theological Seminary at Princeton, a member of the famous Breckenridge family. It is reported that he lost his presidency at Lafayette because he dismissed a professor of philosophy. This is the conflict which caused the founding of the American Association of University Professors (AAUP). Dr. Warfield strengthened Miss McKeag's beginning efforts and appointed able and brilliant women to the faculty, so that, by 1923, graduates of Wilson College were accepted as members of the American Association of University Women. When Dr. Warfield retired, except for four men, all the faculty were women. Salaries were low, but there was a regular pay scale with definite increases planned. Salaries were not based on sex or dependents. Wilson had an excellent business manager. Not a penny was wasted. The best food from surrounding farms was served in the dining room. In June 1936, Dr. Warfield retired and died before leaving the president's house. Dr. Warfield was an austere person, a benevolent autocrat. During his administration, the best side of the faculty emerged. Pettiness, in general, did not.

In the summer of 1936, Paul Swain Havens, 33 years old, a Princeton graduate, a Rhodes Scholar, a teacher of English at Scripps College in California, an inexperienced administrator, became President. His mother had graduated from Wilson. Her college roommate, Mary Belle McElwain, the Godmother of Paul Havens, was a member of Wilson's Board of Trustees. She was a Classics Professor at Smith College. Two years later Margaret Disert, Class of 1920, a cousin of Mary Belle McElwain, the registrar and recruiter of students, was appointed Dean against the express wishes of the faculty. The die was cast.

His second year there, Paul Havens attempted to revise the curriculum. Elizabeth Rogers, Professor of History, an authority on Sir Thomas More, daughter of a distinguished scholar, upon whom had been conferred an honorary doctorate by Oxford University, led the opposition. Her courses in history were outstanding and attracted many students. The proposed new curriculum would have greatly affected the history courses … **(end)**

There were attempts in the 1970s to identify the challenges and to address them. The following is taken from the writings of Anne Pearce Lehman, '49:

In the 1960s, life and ideas about a college education in the United States were in turmoil. High school girls no longer saw a reason for attending a same sex college. President Paul Swain Havens had come to Wilson in 1936 as the youngest college President in the United States. He knew that the situation that had created the necessity for women's colleges had changed during World War II. Women had shown that they could run the farms, work in the factories, and successfully break the Nazi and Japanese codes. These women had been specifically recruited from the colleges known as the Seven Sisters and the Three Little Sisters. And Wilson had contributed their Dean, Margaret C. Disert, '20, to the WAVES. The women's colleges were asked to make room for some of the millions of men returning, eager for an education. . . .

In the Fall of 1974, Mary Redington Galbraith, '60, and Carla Dean Day, '63, from the Washington Club, presented on campus a symposium "700 by '76" with Luther Hoopes, a consultant who had been hired by Hood College to help increase enrollment; the Assistant Director of Admissions at Trinity College, Hartford, Connecticut, a graduate of Harvard named E. Max Paulin; and

Congressman Bud Shuster, Franklin County's Congressional Representative, the three having been identified and recruited by Bill Day, Carla's husband. Faculty, administration, Trustees, and alumnae were invited to attend and participate. Dr. Charles Cole, the College President, concluded his remarks by quoting George Washington: "Let us all get into the boats." Luther Hoopes had been instrumental in convincing Hood College to go coed. Congressman Shuster urged continued work and offered what help he could, and Mr. Paulin discussed the necessity for publicizing the College and considering changes that would not be merely "change for the sake of change." Discussion and questions followed the presentations. Some alumnae, particularly from the Pittsburgh and Philadelphia contingents, were very upset with our shining a light on the various less-than-good conditions at the College.

As a result of the symposium, the various constituencies of the College began to communicate with each other more freely. Although probably not a direct result of the symposium, Dr. Cole left the College abruptly before the end of that academic year, was replaced temporarily with Acting President Dr. Lawrence Dennis, and Margaret Waggoner was chosen in July 1975 to lead the College.

Under President Waggoner, the One-Plus-One program was put into motion. In this program, each alumna, faculty member, and Trustee was to recruit one prospective student.

Wilson women have always had a unique alchemy of love, service and openness that forges close friendships, unlike at many other colleges. Our bonds cover a multitude of generations before and after our own time, providing a sense of belonging and togetherness. I think this is Wilson's strongest achievement. **(end)**

Chapter One
SAVE WILSON!

In many ways, the story of Save Wilson has its roots in a lengthy newspaper article written by David Dunkle and published on January 9, 1979, in *The Public Opinion.* **(Reprint permission granted.) It is important to note that the interview with Dr. Waggoner upon which this article was based was in late 1978. It is quoted in full here:**

OUTLOOK IMPROVED: NEXT FALL LOOKS VERY GOOD.

A picture of Dr. Margaret Waggoner forms the centerpiece of the article and under her photo is the quote, "It is important to know that we have managed to maintain faculty strength over the last two years, even with a low (student-to-faculty) ratio and we still balanced the budget."

> Maybe it's a case of Midwestern stubbornness winning out in the face of long odds. Or maybe it's just the result of careful management and patient planning paying dividends. Either way, it's beginning to look like Dr. Margaret Waggoner has led Wilson College through its greatest crisis and possibly into an era of expansion.
>
> Not too many years ago, many people were writing off Wilson as a hopeless cause— an educational anachronism whose time had passed. More and more all women's colleges were closing their doors or making the switch to a coeducational setup.

Now, although problems still remain, the light at the end of the tunnel seems to have become a steady glow.

"In 1975, we began a major effort to strengthen Wilson in every aspect," Waggoner says. "This included many things—recruitment of students, adding the best possible faculty when additions were possible, even plant and management efficiency."

The Iowa-born president has proven to be a tough and able administrator—willing to make difficult and unpopular decisions for what she considers the best interests of the College.

Two items needed immediate attention—low student enrollment and a rising budget deficit.

Currently, the enrollment is 222 students, which is still low but substantially higher than it was when she took office on July 1, 1975. And she says, "next fall looks very good— we have in hand 12,000 inquiries for next fall. That's about twice the maximum we have ever had."

She admits that inquiries "are a long way from matriculated students," but says she hopes for as many as 150 freshmen come September. That accomplishment takes on more significance considering that the total number of college-age students available is declining every year.

Her approach to getting Wilson back on its feet has been wide-ranging. In every area, she says, there has been an effort to cut costs without cutting effectiveness.

"It is important to know we have managed to maintain our faculty strength over the last two years, even with a low (student-to-faculty) ratio, and we still balanced the budget," she says with satisfaction. "This took great effort. The administration is very austerely staffed in order to maintain the faculty, which is, after all, the heart of the institution."

The College currently has 43 full-time faculty members and seven part-time ones, which breaks down to an overall student-faculty ratio of about five-to-one. She cites statistics which indicate the average ratio for a private four-year college is a little over thirteen-to- one. Public colleges and two-year institutions are substantially higher than that.

She does not believe there is an "ideal" ratio, saying, "It's impossible to say. The effective ratio in different curriculums varies. Besides, individual attention is part of the character of this institution, and we want to maintain that always." The importance of the student still occupies the highest priority at Wilson. "Management may be the watchword and the faculty may be the 'heart,' but the student is the product, and any school rises or falls on its success in providing a quality education," Waggoner said.

"Our students have been able to get into the (graduate) schools they want," she says, pointing out that half of the College's graduates go on to some form of graduate work.

"It's hard to be exact about this because some students wait a year before going on."

Career planning, extra-curricular activities, financial aid and steady upgrading of the curriculum are the main ways the College tries to prepare students for life after graduation.

"First of all, we are a liberal arts college, and I'm convinced that is a very important kind of education," she says. The main reason for this, she feels, is because it exposes students to a wider range of subjects and ideas than a more specialized education can match.

"We try to provide the student with the means to move from college into whatever area she chooses to work in. We also try to provide her with enough background that she will have the ability to change her mind and take advantage of new opportunities."

With tuition at the school creeping toward the $5,000-a-year mark, finding qualified students with the ability to pay has become a difficult challenge. For this reason, she says, about two thirds of Wilson's students receive some sort of aid—be it federal, state, or one of the 100 jobs Wilson itself offers.

Students work in the library, the cafeteria, the stables, the offices and the language lab, and the money they earn is applied toward tuition.

"Basically, we put them anywhere there is a job a student can do. We try to get them to move around a bit and learn different things. One exception to that is where a job requires a special skill."

Colleges in financial difficulties often look to extra-curricular activities as prime candidates for budget cuts, but Waggoner says Wilson will not take that route.

"Those activities are an integral part of the educational experience and the development of the student. The student learns how to tackle something on her own and carry through. She learns how to work with other people, how to organize and how to lead.

"I think this is very important. There is an indirect effect here, too, I think. As a result of this participation, they might be more willing to try things after they leave here that they might not otherwise have attempted."

With operating costs of $2.7 million a year, the College is still very dependent upon the contributions of alumnae. In fact, the timely arrival of an anonymous donation, and an estate bequest totaling $1.5 million in 1977, may have made the difference between life and death for the school, which was struggling at the time to make ends meet. Conditions have improved, but money for new programs is still in short supply. For this reason, curriculum expansion is a very careful undertaking.

The College did purchase Penn Hall for $1.1 million in June 1973 and is making use of some of those facilities. Waggoner says the gymnasium, the fine arts building, and three residence halls are currently in use.

"The other residence hall and the theater have not been renovated and are not in good shape, but we are seeing a use for them, as well."

Plans also call for moving the Language Lab from its present location in the library to South Hall, site of the old health center, which has also been moved closer to the residence halls.

She talks about the importance of the bio-chemistry curriculum.

"Thirty-seven percent of the seniors last year were science majors and 40 percent were science majors the year before that. This is a high percentage for any institution and it's very important because a student can go from that into many areas of health sciences."

She calls the art faculty "first rate" and says the study of the Classics is "very strong."

"Actually, we try to be sure all areas of our curriculum are as strong as you can make them," but she says there is always room for improvement.

Probably the most worrisome thing in the College's future right now is finding a way to comply with the federal government's new regulations regarding handicapped students. The College has until the end of June 1980 to reach compliance, despite the fact there are not any handicapped students currently enrolled.

The Rehabilitation Act requires that all buildings be accessible to handicapped students. "This means that a student who is, say, in a wheelchair, must be able to enter anywhere she needs to go. To do this, we are putting in ramps and elevators."

The estimated cost of the project is $100,000, and she says that promised federal funds "are very limited and will not be forthcoming for some time."

Despite this, she says, "we're going to try to make it [the deadline]."

With the financial picture at least stabilized, the number one priority for the future is to continue increasing enrollment. Waggoner lists 720 students as the "maximum number," but says "the present campus could hold about 600 students. That would be a good number." **(end)**

One month and ten days later, the announcement to close the College was made with not a hint of this momentous decision given to anyone other than the Board of Trustees—not the alumnae, not the students, not the staff, not the faculty, not the Chambersburg community. The impact of the newspaper article in conjunction with the total surprise of the announcement fueled the agony and the fury and a sense of betrayal of the alumnae who became actively involved in Save Wilson College.

On February 19, 1979, there was a convocation scheduled at noon at Wilson College, with President Margaret Waggoner presiding and Chairman Martha Walker. They announced, to everyone's surprise and shock, the closing of the college.

There were critical events leading up to this totally unexpected announcement.

On **February 3, 1979,** the Board of Trustees met and learned the news that against a hoped-for goal of 150 new students, there were only 50 confirmed freshmen for the Fall of 1979. President Waggoner felt that the alumnae giving would not produce the amount needed to keep the College in business.

The Board took two actions: (1) to obtain the advice of a panel of experts with the understanding that the Board officers and the President were to report back to the full Board at a meeting called for February 17, 1979; and (2) that no other constituencies would be informed of the crisis.

Martha Walker, Jane Stewart, Alice Beeman, Dick Hough and Mary Patterson McPherson were the Trustees recommending names for the panel. The panel was chaired by Dr. David Truman, the Director of the Russell Sage Foundation, and included John Butler from the fund-raising firm of Barnes and Roach; Dr. David Robinson from the accounting firm of Peat, Marwick and Mitchell; and William Ihlenfeldt, Vice-President of Admissions for Northwestern University, who participated on the telephone. They met for six hours and deliberated using materials provided to them by the President.

This panel then met with Dr. Waggoner in New York City for three hours on **February 9th,** and reviewed many documents, including a four-page news release announcing the closing of Wilson, marked "Release at 12:00 noon, Monday, February 19, 1979."

On **February 14th,** Dr. Truman met with the President and four officer Trustees: Martha Walker, Richard Hough, Alice Beeman and Jane Stewart. He advised them that the panel's opinion was that it was not practical to continue Wilson beyond June 1979. The Trustees asked the President to seek another opinion on admissions and to prepare a resolution to close Wilson that would be proposed for consideration at the next full Board meeting.

Thomas Huddleston, from the admissions office of Bradley University, was consulted during the three following days, as were attorneys Thomas

Menaker and Attorney Lefever, by phone, on the form of the closing resolution prepared by the Board officers. The President advised that a *cy pres* (meaning to alter the terms of a charitable trust) proceeding would be necessary before the actual closing of the College, and she requested that Mr. Lefever contact the state attorney general's office for the purpose of informing it of the Board's intention to file a *cy pres* proceeding. The President was told that she needed Board approval of the resolution to close the College before the attorneys could contact the attorney general's office.

On **February 17, 1979,** the President met with the Board officers to report on the call with Thomas Huddleston, who recommended proceeding with the closing of the college. At 2:40 p.m. on February 17, 1979, twenty Trustees out of twenty-four met at Girard Bank in Philadelphia. They received the President's report from the expert panel, and Chairman of the Board, Martha Walker, reported on the February 14th meeting with the chair of the panel, Dr. Truman. Following a Board discussion, a motion was made by Chairman Walker and seconded by Marguerite Thomas to adopt the resolution to close the College and to convert the assets to the Wilson College Foundation as of July 1, 1979. The resolution passed with no "nay" votes and one abstention.

On February 19, 1979, at 11:55 a.m., Betsy Diely, the President of the Alumnae Association and a member of the Board of Trustees, placed a call to Nancy Besch, the immediate past president of the Alumnae Association. Betsy Diely said "I hope you are sitting down. In five minutes there is a convocation for the whole College community in the chapel where the announcement is going to be made that the Board of Trustees voted to close the College, effective June 30, 1979. Indeed, five minutes later at 12:00 noon, at the convocation in Thomson Hall for the entire Wilson College community, the Chairman of the Board made the announcement that, due to declining enrollment and financial problems, the College would close on June 30, 1979. No prior information at all had been given to the alumnae.

Chapter One: Save Wilson!

In Nancy Besch's words as she recalled that day:

I had no clue … In fact, I had recently received a copy of the January *Public Opinion* article that made it sound as though the College was really moving forward in a very positive way. That was like a double whammy. I had been President of the Alumnae Association prior to Betsy, from 1973-1976, and she had followed me, serving from 1976-1979. Betsy, who at the time was 35 years old (16 years Nancy's junior), was really torn because she wanted to abstain from voting on the closing since she was a voting member of the Wilson College Board of Trustees by virtue of her elected position as President of the Alumnae Association. The Trustees wanted a unanimous vote in favor of closing and she was under a lot of pressure. She called me as a courtesy. She was in a quandary.

My first instinct was absolutely a feeling of betrayal the likes of which I had never felt before. I immediately called Eleanor "Ellie" Martin Allen, '49 (a friend from childhood and for years together at Wilson). The two of us just commiserated, asking each other how this could have happened and what we could do. I'm sure it was on the television that day, but any news coverage had no effect on me. Ellie's daughter, Melissa, was a Junior at Wilson and did call Ellie later that afternoon with the news. Later we heard that a few of the Trustees would be coming to the campus on February 24th, and Ellie and I decided to go. We knew enrollment had been declining, but we weren't satisfied with what they told us and the fact that school officials had not contacted anyone ahead of time. I was immersed in preparations for the 100th anniversary of the Alumnae Association to be celebrated in June, and I thought I was in touch with what was going on. **(end)**

February 19, 1979 Press Release

**FOR FURTHER INFORMATION:
THE PRESIDENT'S OFFICE**

RELEASE AT 12:00 NOON MONDAY, FEBRUARY 19, 1979

CHAMBERSURG — Wilson College Trustees announced Monday (February 19) that the College will cease operations as a college at the end of the current academic year.

Martha B. Walker, Chambersburg attorney and Chairman of the Board of Trustees, presided at an all-campus convocation Monday noon and announced the Trustees' decision to close. She emphasized that Wilson College is not bankrupt. The decision to close, she said, is based on Wilson's declining prospects in a time of rising inflation and lowered college enrollments everywhere.

"The Trustees are proud of Wilson's tradition of academic excellence and of its ability to give its students a complete and rich educational experience," Mrs. Walker explained. "We believe it better to close the College altogether rather than cling to a precarious existence and to be forced to weaken our educational offerings."

Two weeks ago, at their regular winter meeting, the Board of Trustees asked Wilson President Margaret A. Waggoner and Board Chairman Walker to convene a panel of outside experts to review data on the College's finances and enrollment, matters of increasing concern to the Trustees for several years. This panel included nationally recognized leaders in educational administration, admissions, financial management and educational fund development. The panel conferred both with President Waggoner and with the four officers of the Board of Trustees—Mrs. Walker, Chairman; Richard A. Hough, Vice-Chairman; Alice L. Beeman, Secretary; and Jane Stewart, Assistant Secretary.

Panel members confirmed the Trustees' own assessment of Wilson's situation. The officers presented the recommendation to close to the entire Board of Trustees at a special meeting in Philadelphia on Saturday, February 17. The formal resolution for closing was adopted at that time, and President Waggoner was instructed to proceed with the necessary steps to complete this spring's academic program and to close the College thereafter.

In their resolution of closing, the Board of Trustees also declared their intent to establish the Wilson College Foundation, Mrs. Walker announced. This foundation will continue to work toward the historic goal of Wilson College—the liberal education of women for excellence, for leadership, and for service. It will do so by such means as educational research and development, undergraduate scholarships to women, and other appropriate programs. The foundation will be endowed with assets remaining when the closing of the College is completed. College endowment funds restricted for certain purposes by the donors, such as scholarships, will be carried over into the Wilson College Foundation and continue to be used for the purposes indicated, Mrs. Walker stressed. Mrs. Walker added that no plans have yet been made for the sale or other use of the campus physical plant. The Trustees of the College are aware that the College has been an important economic and cultural resource for the community of Chambersburg. The needs of that community will be kept in mind, she said, as alternatives for disposition are studied.

In explaining the decision to close, Mrs. Walker said the decision had been forced upon the Trustees by two developments, the full import of which became clear only in recent weeks.

The first is the inability of the College to attract enough students for next fall's freshman class. Last October, College officers were optimistic because a larger-than-usual number of high school seniors had indicated an interest in Wilson, asking for College publications and other information. By the end of January, however, these inquiries had not materialized as applications for admission. Historically, by January 31, the College has received at least half, and usually more, of the total number of applications needed for the next fall's class. This year, the number is well below half of the total needed for a class large enough to continue operation of the College.

Secondly, like all private colleges, Wilson is heavily dependent upon gifts and grants from individuals, foundations, corporations and other donors. Year-end gifts, those received in December, are traditionally heavy and constitute a major portion of the annual total of gifts to be received. In 1978-79, such gifts and others to Wilson, are lower than in previous years.

"We are not sure of the reasons for either of these unhappy developments," Mrs. Walker said. "Regardless of explanations, however, the Trustees were faced with the reality of an enrollment below our needs for next fall and with a decline in gifts to the College.

These hard facts, coupled with the Trustees' commitment to maintaining a standard of educational excellence at Wilson, led directly to the decision to close."

In reaching that decision, Mrs. Walker said the Trustees also considered the following factors:

(1) A high rate of national inflation is continuing to drive up college operating costs and to force comparable increases in tuition and fees. As tuition goes up, public institutions become more competitive. Likewise, as tuition rises, so do demands upon college resources for student aid—grants, loans, jobs. During the current year, for example, about two-thirds of Wilson's students receive some financial aid, and 53

percent of the necessary money for aid comes from College funds. Furthermore, inflation steadily pushes up the dollar amount that each student needs.

(2) College enrollments nationally are entering a period of decline, expected to last at least until 1990. Because of lower birthrates, the number of young people in the college-age population—18-22 years—will drop sharply in the 1980s. In Pennsylvania and other northeastern states from which most Wilson students come, the decline is predicted to be about one-third. Three severe winters in a row, combined with general inflation and the energy crisis, have contributed to soaring costs of operating the College plant. Some of the Wilson buildings are old and costly to maintain. The increasing cost of replacement of worn-out or outdated educational and plant equipment is another source of growing pressure on College funds.

(3) Compliance with federal laws and regulations has thrust new costs upon the College. Wilson's estimated cost to comply with federal requirements for making all its facilities accessible to the handicapped, for example, is more than $150,000. This year's new social security taxes upon employers, with further increases scheduled the next two years, are causing significant increases in personnel costs. The new federal minimum wage increase has also pushed up labor costs, and the removal of the mandatory retirement age will add to faculty costs.

(4) A national trend toward "career education" and toward job training programs has added to the difficulties faced by all liberal arts colleges such as Wilson. While Wilson has kept its curriculum flexible, its program is rooted in the liberal arts and its faculty is dedicated to that tradition.

(5) Wilson College opened the spring semester with an enrollment of 214. The optimum size for the student body, considering the educational program offered by the College and the physical plant available, would be about 700. A strong program of student recruitment has been undertaken each of the past several years, resulting in an upswing of inquiries from prospective students. Nonetheless, applications for next September's entering class are considerably below the number required if the College is to be large enough to continue to offer a full program of studies in an educational environment equal to that which Wilson has offered in the past.

"Wilson College has tried for several years to rebuild its enrollment and its financial resources so that we could continue the proud tradition that has been ours for more than a century," Mrs. Walker said. "Under the leadership of President Waggoner, a great deal of progress has been made. But the external forces—inflation, declining college-age population, disinterest of young people in liberal education, expensive federal requirements and regulations—all of these are beyond our power to change."

Mrs. Walker added that the Board of Trustees, in adopting the resolution to close, had also adopted a special resolution of appreciation to President Waggoner for her unstinting devotion to Wilson College, for her leadership of the educational community, and for her skill in management of the College's physical and financial resources during a period when they were stretched to the limit. "Without President's Waggoner's work, the decision to close would have been forced upon us much sooner," Mrs. Walker said.

At the campus convocation Monday, Mrs. Walker asked the President to explain steps approved by the Board to meet the special needs of faculty, students, and alumnae. Dr. Waggoner said that she would confer later this week with members of the faculty and staff about termination arrangements. The Board of Trustees will continue the regular monthly salary payments to all faculty through August 31, 1979. After regular salary payments cease, the College will pay unemployment compensation to both faculty and staff under the special provisions of Pennsylvania law for colleges and other non-profit organizations. In addition, help will be offered through such means as assistance in preparing resumes, arranging job interviews, obtaining references and recommendations, and the like.

"Students now in their senior year who complete their academic degree requirements on schedule will receive Wilson College degrees at Commencement on May 27," the President said. Students in freshman, sophomore, and junior classes will receive individual counseling on transferring to other colleges and continuing their educations.

"The College will arrange for the permanent maintenance of student and alumnae records," Dr. Waggoner said. Such records will remain accessible to those who need transcripts, copies of letters of recommendation, and similar items.

Wilson College was founded in 1869 as a college for women. Its academic reputation has always been excellent, and many of its graduates have achieved positions of distinction in the professions, in business and government, and in the arts. Students have come to Wilson from everywhere in the United States and from many other countries. The 6,500 alumnae live all over the world.

In 1974, with the appointment of Margaret Waggoner as President, the College undertook a broad program of reorganization and rebuilding of institutional strength. Both actions were necessary because enrollment had been dropping steadily since 1965 and because the College had begun to draw upon its unrestricted endowment funds to meet current operating costs. In the four years since, the pattern of declining admissions has been reversed, but new enrollments have not grown as College leaders had hoped. Balanced budgets were achieved in each of the last two years, but the margin was slim. There has been some increase in the endowment.

"Wilson's alumnae and other friends have been generous with their gifts," President Waggoner commented. "However, the gap between income from student fees and the total required to keep this College operating is more than we can expect our friends to meet on a continuing basis."

Wilson College receives almost no support from federal and state tax sources. Some of its students benefit from federal grants, loans, and work-study funds.

Wilson has a small endowment fund, most of which is restricted for specific uses, such as scholarships. These restricted funds, plus proceeds from the sale of the campus plant and equipment, will become the endowment of the Wilson College Foundation. Current operating funds of the College, plus reserve and unrestricted endowment funds will be used to meet current obligations and to satisfy costs incurred in the closing of the institution. **(end)**

EVENTS MOVED QUICKLY AFTER THE ANNOUNCEMENT ON FEBRUARY 19, 1979

After the convocation, calls from students alerted some members of the Alumnae Association Board, and President Diely asked Carolyn Burger, who was one of the alumnae on the Board of Trustees, to call a meeting of Alumnae Board members on March 3rd. The agenda was to decide on the future of the Association and to determine the path forward.

Also, on February 19, 1979, a letter and a copy of the press release quoted above were sent through the US mail third class to all alumnae. The letter said:

Dear Wilson College Alumna:

It is our sad duty to inform you that the Board of Trustees has decided that it is necessary to close Wilson College, effective at the end of the current academic year. Enclosed is a copy of a press announcement released today, explaining the reasons for the Trustees' decision.

As an alumna, there are several things that you especially will want to know:

- Your Wilson College degree remains valid. It can continue to be used, indefinitely, in applications for jobs and for admission to graduate and professional studies.

- Arrangements will be made for the permanent maintenance of Wilson College student records. Thus, transcripts, placement office letters of recommendation, and similar materials will continue to be available to you. You will receive detailed information about this later.

- Students now enrolled as seniors may complete their studies and receive their Wilson College degrees in May. Students in other classes will receive individual counseling and help in transferring to other colleges and in planning the continuation of their education.

- All faculty members will receive full salary through August 31, 1979. Thereafter, employment compensation will be paid by the College and administered through the state employment compensation system, as required by the laws of Pennsylvania.

Each person is evaluated individually for such compensation. The College will also actively assist faculty and staff members to locate other employment. It will help them prepare resumes, arrange interviews, and obtain recommendations. For those who may wish to seek non-teaching employment, some professional counseling may be provided.

- The College will continue normal operations for the remainder of the academic year. All scheduled campus events, including the alumnae reunion on June 8-9, will be held. Alumnae gifts will continue to be needed to make this final year at Wilson an educational experience for our students equal to that which Wilson was able to give preceding classes and also to help meet continuing obligations to faculty and staff.

We want to assure you that the Trustees gave every possible consideration to alternatives to closing: co-education, adding vocationally-oriented programs and courses, opening branch campuses in urban centers, and the like. The ultimate result of any of these options, even if otherwise feasible, would be to change the essential character of this College. We believe your commitment to the Wilson College tradition of liberal education and excellence is similar to that of the Trustees themselves. You will therefore understand our belief that it is better to close the College than to adopt measures whose chance of success is dubious and which, in any event, would make Wilson unrecognizable to those who have known and loved it in the past.

Finally, we believe you will be interested in the use to which the Trustees propose to put the assets of Wilson College remaining when all closing costs and obligations have been satisfied. The Trustees have formally stated their intent to establish the Wilson College Foundation to continue work toward the historic aims of Wilson for the liberal education of women for excellence, for leadership, for service. Such work might consist of undergraduate scholarships for women, educational research and development, and such other programs as are consistent with the Wilson College tradition.

Wilson College has been in operation for more than a century. It has a history and tradition of excellence and service of which alumnae can always be proud. We believe its name and achievements will continue through the lives and accomplishments of its alumnae, as well as through the activities of the Wilson College Foundation.

Sincerely,

Martha B. Walker, Chairman, Board of Trustees and
Margaret Waggoner, President **(end)**

On **February 20th**, some students called many of the area alumnae and asked them to join in a protest rally to be held on **February 21st**.

On **February 21st**, the Director of the Alumnae Association called most of the Board members of the Association to an informal meeting of alumnae on **February 24th**, when Chairman Martha Walker shared information about enrollment and finances. The recruiting had been done largely through Student Search by purchasing 75,000 names which resulted in 12,000 inquiries. As of January 31, 1979, the College had received 83 applications, out of which they accepted 27, and had six (6) deposits. This led them to estimate 30-40 enrollments in the fall of 1979. At the same time in 1978, the College had 131 applications, resulting in 63 enrollments in the fall of 1978. The endowment was $3,818,000, out of which $2,500,000 was restricted. With the closing of the College, they owed $500,000 for the Housing and Human Development (HUD) mortgage on Prentis and $750,000 on Disert and Rosencrans (all dormitories); $800,000 in unemployment payments; and $200,000 in interim costs, for a total of $2,250,000. The College had, as of January

1979, a $400,000 operating deficit. Fundraising was falling short—only $600,000 thus far against a $1.2 million goal. If the College remained open, they were anticipating an operating deficit of $1,000,000 for the 1979-80 academic year (taken from notes of that meeting).

On **February 24th**, there were also these meetings:

- The Wilson College Government Association Executive Board and some alumnae met and discussed various strategies, summarized as follows: generating a petition (thus far they had 151 names); making a report to Middle States; sending out information for media coverage; having general assemblies; Presidential meetings at the College; a hotline staffed by students; a special issue of the College newspaper for alumnae; phone calls to alumnae, trustees, parents, friends.

- Concerned alumnae in Laird Lounge met where they developed a list of questions for the Coordinator of Alumnae Affairs to ask the alumnae Trustees.

- Thirty alumnae and a faculty member met in the dining hall with Trustees Martha Walker, Jane Stewart, Betty Blackadar, and Tracy Work. Students were not admitted to this meeting. Several points were made dealing with the rising costs as a result of the new rulings of the Occupational Safety and Health Administration (OSHA). The faculty member made the point that the human factor is missing on the part of the President and the Trustees; that there was no confidence in the President. Changing to be more career oriented seemed to not be on the table. Trustee Betty Blackadar then met with students and alumnae and gave a report of the meeting with Trustees that had just occurred.

As a result of these meetings, neither the students nor the alumnae present were satisfied with the explanations provided by the Trustees for voting to close the College. There was distrust of both the President and the Trustees. Many doubted that other options were really considered or that all had been done that could have been done to attract students, including better use of alumnae and the connection with the Presbyterian Church. Some felt that perhaps the Board of Trustees had not received all the information it might have in order to make a good decision.

On **March 3rd**, there was first a meeting of the Alumnae Association Board, at which time they resolved to continue the Association and to request a meeting with the Trustees within two weeks; and then a mass meeting of 300 persons.

Quoting from hand-written notes of the first meeting:

An unofficial gathering on March 3, 1979, of members of the Alumnae Association made the following statement:

Our goal is to encourage the Board of Trustees of the College to reverse their decision to close the College, and we challenge their decision.

We propose that there is a definite need for further investigation into the criteria upon which the board of experts based their suggestions, and upon which the Board based their decision.

We propose that the efforts that the College has made to recruit students should be re-evaluated thoroughly. We will support an effective recruiting program and volunteer our efforts.

We propose that the alumnae be polled to determine resources for recruitment, resources for communication, professional resources and financial resources.

We propose that communications be upgraded. We feel that there has been an ongoing lack of communication, and that was exhibited in the unprofessional conduct in informing the alumnae of the Board of Trustees' decision.

We propose that there should be an examination of the curriculum and that suggestions submitted by the Middle States [accrediting association] be implemented.

We propose that the majority of vested interest in the College is from the alumnae. The alumnae have the strongest investment in the matter of the affairs of the College.

We propose that we exhibit a vote of no confidence by the alumnae in the vote of the Trustees to adopt the option of the panel of experts to close the College.

We propose that the alumnae support the formation of necessary committees to implement these proposals, and further that a directing committee be established to work on details and formalize a concrete proposal to present to the Board of Directors of the Alumnae Association for consideration of further efforts. **(end)**

The afternoon of March 3rd, there was a mass meeting of 300 persons alerted by phone that week, including alumnae, faculty, and students. Nancy Besch, immediate past President of the Alumnae Association, was asked by Betsy Diely to convene the meeting since Betsy was on the Board of Trustees and she had voted to close the College and would not be considered credible.

There were two major motions that passed: 1) To form the Save Wilson College Committee, and 2) To elect Nancy Besch as Chair of the Save Wilson College Committee.

Quoting from the notes of Nancy Besch:

We needed committees ... Our mission statement was to make sure Wilson College stayed open. It was not formalized, but that was the gist. The outrage was universal. There were no naysayers in the group ... You have to remember that I didn't know any of the members of that Save Wilson Executive Committee except for Eudora Roseman, '63. I had never met Dr. Marilyn Mumford, '56, a professor of English at Bucknell University, or Carolyn Smithson Berger, '62, an executive with AT&T. I knew Betsy Diely only from conversations we had had when I was going out of office and she was coming in as Alumnae Association President. Nobody was blaming anybody during the spring of 1979, and the whole time of the Save Wilson effort. I never had any ill feeling against any of the members of the Board of Trustees. **(end)**

With Save Wilson established and Nancy Besch as Chair, the next six days were whirlwinds of activity. The group established the C. Elizabeth Boyd Fund to pay for legal and mailing expenses. Task forces were established for admissions, curriculum, finances, and public relations and leadership. A written request for a meeting between the Alumnae Association and the Board of Trustees was hand-delivered by Carol Tschop to Chairman of the Board, Martha Walker, under the signatures of Alumnae Trustees Tracy Work, Betsy Diely, and Betty Blackadar.

The Alumnae Board, at their **March 3rd** meeting, drafted a letter, dated March 6, to be mailed to over 6,500 alumnae advising them of the actions taken on March 3rd—specifically, the formation of the Save Wilson Committee, with Nancy Besch as Chair, and the formation of the C. Elizabeth Boyd Fund to raise needed money for expenses. However, the alumnae were denied use of the College addressograph system for mailing this letter. President Waggoner told alumnae members Joan Edwards and Carolyn Shaffer, that she would discuss its use with the College's attorney.

On **March 5th**, President Waggoner was sent a certified letter from the Leadership Committee of Save Wilson requesting copies of the documents shown to the panel of experts chaired by Dr. Truman ... In a follow-up phone call on **March 6th** by Joan Edwards to President Waggoner, Joan was told that the documents requested in the certified letter would be prepared, after discussion with the College's attorney, and that this process will take some time. On **March 12th**, the Leadership Committee received a written response from Dr. Waggoner stating that a report to the alumnae was being prepared.

On **March 5th**, Chairman of the Board of Trustees, Martha Walker, called a special meeting of the Trustees for **March 10th**, to be held in New York City. Indeed, on March 10th, four of the members of the Alumnae Association—Carolyn Burger, Marilyn Mumford, Eudora Roseman, and Julia Billings—made a one-hour presentation. The presentation showed evidence of shortcomings in admissions and in outlining proposals to aid the College in other areas, including raising $500,000. Approximately 40 Wilson students arrived by bus and demonstrated outside the AT&T Building, singing the *Alma Mater* during the meeting. Richard Hough, Vice-Chair of the Board, was a high-level executive of AT&T. At this meeting there was a unanimous vote by the Board of Trustees NOT to reconsider the original decision to close the College.

March 6th-8th: Under the direction of Carolyn Shaffer, local alumnae, spouses, students, and friends hand-addressed, folded, stuffed, and stamped 6,300 letters in Riddle House at Falling Spring Presbyterian Church, using a mailing list obtained by an unidentified person who had anticipated that the use of the addressograph would be denied. Copies of the above letter were sent also to the Board of Trustees, the Wilson College Government Association, the Dean, President, and Faculty.

Addressograph story written by Marie Beck:

Lynn Sharpe, '50, and Joan Foresman Edwards, '58, left William Coffield's office at the Chambersburg Chamber of Commerce more downhearted than they expected to be. In his distinctive

Maine accent, so out of place for the central Pennsylvania town he had served for many years, the white-haired executive director of the town's business consortium had little comfort and no help to offer in the alumnae effort to save the College. Coffield, though gracious, bluntly told the two women that Wilson College—a fixture in the community for 110 years—had no appreciable impact on the Chambersburg economy and had not been an economic contributor for many years. Stunned by Coffield's assessment, the two could scarcely believe that the 400-600 students who arrived each fall, checkbooks in hand, and the ancillary employees that lived, worked and purchased goods and services in the community, didn't make the College an entity worth fighting for. The takeaway message they heard was the suggestion that perhaps the time had come for the old girl to go.

Disheartened but not deterred, Joan drove the two miles from Coffield's limestone office building near the town's historic center back to the campus to report to Linda Crick, '73, at the Alumnae office in Laird Hall.

"Quick, get down to the post office," Joan remembers Cricky saying. "Carolyn needs your help." Joan had no idea what kind of help Carolyn needed, but she dashed through "the Tunnel," a corridor that served as the below ground connection for six of the campus buildings and the quickest way to get from the Alumnae Office to the campus's basement post office. When she arrived, Joan saw Carolyn Trembley Shaffer, '50, lifting heavy wooden drawers full of 4 by 4-inch light steel plates bearing addresses of alumnae and others on the College's mailing list. The small plates fit into the cumbersome addressograph machine that took up a sizable chunk of real estate in the small post office. In the days before mail merge and laser printer, the embossed plates, manually inserted into a bulky machine, enabled large quantities of envelopes to be stamped with the recipients' address. The wooden trays holding the names and address plates for more than 7,000 Wilson alumnae and friends of the College were the key to reaching the alumnae.

Having learned that the alumnae office staff had been forbidden by the President to use College resources to assist the alumnae "insurgents," Carolyn had thought of an alternative. She asked the Reverend William Harter of the nearby Falling Spring Presbyterian Church if the alumnae could use the church's addressograph.

"That is, of course, unless that would get you into trouble," Carolyn offered.

"You're a Presbyterian, aren't you?" Harter replied. "Don't you know Presbyterians are always getting into trouble."

While Carolyn and Joan wrestled with the trays, President Waggoner's secretary Alice Bigham Mower, '47, a Wilson alum herself, happened to walk by. Alice did an immediate about-face and scurried back to her office. As soon as she glimpsed Alice, Joan thought, "Uh-oh, the jig is up. She's going back and tattle."

They hadn't much time. Carolyn was already breathless from multiple trips through the heavy double doors and up two-dozen cement steps, and Joan found she was working up a sweat in the hauling despite the early March temperatures. They had loaded nearly half of the trays into the back of Carolyn's station wagon when a fuming Margaret Waggoner came storming down the Esplanade, a covered walkway linking the aboveground buildings.

She demanded that they return the addressograph trays immediately. "These are the property of Wilson College," Joan remembers the square-jawed president saying. Carolyn, a no-

nonsense Baltimore County mother of three, had learned of the closing on February 19, when her daughter, Barbara, a Wilson student at the time, called home crying with news of the College's closing. Carolyn's own outrage was crystallized by her daughter's tears. As treasurer of the Alumnae Association she was aware of how much of the alumnae operation was supported by the alums. She boldly informed the president that the Wilson College Alumnae Association had purchased the equipment years before and that the address plates were the property of the Association and not the College. Possession being 9/10ths of the law aside, when Waggoner threatened to call the police, Carolyn and Joan relented and began the doleful process of lugging the addressograph trays back down the steps into the bowels of the post office …

It never occurred to Joan until she got home that evening and related the events of the day to her husband Jerry how close she and Carolyn might have come to being hauled down to the Borough Hall police station. The look on Jerry's face was enough to make her think that they might actually have been arrested. "My God. What have I done?" she thought to herself. "Then I was really worried."

In a March 24, 1979 *Public Opinion* editorial, headlined with the word "Shame!" local newspaper columnist Paul B. Ambrose chastised College officials, but did not identify Waggoner by name. "Shame on the Wilson College official or officials responsible for denying the Alumnae Association the use of the metal address plates that would facilitate communication with the College's far-flung alumnae." Quoting from the Ambrose editorial:

> "Just like the little girl who takes her dolls away from the playmates and goes home when she can't have her own way,

we now have a Wilson official locking up the address plates because the Alumnae Association has enough College loyalty to question the "wisdom" of the Board of Trustees' decision to close down the century-old institution."

Those opposed to the closing of the College had silent allies... but one anonymous College employee saved the day. In the first raw week of shock and dismay that came with the announcement of the College's closing, a College employee acting on her own had secretly photocopied the entire College's mailing list—all 7,140 addresses.

These names and addresses were worth more than gold to those who rallied to save the school. Using this database, Wilson volunteers would be able to mobilize distant alumnae so the Board of Trustees could be pressured to reverse its decision. This mailing would be the first to directly ask alumnae for donations to fund the campaign. But before there could be a mailing, Carolyn had to use her personal credit card to purchase the necessary paper, labels, and envelopes from a local merchant, since the Alumnae Association, in the wake of the announced closing of the College, no longer had access to its own funds.

The word eventually got out with newsletters written in Chambersburg, driven by a volunteer to Acorn Press Inc., in Lancaster, Pennsylvania, a family business owned by Eudora "Dory" Roseman, '63, and her mother Elizabeth "Betty" Colt Roseman, '35, and her brother. Because time was critical, Dory would run the presses after regular hours. Ink scarcely dry, the copies would be driven back to Chambersburg. Often couriers employed a pony express system arranging to meet someone halfway between Lancaster and Chambersburg and transfer the goods. Envelopes were hand-addressed by alums around a dining room table in Philadelphia and returned to Marcia Kirchhoff

Rodenhaver, '49, Chambersburg home for stuffing. Some of the missives were even stuffed by alums in Baltimore. The very first mailings were all individually sealed and stamped with stamps that had to be licked and applied in the day when that was how one put a stamp on a letter.

Later an unheralded volunteer laboriously typed a complete list of alumnae addresses that could be copied onto mailing labels, and Bob Harrison '50…offered the use of a postage meter at the local bank where he worked which could be used after hours. The bank was reimbursed for the cost of the postage …" **(end)**

On March 6th, the first Alumnae Association Newsletter addressing the closing was sent and is quoted as follows:

Dear Wilson Alumna,

As you know, on February 17, 1979, the Board of Trustees voted to close Wilson College on June 30, 1979. As representatives of the Alumnae Association Board we are writing this letter to inform you of actions taken on Saturday, March 3rd, at a special meeting of the Board. The voting members of the Board of Directors unanimously passed a motion requesting a meeting with the Board of Trustees within two weeks in order to provide them with additional information pertinent to the closing of the College. We believe they did not have the requisite data during their deliberations to make a decision in the best interests of the College. We further believe that had this information been available for the meeting, the decision to close the College would not have been made. The express purpose of this meeting is to persuade the Board of Trustees to reconsider its decision.

In compliance with the Trustees' bylaws, three alumnae Trustees have requested a special meeting of the Board of Trustees. These Trustees are Mary George Work, '29, Betty Fenner Blackadar, '42, and Elizabeth Hanning Diely, '64 (Alumnae Association

President and voting Trustee). This meeting will occur within two weeks.

A letter has also been sent to each Trustee detailing the alumnae concerns, especially regarding the proposed Wilson College Foundation. As a result of an informal gathering of more than three hundred alumnae and College friends on March third, task forces have been established to investigate such areas as public relations, admissions, curriculum and the current financial condition of the College.

As the Alumnae Association has been totally funded by the College since 1969, there are no moneys available to support unforeseen and unbudgeted expenses. Therefore, a fund has been established to cover such items as this first class mailing to all seven thousand members of the alumnae body. Any donations may be sent to this fund which was established by the assembled alumnae on March 3rd. (C. Elizabeth Boyd Fund with Mrs. Hege Sheller, the Local Administrator and her address to which to send donations.)

A voluntary alumnae group will be personally responding to your individual letters very soon. We have enclosed lists of the members of the Board of Directors of the Alumnae Association and the Board of Trustees. You are urged to communicate your questions and concerns as soon as possible. Your Board of Directors voted unanimously to continue the Alumnae Association, and its future organization and direction are currently under study. Reunion plans for June 8-10 are completed, and you will shortly be receiving both Reunion Weekend information and an Association ballot. We need your continued support during these difficult days ahead. Cornelia M. Lentz, Vice-President, and Jane T. Ensminger, Presidential Nominee 1979-1981, Alumnae Association **(end)**

Chapter One: Save Wilson!

On March 13th at 10:00 a.m. in Gettysburg, Pennsylvania, Betty Boyd, Nancy Besch, Carolyn Burger, Carolyn Shaffer, Jane Sheller, Dolly Swisher, and the Coordinator for Alumnae Affairs met with Lawyers Swope and McQuaide. McQuaide was the lawyer to be assigned to handle the Alumnae Association's case against the Board of Trustees with Swope as his advisor. I have summarized the following from notes taken at that meeting.

> McQuaide's feeling was that the case should be tried through the Court of Common Pleas, using the non-profit corporation code and the fiduciary code. The sections of the Law that would be appealed were promulgation in 1975 so there were few legal precedents. The Alumnae Association had to convince the judge that he has reason to take jurisdiction in a matter concerning a private corporation and to determine what the burden of proof is and to assume responsibility for it.
>
> The heart of the case ultimately involved two key issues: (1) Money—demonstrate that the money situation at the College was handled poorly and that the Alumnae Association can handle it better. That meant raising adequate funds, possibly through a pledge campaign; (2) Students—demonstrate that Wilson's recruitment effort was handled poorly and the AA can handle it better and change the enrollment picture.
>
> It was agreed that the Alumnae Association had to find their own expert witnesses to testify in the areas of admissions, public relations, and curriculum and not rely on past experts such as Rex Moon.
>
> It was noted that the money had stopped coming in from the Presbyterians, although Wilson was earmarked for $180,000 from the Major Mission Fund of the Presbyterian Church (USA). One of the ways of gaining exposure was through the Synod School, formerly, but no longer, held at Wilson.

Legal Considerations

1. They needed a member of the Board to request an audit—probably Jean Zehner—since it is better to ask a friend than demand through legal channels.

2. There must be an underlying lawsuit in order to demand discovery, so best to go ahead and initiate the lawsuit in order to get the needed information.

3. The Alumnae Association must convince the judge that they do have a case, and they must establish that the facts warrant some action of the Court to prevent the closing of the school. They could ask for the removal of the Board of Trustees, but ultimately the Court decides the manner in which the *status quo* would be maintained—including having the College stay open and having the responsibility to report to the Court or to a court-appointed receiver.

4. The Board of Trustees can file a cross-petition requesting that the Court uphold their decision to close the College.

In short, McQuaide believed that the Alumnae Association had sufficient standing to file in Orphan's Court (dealing more in state than in federal law) and to get an immediate *ex-parte* or one-sided injunction, also called a restraining order, that requires a hearing within five days if the judge were convinced. McQuaide had been in touch with the faculty lawyer, John Killian, but it didn't seem particularly beneficial to work with them at this time. McQuaide believed that there would be no difficulty in establishing at a hearing that there would be irreparable harm done if Wilson would close without further investigation.

The status of the C. Elizabeth Boyd Fund was discussed as he was not sure the way it was described would permit tax-exempt status. The possibility of rescinding the agreement between the College and the Alumnae Association was discussed since everyone thought it would be beneficial to be an autonomous association.

They needed plaintiffs—a Trustee who did not vote for the closing, donors, students, parents of students, alumnae. McQuaide needed a copy of the original charter and the group needed to obtain pledges from alumnae that would be strictly conditional, using terminology such as "if and only if the College remains open as a teaching institution."

Wes Oler, an attorney in Carlisle, would be helping with the research and writing in preparation for the hearing. McQuaide charged $45/hour and he was already owed $1,500.

On March 14th, the decision was made on the part of the Alumnae Association to retain an attorney and to file a lawsuit in order to obtain a court review of the decision to close the College. This was announced by Carol Tschop in the local media.

On **March 18th**, the Save Wilson Committee was established as an ad hoc committee of the Alumnae Association. Committees and chairmen were appointed: Selections, Jane Fox; Admissions, Dolly Swisher; Communications, Carol Tschop and Joan Edwards; Curriculum, Phyllis Ganz; Financial, Carol Bauer; legal, Eudora Roseman; Liaison, Carolyn Shaffer; Retention, Joyce Morrison; Steering Committee, Nancy Besch, Chairman, with members Carolyn Burger, Jane Ensminger, Marilyn Mumford, and Marie Williams. The Preservation of the Wilson College Trust pledge campaign was initiated, and there was resolution passed unanimously to call a mass meeting of the alumnae on campus on May 5th.

By the time of the March 18th meeting, work had already been done to examine the admissions process. The admissions report given to this group speaks to the process and failures of the admissions efforts to yield a class for the fall of 1979. This is critical since it helped established the legal case of Save Wilson.

Eudora Roseman gave the first part of the report and it is quoted in part as follows:

In order to understand Wilson's failure to attract new students for the 1979-80 academic year, it is necessary to understand the system employed by the Admissions staff. This system utilized four major steps: Student Search, System Six mailings, prospectus with application, and the catalog...

I. Student Search

    a. April 1, 1978: personal-looking letter sent to 70,000 young women whose names were purchased from Student Search. This letter, designed by Epsilon, used the person's first name in the greeting and appeared to have been signed personally by John Mason. The mailing also included a reply slip and a small brochure.

    b. August 28, 1978: A similar letter was sent to the 63,000 young women who did not reply to the first letter.

    c. Mailing lists: Responding to either of these initial letters placed the prospective student on two mailing lists, with a third mailing to students with certain selected interests.

        i. Newsletter mailing list which included a financial aid brochure.

        ii. Alumnae tea mailing lists for as many students as possible to receive invitations to alumnae teas in their area—46 students reached.

        iii. A letter to prospective students with expressed

interest in law, medicine, dance, psychology, or music was sent. The staff members spoken to were unsure as to how many letters were sent or whether the process was ever completed, but more research showed that the letter went to 4,000 students, but those may not have been interested in Wilson. The students were chosen from the original pool of 70,000. The letters they received did not necessarily correspond to reply cards from them with specific questions and comments.

A critical issue is that of "dead inquiries." A dead inquiry is any inquiry not answered within thirty days. It is unlikely that a dead inquiry will yield an application, or so say admissions people. One admissions staff reports that the high volume of inquiries caused an almost two-month delay in mailing responses, thereby creating literally thousands of dead inquiries.

II. System Six Letter: If a student returned the reply slip in the initial Student Search letter, she received a mailing containing the following items.

   a. A personal-looking letter

   b. Three-minute summary of Wilson College with a map of the campus and the surrounding area.

   c. Reply card. There seem to have been several versions of the reply card, but each version gave some opportunity to ask questions or make comments.

III. Prospectus and Application:

   Everyone of the 12,000 students who responded to Student Search also received the prospectus and application.

On January 29 and February 15, 1978, Wilson College attempted to begin the process of replying to questions and comments on the reply cards. The total number of responses from the Admissions Office to the students who had returned the reply cards was 163. It had been six months since most of the reply cards had been received. (Copies of each reply card and letter of response are in a safe deposit box.) <u>The remaining 1,416 students who were interested enough to reply on two occasions never received a response from Wilson College!</u>

IV. Catalog:

Each student who returned an application was sent a catalog. At least one applicant (daughter of a faculty member at Dickinson) reported that she never received a personal acknowledgment of her application.

<u>Failure of the System</u>

The information presented in this report demonstrates that the recruiting effort at Wilson suffered from the following important weaknesses:

I. There was no process designed to convert inquiries into applications. Without the elaborate follow-up procedures utilized by other institutions, the predicted conversion ration could not be accurate.

   a. The inquiry response was greater than expected, and the Admissions Office was unable to handle the volume.

   b. Emphasis on solving the problem of low initial inquiries may have obscured the need to continue our commitment to intensive personal contact.

II. The system lacked the personal quality which has always been the hallmark of Wilson College. This lack was particularly evident in that only 163 of the 1,579 persisting inquiries received a personal response.

    a. Faculty were not asked to answer questions about major fields and curriculum. In the past years they had been effective in this role. The bulletin "using the Student Search Effectively" reports that departmental brochures were an important part of recruiting. "In a survey of students done in 1976, . . . 87 percent reported they read those materials that seemed of interest, but 11 percent of the students reported that they read all of the college material that they had received. The student surveys make it clear that materials that are related to the student's intended major are read by the students." It is clear that such faculty input was critical in the recruiting effort.

    b. There was a marked incongruity between the espoused personal philosophy of the College and the recruiting approach which introduced students to Wilson. Failure to answer questions of prospective students demonstrated a marked lack of personal attention to individual concerns.

    c. Alumnae and students could certainly have been used to answer the large volume of replies, but they were not informed of the crisis.

III. The Admissions Staff was not used effectively.

    a. Salaried Staff

        i. There was no particular person assigned to

answer questions of prospective students.

ii. There was no particular person responsible for encouraging campus visits or for calling them on the phone.

iii. The bulk of these undelegated responsibilities fell mainly on Kathy Haines who was already responsible for the daily operation of the office. Kathy did appeal to John Mason on several occasions for assistance, but no major relief was provided.

iv. Deborah Cramer's sole responsibility was to organize teas for prospective students in alumnae homes. By early fall it was obvious that this was an ineffective use of Debby's time. . .

v. Lynn Williams' sole responsibility within the recruitment process described herein was the production of the "Wilson Update."

vi. Gloria Weagly was responsible for operating System Six.

b. Student Workers

i. Student workers had been scheduled inefficiently. A different student worker was scheduled for each hour of the day. Not only was student production limited by this arrangement, but it also hindered the effectiveness of Kathy Haines who had to give instructions to another worker at the beginning of each hour.

ii. Because of personality clashes between Silver Key (an honor society for students working in admissions) and members of the admissions staff, the club was not utilized to its former degree.

IV. Inadequacy of selected printed materials.

    a. departmental brochures to be used in recruiting were never printed. An information sheet to gather data was distributed to faculty in preparation for this project but the brochures never materialized.

    b. A film was to have been made to portray campus life. The film was apparently never completed.

    c. One of the initial mailings—the reply slip—seemed to us to make a very poor initial impression of the College.

By July 1 (1978), Wilson College had received at least 900 cards asking for further information about the College. It was six months before even 163 of these 900 students received a personal response. One can only wonder how many applications would have been generated by an admissions system which utilized the efforts of the entire Wilson community or one which maximized the efforts of the admissions staff! In brief, the admissions effort in this critical year was seriously deficient.

CONCLUSION

In retrospect, Student Search was successful in generating inquiries for Wilson College. The failure occurred in converting inquiries into applications. We have demonstrated some of the major weaknesses in Wilson's recruiting effort, highlighting the lack of a system of personalized follow-up to inquiries. Ironically this phase in recruitment had been Wilson's strength in the past. There is, therefore, every reason to believe that Student Search combined with a well-planned and executed system of follow-up would yield the freshman class that we need to continue as a viable institution. **(end)**

On **March 19th**, a press release was sent out to the area media outlets announcing the formal establishment of the SAVE WILSON COMMITTEE, and the second Alumnae newsletter was written in Pittsburgh, printed in Lancaster, delivered to Chambersburg, and mailed!

Quoting from the press release:

Nancy Besch, Camp Hill, PA, was formally elected Chairperson of the Save Wilson Committee at an at-large meeting of the Wilson College Alumnae Association held yesterday (3-18-79) in Lancaster. A past president of the Alumnae Association, Mrs. Besch is currently serving on the Camp Hill School Board and as Chairperson of the Hemlock Girl Scout Council.

Appointed by the President of the Alumnae Association Board of Directors, Mrs. Elizabeth Diely, the Save Wilson Committee subsequently authorized the establishment of eight sub-committees to pursue information and alternative means of operating the College. These committees will explore development and finance, admissions, curriculum, communications, selection of personnel, retention of students and faculty, liaison relationship among students, faculty and the Presbyterian Church, and legalities. An executive committee chaired by Mrs. Besch will coordinate and oversee their efforts.

During the meeting yesterday, alumnae who attended the March 10 meeting of the Board of Trustees in New York City presented an overview of the proceedings of that meeting and the information reviewed at that time. According to Carol Burger, a member of the Alumnae Association Board of Directors and one of the presenters, the alumnae were not permitted to have legal counsel present or to ask any questions of the Board of Trustees. They were also to be provided with a tape recording of the proceedings, but as yet have not received it. The alumnae's presentation included detailed information regarding admissions, recruitment of students, curriculum, public relations, and the decision- making process involved in closing the College.

The Board of Directors of the Alumnae Association also formally resolved to establish the Preservation of Wilson College Trust, a tax-exempt trust designed to receive pledges of monetary support to continue the operation of Wilson College as a teaching institution. **(end)**

On March 20th, a second Alumnae Association newsletter was sent to the alumnae, quoted here.

Dear Wilson Alumna,

On March 10, 1979, the Board of Trustees agreed to meet with four representatives of the Board of Directors of the Alumnae Association in New York. They were Julia Billings, '38, Carolyn Burger, '62, Marilyn Mumford, '56, and Eudora Roseman, '63. The purpose of the alumnae presentation to the Trustees, was to provide additional facts, figures, ideas and good "alternatives" so that the Trustees might "reconsider" their decision to close Wilson. <u>Many</u> documented administrative failures were disclosed in research done by our alumnae and current students. For example, the fact that the Admission's "Student Search Program" had 1400 "second inquiries" from prospective students which went unanswered from May '78 until January '79. How could a Freshman class be expected for '79-'80? Another fact is that the teacher certification at Wilson is in jeopardy. Another fact is that Wilson's "Self -Study" was not geared to the two most pressing problems facing Wilson—enrollment and financial status. This may be the most damaging of any of the administrative failures, as in fact the Middle States Accreditation Report indicates. In the limited time of one hour (restricted by the Trustees), the Alumnae presented these facts and <u>many</u> others. The decision of the Trustees was <u>not to reconsider</u>. It is also interesting to note that the "panel of experts," as referred to in your Wilson letter of February 19, were <u>never on campus</u> to research Wilson's situation, nor did they present anything <u>in writing</u> before or during their presentation to the Board.

March 18th, in Lancaster, 24 alumnae were present to improve and organize alumnae efforts. I only wish I could express on paper the feeling I had during that meeting, surrounded by women with brilliant ideas, good organization, and exuberant enthusiasm, working together on this very difficult task. (In addition to this group, people such as Paul Havens, Margaret Disert, Book Leitch, Phyllis Ganz, Betty Boyd, Past Wilson Trustees, the Wilson faculty, "former" faculty, and at least one current Trustee are backing the Alumnae Association's goals.)

Results of the March 18th meeting are as follows:

-A radically innovative admissions policy was proposed, which will become public as soon as we have a decision by the court.

-In addition to the C. Elizabeth Boyd (contributions used to pay attorneys' fees and to send mailings to alumnae), we are establishing "The Preservation of Wilson College Trust." This is a legal Trust which allows gifts to be <u>tax exempt</u> and to be <u>matched</u> by outside sources. Gifts for this trust will be used for the purpose of revising Wilson College <u>if</u> it continues as an educational institution. Our attorney explained we must be able to prove two things: (1) That alumnae can handle student enrollment; and (2) That alumnae can get sufficient funds to operate the College. We need an <u>immediate</u>

response of "pledge" to the Trust, for proof to the court we can get financial support. Please use the enclosed pledge card for Trust contributions. (Incidentally, DO NOT send gifts addressed to Wilson College, as such money is being used as unrestricted funds to help pay for the closing of the College.)

- Selected alumnae are willing to do "road shows" in your area, to explain in detail what has happened at Wilson and what the alumnae are doing. If your Alumnae Club or any "group" of alumnae would like such a presentation, please contact Nancy Besch.

-A Save Wilson Committee was set up to organize our efforts and allow for the most effective use of alumnae talents. Please use the tear-off section below to indicate your committee preference if you plan to work on the Save Wilson Committee. Your ideas and assistance may be instrumental in the outcome of Wilson College.

<u>SAVE WILSON COMMITTEE</u>

Chairman: Nancy Adams Besch

Steering Committee: Carol Smithson Burger, Jane Troutman Ensminger, Marilyn Mumford, Marie Williams

Admissions: Dolly Swisher

Communications: Carol Tschop/Joan Edwards (P.R. interior and ext., Tel-Co Mail Network—reaching all alumnae in 24 hrs.)

Curriculum: Phyllis Ganz (Middle States, teacher certification, overall)

Financial: Carol Phillips Bauer (fund raising, trust fund, development)

Legal: Eudora Roseman (Coordinate activities of attorney and Save Wilson Committee)

Liaison with Constituencies: Carolyn Trembley Shaffer (Faculty, Students, church, Chambersburg community)

Retention: Joyce Morrison (Keeping students on campus, current and future)

Selection: Jane Taylor Fox (Nominating Trustees, administration, Alumnae Director)

It is critical we have near 100% alumnae support. Please contribute your talents by completing the tear-off form and contacting one of the committee chairmen. WILSON WOMEN ARE KNOWN AS LEADERS; and we will prove this by uniting to save Wilson College. Leslie Gottschalk, Class of 1974

Note: March 24th, Wilson Charter Day plans meetings at Bellfield Presbyterian Church, Pittsburgh, PA, Bryn Mawr Presbyterian Church, Bryn Mawr, PA, 10:30 a.m.

Please show your interest: Return to Nancy Besch: Do you support the movement to keep Wilson open? Are you interested in working on a Save Wilson Committee? Which committee?

Do you think we should consider changing the curriculum to some pre-career oriented courses? Do you think we should consider going co-ed? **(end)**

Taken from the writings of Joan Edwards entitled "The College That Refused to Die: The Untold Story of Wilson College." It is the account of the organizational meeting which she titled *Wild Days* **and was first drafted November 10, 2014.**

On March 18, Edwards and Tschop had just been named Co-Chairmen of the Communications Committee. The committee was given responsibility for public relations and internal communications, including alumnae newsletters and setting up a national telephone tree. "We went home thinking 'now what do we do?'" said Edwards. While Margaret "Peggy" Felton Kilmer, '66, was drafted to set up a telephone network so that the committee could disseminate information and rally support, nothing in Edwards' background had quite prepared her for the ensuing media attention.

Queries were coming in from local, regional and national news organizations, and those fighting to save the College needed a strategy and practical guidance in handling the press. Tschop had written one or two of the initial press releases for local outlets, and, because of her work promoting college and community theatre productions, she had connections at several of the nearby radio stations. Edwards said, "Carol actually hand delivered her hurriedly written press releases to the local newspaper and radio stations on her way to her 'real' job. Two days (March 20) after the meeting in Lancaster, I found myself doing my first gig as a spokesperson for the Save Wilson Committee on Molly Messner's popular Chambersburg area radio program, *The Molly and Me Show*.

Edwards also had her first encounter with a major press outlet when she met with veteran *Pittsburgh Post-Gazette* reporter Jane Shaw on March 21st. President Waggoner had invited Shaw in January to visit the campus and write about the College's progress. Now, three months later, the story was quite different. ... "Shaw came directly from meeting with Waggoner, and fortunately I was armed with plenty of correct information garnered from my fellow Save Wilson Committee members," Edwards recalled. ... The reporter questioned Edwards at length about the viability of the College during a two-hour lunch meeting at the local Holiday Inn. Shaw apparently wasn't feeling any deadline pressure even after the interview. The article about Wilson did not actually appear until May 21st, before the judge's ruling. "This whole incident is a wonderful example of how the alumnae network responded and contributed enormously to the cause ... Every member of the Save Wilson Committee can tell you numerous stories like this."

The most valuable public relations help came from a more experienced source in the form of a former newspaperman-turned-ghostwriter who was married to 1962 Wilson graduate Ellen Beswick, '62. Drew Farnum Steis was a former United Press International reporter, who was a stay-at-home dad and freelance writer in the Washington, D.C. area. "On March 25th, I got a phone call from Drew explaining that his wife urged him to offer his expertise after reading our 'help wanted' ad in the first Save Wilson newsletter that had just been mailed to alumnae three days before. "I want to come to campus to meet with you," Edwards recalls his saying. She telephoned Tschop, Crick, and Swisher and arranged to meet him the next day, March 26th, in Patterson Lounge, a genteel parlor and meeting room just steps away from the Alumnae Office on the College campus "After we met him, we knew he had the professional experience that we needed. He brought the list with 43 editors' names, addresses and phone numbers. There was no Internet or Google in those days. It would have taken us weeks to gather that information. As it turned out, in his work for UPI he knew a lot of these people."

In addition to the print media contacts, Steis told the women he could supply a listing of every major TV and radio station in the country, and offered his expertise to help mount a national media campaign as the Communications Committee had been assigned to do. "It was truly an answer to prayers," Edwards recalls. "This was the day before we filed suit, and Steis knew that the press would show up hoping to interview our attorneys. He said 'you two need to be at the courthouse with the press releases and hand them out to the reporters.'" Steis' calm assertiveness and specific direction instilled confidence. "He called Nancy Besch to confirm facts and wrote a press release on the spot before leaving for his home in Virginia," Edwards recalled. Tschop, who had a full-time job, was not able to join Edwards the next day, but with Steis' words echoing in her ears: *you just want to be a presence and you need to look and sound official,* Edwards made her way to the courthouse Edwards had printed fifteen to twenty copies of the press release "and I know I gave out every one of them."

The very evening after the meeting with Steis, Edwards attended the local Franklin County Wilson Club's dinner meeting. She noted in her journal that the meeting, held to celebrate the College's Charter Day, included many alums who had helped stuff envelopes in the immediate aftermath of the announced decision to close the College. "I had been invited only a few days before to make remarks on behalf of the Save Wilson Committee, and, of course, my surprise announcement was that the alumnae suit would be filed the next day (March 27th)," Edwards recalled. "After I spoke, Martha Walker, the Chairman of the Board, who was attending the meeting, … was granted an opportunity to respond and defend the Trustees' decision to close the College. There was a question and answer period and opinions were expressed, but everyone was civil, despite this incredibly unique and poignant circumstance. In the end, someone made a motion to support the Save Wilson Committee, and it was passed."

"We went through office personnel like a baby through diapers—very few could stand more than a few days in a row without suffering battle fatigue. We were open nine hours a day, six days a week, and there was no let-up in the activity. Two phones were in use constantly—as evidenced by the telephone bill. But most of the calls came in from the alumnae who wanted to know what was happening and from the news reporters.

"Then there were the people who dropped in. A steady stream, and we always dropped what we were doing to talk with them. Students and faculty kept us posted on what was happening on campus. Reporters shared information with us, the townspeople bought our bumper stickers, signed our petition, and signed our pledge cards. Most simply wanted the campus there—they used the tennis court or strolled on the banks of the Conococheague. Then there was the plumber who kept me a half-hour after closing and he gave me a dollar; the little boy about 9 years-old who said he heard Wilson needed money and dropped 36 cents into Madelon Nordquist's hand then hurried off; and the meter man who quietly asked how we were doing, and then told how his ancestral roots were in the McClure farm. What a lift we had that day." **(end)**

On March 27th, Save Wilson filed a petition in Orphan's Court, Franklin County, with Robert McQuaide as the attorney. A press release about this was sent to 43 major newspapers, wire services, and area TV and radio stations.

In response to the press release as it appeared in the *Public Opinion*, Alice Bingham Mower, '47, a resident of Chambersburg, wrote a letter to the editor quoted as follows:

According to the lead article in the *Public Opinion* of March 27, 1979, a news release put out by the Save Wilson Committee states that the suit was initiated by a "core group of individuals who represent the 6,500 members of the Wilson College Alumnae Association, faculty, student body, staff and prospective students."

I strongly resent the assumption of the "core group" that it represents me, and wish to go on record in support of the decision of the Board of Trustees to close the College and in support of the dedicated administrators who have been wrongly accused of mismanagement.

If you are not in sympathy with the suit, have the courage of your convictions, and resent the assumption of the "core group" that it represents you, speak out against the suit and come to the defense of the administration and the Board of Trustees through letters to the Board of Trustees, the directors of the Alumnae Association, and this newspaper.

Granted—all of us alumnae, as well as members of the College community and the larger community, are devastated by the fact that the College will close, but the facts speak for themselves and we must accept the inevitability of the demise of Wilson. It is most unfortunate that its passing is to be marred by the present circumstances and it is evident that the Save Wilson Committee has failed to consider the irreparable damage their actions are causing in the way of forcing the members of the Alumnae Association, faculty, student body and administration to split into opposing factions." **(end)**

On March 30th, there was a news release announcing May 7, 1979 as the date of the hearing on Wilson College. Nancy Besch, newly identified Chairman of the Save Wilson Committee, was quoted in that very first official press release, her firm voice coming through:

"We do not feel that the present Board of Trustees was fully informed or took into consideration several viable alternatives that would permit the College to continue ... In fact, there are strong indications the Board was misled by being given incomplete information about the College's current situation."

Looking back, Edwards notes that "none of us, least of all Drew Steis himself, had any idea how deeply he would become involved with the fate of Wilson College in the months to come." And then Three Mile Island happened!

As told by Joan Edwards and Nancy Besch:

Three Mile Island: On Thursday, **March 28**, at 4:00 a.m., a little more than twelve hours after Edwards was handing out press releases and only sixty miles from those Franklin County Courthouse steps, equipment failure and operator error resulted in the worst commercial nuclear reactor accident in American history. The Three Mile Island nuclear reactor near Middletown, Pennsylvania, was located only twelve miles from Besch's Camp Hill home.

Attention quickly turned to the threat of a nuclear calamity. Fears of a possible meltdown of the nuclear reactor, radiation exposure and widespread contamination triggered a rolling panic, calculation of the radioactive fallout, and hastily devised evacuation plans.

Amidst official reassurances and media speculation, the public nervously watched camera footage of steam rising from Unit 2, one of Three Mile Island's four conical towers perched on an island in the Susquehanna River. As the world watched in fascinated horror speculating on the impact of an East Coast nuclear meltdown, Besch was preoccupied with telephone calls, rallying support and strategizing about the alumnae's legal options. But Nancy's husband, who had hurried home from Washington, was glued to news reports of developments at Three Mile Island, newly terrifying news.

At first, only those living within five miles of the reactor were encouraged to evacuate but the recommended perimeter was growing. As Nancy Besch recalls, "That Saturday night I was talking to Carol Phillips Bauer, '58, a college professor living on Long Island, New York, who chaired the Financial Committee of Save Wilson and was the mother of a Wilson freshman, when Earl came in and announced that we were evacuating to

Chapter One: Save Wilson!

Allentown. Right NOW!! I took my pocketbook and swept up all of the Wilson College stuff on my dining room table. My 14-year-old daughter, Diane, grabbed her pillow and her bag and we left at 10:00 p.m. I never took a picture, memento, anything but my materials relating to the Wilson suit ... and to think, we may never have been able to come home again. I suppose I grabbed a toothbrush, but I don't remember if I did even that. Diane never questioned this because I was so immersed in everything related to Wilson. This was just what she expected ..."

Meanwhile, back in Chambersburg, Edwards was pondering the looming nuclear accident that effectively eclipsed the story about a group of alumnae taking a college's Board of Trustees to court. "The day we filed suit, I remember thinking that every reporter in the world is covering Three Mile Island. How do we get them to drive the fifty miles to Chambersburg? We still had the attention of *The Public Opinion* as well as Dan Cupper, from the Harrisburg *Patriot-News,* and the Hagerstown WHAG-TV news anchor, Pat Ciarrocchi, but no one else was calling us. I had this feeling we'd missed out."

Wilson's only direct connection to Three Mile Island was when it became an evacuation site for Middletown area nursing home residents. With the evacuation of fragile Harrisburg area residents to the College's dorms, the crisis in Middletown seemed more real to those just outside the affected perimeter. Like Besch, Edwards, distracted by her work on behalf of Wilson, relied on her husband to keep an eye on Three Mile Island and be vigilant about her family's safety. Edward's primary focus was completing the Steis "to do" list.

Edwards recalls Steis' favorite expression was "Read my lips, Joan." She thought with all of his newspaper experience that he would be the one to take the committee's message to the press.

But Steis was adamant: "the face of the Save Wilson Committee *has* to be a woman and you need to establish a relationship with these reporters." According to Edwards, "Drew also urged us to start a community petition drive in support of our efforts to keep the College open. One of our volunteers, Chambersburg resident Janice Kohler, '57, went out and bought dozens of yellow legal pads and organized a team of alumnae to help her circulate petitions for Chambersburg and for the faculties at Wilson, Dickinson and Gettysburg. She had all these different categories, and she got 4000 signatures."

Save Wilson College Headquarters: Edwards credits Steis with the brilliant idea to find a physical location for Save Wilson Committee operations. (Steis had been hired as a consultant by Save Wilson on **April 12th.**) "We had been working out of people's kitchens," remembers Edwards. Marcia Kirchhoff Rodenhaver, '49, who lived in a spacious house a block from campus, had invited volunteers to work at her dining room table, but they needed more space, "Drew said to me, 'Joan this is just like a political campaign. The Save Wilson Committee needs a headquarters, to establish a presence and someone who always knows the right thing to say. ... I want you to find an office storefront downtown with two telephone lines, and I want it tomorrow.' My first response was, 'How can we afford that?' We were stuffing envelopes at an alumna's home at the time, and someone said to call longtime broker Joe Ausherman. He offered a little office on North Main Street right across from the Coyle Free Library, next door to The Little Shop, where generations of Wilson women bought elegant clothing and high- end sportswear. It was a single room, less than 20x20 feet square with a large window, a bathroom, and back porch, and to my relief (knowing how little money we had to work with) was immediately available for $125 a month. I remember thinking

Chapter One: Save Wilson!

I wanted to ask if he would donate the rent, but I had not yet developed the shameless chutzpah that not much later became part of my persona, for good or for bad ... I called Nancy to get approval to incur the expense."

Edwards next task was to secure telephones. "I called the phone company, and the woman on the other end said it would take two to three weeks to establish service." Edwards was crestfallen as she explained the urgency. "Oh, this is about Wilson College," Edwards recalls the service department employee saying, mentioning that a family member had taken classes at Wilson at one time. "Yes, I can help you," the woman said. "It's an important thing you are doing." "We got our phone service, and I was rather proud of myself when I called Drew to report mission accomplished."

From the moment the lease was signed, the pace accelerated. Edwards brought in a two- drawer filing cabinet, a portable typewriter and various office supplies her daughters had once used at home "playing school." Wilson's physical education teacher and gymnastics coach, Joyce Donatelli, showed up at the empty storefront with a card table, chairs and a coffeemaker. Donatelli's contributions to that bare space were particularly welcome ... "We arranged for news coverage of a ribbon cutting for the Save Wilson Headquarters on **April 16th,** the day after Easter," said Edwards, who remembers the venerable snowy-haired former Wilson Academic Dean, Margaret Criswell Disert, '20, and the young bespectacled Wilson College Student Government leader, Gretchen Van Ness, '80, posing side by side at the ceremonial Headquarters' opening. Among the participants were Greater Chambersburg Chamber of Commerce Director, William T. Coffield, who had earlier rebuffed initial effort to aid the group and expressed his candid opinion that the closing was inevitable, showed up for the ribbon cutting.

The Committee now had a centralized workplace, a single phone number, and a communication system where everyone could be in touch with each other. The tiny room became a beehive of activity immediately. The Save Wilson Committee Headquarters remained open six days a week, nine hours a day for the next six weeks.

Steis spent four to six hours each day at the new headquarters, commuting to Chambersburg from Great Falls, Virginia. "He pounded out a press release or more a day on this little portable typewriter that had to have been twenty five years old," recalled Edwards. "In between, he gave us basic instruction about how to deal with the reporters, and how to generate copy for the press and our alumnae newsletters."… "As the Save Wilson effort went into high gear on all fronts, we were working day and night scheduling volunteers to help. The two phones were now ringing constantly. Within a couple of weeks Carol and I were feeling overwhelmed and we talked to Nancy Besch about enlisting a paid office manager. At the suggestion of one of our volunteers, we hired Madelon Nordquist, a former faculty wife, who was so efficient in that role that the College later hired her to work in the public relations office." Drew was a terrible speller, according to Edwards, "but Madelon would retype his releases and see that they got copied somewhere."

Each morning, Nordquist would come in and, after consulting with Steis and Edwards or Tschop, she would assign one volunteer to recruit enough women for the next day. Usually four to six volunteers were needed on a daily basis, drawn from a pool that eventually numbered around fifty. Most were alumnae or retired Wilson faculty and staff. "One of the regulars was a high school girl who walked in one day and offered her help," said Edwards. "She loved the work and spoke of a future in public relations." Nordquist designed and posted on the wall detailed instruction sheets for each routine procedure, which saved time and confusion for the ever-revolving team of part-time helpers. Tasks included preparing press releases and newsletter mailings, opening incoming mail, answering the phones, typing and filing, running errands, and talking to the dozens of people who dropped by the office each day.

Volunteers helped select the lead story of the day from the daily kaleidoscope of events as they unfolded and did research for Steis as part of the releases he wrote when he was at the office. "Later Carol or I and Anne Coffin, '65, were able to put them together," said Edwards. "The stories came from a variety of sources: students, faculty and other committees. As we developed a relationship, reporters would call us to give them a response to events we were not yet aware of." Bob Vucic, the amiable Pennsylvania reporter for *The Morning Herald*, a neighboring Maryland newspaper that covered Franklin County, had an office upstairs, and he would sometimes come down to exchange information with volunteers. A few times Waggoner's attempts to manage the press backfired. She had fired her PR person, and, as a result, penned her own releases.

Edwards' crusade to help save Wilson became a family affair. "My daughter Jill, who was eleven years old at the time, came in one day when nobody was home to stay with her, and I asked her to make a large sign for our front window with Magic Marker—SAVE WILSON COMMITTEE. I looked up and realized she had spelled 'committee' wrong. I corrected it later, not wanting to hurt her feelings ... In retrospect, Wilson's crisis had a profound lasting effect on our entire family."

In the headlong rush to implement another of Steis' recommendations, Edwards ordered bumper stickers that read: "Save Wilson College." "Turns out we were 'green' before anyone really knew what that term meant. Because the SWC was on a very limited budget, I ordered the least expensive ones I could find. As winter snows gave way to spring showers the printing on the blue and white bumper stickers washed away. Turns out they were printed with biodegradable ink," said Edwards, chuckling at their folly. "We ordered 1,000 of them and I still have some at home. Can't bring myself to throw them away." Besch and Edwards, who had only passing awareness of each other in the years before, were now in daily contact as the office became the central clearinghouse for receiving and disseminating information from Wilson supporters across the country.

Norquist and Edwards developed a clever system to ensure that nothing got lost in the chaos. On one wall of the headquarters hung dozens of large brown envelopes, each labeled with the name of key campaign figures. Phone messages and notes were dropped into the proper envelope, then checked daily, and the contents mailed or information called in to the person who needed to receive it. This was a critical component to maintaining communication among Besch and representatives traveling throughout the region drumming up support and volunteers based in Chambersburg.

"You have to remember," Edwards said, "this was the era before computers, answering machines, voicemail or cell phones, and long-distance calls cost a *lot* of money. In an extraordinarily short period of time—from the day of the announcement of the College's closing (February 19th) to the filing of the lawsuit (March 27th) against the College's Board of Trustees—the alumnae working together had established the basic committee structure, identified key leaders and created an effective internal mechanism to coalesce support and mobilize opposition. All the key committees were up and running in a matter of a few weeks. It was really remarkable." **(end)**

The first road show of Save Wilson was in Philadelphia on March 24th, and is illustrative of others. Nancy Besch, Marilyn Mumford and Kathy Torpy of Save Wilson attended a meeting at the Bryn Mawr Church of the Philadelphia Alumnae Club, chaired by President Meredith and attended also by President Waggoner. It was made clear that the club would continue in spite of the closing of the College. It is important to say here that this was not a unanimous feeling. There were many alumnae—and some in the Philadelphia Club—who felt that closing the College was the best thing to do and that ceasing the work of the Club would be appropriate. Summarized from the notes of Nancy Besch, President Waggoner made the following points:

- Declining enrollment
- Deficit spending
- Dr. Waggoner's tenure began July 1, 1975. In 1974-75 the Board was concerned about whether the College should continue. At that time there was an operating budget deficit and efforts had been made to cut the deficit. 1970-74 had been difficult years. In admissions they began the "One Plus One" program. Students were asking questions about the future. There were curricular changes made.
- In fall 1978, there had been 4,000 inquiries in early fall but by December applications were coming in very slowly. At the end of the day they had 12,000 inquiries and they needed 150 students for the fall of 1979. There would be real trouble if enrollment did not increase since they had $1.25 million in operating costs.
- Concerning the closing:
    » Students, faculty and staff would be helped with relocation
    » All alumnae records would be maintained.

» Dr. Waggoner hoped that the alumnae would look at the facts of the case and help make the final semester successful.

It was noted that Westmoreland County was now forming a club with total support for Save Wilson. There was help coming from many sources concerning both the business and the curricular aspects of the College.

In discussion with Dr. Waggoner, the Club was told that all but one Trustee had attended the Board meeting of February 17, 1979, when they voted to close the College. At the March 10th meeting of the Board in New York City, the Board refused to reconsider their vote to close the College. The confidentiality maintained in both the February 3rd and 17th meetings of the Board was decided on because the Board felt they needed to do their deliberations in private. When they determined the situation had reached crisis proportions they felt, on February 17th, that they had to make the announcement quickly for the sake of the students, staff and faculty. Concerning enrollment, Dr. Waggoner noted that various techniques tried were not working well. Student Search, yielding thousands of names, produced very few inquiries that turned into enrollments. This was despite extensive financial aid in the face of rising average need—*i.e.*, $3700/per student to $4950 to $5570.

Dr. Waggoner noted that the decision not to contact alumnae was not an easy one. "If alumnae had been asked, of course, they would want the College to remain open." The new foundation would have a Board of Trustees; operating costs would be met, and the assets would be the restricted funds left in the current endowment. Dr. Waggoner felt that alumnae would donate to the foundation if the mission were well stated.

Concerning faculty, Dr. Waggoner said that the faculty would receive their salaries and, by announcing the closing now, would have time to look for new jobs. There would not be severance, and they would not have a year's notice. **(end)**

On April 2nd, the Steering Committee met in Lawrencevillle, New Jersey. Nancy Besch reflects upon those hectic days with amazement. She and the Steering Committee "were meeting weekly and traveling the Mid-Atlantic addressing groups of angry and bewildered alums, fending questions from the media as well, and coming up with a legal strategy to block the closing." As the organization's leader, she was also working to address the "what after" questions of how the College would operate and who would be the next Wilson President *when*, not *if*, the alumnae won the court case and succeeded in keeping the College open. The Steering Committee made plans for Save Wilson Road Shows.

Also, on **April 2nd**, a cover letter from Chairman Martha Walker accompanied a twelve-page statement by the Board of Trustees under the signature of Chairman Walker, which was mailed by US bulk mail delivery to all alumnae. Some of these mailings did not arrive for 6 weeks or more.

April 2, 1979

TO: Alumnae of Wilson College

FROM: Board of Trustees of Wilson College

In the weeks following the February 19 announcement of the decision of the Board of Trustees to close Wilson College at the end of the current academic year, many alumnae have written or telephoned Trustees and officers of the College. Some have praised the Board for its courage in facing the unwelcome facts and for making a painful but necessary decision; others have been sharply critical. Some alumnae have organized a "Save Wilson College" campaign.

Questions have been raised both about the reason for the decision to close and about the process by which the Board arrived at that decision. Unfortunately, considerable misunderstanding and some misinformation have confused the situation.

In the belief that Wilson alumnae will want to form their opinions and determine their course of action on the basis of accurate information, we have prepared the enclosed statement. It provides a chronology of our meetings and decisions in the past two months and offers for your review the essential data upon which the Trustees based their decision.

We invite your thoughtful consideration of this statement. Martha B. Walker, Chairman Wilson College Board of Trustees

A STATEMENT BY THE BOARD OF TRUSTEES OF WILSON COLLEGE

On February 17, 1979, The Board of Trustees of Wilson College adopted a formal resolution to close the College effective at the end of the current academic year, on June 30, 1979. Since that decision was announced, there have been many questions from alumnae and other friends, as well as from the campus and Chambersburg communities, about the reasons for the decision. This statement has been prepared in response to those questions.

BACKGROUND

Wilson College is a liberal arts college for women, located in Chambersburg, PA. It was founded in 1869, enrolled its first class in 1870, and has been in continuous operation ever since.

The College recorded its peak enrollment in 1967-68, with a total a total of 722 students. Wilson's largest freshman class was 252, admitted in September 1965. Since 1965, unfortunately, the number of entering students has steadily and precipitously declined.

Chapter One: Save Wilson!

The smallest entering class was 41 in September 1976, while the entering classes of 1977 and 1978 have totaled about 65 students each. In the spring term of 1978-19779, total full-time equivalent enrollment is 214.

During these years of enrollment decline—1968 onward—the College, has, not surprisingly, also encountered increasing financial problems. From 1968-69 through 1975-76, the College operated at an annual deficit, the largest being $862,546 in 1974-75. These deficits forced the College to tap its reserve funds and unrestricted endowment funds. Between July 1, 1970, and June 30, 1975, the Trustees transferred $4,320,000 from endowment principal to the operating funds in order to cover deficits.

In 1974-75, the Board of Trustees recognized the growing severity of Wilson's problems and commissioned a major study of the College's potential for the future. One of the "alternative futures" listed in the study was: "Closing the College immediately and establishing a working foundation to support scholarships for young women to attend college at a place of their choice." The Trustees considered several other alternatives at that time, but their ultimate decision was to try again to restore Wilson to its former health and strength as a liberal arts college for women. The Trustees made a deliberate decision to remain a college for women and to remain a college stressing liberal education. They chose a new President whose philosophy of education was consonant with those decisions.

In the three-and-one-half years following those decisions by the Trustees and under the leadership of President Waggoner, substantial progress was made in re-structuring the curriculum, revitalizing the faculty, recruiting students, and enlarging the College's financial resources. Major cost-reduction efforts were undertaken through staff realignments and reduction. Financial support from alumnae, foundations, Trustees, and other friends of the College was increased. The College was reorganized, from twenty departments into four divisions – Fine Arts, Humanities, Social Sciences and Education, and Natural Sciences and Mathematics. Wilson's faculty, though reduced in total number, was strengthened by the appointment of a number of able young scholars and by the addition of part-time and temporary appointments. Student internships and a major program of career counseling were developed to assist students. Students were given a stronger role in their own governance through the Wilson College Government Association. A program of continuing education for adult women was strengthened. Improvements in plant and equipment were achieved.

In crucial areas of student recruitment and retention and of financial stability, there was also progress. The downward trend of enrollment of new students halted. The budget was balanced for two years, thanks both to the improved management of College resources and operations and to successful fund-raising efforts.

Despite these efforts, however, and despite the substantial progress, the final "corner" was never quite turned so that Wilson could face the future with certainty. New enrollments in the fall of 1978 fell below projections and the attrition rate among returning students went up. Alumnae and other donors, perhaps wearying of the prolonged effort, fell behind projected goals in gift and grant support. And the major student recruitment effort designed to enroll a class of 150 freshmen for the fall of 1979 faltered, despite its initial success in stimulating inquiries about Wilson from prospective students.

THE FEBRUARY 2-3, 1979, MEETING OF THE TRUSTEES

It was against this backdrop that the Board of Trustees gathered on campus on February 2-3, 1979, for their regular winter meeting. As committees met and reviewed data and as the full Board assembled, the following facts were considered.

ADMISSIONS: In September 1978, the College enrolled 63 new freshmen, well below the projected 120 on which the preliminary operating budget for the year had been based. During the spring and summer months of 1978, a revised and enlarged recruitment effort was undertaken with the goal of enrolling a class of 150 in September 1979. Central to this effort was the use of names of college-bound high school students obtained from Student Search, a service of the College Entrance Examination Board. This process brought approximately 10,000 inquiries about Wilson College from high school seniors who have the apparent academic qualifications for admission. (Other means of generating inquiries produced about 1700 inquiries.) Based on historical ratios of inquiries to applications to actual enrollment (see Table I), this volume of inquiries was adequate to produce an entering class of 150 in the fall of 1979. It was this volume of inquiries, as reported to the Trustees in November 1978, that had caused the Board to be optimistic about the College's future.

Experience over a long period of years has shown that by the end of January, Wilson has received applications from twice as many or more prospective students than may realistically be expected to enroll the following September. (Some applicants are not admitted, and many students apply and are accepted at more than one college.) On January 31, 1979, only 83 applications, many of them still incomplete, had been received and 10% below that in 1977. And it was less than 30 percent of the number needed to produce an entering class of 150 in September. Two weeks later, when the Board held its February 17 special meeting, the number of applicants had grown by only 18. It was clear from these figures that Wilson could expect an entering class in

September 1979 of only about 60 to 65 new freshmen. The harsh reality that the Board had to consider was that for the third year in a row, Wilson would be admitting a class much smaller than needed to build up a total enrollment which would make the College educationally and financially healthy.

Added to the distressing information about enrollments was the faculty's and Trustees' continuing concern about retention of students. Forty percent of the entering class of September 1977 did not return to Wilson in the fall of 1978. Informal surveys of this year's freshman class, taken by students themselves, indicated that the attrition rate between May and September of 1979 was also likely to be high.

The poor prospects for new enrollments next September and the effects of increasing attrition among current students meant that the College in 1979-80 would even smaller than in 1978-79.

TABLE I: WILSON COLLEGE ADMISSIONS OFFICE STATISTICAL COMPARISONS

CLASS ENTERING	ACTUAL					PROJECTION
	9/74	9/75	9/76	9/77	9/78	9/79
1. Total Inquiries	5100	620	3000	3000	3700	11,000
2. Applications	264	254	157	158	185	550
3. % Application to Inquiries	5.2%	4.1%	5.2%	5.2%	5%	5%
4. Acceptances	225	221	109	126	151	412
5. % Acceptances to Applications	85%	87%	69%	89%	82%	75%
6. New Enrollments	111	105	41	65	63	150
7. % Enrolled to Inquiries	2.2%	1.7%	1.4%	2.2%	1.7%	1.4%
8. % Enrolled to Applications	42%	41%	26%	41%	34%	27%
9. % Enrolled to Acceptances	49%	48%	38%	52%	42%	36%

November 4, 1978

FINANCES AND FUND RAISING: In 1976-77, after seven straight years of deficits, Wilson College achieved a balanced budget—by a margin of $7,327 on a total of approximately $2.5 million. In 1977-78, the budget was again in balance by a margin not much greater. For the 1978-79 year, the budget as revised after September enrollment figures were available anticipated a small deficit. (See Table II)

The Trustees looked at these figures, however, with the realization that the 1976-77 balanced budget had been achieved only by the most stringent cost-cutting efforts and with the aid of a gift of $500,000 from an anonymous donor. The 1977-78 balance was achieved by transferring into operating funds some $400,000 from an unrestricted bequest which the Trustees had originally intended to place in the endowment fund. Though other large gifts and bequests might reasonably be expected to come to Wilson in future years, it would be unrealistic and irresponsible to budget on the assumption that such gifts would be received every year.

TABLE II: WILSON COLLEGE OPERATING BUDGET

INCOME Educational and General	ACTUAL				PROJECTION
	1974-75	1975-76	1976-77	1977-78	1978-79
Fee income	$869,021	$828,674	$676,940	$680,928	$712,575
Aid income	$182,026	$170,111	$166,168	$193,667	$221,301
Aid awards	$255,479	$286,996	$182,425	$193,667	$221,301
Net Fee Income	$795,568	$711,789	$660,683	$680,928	$712,575
Endow & Trust	$121,571	$ 93,176	$128,530	$187,556	$177,558
Gifts and Grants	$367,353	$618,475	$1,153,702	$1,202,893	$1,275,000
Other	$ 87,167	$ 76,143	$ 55,335	$ 63,919	$ 88,571
Subtotal:	$1,371,659	$1,499,583	$1,998,250	$2,135,296	$2,253,704
Auxiliary Enterprises	$609,682	$597,330	$469,413	$403,432	$372,325
TOTAL:	$1,981,341	$2,096,913	$2,467,663	$2,538,728	$2,626,029

EXPENSE	ACTUAL				PROJECTION
General Admin	$197,249	$112,185	$ 88,322	$ 80,941	$ 98,290
Student Services	$ 60,071	$ 51,728	$ 57,241	$ 63,037	$ 64,010
Development and External Affairs	$286,377	$259,276	$261,796	$300,285	$306,539
General Institutional	$205,898	$201,190	$207,089	$197,002	$235,317
Subtotal:	$749,595	$624,379	$614,448	$641,265	$704,156
Instructional	$992,927	$886,782	$867,663	$907,024	$949,849
Physical Plant	$373,939	$408,228	$392,448	$421,320	$467,384
Subtotal:	$2,116,461	$1,919,389	$1,876,599	$1,969,609	$2,121,389
Auxiliary Enterprises	$769,489	$665,492	$619,483	$585,034	$582,421
Subtotal:	$2,885,950	$2,584,881	$2,496,082	$2,554,643	$2,703,810
Transfer to Fin Aid Student wages	$ 42,063	$ 45,080	$ 35,746	$ 47,364	$ 56,461
TOTAL:	$2,843,887	$2,539,801	$2,460,336	$2,507,279	$2,647,349
RESERVE (DEFICIT)	($862,546)	($442,888)	$7,327	$31,449	($21,320)

(Note: General Administration: Board, President, Dean and Business Office; Student Services; Student Services, Financial Aid, Career Planning and Placement, Registrar, Activities and Transportation; Development and External Affairs: Admissions, Publications, Public Information, Development, Alumnae; General Institutional: Communications, Audit, Legal, Investment, Dues, Commencement, Lectures and Concerts, Staff Benefits, etc.; Instructional: Compensation, Supplies and Equipment, Library; Auxiliary Enterprises: Food Services, Dormitories, Health Center, Bookstore.)

Looking at the January 31, 1979, report on fundraising for the current year, the Trustees saw that approximately $1 million was still to be obtained by June 30 to reach the year's goal of $1,275,000. They also saw that the Annual Alumnae Fund, an important segment of the total goal, was lagging behind last year's figures, both in dollars and number of donors, and that the total gifts received from other friends of the College was likewise behind last year's figure of the same date (see Table III). The most optimistic estimate offered by the Board's Committee on Public Relations and Development was that gifts and grants to the College would fall short of this year's goal by at least $450,000. The effect of such a shortfall upon the College budget would be to send the deficit upward from the modest amount projected last fall to a half-million dollars or more. Further, assuming no decrease in enrollment, projections for the 1979-80 year indicated that to balance the budget the fund-raising goal would need to be at least $1.6 million—a substantial increase over the current year's unrealized goal.

To this information, the Trustees were forced to add their knowledge that the national inflation rate continues at a high level. A tuition increase had already been authorized for the coming year, but with all operating costs rising, the additional income produced by the rise in tuition would be far from adequate to meet the need. And the effect of the worsening energy crisis, with its possible effects upon all costs, but especially those for fuel oil was very much in the Trustees' considerations.

TABLE III: SUMMARY OF ANNUAL GIVING

	1977-78 Total	Jan. 31, 1978	Jan. 31, 1979
Annual Alumnae Giving			
Gifts and grants	$313,913	$133,818	$126,216
Number of Donors	2,503	1,484	1,335
Annual Giving – Non-Alumnae			
Gifts and grants	$892,089*	$48,699	$27,751
Number of donors	287	93	138

*Includes $400,000 of an unrestricted bequest originally intended by the Trustees to be added to endowment but later transferred to current funds in order to meet operating budget needs for the year.

PHYSICAL PLANT: Needs and progress on maintenance of the physical plant of the College were also reviewed. This included consideration of the sale, rental, or demolition of the Penn Hall dormitory and theater buildings. These buildings have been unoccupied and unheated since Penn Hall was purchased in 1973 and are consequently rapidly deteriorating. The College has sought in vain for the past two years to find suitable non-college uses for this property. The plant report included information about damage to roof, gutters, campus plantings, walks and roads by recent severe ice storms and the expenses—unanticipated in the budget—for clean-up and repair, and the extent of the need for repointing of buildings and the cost of this repair. The Trustees were aware of other costly deferred maintenance needs, for both plant and educational equipment, that remained outstanding in spite of the major efforts since 1975 to reduce the backlog.

FACULTY: The Board's Executive Committee held its regular meeting with the faculty's Committee on Cooperation with the Board of Trustees. Several items discussed in this meeting were of particular significance to the Trustees. There was a report on the threatened withdrawal of approval of the College's teacher certification program by the Pennsylvania State Department of Education (later modified after College negotiations with the State Department, but not entirely removed). There was a report on the faculty workload, which brought home to the Trustees the fact that the College has a full-time faculty of only 43, aided by eight part-time appointees, endeavoring to cover more than twenty disciplines and a number of interdisciplinary and inter-institutional programs.

The faculty committee also reminded the Trustees of their financial needs, requesting consideration of a general salary increase of 15% plus a cost-of-living adjustment. And they noted that the continuing financial difficulties of the College make funds for faculty development—research, attendance at professional conferences, sabbaticals, and the like—almost impossible to obtain.

NATIONAL TRENDS: The Board had also an awareness of national trends in the economy and in higher education, which are certain to affect Wilson College adversely. Among them are a high rate of inflation that continues to drive up College operating costs and to force increases in tuition and fees, as well as to increase the need for funds to provide student financial aid. Perhaps even more significant are the national population studies which show that, because of lowered annual birthrates, the number of young people in the college-age population will drop sharply in the 1980s. In Pennsylvania and other eastern states from which Wilson draws most of its students, the population decline is expected to be a much as 33 percent. Finally, liberal education as known and practiced by Wilson College, is less sought after by both high school seniors and their parents than formerly. Career education is the motto of the times. The Wilson College Board of Trustees, supported by the faculty and alumnae, made a conscious decision in 1970 to remain a college for women. In 1974, following a study of the entire campus situation by an outside consultant, the Board was determined to remain a liberal arts college. Both decisions might now be reversed, but only if capital were available for extensive and expensive revision and additions to the campus plant, equipment and faculty.

EDUCATIONAL ENVIRONMENT: All of the above factors led to the Trustees to question whether Wilson College now has, or can expect to have in the future, the kind of educational and cultural environment which they want for Wilson students and faculty.

Here is a student body of 214. Here is a faculty of 43, stretched over more than 20 disciplines and endeavoring also to do all the student advising and committee work expected of faculties at much larger institutions. Here is an administration reduced in numbers to an absolute minimum, with a support staff also at minimal levels. Here is a physical plant, designed for 600 to 700 students, requiring increasing amounts of maintenance and replacement as buildings and equipment age and become outdated. Here also is a plant requiring substantial renovation (estimated at over $150,000) to meet new Federal requirements to meet the needs of the handicapped students. And finally, here is a financial situation requiring an annual gifts-and-grants goal of approximately one-half the College's annual operating budget. A substantial portion of those gifts and grants must come from alumnae body number only 6,500 spread throughout the nation.

CONCLUSION: It seemed to the Board at its winter meeting that it would not be true to its trustee and fiduciary responsibilities, if, in the face of these facts and future prospects, it did not consider closing the College. Yet the Board was unwilling to take this step immediately or to do so without a review by others able to look more objectively at the College than the Trustees.

The Board therefore instructed the President to arrange for a review of the data on admissions, finances and educational environment by a group of consultants, chosen for their experience and expertise in related fields. The Board was asked to suggest possible consultants, and the officers of the Board, in consultation with the President, then selected those to be invited to serve on the consulting panel. The Board further instructed the officers to prepare a recommendation for consideration by the Trustees at a special meeting to be held on February 17, in Philadelphia.

THE CONSULTATIONS

The officers chose a panel chaired by Dr. David Truman, recently retired President of Mt. Holyoke College, now serving as Interim President of the Russell Sage Foundation.

Assisting him were Mr. John Butler, Executive Vice-President of the Philadelphia fund- raising consulting firm of Barnes and Roche; Mr. Danial Robinson, member of the public accounting firm of Peat, Marwick and Mitchell; Dr. William Ihlenfeldt at Northwestern University; and Mr. William Huddleston, Director of Admissions at Bradley University and a frequent leader of national seminars on college admissions. In the week following the Board's February 2-3 meeting, President Waggoner met in a full day's conference with Dr. Truman, Mr. Butler and Mr. Robinson. These four reviewed and discussed together detailed enrollment, financial, and management data from the past three years. Extensive telephone conferences were held with Dr. Ihlenfeldt and Mr. Huddleston.

The data considered by the consultants included complete admissions reports for the past three years and the printed material (brochures, catalogs, letters) that has been part of the recruitment effort; budgets of the past four years and tentative projections for the coming year; fund raising reports and materials of the past three years. At their meeting with President Waggoner, the consultants also discussed such broad questions as whether Wilson's fund-raising potential is sufficient for a year-after-year effort; whether a college as small as Wilson and located in a small city can attract the caliber of professional staff needed; and whether Wilson on a long-range basis can provide the kind of educational/cultural environment that will attract sufficient students to make the College educationally and financially viable.

Perhaps it should be stressed at this point that the panel of consultants was not asked whether Wilson College should close. The consultants were asked to review our admissions and financial data and to give their opinion on the likelihood of Wilson reversing what seemed to be a steady decline over the past dozen years or more. The decision to close was made by the Trustees, and they accept full responsibility for it.

On February 14, the four officers of the Board of Trustees (Chairman Martha Walker, Vice-Chairman Richard Hough, Secretary Alice Beeman, and Assistant Secretary Jane Stewart) met with Dr. Truman in his New York office. They were accompanied at this conference by the President. A report on this conference and subsequent meeting of the officers was made by Mrs. Walker to the Board at its meeting on February 17.

THE BOARD'S SPECIAL MEETING ON FEBRUARY 17, 1979

On Saturday, February 17, 1979, the Board of Trustees assembled for a special meeting in Philadelphia. The purpose was to hear the results of the consultations and the recommendation by the officers and to reach a decision upon the future of the College. Twenty Trustees were present; five were absent.

Martha B. Walker, Chairman of the Board, reported on behalf of the officers on their conference with Dr. Truman and the report of the opinions of the other consultant. Some highlights of Mrs. Walker's report are these:

1. Both of the admissions' experts consulted felt that Wilson could not attract sufficient students to meet our need for an enrollment of 600-700 students. Mr. Ihlenfeldt said that even if all possible expedients were tried—lower admission requirements, introducing pre-technical and career courses, introducing coeducation, perhaps starting extension courses or branch campuses in urban centers— even if all these were tried, Wilson was not likely to attract more than 325-350 students as a total enrollment. Mr. Huddleston's suggestion was that Wilson should proceed as though it were starting an entirely new college; study the potential market to determine what students and their parents want, re-design the College to meet those wants, and recruit a freshman class in 1981. If these things were done, his estimate of the maximum potential enrollment was 450. But this would not be reached for some six years.

2. The consultants said Wilson's fund-raising program is sound, but that the College is simply not likely to attract the major donors necessary unless enrollment can be improved. Considering the size of the College and alumnae body, Wilson has done quite well. They said it is a "miracle" that Wilson has balanced its budget the past two years.

3. The consultants were concerned about the deteriorating internal environment of the College. The constant pressure to recruit new students and uncertainty about the College's future inevitably lead to a decline in morale and optimism. This in turn makes it more difficult for the President and others to recruit new faculty and staff of the ability and experience needed.

4. Dr. Truman spoke especially of the responsibility of the

> Trustees to protect the remaining assets of the College—indeed, not to "fritter" them away on a nearly hopeless effort to keep the College going in any form. If the Trustees decide to close, he said it was important to make the decision soon and to inform the College community in order to provide time for such necessary matters as relocation of faculty, transfer of students, and orderly closing of the College.

Mrs. Walker summarized by saying that she felt that the panel had told the officers and Trustees that there are no panaceas and that they have no bold new ideas to offer us.

Mrs. Walker said that the recommendation of the four officers is that Wilson College must close.

Following Mrs. Walker's report, the Board discussed at length the officers' recommendation to close the College at the end of the 1978-79 academic year (June 30). They noted that none of the five consultants had been optimistic about Wilson's chance of surviving, no matter what heroic measures were undertaken—re-vamped curriculum, changes in the marketing of the College and recruiting of students, acceptance of co- education, etc. They noted also that even when some hope had been expressed about such measure, it was tempered by caution about the funds and time needed for undertaking major innovations. The Trustees also were aware that the immediate possibility of closing had not been discussed with faculty, students or alumnae other than those alumnae who serve as Trustees. This matter had also been considered at the February 2-3 meetings. The decision to keep the matter in confidence was taken because of the concern that discussion or rumors of an impending closing would have a devastating effect upon student recruitment and retention and fund-raising, and would foreclose any alternative solutions that

Chapter One: Save Wilson!

might have been proposed.

The Trustees also considered delaying the decision until the end of the academic year. However, it seemed wiser and fairer to all concerned to take decisive action now. The College was involved in the recruitment and hiring of new faculty. March 1, by Wilson College Bylaws, is the date on which renewal of faculty contracts for the coming year for faculty holding a first-year appointment must be agreed upon. If students are to find other colleges meeting their needs and willing to accept them as "transfers" next September, it is important that such negotiations start now and that deadlines for transfer applications be met. And certainly, for faculty and staff who need to locate other employment, the maximum possible "lead time" is essential. The Trustees likewise felt that continuing to operate the College for another year, when in their best judgment such operation could not be successful, would mean wasting the remaining resources of the College and avoiding their own trust and fiduciary responsibilities.

After considering what they genuinely believed to be all possible alternatives, the Trustees adopted the resolution of closing. The vote was unanimous except for one abstention.

There were no "nay" votes. Text of the resolution follows:

Aware of the deteriorating situation with regard to admissions, retention and enrollment as well as voluntary gifts and grants and of the jeopardy in which the continuation of the College as an excellent and effective college for women is placed, the Board of Trustees of Wilson College hereby resolves and gives notice that classes shall be suspended at the end of the academic year 1978-1979, and that the Board of Trustees shall begin at this time to take those steps necessary and which it deems appropriate to conclude the operation of the College in its present form.

It is agreed by the Board that, as of 1 July 1979, the corporate entity in which Wilson College now conducts its functions shall change its corporate name to the Wilson College Foundation and that the assets of the Foundation, other than those needed for the administrative functioning of the Foundation, that are not already in such form shall then be converted, over such period of time as to the Foundation shall seem necessary and prudent with a view to maximizing values, into endowment of investment-type assets producing an appropriate return.

The purpose of the Wilson College Foundation shall thenceforth be to continue to work toward the aims of Wilson College when an operating educational institution and to administer the assets of the Foundation in a manner as nearly as possible to fulfill the purposes fulfilled by Wilson College when an operating educational institution. The purpose of Wilson College as stated by its founders and continued to the present time has been to provide for women the opportunity for a broad and thorough education of the highest quality. As stated in its first catalogue, "the aim of the institution is . . . to provide in its course that thorough and effective discipline, which shall develop the mental faculties, and secure both habits of thought and real scholarship." From the beginning, there has been particular concern that the development of character be an integral part of a Wilson education. Hence the purpose of the Wilson College Foundation shall be to foster the liberal education of women for excellence, for leadership, for service. This goal may be pursued by the Foundation by such aid to the undergraduate education of women as it may deem appropriate to furthering the aims of Wilson College, including but not necessarily limited to educational research and development and scholarships for the undergraduate education of women.

ANNOUNCEMENT OF THE DECISION

The Trustees thought that it was essential that the first announcement of the decision to close be made directly to the College community of students, faculty and staff. For that reason, President Waggoner called an all-campus convocation for noon on Monday, February 19. As Board Chairman, Martha B. Walker made the announcement of the Trustees' decision.

Immediately following the convocation, a press announcement was released. This detailed statement was distributed to both local and national media, print and electronic.

In the week following the February 17 meeting and decision, the College also sent special letters to a large number of groups having a special interest in the matter. These included the parents of current students, emeritus faculty members, members of the Board of Directors of the Alumnae Association, the total alumnae body, leaders in the Chambersburg community and the Presbyterian Church, and foundations that have supported Wilson. Preparation and mailing of these letters, handled on campus, necessarily took several days, and thus not all interested persons received the information at the same time.

On the campus itself, President Waggoner immediately set in motion procedures to aid underclassmen to transfer next fall to other suitable colleges, to assure seniors that they would be able to complete their studies and graduate in May, to assist faculty in locating possible openings at other colleges and submitting their qualifications for consideration, and, to the degree possible, to assist non-teaching staff to locate other employment.

THE MARCH 10 SPECIAL MEETING OF THE BOARD

The news of the closing was a particular blow to alumnae. Wilson College alumnae have demonstrated their loyalty and devotion to the College over many years. Without their support, Wilson surely would have closed much sooner. Because they found it difficult to understand and to accept this decision, the directors of the Alumnae Association requested a special meeting of the Board to hear presentations by several alumnae representatives. This request was granted, and the Board reconvened on Saturday, March 10, in New York City. Four alumnae representatives were present to make formal statements to the Board and to request review and reversal of the decision to close the College. Twenty Trustees were present; five were absent.

The alumnae representatives focused on admissions, curriculum and related concerns. They expressed the belief that Wilson could still overcome its admissions problems through greater personalization of recruitment and by employing outside experts to design and implement a sophisticated national program of advertising and student recruitment. They said that they believed the curriculum can be updated and new programs implemented in career-oriented fields of study. And they offered direct alumnae volunteer assistance and participation in administration of the College if it were re-opened and if some re-staffing were needed.

After hearing the alumnae presentations, the Board again reviewed and discussed at length all the data and their implications for the future. At the conclusion of this discussion, the Board reconfirmed its previous decision to close Wilson College effective June 30, 1979. The vote was unanimous except for a single abstention. There were no "nay" votes."

CONCLUSION

In considering whether to close Wilson College, the Trustees have kept in mind the needs of the faculty, staff and students. According to several recent court decisions, a college that is closing has no legal obligations to its faculty beyond the actual closing date. The Board of Trustees have agreed to pay all faculty members through August 31.

Unemployment compensation beyond that date is being paid by the College under terms of applicable Pennsylvania law. Some faculty are contesting this arrangement, arguing that the College should provide one full year's notice and pay. This matter is under negotiation with the aid of the College's legal counsel and counsel retained by the faculty. The cost of such negotiations and of any lawsuits that may ensue will of course be part of the closing costs of the College.

It is the opinion of the Trustees that all debts and obligations of the College can be satisfied. Beyond current operating costs and obligations to faculty and staff for unemployment compensation, these include a debt of approximately $1,250,000 to the Federal Department of Housing and Urban Development and to banks to satisfy loans received for construction of Disert, Rosenkrans and Prentis residence halls. To meet these obligations, the College will use its unrestricted endowment and reserve funds, totaling $1.3 million. It will also be necessary to derive funds from the sale of the physical assets of the College—equipment, supplies, buildings—as soon as College requirements permit. Any funds remaining after all debts and obligations are satisfied, plus the restricted endowment (approximately $3.4 million) will be used to establish the Wilson College Foundation. After they had reached the decision to close the College, the Trustees decided to establish the Wilson College Foundation. It is expected that the capital fund of the Foundation will be small, but that it will nonetheless provide sufficient annual income to assist in the liberal education of women—the historic purpose of Wilson College. Restrictions placed by donors upon funds now held in the Wilson College endowment will be observed by the Foundation.

At meetings later this spring, the Board of Trustees will determine the procedure for establishment of the Wilson College Foundation under the governance of a small board of directors. Suggestions of persons to serve as directors will be sought from presidents of women's colleges and officers of similar foundations. Suggestions also will be sought from Wilson College alumnae. The Foundation's board of directors will then be empowered to employ necessary staff—probably a part-time professional director and necessary secretarial assistance.

In making this written statement, setting forth the reasons and the background for their decision, the Trustees believe there is little more to be said. They urge all friends of the College to accept the decision and to refrain from efforts to place blame or to identify mistakes of the past. All of us mourn the passing of Wilson College, but we take comfort in the knowledge that it has served many generations of young women and that it has met the educational needs of its students and alumnae for 110 years.

Suit has been brought in the Court of Franklin County against 24 of the Trustees of Wilson College by three alumnae, four students, one faculty member, one Trustee and one prospective student, asking removal of these Trustees and their replacement by qualified persons nominated by the plaintiffs and that there be a permanent injunction against the decision to close the College. The suit further asks that there be a temporary injunction imposed, pending the result of the litigation, upon all steps to implement the decision to close. Judge John Keller denied the request for an immediate temporary injunction. A hearing on the remainder of the requests is expected in about a month, following the filing of preliminary objections.

It is the opinion of the Board and its counsel that the case is without merit but that it would be inappropriate to comment further before the hearings. **(end)**

In the two special meetings of the Trustees on **February 17, 1979, and March 10, 1979,** no Trustee voted "nay" on the motion to close the College, and only two Trustees were unable to attend either meeting to participate in this difficult decision.

From the personal journal of Nan Clarkson concerning the March 10, 1979, Special Meeting of the Board:

... Emerging from the taxi, I saw familiar faces. There were alumnae of Wilson—awaiting the arrival of the Wilson bus ... and soon after that, we heard shouting and there it was, an old yellow school bus, careening down Broadway with girls spilling out of its windows, a full load. They piled off, full of holiday spirit. Perhaps it was the sight of me that sobered them, and then someone said, "Oh-oh look who's coming!" and there a block away, coming fast, were Mimi Wood and Margaret Waggoner. They looked fairly grim. As we went into the giant building through the revolving door, we heard them singing the Alma Mater: "Neath a group of pines and maples, by a gently flowing stream" sounded tragic in that concrete canyon. Perhaps "pathetic" is a less pretentious word. They had come all that way—surely a five- or six-hour trip on that bumpy conveyance—to plead for us Trustees to reconsider the decision to close the College. In my heart of hearts, I knew that wasn't going to happen ... up on the 13th floor. Greeted everyone in the huge Board room. There was no coffee or tea or any spot of warmth, just a huge room ... Quite a good number were there.

Kay Sweeney was up from Florida, most of us had flown in just for this meeting. It had been called by three alumnae Past Presidents—Mary Work, Betty Blackadar and Betsy Diely.

After being convened, we discussed how we would handle the time apportioned to the alumnae who were the representatives chosen to address us with what they called new information. We determined that we would not discuss with them but would, rather hear them, then excuse them, then formulate questions, then ask them back in to simply answer our questions.

Around the table, we all sat in comfy leather chairs, our papers before us. The six alumnae filed in, a fine-looking group of women, several of them youngish. Altogether, from beginning to end, I was impressed with them and felt a response of true sisterhood toward them. One looked very grim.

The first speaker was also the leader of the group. She is a young woman who is articulate, poised and cool. Her style was expressed in the impromptu way she made use of a painting in the Boardroom to close her part of the presentation. "That painting shows a linesman," she said, directing our attention, "and you can see he is fighting his way through a terrible storm to bring help to a line that's down. We're like that linesman; we've come to help save Wilson College."

The next two speakers were not memorable. One ... dealt with the explosive matter of "the 1500 cards." Supposedly 1500 prospective students were left without proper prospecting. (Margaret later had an adequate explanation for this. I think it was that they were the ones pulled from the first replies who did not seem adequate to do the job. Later, desperate, and so sent out letters to them in January. True or not, it certainly makes sense—though why didn't someone save them all this trouble and tell sooner?)

The next speaker spoke to the question of how we might effect a turn-around even after announcing the closing of Wilson. She alluded to Colorado College for Women and one other which have done this. She spoke of warmth needed to find faculty, students, alumnae and all to effect a critical involvement—spoke of the indomitable "spirit of Wilson that transcends us all."

Then the fourth speaker stood up. She was unrelievedly grim, and I rather suspect she felt that her position gave her more expertise than most of the Trustees lining that long table were willing to grant her. In fact, much as my own instincts toward her were sympathetic, admiring of her rapier-keen observations and her relentless case study, I suspect that most were put off by her manner.

She spoke of lack of imaginative leadership and lack of candor. She asked why the Middle States evaluation wasn't worked on immediately, why the Moon Report wasn't heeded. "Students today," she said, "are very career oriented. The Wilson curriculum doesn't reflect this."

The leader of the group closed with a stern but gracious series of jeremiads: "loss of quality of life to Chambersburg as well as loss of 116 jobs; 52% of last year's freshmen class didn't return; ... how did you make that decision in two weeks?" ... she made a fine closing salvo.

They then all filed out. No one official said anything. One of the male Trustees got up and thanked them. I called out a thanks to them.

The talk now centered on questions for them. Already my sense of the meeting was negative: those who were planted behind the President and the Chairman weren't about to bend; the rest of us hadn't the energy or the zeal to fight for what seemed more than ever "a lost cause." Because the sad fact was that, though the alumnae speakers were indeed

compelling in their energy and zeal, they had brought us no new visions of "how to"—only a catalogue of grievances, albeit grievous ones. Our questions for them were very specific, and the Chair of the Board asked them; she behaved in her most unsmiling, lawyerly way. On the other hand, the answers were disappointing. When specifics were asked for, we were given generalizations. Where did you get your information about the 1500 cards?

Answer: the Admissions Office. About the two colleges that had turned around after announcing closing? Answer: they admitted they hadn't yet gotten any answers from Colorado College for Women, and then the other was a co-ed college in Pittsburgh that they hadn't yet contacted.

In answer to our question about how they proposed to help admissions, fund-raising and interim services they could provide, their replies were

123

fervent, but no new ideas were given that hadn't been thought of or tried. The plain and simple facts are that it's too late, I think.

Before they came in, a Trustee said, "I don't think we need to treat these people as if they are a foreign body. In all my years I've never heard a better presentation. He also broke our agreement not to ask questions. He quizzed them on the addressograph matter so that the responsibility for that tasteless affair was put at Margaret's door. Margaret defended herself as usual; how could she know that it was a bona fide letter from the Alumnae Board? An alumna Trustee who headed the Alumnae Association spoke up to to say that the President hadn't even tried to find out. If she had, she'd have discovered it was signed by an officer of the Board and went out with her (the President of the Alumnae Association) full approval. Small matter but multiplied over and over it becomes a giant accusation.

An alumna of the small group had said that "if the closing of the College is due to poor administration, then it can be saved." As they left the room this time, we went into an executive session, and yet, even with the President gone from the room, her staunch supporters formed an effective presence.

I finally said in a very choked and uncharacteristic way some of the things that I didn't want to say but had to—how deeply I felt the wrongs that had been pointed out to us, the insult for the alumnae in not telling them and in sending their letters about the closing by third class mail (a saving of $1500 in postage that may have cost Margaret Waggoner her career as perpetual guardian of the Wilson College Foundation). The errors of taste and judgment embodied in the fact that fund-raising for the W.C. (foundation) fund was going on under the President's direction at the time when all her energy and time should have been for ministering to the agony of the College in its state of crisis.

Then I said that since no one else seemed about to do it, I reluctantly brought up the possibility of keeping the College open at least til

September, just to allow all the concerned factions the honor of at least trying to bring off the miracle they feel so certain could happen. When I said "reluctantly," it was because I had to admit I had no magic, nor did I have a whole lot of faith that anyone else did. But what would it cost us? "A lot," said the Vice-Chairman of the Board, with a snort. Please don't intimidate me, I smiled. Another woman Trustee said, "Let her speak—after all, Nan is playing the Devil's advocate, and I for one want to explore the idea." The idea did not get adequate play by starting too soon to implement the action! The Chairman had said, "Well, if you do that, you'd do it without Margaret." So we got off track by a Trustee's saying, "Well we need an executive officer. Who here would be willing to provide leadership for the interim period?"

"What would students do if they showed up and there weren't enough to open the College? Answer: they'd have risked and lost. But 15 have signed that they'll be there in the fall. Why not let them try to get another 150? If they cannot, and we close anyway, there are any number of unfilled colleges who'd welcome them. What about faculty? They're leaving already? Answer: We have to pay them until Aug. 31 anyway. Lots will not have jobs by them. A skeleton force would keep things going for the month or so until you could bring in the cream of the considerable crop of unemployed faculty members."

The idea died aborning. The only fact that really doomed it was a Trustee's financial stand: "The cost would be insupportable. You couldn't just close down in that case—you'd have to keep going at full steam all summer."

Well, yes, that's what they were asking for. When it came time for the vote, an alumna trustee asked about abstaining. "I wear two hats," she said, obviously in high stress ... "you are first and foremost a Trustee of Wilson College," said the Chairman. "You can vote yes or no but you cannot abstain." Nevertheless, she did abstain. I cannot help wondering if I had jumped on the chair and said you've no right to tell a Trustee how to vote and I intend to abstain too because I simply don't think I'm sure enough

125

this time and wish we would put off this vote until another meeting. After all, this College has 110 years of history, and there are many voices raised to save her now. We've seen how our judgment has been observed by the fury of the opposition. Let's all abstain!

The Chairman read a long letter blaming the choleric faculty for its lack of leadership and its hand in bringing about its own decline and fall. Who wrote it? I asked. "It is unsigned," the Chairman said, after reading it. "An anonymous letter isn't worth anything," I said. Others agreed, but the damage was done.

It was late—7:00 ... we were all gray with tiredness and a kind of defeat. The students were on the street singing and we had to face them.

Stanley Stillman (a Trustee also) and I went down. I had my arm in my sling and my whole body felt as vulnerable as my elbow, full of pain. When we came out of the revolving door into the darkness, the busload (of students) were grouped there singing the Alma Mater, softly, many in tears. The President of the Wilson College Government Association broke ranks and came over to me, grasped my arm gently—her face a question mark, so sad. I feel terrible, was all I could say. My tears said the rest. Then Stanley and I turned and walked away. The music following us for blocks. I shall never forget the sadness of that time. Another trustee who was an alumna wrote that she saw the same thing, but she was with a larger group. She said she wanted to join them "but their faces were full of hate. We were the enemy."

Indeed, when the book has been closed on Wilson, I wonder just how much a violent kind of anger, even viciousness, contributed to the lack of Save Wilson passion among us alumnae Trustees. Several of us were at the Wilson meeting when a staff member was careening around shouting insults and innuendos. Stealing those 1500 cards probably did more harm than good. Their rage may have stifled the sisterhood among us. Perhaps they can do it without us Trustees. But I do not believe it, alas and alack. (pp. 149-158, Vol VII, Personal Journal)

Chapter One: Save Wilson!

Nan Clarkson wrote in her Personal Journal:

March 29: *A letter to a classmate, which reads in part:*

You are right that the Trustees, having all financial and enrollment facts before them, acted with what they deemed "fiduciary responsibility." What we had no way of knowing was the response our decision to close the College would evoke: the rage, the motivating power it would release in the, literally, hundreds (they say even thousands) of alumnae now actively engaged in the "Save Wilson" activity. Whether there is an equal perseverance, energy and know-how to carry this groundswell beyond a brief upheaval of revival, who's to say? (p. 160, Vol VII, personal journal)

That same day: *The drama intensifies. An alumna Trustee went to Wilson as a part of the Executive Committee yesterday. I called at night for her news. We are individually, each Trustee, being served with an injunction. I'll receive it either by the sheriff's office or by registered mail, probably today. Saddest of the news here is that the names of those bringing us to court include two of our Trustees, both old and dear friends, having served faithfully along with me on the Board of Trustees.*

Two separate groups are investigating purchase of the campus: Vale Institute of Pittsburgh and an old folks' home type of organization. The President is speaking of leaving. The students have asked Carolyn Burger, an alumna active in Save Wilson, to speak to them at graduation. She speaks about all of this in a way that gives me pause. She often adds on a rather grim little ending to reporting a sequence of events—e.g., "of course, they're totally biased" or "of course, we're the enemy."

... I think what appalls me is that evidently the Chair and the executive committee as a whole are refusing to pay any attention at all to the Save Wilson Committee. Even (another alumna Trustee) who has always for me been the Wilson lady incarnate, believes we cannot survive on financial grounds. My insecure instinct gropes around questions such as: But we aren't bankrupt; why not try for one more year to see if there's anything to what these alumnae are trying to prove to us? Why do we

consistently avoid any substantive discussion about the President's performance? Is it because the President's supporters on the Board are so frighteningly formidable? Yes, partly. Is it because firing her would seem to affirm several years of doubt and vulnerability on our parts? Because a segment of the Board would resign? Including the Chairman? Whether or not the President is indeed guilty of the grosser misdemeanors laid at her feet by her detractors, one thing we're sure of: she has become the scapegoat and serves now as a terrible irritant. Her obvious financial skills do not outweigh her abusive personality, which has managed to alienate just about every faction of the campus faculty, to say nothing of the ranks of alumnae.

The charges against her are very serious. Yet we refuse to look into them. Having done so for years now—left all our concerns in the hands of the Vice-Chairman who has evidently never transmitted them to her in a way that caused her to change in even the slightest noticeable way ... The President herself questioned whether she should resign, but the Chairman of the Board talked her out of it. The Chairman is exhausted and very pregnant and is going off to Williamsburg for a week. This rankles, for after all, this was the very reason (the vulnerability as to this heavy time in her life, i.e.) that I went out on a limb back last fall to suggest that there might be others more ready at this crucial time in Wilson's life to shoulder the demands of that office. For this, I was soundly reproved ... and my voice silenced.

We continue to defend a person—who is right rather than what is right. In a frank discussion with the Chairman, she said that resignation would have been good before the litigation, but now it would appear as a real sign of weakness, as if we were admitting, too late to retrench, our inept handling of the Presidential problem ... I assured her that I would never be disloyal to the Board, as she worried I might. If so, I would resign. The Chairman really believes that Wilson cannot be saved, and she also believes that the Save Wilson people made a big tactical mistake by deciding to sue each of us separately rather than as a body ...

Chapter One: Save Wilson!

Nancy Besch called. She was hoping, I think, to see how I felt about the injunction, but more importantly, to reiterate her assurance that the Save Wilson Committee truly wants to work with the people on the Board who feel Wilson could be saved. With the fuzzy outlines of a friendly discussion (in which it struck me that I was being more careful than she), I believe she gave me to understand that if the President were to resign and if some of the more rigid Board members were to resign, the committee—no, the plaintiffs in the lawsuit—would drop the suit. I told her that if there were to be any hope of this, there were two crucial alumnae on the Board who had been devastated by the hostility oh yes, I also suggested to Nancy that the best thing her group could do was to articulate their strong leaders— i.e., list alumnae ready and willing and free to take on these new jobs I did not for a moment regret talking to Nancy. I trust her, and feel as much an alumna as a Trustee.

Another trustee who called is willing to put her name on a list of Trustees who wish to talk further with the alumnae group. I called yet another, and he is willing to allow his name to be used too. That is helpful in the extreme, for these two are impeccable Trustees—loyal, respected by all for their specific gifts to the College and their financial clout.

I don't want to wait too long to declare my true feelings. And yet, I do not yet know my true feelings. If there's a chance that Wilson could be saved, I'm for trying to save it. However, with only a smidge over two million left in unrestricted endowment, that's problematical. Worth the risk, however, to my mind.

May 2, 1979: *Today I did something that I am deeply divided about. Through another alumna, I made the suggestion that one of the alumnae Trustees be subpoenaed to answer questions about admissions at Wilson. She knows a great deal about the mis-management in that office, and has herself spent hours working for enrollment. ... This is the bit that I could do toward helping the "Save Wilson" people. ... This Trustee is in a unique position to at least reveal the director's ineptitude and the*

President's coddling of his student search. (The Trustee's) distress at the mishandling deserves to be a part of the total picture and yet it may well be too late to do anything about it. Forgive me. If the "end" of Wilson's possible survival justifies means, that fills me with guilt. I stand there. (pp. 162-166; 170, Vol. VII, personal journal)

On April 17, 1979, President Margaret Waggoner agreed to allow the alumnae to use Laird Hall for the May Day Rally after students invited the alumnae. No housing nor parking on campus was to be made available to alumnae. On this date, a petition drive was launched in the local area, and Save Wilson bumper stickers were ordered. $386,000 in cash and pledges had been raised to date. By April 20, 1979 the amount was $432,000 and by April 30, 1979 they were up to $609,000!

On April 21, 1979, the Wilson College Alumnae Newsletter #3 was sent. It is quoted in large part as follows:

SAVE WILSON COMMITTEE FILES CLASS ACTION SUIT

After the Board of Trustees voted on March 10 "not to reconsider" their decision to close the College on June 30, the Save Wilson Committee and its attorneys decided to try to reverse that decision through court action. Robert L. McQuaide filed a petition on behalf of the five-member law firm of Swope and Frazer of Gettysburg. It was also signed by J. Wesley Oler, Jr., of Carlisle.

The petition was filed in Orphans' Court of the Court of Common Pleas on March 27; the hearing will begin on May 7, at the courthouse in Chambersburg.

The suit seeks to remove 24 members of the Board of Trustees and to obtain a permanent injunction, at conclusion of litigation, against closing the College.

The petition charges the Board of Trustees with 17 counts of mismanagement. Among the most important are these:

–Failure to "fully implement a report submitted to the faculty, administration, Trustees and students for use in 1979-1980 and following school years by the Commission on Higher Education of the Middle States Association of Colleges and Schools, choosing instead to terminate the College less than a year later, notwithstanding a degree of optimism expressed by the report as to the College's financial picture";

–Failure to "adequately and competently recruit new students or to fully utilize alumnae in the recruitment effort";

–Failure "... to sufficiently curtail expenditures in view of income... " and to secure adequate funds to meet general operating expenses;

–Failure "... to adequately reorganize and maintain a competent and effective administrative staff . . ." and to ". . . devise and implement a plan for faculty retrenchment as the facts and circumstances warranted..."

The suit also states that "qualified persons are available to exercise the duties of trustees in place of respondent trustees." The Save Wilson Committee has begun massive fund- raising efforts to supply sufficient money to help meet operating expenses of Wilson College should the Court order the institution to stay open.

STATUS OF SAVE WILSON COMMITTEE

In response to the question, "Is the Save Wilson Committee" official? THE ANSWER IS YES. The Committee was duly constituted as an ad hoc committee of the Alumnae Association by a unanimous vote of the Board of Directors of the Association on March 18, at the direction of Elizabeth H. Diely, President of the Alumnae Association.

RESPONSE TO TRUSTEE LETTER

Recently all members of the Alumnae Association were sent a 12-page document from the Board of Trustees addressing certain issues relative to the closing of the College. This statement, while accurate in many of its particulars, also contains significant distortions and misrepresentations, which will be addressed in detail at the general meeting of the Alumnae Association on May 5, at the College.

SAVE WILSON COMMITTEE HEADQUARTERS OPENED

The Save Wilson (College) Committee has opened a headquarters in Chambersburg at 127 North Main Street. This office will coordinate all of the public relations and publicity efforts as well as all facets of the legal battle to keep the College open.

Nancy Adams Besch, '48, who was elected Chairman of the Save Wilson Committee, stated that, "The flood of mailgrams, letters, contributions, and telephone calls offering help forced the Save Wilson Committee to open a headquarters in downtown Chambersburg near the Wilson campus. The surprise February 19th action by the Board of Trustees to close the College, without consulting the 6,500 alumnae or the faculty, staff, or students, has angered many people. We have had hundreds of offers of support from civic, business and religious leaders, from parents of students, and from other friends across the country. The Save Wilson Committee was literally swamped by offers to help and to provide financial support."

HOURS OF OPERATION AT SAVE WILSON HEADQUARTERS

The Save Wilson Committee Headquarters is staffed by volunteer alumnae, faculty, students, and friends of Wilson College, <u>Monday through Saturday</u>, from 9:00 a.m. to 6:00 p.m.

At headquarters, you can obtain information on the various measures being taken to save the College. Copies of a petition urging President Waggoner and the Board of Trustees to reverse their decision may be obtained at the headquarters. The office is also accepting contributions to finance the continued efforts of the Save Wilson Committee.

PROFESSIONAL STAFF HIRED

A professional public relations and publicity person has been retained by the Save Wilson Committee to assist Joan Edwards, '58, and Carol Tschop, '72. He is Drew Steis, husband of Ellen Beswick, '62, of Washington D.C., who has been retained on a part- time basis to direct the public relations and publicity campaigns of the Save Wilson Committee. Mr. Steis brings a wealth of experience to the alumnae effort. He worked at United Press International for seven years and was Washington Bureau Chief for the *Boston Herald Traveler* for four years. He worked for a member of Congress for four years and served as a private consultant for two years. The Save Wilson Committee is pleased to welcome him aboard and to have the benefit of his considerable expertise in the public relations sector.

A WORD OF CAUTION

Communications Co-Chairs Joan Edwards and Carol Tschop have stated that "While we are in this period of litigation, the Committee needs to retain absolute credibility and cannot be vulnerable to charges of libel and slander. You are cautioned to use discretion and to refrain from 'name-calling' in letters to classmates that may have wider circulation than you intended."

EMERGENCY FUNDRAISING UNDERWAY

The Finance Committee of the Save Wilson effort has announced a goal of $4,000,000 to be raised in the next few months. To date, we have raised $395,000 in pledges to the Preservation of Wilson College Trust. This is an impressive achievement, but IT IS NOT ENOUGH. According to Carol Phillips Bauer, '57, secretary of the trust fund, "The goal can be met if enough alums are sufficiently committed to saving the College that they will make a more generous pledge than they have been used to, particularly in this crisis three-year period. THE TIME FOR ACTION IS NOW."

The urgency of the fundraising effort is related to the court case. The most persuasive evidence we as alumnae can offer the court is the pledge cards indicating our willingness to back the College with financial support. The Steering Committee and Robert McQuaide, the attorney who will represent us in court, would like to be able to show the judge a huge stack of cards from a significant proportion of the total alumnae body. Last year, only 39% of Wilson alumnae gave to the annual fund. This year, the life of our College is at stake. We must think in terms of a crisis. It is crucial that every available source of funding be tapped.

Here are a few suggestions:

1) Alumnae pledges: send in your pledge card NOW if you have not yet done so. Consider increasing you pledge if you can manage it. Urge classmates, roommates, big and little sister classes to do the same. PLEDGE CARDS MUST BE RECEIVED BY MAY 5th in order to be acknowledged in court, although of course they will be gratefully received at any time.

2) Parents of alumnae: many parents of alumnae have already volunteered their financial support of the Save Wilson Committee. This important source of funds should not be overlooked. Make sure parents understand that donations

should be sent to the Preservation of Wilson College Trust, c/o Carol Bauer.

3) <u>Matching gifts:</u> Give a pledge card to your employer or your spouse's employer. Many businesses are willing to support this effort, but they can't pledge their support if they don't know who we are or what we're trying to do. Make sure your employer understands that <u>pledges will not be collected</u> unless Wilson College remains a teaching institution.

4) <u>Public and private foundations:</u> if you have suggestions in this area of fund-raising, contact Marie Williams, '62, or Marilyn Mumford, '56.

5) <u>Friends of the College:</u> so many of you have requested extra pledge cards that we are enclosing one with this letter, along with a sample letter for you to send to a non-alumna friend. Or you may prefer to write a personal note. The importance of this is to increase the base of financial support.

6) <u>Presbyterian churches:</u> church officials are well aware of our crisis and many contacts have been made at the Synod level. You may send names of ministers, etc., to Nancy Besch.

CLARIFICATION OF THE C. ELIZABETH BOYD FUND

Many alumnae have asked for a clarification of the difference between the Preservation of Wilson College Trust and the C. Elizabeth Boyd Fund, both of which are fund-raising activities of the Save Wilson Committee. The C. Elizabeth Boyd Fund was created on March 3rd by resolution of the alumnae who gathered at the College to discuss what could be done in response to the Trustees' announcement.

The purpose of the Boyd Fund is to pay for <u>legal and mailing expenses</u> of the Save Wilson Committee. These are the only two expenses for which moneys have been expended from this fund. Although contributions to the Boyd Fund are not tax-deductible, <u>additional cash donations are needed</u> to underwrite additional mailings and to pay the attorney fees as they occur. An accounting of the Boyd Fund as of April 7th appears below.

Contributions to the Preservation of Wilson College Trust, on the other hand, are <u>made in the form of pledges rather than cash,</u> and will be applied to the operating costs of the College <u>only</u> in the event that the court decision is in our favor and Wilson remains a teaching institution. (These pledges will <u>not</u> be collected if a foundation is created from the liquid assets of the College.)

<u>Accounting of the Boyd Fund to April 7:</u> Received—$21,178.15; Expenditures—$13,584.85: Printing—$463.80; Envelopes—$75.00; Postage—$2,046.05; Legal fees—$11,000. Balance on hand as of April 7: $7,593.30.

BUMPER STICKERS AVAILABLE

Bumper stickers reading "Save Wilson College" in blue letters on a white background are available to clubs and individuals from the Save Wilson Committee Headquarters. They cost 35 cents and can be sold for $1.00 to interested alumnae and friends...

"MAY DAY * MAY DAY * MAY DAY"

Members of the Steering Committee of the Save Wilson Committee have received notification from the Wilson College Government Association inviting alumnae to return to campus on Saturday, May 5, to participate in the activities of May Day weekend.

The letter from the students reads in part, "In view of the fact that the coming May Day weekend may be our last, and there has been some confusion about who will be welcome on campus ... WCGA and the May Weekend Committee would like to take this opportunity to extend our warm and unqualified invitation to you and all alumnae to share this special weekend with us. I speak for all the students when I say that we look forward to seeing you and all the alumnae on that day. Please spread the word!" signed by Gretchen Van Ness, President of WCGA.

SAVE WILSON COMMITTEES WORKING TO PREPARE EVIDENCE FOR USE IN COURT

CURRICULUM COMMITTEE: Chair, Phyllis Ganz, '50; Steering Committee liaison, Marilyn Mumford, '58. The Curriculum Committee met on April 7th in Chambersburg with members of the Wilson College faculty. The committee has defined its task as falling into four areas: (1) preparing a statement of rationale and objectives for the curriculum; (2) identifying expert witnesses on curriculum who are willing to testify on content; (3) preparing short-range proposals that could be implemented in the 1979-80 school year, if the court decides in favor of Save Wilson; (4) preparing long-range proposals that will attract greater number of students to the campus.

SELECTION COMMITTEE: Chair, Jane Fox, '59; Steering Committee liaison, Carolyn Burger, '62. The Selection Committee has met three times in Pittsburgh. Its task is to prepare a list of potential Trustees to be presented to the Court in the event the decision is made to keep Wilson open. If you have a candidate in mind: (1) make a personal contact to determine the candidate's willingness to serve, degree of commitment, and ability; (2) if the person seems a strong candidate to you, send his/her name; (3) ask the person to submit a resume or curriculum vitae and a statement of his/her willingness to be a Trustee.

... ALL NOMINATIONS MUST BE RECEIVED BY MAY 1st IN ORDER TO BE USEFUL! The Selection Committee is also preparing a list of nominations for Interim President of the

College.

LEGAL COMMITTEE: Chair, Eudora Roseman, '62; Steering Committee liaison, Marie Williams, '62. The Legal Committee is responsible for coordinating efforts of the Save Wilson Committee with our attorneys. Each member of the legal committee serves as liaison to one of the other seven committees within the structure of the Save Wilson Committee. The Legal Committee met on April 1st in Lancaster with Robert McQuaide, our chief counsel. It is his opinion that those who want to help can best serve by sending in their pledge cards, by encouraging others to contribute to the cause, and by recommending persons to serve as potential Trustees.

ADMISSIONS COMMITTEE: Chair, Dolly Swisher, '73; Steering Committee liaison, Carolyn Burger, '62. This committee has divided its task into two areas: (1) to meet legal needs by determining the extent of "failure" in past recruitment of students; and (2) to develop a number of innovative approaches in admissions whereby a student body can be secured in coming years. The committee will be ready to recruit students as soon as the court decision is made.. If you have information or ideas relevant to this subject, send them. The Admissions Committee met twice in Philadelphia on April 4th and April 18th. **(end)**

On April 24th, a statement was issued by the Faculty Committee on Cooperation with the Board of Trustees of Wilson College. It is quoted as follows:

The Board of Trustees of Wilson College issued a statement dated April 2, 1979, that, in the words of the Chairman of the Board, "provides a chronology of our meetings and decisions in the past two months and offers for your review the essential data upon which the Trustees based their decision [to close the College]." In her letter addressed to the faculty and students of Wilson College, the Chairman, Martha B. Walker, further states that "unfortunately, considerable misunderstanding and some misinformation have confused the situation." This committee agrees but must add that any objective review of the statement by the Board will demonstrate that a principal source of the misfortune, misunderstanding, misinformation, and confusion is to be found in the document the Board itself has issued. Segments dealing with matters about which faculty are particularly knowledgeable are in several instances demonstrably contrary to fact, and in others, highly misleading. Faculty on this committee are embarrassed that, in an academic community in which students have chosen to live by an honor principle, faculty must reject major portions of a document because language which purports to be an explanation becomes, in fact, language of manipulation.

The <u>two most critical problems</u> facing Wilson College are <u>finances and enrollment</u>; and Wilson, like many private colleges in our nation, has been facing these problems for several years. We maintain, however, that in <u>recent years the College has yet to attack these problems with responsible and effective leadership, to say nothing of dynamic and innovative leadership.</u>

We emphasize very strongly, however, that our aim here is not simply to add to the charges that the College has suffered under ineffective leadership in the battle to remain a school of high academic standards; rather, our aim is to provide evidence that, under the present Board and President, the battle has not yet begun.

To see this point, we need only to address ourselves to the items listed as examples of "substantial progress" made "under the leadership of President Waggoner."

(1) The Board states that "substantial progress was made in

restructuring the curriculum." The faculty is not aware of any fundamental restructuring that has occurred in the last 3½ years. The Dean of the College chairs the Curriculum Committee, and she must shape ideas into reality. With four Deans in 3½ years, restructuring has been impossible. This year the faculty was hard at work at curricular revision, which was abruptly halted by the announcement on February 19 of the closing of the College.

(2) The Board states that substantial progress was made in "revitalizing the faculty." About 40% of the faculty has been employed at Wilson for three years or fewer. "New" is not a synonym for "revitalization." Revitalization occurs when vital ideas, whether projected by youthful or experienced faculty, staff or administrators are given form by competent leaders. Eight faculty have resigned since 1975. Over the vehement objections of faculty, alumnae, and students, loyal and mature faculty members were denied tenure in 1975, and this number includes one who shortly before had received the Lindback Foundation Award for excellence in teaching! These terminations were not retrenchment; the positions were filled by new faculty members.

(3) The Board states that substantial progress was made in "recruiting students and enlarging the College's financial resources." Examination of the data in Table I of the Board's statement reveals that in fact no progress has been made in student recruitment. While the President has publicly congratulated herself on improving admissions figures, this past fall the new student enrollment was 40% below that in 1975, when Dr. Waggoner arrived at Wilson. At that point the Board chose to hire as Director

of Admissions a very young person who had had no prior admissions experience. In the last 3½ years, faculty have been permitted no significant input into admissions policy. Just this past year the Dean of the College was denied access to information on the newly instituted Student Search admissions program and to the Standard Achievement Test scores of students. Faculty were told that principal efforts in student recruitment were to be directed toward Student Search and that other efforts were to be deemphasized as unproductive. Students and faculty were assured that, even by conservative estimates, these efforts would result in a new freshman class of 150 students!

(4) The Board states that "major cost reduction efforts were undertaken through staff realignments and reduction." The administrative staff has indeed been reduced in an attempt to control expenditures, but the turnover in personnel holding critical staff positions has been disgraceful. For example, in the past 3 ½ years, the College has seen four Deans, three Admissions Directors and heavy turnover in admissions staff, three Business Managers, two alumnae affairs directors, three public information heads, and heavy turnover in the development office staff. The Board of Trustees, in good conscience, cannot claim that it has done everything possible to save this College when continuity of management has been nonexistent. How could any faculty evaluate adequately and consistently the curriculum of a college, and how could it hope to have its efforts publicized, if it must begin each new year with a different dean or different information officer? How can recruitment officers learn enough to sell the College's program or to maintain a strong program of recruitment

under these circumstances? How and where can any genuine coordination occur?

(5) The Board states that "the College was reorganized, from twenty departments into four divisions." We simply note that the College was reorganized into a divisional structure well before Dr. Waggoner became President. Departments had surrendered their traditional autonomy. Curricular changes were to be examined from a divisional perspective before submission to the faculty as a whole. Department chairpersons—in many cases senior professors of long experience—surrendered prestige and influence that is a measure of achievement in almost all colleges in the nation in order to clear the way for effective administration. The faculty could not anticipate that, while it had reduced its departments to four divisions, it would have to try to effect its decisions through four separate Deans in 3 ½ years.

(6) The Board states that "student internships and a major program of career counseling were developed to assist students ..." The internship, career counseling, and placement programs have been strong for many years. The Committee is aware that, through the dedication of the present director, she was aided very often by alumnae who have demonstrated their loyalty by assisting in these efforts by returning to campus to counsel students.

(7) The Board states that "students were given a stronger role in their own governance through the Wilson College Government Association." Contrary to the Board statement, there has been no essential change in student government in the last 3½ years, and the role of the WCGA has traditionally been strong. Students representation on faculty and Board committees was instituted well before

Dr. Waggoner's arrival.

(8) "A program for continuing education for adult women was strengthened." The last person who acted as coordinator of continuing education students resigned in the summer of 1978 and was not replaced. Although the academic advising function has been centralized, there is no single person responsible for the coordination of the affairs of these students. Also, there has been a contraction of recruitment efforts.

(9) "The downward trend of enrollment of new students halted." Again the data in Table I of the Board's statement indicates that the downward trend has continued. Why does the Board state in one place that progress has been made in student recruitment and enrollment and in another place that the decision to close the College was in large measure based on declining enrollments? The Board justifies its decision to close the College by contradictory statements.

The Board also cites a decrease in alumnae giving for this year. Gifts and grants received from alumnae by January 31, 1979, were 5.7% below the amount received from alumnae by January 31, 1978. Is this decrease an indication of a real failure on the part of alumnae? Gifts and grants as of January 31, 1978, were only 43% of the total received in the 1978- 1979 academic year, so we must expect that this year most gifts had not yet been received by January 31. Furthermore, at a meeting of the Development and Public Relations Committee of the Board on February 3, 1979, the Director of Development and Public Relations said that she was confident that alumnae gifts and grants would reach the goal for 1978-79.

The alumnae—and indeed most of the College community—

had been led to believe that the College had "turned the corner." After David Dunkle, a reporter for the *Public Opinion*, interviewed Dr. Waggoner, he reported on January 9, 1979, only six weeks before the announcement of the closing, that "... it's beginning to look like Dr. Waggoner had led Wilson College through its greatest crisis and possibly into an era of expansion."

In November 1978, at a meeting of the Faculty, Dr. Waggoner presented a summary of the College's operating budget (Table II in the Board's statement). At this meeting, Dr. Waggoner expressed frustration over certain aspects of the financial picture of the College.

In 1974, the Academy for Educational Development, Inc., presented to the Board of Trustees a report titled "Survival for Wilson College: The Time for Stewardship and Sacrifice." In the chapter headed "Management Weakness at Wilson College," the Academy listed several problems, including: (1) "A great many of the major and minor decisions have been centralized in the President's office." (2) "There has either been limited delegation of responsibility along with job assignments or individuals have been unable or reluctant to assume individual initiative and responsibility." (3) "There has been substantial turnover in very important positions crucial to academic leadership, to the conduct of external affairs, and to the organization of student life on the campus."

Four years later, in June 1978, the Middle States Association of Colleges and Schools [the group that accredits the educational program of the College] in its Report to the Faculty, Administration, Trustees, Students of Wilson College stated: (1) " ... the Dean's office has suffered a high turnover (five Deans in five years) ..." (2) "There appears to be a need for more communication and interaction among the administrative staff." (3) "A more open administrative style, greater visibility on campus of major administrative officers, more open and frequent channels of communication, and greater involvement of the faculty in the decision-making process are some of the possibilities which should be explored to promote faculty leadership; cement administration-faculty relationships; and maximize the contribution of both to the College." (4) "There is a clear and urgent need for more delegation of authority." (5) "Administrators must know to whom and for what they are responsible; they must be given the authority to dispense these responsibilities."

Clearly, the Board was told by unbiased experts, in 1974, that there were severe management problems. In 1978, the Board was told, in effect, that the situation had not changed. Again we repeat our assertion made at the outset of this statement under the present Board and President, the battle has not yet begun.

In its statement, the Board claims to have "considered delaying the decision [to close the College] until the end of the academic year." We are outraged that the Trustees even considered the possibility of waiting until the end of the year. As it is, students and faculty have had less than four months' notice and are frantically trying to relocate at other institutions. Because of this inexcusably late announcement, it is no surprise that, to date, only a few faculty members have been offered regular, full-time academic positions.

Further, the Board has told the faculty that the Trustees' By-Law requiring one year notice and pay "if termination of employment before the end of the period of appointment is based upon institutional considerations such as the discontinuance of a program or financial exigency ..." will not be honored, even though the College is not bankrupt. In a letter to the Chairman of the Board and the President of the College, the American Association of University professors wrote, " ... based upon our current understanding, the announcement by the College concerning the decision to close does not equitably treat the faculty in terms of its entitlement to notice and severance salary consistent with standards commonly accepted in the profession and also accepted in the By-Laws of the Trustees of Wilson College."

Another such issue arises for students in their junior year who face a particularly severe problem since most colleges require two years residency for graduation at their institutions. Dr. Waggoner assured the juniors that it is possible for them to receive a Wilson College degree in 1980 after completing their Wilson program at another institution. Since the Board denies its obligations to the faculty, we must be wary of assurance by the Board that juniors can, in fact, receive a Wilson degree in 1980. In response to faculty concerns, Dr. Waggoner has written, "... students are being held hostage by the faculty. Such abuse of students by faculty is a disgrace to the profession."

It is unfortunate that Dr. Waggoner refuses to recognize the genuine concern that faculty have for our students. The faculty comprising the freshmen-sophomore advising staff have sent over 200 letters of recommendation to admissions offices; other faculty members have sent numerous letters and have even telephoned admissions offices to ensure placement of our students. There appear to us to be serious risks for a student who enrolls in another institution with the intent of receiving a degree from a nonexistent college. The Board is unwilling to inform students of those risks or to clarify the bases upon which a degree can be awarded legally and financially by a nonexistent college. We are told in effect that the Board knows best. In view of the Board's handling of the problems of the College, we must wonder if the Trustees really know best.

Recent actions of the Board and the President have further alienated faculty, students, alumnae, and even many on the administrative staff, and the situation is rapidly deteriorating. Alumnae have been denied access to alumnae address plates. Alumnae have been banned from campus over May Day Weekend, ostensibly because the President does not want to overtax the staff. Genuine faculty concerns are labeled a disgrace to their profession. Administrative staff who believe that the College can still be saved are told they could lose their jobs because of conflict of interest.

We are proud of the contributions that Wilson College and her alumnae have made to the nation and, until recently, we have taken pride in her leaders. On the very weekend that this committee was in good faith presenting reports to the Trustees on plans for faculty development in accord with the recommendations of the Middle States accrediting body, the Board, unknown to the faculty, was apparently setting in motion plans which were to result in the death of the College. No wonder, then, that we deeply resent the Board's funereal comments that "there is little more to be said," that "all of us mourn the passing of Wilson College," but that "we take comfort in the knowledge it has served many generations. "Then, over one hundred years of vigorous faith in the ideals of a liberal education for women are provided with a coffin—the Wilson College Foundation.

The alumnae clearly recognize that Wilson lives in the hearts and minds of those who know her, and they are determined to make their college live, not to become a living memorial. We wholeheartedly support their efforts.

Wilson College deserves it!"   April 24, 1979 (**end**)

April 26, 1979. Letters were sent to honorary degree recipients by Nancy Besch requesting support. The letter reads as follows:

"Dear_____:

You may be aware that on February 19, 1979, the Board of Trustees of Wilson College announced that Wilson would cease to operate as a teaching institution on June 30, 1979, after a 110-year history. The Board of Trustees cited declining enrollment and decreasing financial support as primary reasons for closing the College. The Board's announcement came as a great surprise to the faculty, students, and 6,500 alumnae who were not consulted or made aware of the fact that the College was in a period of crisis.

In response to the Board's action, the Save Wilson Committee was duly constituted as an ad hoc committee of the Alumnae Association by a unanimous vote of the Board of Directors of the Alumnae Association, on March 18, at the direction of Elizabeth H. Diely, President of the Alumnae Association.

The Committee's task is four-fold: (1) To develop innovative admissions and recruitment procedures designed to insure future student enrollment; (2) To devise new curricula combining a traditional liberal arts education with career-oriented courses of study; (3) To find and select qualified replacement Trustees and College administration; and, (4) To raise a "substantial" amount of money to cover operating expenses for the coming academic year. Great progress is being made in all of these areas, as they come forward with expertise and pledges of financial support. Because the Board of Trustees refused to work with the Committee in this effort, the Alumnae Association Board of Directors retained an attorney who filed suit on March 27, 1979 in the Franklin County Court of Common Pleas in Chambersburg, Pennsylvania. The petition seeks the removal of 24 Trustees,

Chapter One: Save Wilson!

charging mismanagement and negligence. May 7 has been set as the hearing date.

As Chairwoman of the Save Wilson Committee, I want to make you, as a recipient of an honorary degree from Wilson College, aware of our efforts to prove new leadership and to insure the continued financial health and educational excellence of the College.

If you feel as we do, that there is a real need for women's colleges and that Wilson College, as the oldest four-year women's College in the United States, can and must continue to meet that need, please give us your support in any way you can.

Signed by Nancy Adams Besch **(end)**

April 27-28, 1979. The following tells the story of the phonathon, the broadcast on National Public Radio, and the Trustee meeting on April 28th, to which Nancy Besch was invited. I am quoting from Nancy Besch:

"In April, we had a telethon in New York City on a Friday night (April 27). On Friday afternoon, when I was leaving Camp Hill, I got a phone call from correspondent Stephanie Sheldon from National Public Radio, and she wanted to interview me about the lawsuit.

But she didn't want to record the interview because she wanted to do it live in the late afternoon on the national broadcast of the news program *All Things Considered.* "But I'm just leaving the house to go to Lewisburg," I told her. I had arranged to pick up Mardi Mumford to go to New York City to help with the phonathon. "I'll have to call you on the way," I said. ... As the 18-wheelers roared by, Besch with one hand clenching the

pay phone receiver and the other covering her exposed ear, she told the national news audience (the story) ... Then Besch picked up Mumford at Bucknell, and the two drove on to New York City where there were others from the greater Harrisburg area as well making phone calls to alumnae all over the country for support. "After the phonathon that night, Mardi and I drove directly to Washington, D.C., because the meeting of the Board of Trustees was scheduled in Washington the next morning."

The April 28th Meeting of the Board of Trustees: Besch was the only one invited to join the Board in the Madison Hotel where President Waggoner, nearly all of the members of the Board of Trustees and their legal counsel had assembled to discuss the pending suit. Besch didn't want to be in the position of having to file suit against her *Alma Mater*, but "we knew the only thing we could do was to go to court and appeal the Board's decision." If she was nervous, the diminutive Besch tried to hide it. When she arrived at the hotel suite, the first person she saw was Harrisburg attorney Tom Menaker, the husband of Board of Trustee member Bonnie Menaker. He was representing the College's Board of Trustees. Menaker, a graduate of Duke University Law School, was an influential defense attorney best known for representing the Reverends Phil and Daniel Berrigan, anti-war activists, in the 1972 trial of the Harrisburg Seven. In addition to high-profile cases including the 1974 defense of an Oberlin College athletic director and his wife who harbored fugitive heiress Patty Hearst in a rented Pocono Mountain farmhouse, Menaker also did work for non-profits. Among them was the Hemlock Girl Scout Council, where Besch served as president. They had met often that spring—not about issues relating to Wilson, but about personnel issues involving the Council.

… Again, the majority of the Board voted not to reconsider the decision to close the College, but this time several members of the Board voted to reconsider. **(end)**

Chapter One: Save Wilson!

On May 3rd, an article appeared in Carlisle's *Evening Sentinel*, written by Jim Kershner, titled "Battle Lines Growing Over Wilson Closing": (Reprint permission granted)

"After 110 years, Wilson College isn't about to close without a fight. The main battle opens Monday when a suit to keep the school open by removing the current Board of Trustees will be heard in Franklin County Court. But four developments this week indicate how sharply the battle lines are drawn:

*The Board of Trustees Wednesday filed papers asking that the suit be dismissed because the court does not have jurisdiction, the student and alumnae petitioners do not have the necessary legal standing, and because the suit fails to name Wilson College itself as a defendant.

*Wednesday, 54 of the College's 57 graduating seniors signed a petition stating their "refusal to accept our degrees from (College President) Margaret Waggoner and (Board of Trustees Chairman) Martha Baum Walker at commencement." They requested other officials hand out the diplomas.

*The faculty of the College voted Tuesday evening to request the President to resign immediately and to remove herself from all affairs related to ending the college year and closing the school.

*The student government association has invited the College's 6,500 alumnae to the annual "May Day" festival this weekend, following an attempt by Waggoner to keep the alumnae off campus. Over 1,000 are expected at a Saturday morning meeting organized by the students and the Save Wilson Committee.

Meanwhile, classes are continuing "almost normally" according to a student at the small liberal arts college for women. Students have been busy seeking other colleges since the Board of Trustees announced February 19 that the College would close June 30.

Preparations for the annual dinner-dance, May Court ceremony, talent show and May Fair were proceeding on the scenic, tree-lined 300-acre campus in Chambersburg.

Many of the College's 176 full-time students said they plan to attend the hearing Monday in Franklin County Orphans Court at least between classes. The legal response of the Board of Trustees indicates the suit may end up being decided on legal technicalities rather than on the question of whether the College should be closed or remain in operation. The Board, through its attorney, J. Thomas Menaker of Harrisburg, argues the suit is based on the wrong law. The petitioner—a group of prospective, current, and former students, a faculty member, and a Trustee, represented by Robert L. McQuaide of Gettsysburg—asked the Franklin County Orphans Court to remove the Trustees in accordance with the "Decendents, Estates and Fiduciaries Code" governing nonprofit corporations committed to charitable purposes.

But the Trustees argue that law does not apply "because Wilson College is a nonprofit corporation operating as an institution of higher education rather than a charitable trust."

The hearing begins in Franklin County Orphans Court at 9:30 a.m. Monday and may be continued on succeeding days if it is not dismissed.

The petition signed by the seniors [concerning who gives them their diplomas] was presented to President Waggoner Wednesday afternoon by Cheryl Bauman, senior class President. When asked about the petition this morning, Waggoner's secretary told a reporter, "I really don't have answers to your questions, and President Waggoner doesn't have time to talk to you, so I really can't give you any information." The petition read in part: "Above all, our education has taught us to ask why and seek the truth.

Chapter One: Save Wilson!

It is our feeling that we have been deceived, misinformed, and disregarded by these two women [Waggoner and Walker]. Our conscience will not allow us to respect those who have rejected the Wilson spirit of honor ... therefore, we ask that [Dean Shirley] Van Marter and Dean [emeritus Margaret C.] Disert, two women for whom we have the utmost regard, present us with our degrees at commencement. Let it be clear that we refer only to the ceremonial aspects, not the legal degree conferment."

The faculty resolution calling for Waggoner's resignation follows a long period of tension between the faculty and the administration, according to English professor James Applegate. Last week a Faculty Committee on Cooperation with the Board of Trustees issued a five-page statement that was highly critical of the Board and of President Waggoner. It rejected an April 2 explanation of the closing issued by the Board "because language which purported to be an explanation becomes, in fact, language of manipulation."

The faculty statement concludes with a statement of support for the alumnae and students who have formed the Save Wilson Committee in an attempt to keep the College open.

The Save Wilson Committee, which now claims to have raised about $650,000 in pledges and contributions, is gearing up for a meeting at 10:00 a.m. Saturday, in Laird Hall on campus.

According to Gretchen Van Ness, President of the student government, Waggoner had originally asked the Save Wilson Committee not to hold the meeting at all, because it might interfere with student activities. She later agreed to permit a two-hour meeting, but said the College could not provide housing or parking facilities.

Van Ness then wrote a letter to the alumnae stating: "In view of the fact that the coming May Day weekend may be our last, and there has been some confusion about who will be welcome on campus, ... Wilson College Government Association and the May Weekend Committee ... extend our warm and unqualified invitation to you and all alumnae to share this special weekend with us." **(end)**

May 4th. The *cy pres* petition is filed in Franklin County Court by Martha Walker to have the endowment changed from the College to the proposed foundation.

May 5th. The **May Day Rally boasted 2000 in attendance,** was held on campus, including 600 alumnae who heard reports from the Save Wilson Committee. A raffle sponsored by the local Wilson Club nets $600. The students had invited the alumnae.

The Board of Directors of the Alumnae Association met at 9:00 a.m. on **May 5th**. The main points of that meeting were as follows:

- At the May Day Rally (that day), the Board wanted to make clear to the alumnae that most alumnae board members also held leadership roles in the Save Wilson effort.

- Each Save Wilson Committee Chairperson was to give a brief update of activities and findings since the March 3rd meeting.

- They had not received a copy of the Charter of the Alumnae Association—important to understanding the official and legal relationship of the Association to the College.

- As of June 15, 1979, when the Coordinator for Alumnae Affairs would be leaving, there might be no provisions for paid personnel to staff the Alumnae Office.

- In case of the necessity for reconstituting the Alumnae Association, a member of the Board was asked to prepare a modified Constitutional Revision to present to the Association in June, and one was asked to formulate a new bookkeeping system.

- The Centennial Celebration of the Alumnae Association would go on as planned, but problems needed to be resolved in light of closing procedures.

May 7th-11th. Testimony in the Court Case is heard. The court hearing on Save Wilson ends on May 11, following five days of testimony by 33 witnesses.

May 11th. The Faculty files a $667,000 damage suit against Wilson. (This case never went to court)

May 12th. $1.1 million in cash and pledges had been raised to date. Lili Kraus writes a letter to Nancy Besch offering to donate her $3,000 fee for a benefit concert for Save Wilson.

May 14th. Save Wilson contacts Bill Putch, who offers a benefit performance at the Totem Pole Playhouse on behalf of himself and his wife, Jean Stapleton. The Franklin County Club begins promotion and ticket sales for the matinee to be held on June 3rd.

On May 21st, the special report written by Jane Shaw appeared in the *Pittsburgh Post-Gazette*, entitled "Wilson College's Last Gasp Rage." (Reprint permission granted) It is quoted here in full:

> "The college is not bankrupt. It has had a balanced budget for the last two years and has an endowment of $4.8 million, but on June 30 the 110-year-old Wilson College will close.
>
> The decision by the board of trustees, made at a special meeting Feb 17, has angered alumnae, faculty and students.
>
> The Wilson College Alumnae Association, comprising 6,500 members, has formed the Save Wilson Committee, and has filed a class action suit in Franklin County courts to prohibit the closing of the college in Chambersburg. A decision in the case,

whose five days of testimony ended May 11, is expected by the end of the month.

Many faculty members have joined in the suit, and students have strongly supported the alumnae in their efforts.

"Suddenness" and "secrecy" are the words used most often when these groups discuss the closing. "Necessary" is the word used by College President Margaret A. Waggoner and Board Chairman Martha B. Walker.

"Sudden" because in a recent interview and letter, Miss Waggoner painted a rosy picture for Wilson's future.

"Secret" because alumnae and faculty feel there were never fully informed of the seriousness of the situation.

Wilson College Squirms in Throes of Agonizing Last Gasp

(Continued from Page 1)

"Necessary" because of a low enrollment of 212, lack of incoming freshmen, decline of gifts to the college and increasing expenses.

"It's really not sudden," Miss Waggoner said. "The College has been in bad shape for some time. In the '50s, there were budget deficiencies. In 1975, when Charles Cole resigned as president, it was decided not to close but to give it one more try."

Miss Waggoner, former dean at Smith College with bachelor's, master's and doctoral degrees in physics from Iowa State University, became president in 1975.

"In early December we thought everything was fine, but we came out of January knowing things were not. Their inability to get students and the attrition in our present student body had cut enrollment badly," she said.

In 1974-75, as enrollment fell, one third of the operating budget was deficit. In 1975-76, Miss Waggoner cut the deficit in half. In 1976-1977, she balanced the budget after seven straight years of deficits, largely because gifts and grants to the College doubled. She balanced the budget again in 1977-78, when gifts and grants doubled once more, totaling more than $1.2 million.

"We were trying this year to increases it to $1.275 million. We were looking to gifts and grants for one-half of the income we needed this year," Miss Waggoner said. "That's high for an institution to expect this." (Tuition normally provides 60-70 percent of income.)

"And this year we did not receive the usual amount of year-end gifts. At the end of January, we still had a million of the $1,275,000 to raise.

This raised grave doubts about Wilson's future," she said.

"We had to see this in long-range," Miss Waggoner said. "Could we maintain the quality of education that is Wilson? The conclusion was we could not."

The 25-member board, including 10 alumnae, reacted to the president's report on Feb. 2 by asking her to have a group of consultants review data on admissions, finances and the educational environment. Consultants were selected by the officers of the board and the president.

They were asked to report back by Feb. 17, when a special board meeting was scheduled in Philadelphia.

Although none of the consultants recommended closing, none were optimistic about Wilson's chance of surviving, no matter what measures were taken.

After discussion with these consultants, the board's officers recommended closing the school.

"The committee indicated what traditional alternatives are for colleges in trouble, such as going coeducational, extension courses, adult education, dramatically changing curriculum, branch campuses," said Mrs. Walker, a Wilson alumna.

"The board ruled these out as not being feasible, because of expense and because they probably would not have any effect for several years. They probably should have been considered five or 10 years ago.

"It's easy to say you can change curriculum and become more marketable and attractive, but it's not easily done. And admissions experts said you would have to look at less-qualified candidates than we are taking now."

Another special meeting of the board was held March 10 in New York at the request of the alumnae. Four alumnae representatives formally requested that the college be kept open, but the board reconfirmed its decision to close Wilson.

The action was reaffirmed again on April 28 but this time there were dissenters.

The vote was 15-7, with six of the 10 alumnae on the board opposing the closing.

"There seems to be a pattern of don't let the alumnae know," said Joan Edwards of the Save Wilson Committee, which has almost $1.1 million in cash and firm pledges for the college and $35,000 for the lawsuit.

"The announcement of the closing was made Feb. 19 at noon, and that was the first word anybody had. It was made simultaneously to faculty, students, staff, and the press. But not to alumnae. No official information was given to alumnae until a letter mailed bulk rate was received two weeks after the announcement.

Chapter One: Save Wilson!

"We weren't allowed to ask the board any questions at the special board meeting. In fact, we were asked to leave after our presentation. We were refused the names of the special consultants, although we know they never met as a body, never visited the campus, and did not submit a written report.

"We can't get information about what happened to 12,000 inquiries for admission, although we do know of 1,400 pieces of mail never mailed from the admissions office in response to inquiries."

We have been denied the use of addressograph plates so we could communicate with alumnae. Repeated requests for evaluation of the financial status of the College by the Save Wilson Committee have gone unanswered."

Miss Waggoner said the strong sense of loss among alumnae did not surprise her. "Alumnae of Wilson College are very strongly attached to this institution," she said. "That tells you something about Wilson. I am surprised, however, considering all that has been and knowing the problems of the College that they say, 'Now we should begin to fight.' As if we hadn't been fighting all these years."

The decision surprised the faculty because the administration had been confident of getting 150 incoming students.

"It was a shock," said Shirley Van Marter, dean of the college, of the closing of the College. "It was totally unexpected."

The faculty voted 34-4 to ask for Miss Waggoner's resignation, and a faculty committee has disputed the board's report defending the closing of the College.

"It will be very difficult for the faculty," Mrs. Van Marter said. "The announcement was made too late to make applications. Most institutions have filled vacancies."

The college had held onto the faculty so it would be prepared if it reached the desired enrollment. The 43 faculty members will be paid through the end of their contracts, which is August.

Wilson's 212 students reacted to the closing of the College with protest meetings and demonstrations for a week following the announcement. Fifty-four of the 57 graduating seniors signed a petition requesting Miss Waggoner resign. A group traveled to New York to protest the closing at the second meeting of the board called to review the decision.

"The students are very upset and don't want the school to close," said Janet Serdy of North Hills, a past treasurer of student government. "We feel there are enough reasons for the school to remain open."

Gretchen Van Ness, President of the Wilson Student Government Association, said the students are counting on alumnae to help them fight to keep Wilson open. She recently participated in a ribbon-cutting ceremony opening the Save Wilson Committee headquarters in Chambersburg and is a signer of the court petition.

The seniors have voted unanimously not to accept diplomas from the president of the board or college.

John Mason, Director of Admissions, said the College did all it could.

He said it sent brochures and follow-up mailings to 70,000 students selected because of compatibility with Wilson but got little response.

"We had reason to make a projection of between 120 to150 students," he said. "We needed 120 but the applications did not materialize. We got 60."

Chapter One: Save Wilson!

It is reported 50 applications were received the day after the closing was announced. These were after a statement that the college had closed.

"It's a paradox, but the things we feel are true assets become liabilities: size which permits individual attention and small classes and provides for students' participation in so many activities as she desires; location in a small city with clean air, no crime, none of the problems of a large city," he said.

"But in the mind of the potential student, there's nothing going on."

He said Wilson's decision to maintain a traditional liberal arts program rather than shift to a career-oriented curriculum has also hurt.

"Look at the sheer numbers of students and where they are. They want something different from what we offer," he said.

William T. Coffield, President of the Greater Chamber of Commerce, said Wilson's closing will hurt the local economy and greatly damage cultural life.

"We haven't been able to put a dollar and cents figure on the economic effect," he said. "The loss of spending by faculty, students and parents will be felt, but we'll recover."

"It will be much harder to recover from the cultural loss. The events at the college were open to the public. These included lectures, music programs, drama."

Coffield said the closing of the College was not totally unexpected.

"We felt for the past five years, watching the declining enrollment, that the end was near. But then we had reason to believe the corner had been turned. Enrollment was up last year. Inquiries were good this year. So it was a shock."

Marjorie Parson, publisher and editor of the Public Opinion, Chambersburg's newspaper, agrees the closing will hurt.

"I think it's a serious loss, and we won't really realize the loss until it comes, until it comes," she said. "It will be a great loss of an intellectual force in the community."

"If you don't have students, I don't know how you can keep a college open. I think they did the right thing. 'Close with dignity,' they said, and I agree with that."

Contributing to the dignity will be the establishment of the Wilson College Foundation, which will be endowed with the assets remaining when the school is closed. It will provide undergraduate scholarships to women, sponsor education research and development and underwrite other appropriate programs.

"What I am trying to do in the process of closing is to preserve as much as I can of what has been special about Wilson College and to provide for the use of whatever resources remain." Miss Waggoner said.

Before her plans can take effect, however, the Save Wilson Committee's suit must be settled. It seeks the removal of Miss Waggoner and 24 of the 25 Trustees, including those who now oppose the closing and charges them with 17 counts of mismanagement.

The only Trustee not named in the suit is Jean Colgan Zehner of Fox Chapel, one of the petititoners.

The only other Pittsburgher on the Board is Woodruff Turner, of the law firm of Kilpatrick, Lockhart, Johnson and Hutchinson.

Although still named in the suit, Howard O. Colgan, Jr., Mrs. Zehner's brother, has resigned from the Board.

Mrs. Zehner and her brother were out of the country when the vote to close was taken.

"There are so many things you keep hearing that could have been done," said Mrs. Zehner, a Wilson graduate and a Vice-President of the May Co. "Why didn't they contact the alumnae? Why didn't they contact the Board before announcing the closing?"

"There were alumnae in Chambersburg who offered to be volunteers. They were not accepted. Alumnae who were experts in various fields offered to be consultants at no charge. They were rebuffed.

"I think the solution to the College's situation was to be much more innovative, more in tune with the times, not so afraid to give up standing as a pure liberal arts college."

She acknowledged that many small colleges are in trouble but said Wilson's strong tradition should have been able to keep it going.

"Sure, a lot of small colleges have folded in recent years, but no 110-year-old college," she said. **(end)**

May 22nd. Adelaide Hunt Rowe,'14, has left a bequest of $275,000, announced by Save Wilson, but disputed by President Waggoner, who believed that the bequest should come directly to the College.

May 23rd-24th. Lee Linder, an Associated Press reporter covers the Wilson story in Chambersburg.

May 25th. President Waggoner issues a news release attempting to discredit the Save Wilson claim on the Rowe bequest. The Court issues its verdict that the College must remain open.

May 27th. Commencement

C. Elizabeth Boyd, a graduate of the college and one of the librarians, was one of the most enthusiastic and indomitable supporters, of Save Wilson. The bell on top of Edgar Hall for years had been rung to signal the beginning and the ending of classes. It had been broken and not fixed. Miss Boyd told one of the students that if the lawsuit was won, she would like to ring the bell! In the commotion, the bell did not get rung, but the joy among the students was palpable.

The headlines in the Tuesday, May 29, 1979 issue of the *Public Opinion* read, "**Most thrilling commencement ever.**" Nan Hudnut Clarkson, the new Chair of the Board, opened the commencement and announced that Dr. Donald Bletz would be the Acting President.

Earlier in the month, before the court case was decided, 54 out of 57 seniors had requested that Dr. Waggoner not hand them their degrees—they wanted Dr. Margaret Disert and Dean Shirley Van Marter instead. Their wish was granted. Dr. Nenah Fry was the commencement speaker. Dr. Fry had taught at Wilson and was Dean of the College at Wells College. Forty- four (44) students received their degrees.

Joan Foremen Edwards, '58 wrote at the time of Commencement, May 27, 1979

"How does one describe the feelings—I certainly never felt this way at my own (commencement) 21 years ago—nor have any college seniors before ... or ever again, I suspect. These young women—now alumnae—so extraordinary—the sisterhood between the underclassmen and the "alums" that grew out of crisis—how does one ever express it to those who weren't there? My mind goes back over the past 3 months—has it only been 13 weeks since Wilson's death knell was sounded? One of these seniors called me on February 20th—we were strangers then. I learned only a few days ago who she was; funny how we were too busy to learn the names as we scampered about campus—sisters

Chapter One: Save Wilson!

all with the same purpose. At first I thought of the students as teenagers, like my own at home. But soon I found myself wondering how could they be so intelligent—so mature—why do they often surpass me in what they know—but then again, they are Wilson women. Why in the world did I assume that they would react any differently from the rest of us "mature" Wilson women! In fact, they were way ahead of us! I often think to myself—would we have reacted in our day as these students did? I can't picture myself 21 years ago going to the Alumnae Office and asking for names of Chambersburg alumnae and calling total strangers, plus an incredible number of media people, to appear at a Save Wilson Rally 48 hours after the announcement of the closing. As a matter of fact, I couldn't picture myself appearing at the rally three months ago. I agonized over the dignity of it, and frankly admit my relief when severe icy roads prevented my going. I'll always regret missing it—others went, including Margaret Disert, our beloved Dean—oh, how the students drew strength from her. Each alumna joined the "cause" at her own personal moment. For me it was on March 3, at the almost spontaneous March 3rd rally on campus. I now know from talking with so many of you that my initial reaction of mourning lasted about two days. We all seemed to have learned by telephone within 48 hours! Mourning was replaced by anger gradually. Nan Clarkson later labelled it "creative rage" in her address Reunion Weekend. There were 300 people on campus two weeks later with their rage and creativity ready, and the Save Wilson Committee started that day. It was not only alumnae; it was a meeting of faculty, students, even administrative personnel, and it was the beginning of a revolution. Anger was not a visible factor—commitment to Wilson College—past, present and future—was. All future meeting of alumnae, on campus or away, carried this theme, which speaks highly of Wilson women. The interim is history—months of intense effort by thousands—if you only knew how your letters, phone calls, pledge cards sustained us when our energy and spirits were at rock bottom. Thank God you didn't know how hopeless the situation was at times. It seems so trite to say—we couldn't have done it without you, but it is SO TRUE. Tears were shed at Save Wilson headquarters more times than you would believe just because some alum called or wrote with an encouraging word. It is still happening. You are appearing on campus as a volunteer—gas shortage notwithstanding, but your commitment be it three days or a week or the whole summer, the Class of 1979 keeps the weary, local alumnae going." **(end)**

SAVE WILSON HEADQUARTERS

Chapter Two
THE ALUMNAE VS. THE BOARD OF TRUSTEES

It had been no easy path to the Court of Common Pleas of the 39th Judicial District. The alumnae under the coordination and direction of Save Wilson had not only to select and prepare witnesses concerning why the College should not close, but also had to put together a compelling case that they could keep the College open and functioning should the court rule in their favor. And all of this in under two and one-half months! And limited finances! There was no lack of conviction on their part that what they were doing was right or of their extraordinary determination to win! They were also quite aware of the fact that they might not win.

Special mention should be made of Jean Colgan Zehner, Class of '41, from Pittsburgh, Pennsylvania, who was the Vice-President for Consumer Affairs of the May Department Stores Co. She was on the Board, but due to being out of the country, missed the February 17, 1979 Board meeting when the Board voted to close the College. This gave her standing in the eyes of the court and she was the lead name on behalf of the alumnae.

The courtroom trial began on Monday, May 7, 1979, and ended on May

11, 1979, with the Honorable John W. Keller, Judge of the 39th Judicial District, presiding in Court Room No. 1 of the Franklin County Court House, Chambersburg, Pennsylvania. The verdict was issued on May 25, 1979. Commencement was May 27, 1979.

The Petitioners were: Jean Colgan Zehner, a Trustee who had not voted to close the College; David Platt, a faculty member; Isabel Fulton, an alumna contributing $1,200 unrestricted annually during the last three years; Mrs. J. McLain King, an alumna contributing over $2,000 unrestricted annually; Nancy Besch, an alumna; Karen Devey, a senior; Gretchen VanNess, a junior; Susan Nussbaum, a sophomore; Laurel Bauer, a freshman; Merry Hope Maloy, an admitted student for September 1979.

VS: The Respondents who were Trustees: William H. Alexander, Pauline M. Austin, Alice L. Beeman, Mrs. Alfred K. Blackadar, Elethea H. Caldwell, Mrs. William M.E. Clarkson, Howard O. Colgan, Jr., John H. Culbertson, Robert S. Damerjian, Mrs. Paul R. Diely, Patricia Hicks Hartman, Richard R. Hough, Mary Patterson McPherson, Bonnie Douglass Menaker, Sidney M. Palmer, Jane R. Stewart, Stanley Stillman, Mrs. Edward C. Sweeney, Mrs. Paul J. Thomas, Woodruff Turner, Martha B. Walker, Mrs. Charles O. Wood; Margaret Waggoner, President and ex-officio member of the Trustees.

The lawyers were J. Wesley Oler and Robert L. McQuaide for the petitioners; J. Thomas Menaker for the Respondents; and Bartholomew J. DeLuca, Jr. on behalf of the Attorney General's Office, Harrisburg, Pennsylvania.

Those testifying included alumnae, faculty, Board members, students, outside experts, and staff. Only two out of a total of thirty-three persons testifying had their testimony subpoenaed; two who appeared before the court were not admitted as experts.

Prior to the testimony of the witnesses, the Court spoke: "the Court is well aware of the fact that this case is charged with emotion and strong

Chapter Two: The Alumnae vs. The Board of Trustees

feelings on each side and these are matters that cannot affect the Court in the disposition of the case and the resolving of the ultimate issues." It was also noted that the briefs from the petitioners, the respondents and the Department of Justice were excellent. (p. 2, Court Proceedings)

Perhaps the first ruling of the Court was the most critical: that the burden of proof belonged to the Trustees to show that the College could no longer operate as a college.

All stipulations read into the record were agreed to by both sides regarding the facts; but Mr. Menaker disagreed with some of the stipulations either in terms of the obligation of the Board to act or the necessity of the filing dates (*). These were the key stipulations:

- The Board had commenced closing the College permanently as of June 30, 1979.

- Relocating the faculty and students had begun.

- Prospective students had been notified of the closing.

- The number of faculty members available for the 1979-80 year was not a reason for the vote to close the College.

- "By reason of the need for confidence in the continued existence of a college in order to sustain the interest of prospective applicants, donors, students, faculty and administration, the Board caused irreparable harm, threatening the ability of the College to survive even should the Court, in exercise of its supervisory powers...conclude that the actions were improper." (*) Mr. Menaker objected to the Court's having supervisory powers.

- The Moon Report commissioned by the College and written by Dr. Rex Moon from the Academy of Educational Development, Inc. was submitted to the President and Trustees on November 2, 1974. The Board failed to sufficiently implement the report.

(*) The Moon Report was entered into evidence.

- No amendment to the Articles of Incorporation of Wilson College had been filed with the Corporation Bureau to authorize the termination of the College.(*)

- No court order had been obtained to authorize a diversion of property committed to charitable purposes. (*)

As of May 3, 1979, no *cy pres* proceeding of any type had been instituted. (*) The College did file *cy pres* on May 4, 1979. (pp. 6-13, Court Proceedings)

The faculty received notice on or promptly after February 19, that their employment with Wilson College was to be terminated as of August 31, 1979. (p. 369, Court Proceedings)

TESTIMONY

I am presenting the testimony **by theme** rather than by individual, except for the testimony of Dr. David Truman, which sets the stage.

In all there were 31 persons who testified. 33 were called but two were rejected. Each outside expert was certified by both sides as an expert in one or more areas relevant to the testimony.

I have begun this section with the testimony of Dr. David Truman who led the panel of experts advising the Board of Trustees since, to me, this sets the necessary background for the respondents (Board of Trustees) and helps us place into a context the testimony of the petitioners (alumnae). I follow this with a section on background/history with some relevant information about Dr. Waggoner's early years, as taken from her testimony.

In short, the main arguments of the respondents for closing the College were the declines in enrollment with no hope for improvement in the fall of 1979 and the deficit predicted to rise sharply in 1979-1980, given that gifts and grant income were predicted to fall short by $400-

$500,000, leaving the College with few options for continuing as a teaching institution.

This is countered, in short, by the petitioners, who argue that much more could have been done, and still can be done, to increase the enrollment, and that there are financial resources that have not been taken into consideration by the Trustees.

TESTIMONY OF DR. DAVID TRUMAN

Dr. Truman, President of the Russell Sage Foundation and former President for ten years of Mt. Holyoke College, was the Chair of the panel of experts assembled by the Board of Trustees early February 1979, to report to them concerning their possible action of closing the College on June 30, 1979. His full professional background was presented to the Court, and there was no issue with his being an expert witness in college administration.

Around February 4th or so, "I was called by President Waggoner. She said that the Board of Trustees was concerned about the future of the College and that they were having to deal with the question of whether it could remain open or not, and would I be willing to consult with her and with possibly a group of the Trustees to try to determine or advise them on whether there were any options that they had not considered." (p. 539, Court Proceedings) The Trustees were not asking him to advise them on the issue of closing or remaining open, but whether there were options that needed further exploration.

He did request that all the basic documents over five to six years, involving budget and admissions and diagnostic instruments, be available to the panel. The panel met at Dr. Truman's office for six hours with Mr. Butler (Barnes and Roache, fundraising) and Mr. Robinson (Peat, Marwick and Mitchell, accounting) and Dr. Waggoner. The testimony does not mention that Mr. Ihlenfelt (Northwestern University, admissions) was on the phone, but does mention that Dr. Truman consulted with him.

Documents reviewed by the panel were: Operating Budget Summary and Operating Budget– 1974-1975 through 1978-1979; Main Lafrentz and Co. Audit Reports ending June 30, 1976, 1977, 1978; the Moon Report, dated November 2, 1974; solicitation letters for new students; the letters sent out by the student search program and admissions; alumnae representative manual for the One Plus One program; record of the applications for admission received for that fall of 1979 as of January 31, 1979; Wilson Update 1978.

"I [David Truman] had no question about (the information) on accuracy, and as a matter of fact, President Waggoner asked us before the day was even over whether there was anything else that we would like her to provide that wasn't provided, and we all agreed that no, we had ample evidence on which to base the judgments." (pp. 545-546, Court Proceedings)

"... I think the most striking information was the data on admissions applications for students who anticipated entering in the fall of 1979, plus the data that showed the attrition rate over a period of years at the College ... indication of a rather discouraging picture ... suggesting that there was an increasing problem of students' morale on the campus, and it also suggested in relation to the budgetary material that an extraordinarily high, perhaps unsupportable ratio of students to faculty was developing (five to one) ... good small colleges have a ratio that runs in the area of twelve to one." (pp. 548-549, Court Proceedings)

The point was made concerning the critical importance of alumnae giving to small private colleges. Concerning his observation about the percentage of alumnae who contributed to the annual giving fund, he said "I thought it remarkably high ... with the annual per capita gift running around $100 which is high." (p. 551, Court Proceedings)

Dr. Truman's and the panel's responses were essentially "no," when asked "to say are there things that we ought to be doing that we haven't thought of doing? Are there things that we should improve in the things that we are doing that would have some significant effect on the practicality of the College's remaining open?" Dr. Truman said that the panel "was most impressed with a number of things that had been done . with the ability of the College to have closed, in a very short period of time, a serious deficit situation ... with the growth in the annual giving ... that the admissions program was ingenious, including both its publications and its general design ... we could think of no area where there would be major consequences from a change." (pp. 552-553, Court Proceedings)

Dr. Truman met on February 14th with Dr. Waggoner and the officers of the Board, and basically gave the information as noted above. The Chair of the Board did then ask for judgment about closing the College, and he gave it to her. "It was that it really was not practical or feasible for the College to continue beyond this year, that it would have had the effect, simply of frittering away assets to no real purpose. I must say it is a conclusion that one arrives at with very great reluctance, particularly as a former president of a women's college, it was extremely painful for me to see that kind of handwriting on the wall, but I could see no way out." (p. 552, Court Proceedings)

Cross-examination by Mr. Oler for the Petitioners

Through questioning Dr. Truman, Mr. Oler made the point that Dr. Truman had not been asked nor did he ask for the opportunity to speak with the faculty, with students, or with various administrators; and yet in his other consultations, he had spoken with those constituencies.

No report from Dr. Truman or other members of the panel was ever put into writing.

An interesting question for which Dr. Truman could not even approximate an answer was the amount of acreage on the Wilson College campus. This is highly relevant when thinking of options for the College. He did know that Penn Hall had been acquired and did estimate 8-10 buildings acquired with Penn Hall.

When asked about his use of the Student Search program at Mt. Holyoke, Dr. Truman said it was used in a more restricted way. At Wilson "it was a very broad student search, although with parameters on the qualifications of the prospective students that were fairly restrictive ... with a minimum SAT score of 1200, and in the top 20% of the graduating class. Dr. Truman found that 11,000 names were heartening, but the number of applications (90) not so much. He felt it was a well-followed-up program, but he had not spoken with anyone from the admissions office.

"Well, they had a well-composed letter, initially, making initial inquiry with the opportunity for the students to respond asking for more information. They had the documents ready to be mailed out that had been properly printed up and friendly, rather personalized kind of letter to go out with the next response. They had a whole sequence of publications and communications that were intended to keep the students or the prospective students aware of Wilson and Wilson's opportunities. That is what I meant." (p. 563, Court Proceedings)

The panel had gotten into the timing of the responses, not in the particulars but in a general way.

Dr. Truman: "They were, if I recall correctly, sent out immediately on receipt of the names from the College Board, which usually comes late summer or early fall, and the responses, as soon as they came in or more or less as soon as they were mailed out. There were 11,000 responses which is a large assignment for a small office, so I expect there may not have been an instantaneous reply, so that wouldn't have made any difference."

In essence, the panel knew the system was going on, but had no special tabulation of reply cards. The reply cards were the second response to the school by the student, many with personal handwritten requests for specific information. The panel was not told when applications were mailed or how the inquiries were answered.

Concerning attrition, the panel was told of efforts that were being made to offset tendencies toward attrition. Attrition and a decline in enrollment was a long-term trend at Wilson—at least over a ten-year period. Dr. Truman thought it would be impossible for Wilson to get to 700, and "very difficult in any reasonable time to get as far as 350 students." (p. 574, Court Proceedings) It was his opinion that the school could not operate well financially or educationally or socially with 350-400 students. He was then shown a chart from the Moon Report that indicated that between 1920 and the late 1950s the enrollment was more or less steady between 300-450. A sharp increase took place in the late 1950s and 1960s, such that the high in 1968 was over 700 students. The Moon Report indicated that Wilson should not go above a student population of 500 and that buying Penn Hall was a mistake and that it should be sold as soon as possible.

In short, Dr. Truman and the panel did not offer any suggestions for selling property to help the financial situation. He felt that a liberal arts core integrated with a career orientation would be very difficult.

Mr. Oler: "So am I correct in stating your position that one either pursues a liberal, traditional liberal arts program or one pursues a vocational program and never [the twain] shall meet?"

Dr. Truman: "Never is a long time, but I think essentially I am drawing a sharp contrast between the two, and attempting to mix them is hazardous and probably doomed to failure." (pp. 588- 589, Court Proceedings)

It was also established that he had never participated as an expert in the evaluation of a college that was considering closing; that he met only with officers of the Board and the President for only two hours; and that he did not inquire of Dr. Waggoner whether the various recommendations in the Moon Report had been attempted and what the success was. Finally, he doubted that a change in the curriculum would help at this point in time. He did allow that it was conceivable it might have helped in 1974-75.

On redirect Mr. Menaker asked if Dr. Truman had an opinion about the low yield of applications (98) from the 1,500 inquiries. "I am not sure I have. It seems likely that as the student search device is being adopted, and prospective students are being, therefore, besieged with inquiries of this sort, there is a kind of coupon clipping psychology which distorts any projections you might have ... The stress we felt was in the contrast between the ratio of the 1,500 and the 98, whereas one might, under earlier circumstances, have assumed that there would be a lot more applications by January than that number out of that pool ... the yield from student searches is never terribly high. It is a very expensive proposition and it is very hazardous. ... The problem is that people have a hard time thinking of how else to do it." (p. 595, Court Proceedings)

Testimony by Board Chair Martha Walker concerning meeting with Dr. Truman indicated that he was asked questions about the feasibility of the College "going coeducational, of the College going to ... a Hood College type of curriculum, of being able to raise $1.6 million next year ... until the enrollment was brought up to a point where it could sustain the operation of the College. (p. 1115, Court Proceedings)

A Change in Trustee Meeting Minutes sent to the Trustees Referencing Dr. Truman

In the testimony of Dr. Waggoner, Mr. Oler drew her attention to two sets of minutes sent to Trustees; the later one on March 28, 1979, and the first earlier in the month. The first set of minutes in item #4 of the minutes read (as quoted from testimony): "That (if) the Trustees decided to keep the College open, he urged them that they must commit themselves to a greater investment of energy and personal resources than has been made before ..." (p. 1115, Court Proceedings) Also deleted from page 2 of the final draft was, "Only if the Trustees are willing to gamble and change the essential character of Wilson College can there be any real chance of survival—and that is only a chance, not a guarantee." The second set of minutes omitted this statement. (p. 62, Adjudication and *Decree Nisi*)

BACKGROUND ON ISSUES FACING THE COLLEGE IMMEDIATELY BEFORE AND DURING THE WAGGONER ADMINISTRATION

There were two main reports that were entered as exhibits into the Court Proceedings and that informed some of the testimony for both the respondents and the petitioners.

1. **The Moon Report,** authored by Dr. Rex Moon of the Academy of Educational Development (AED) and submitted to the Board of Trustees on November 2, 1974, played a key role since out of five recommendations for the survival of the College, the main one that would have been the least disruptive had to do with revamping the curriculum to include more career-oriented majors and courses to appeal to a larger number of young women wanting to pursue careers after college. A Board member who testified for the Trustees had been a part of the team contributing to the writing of the 1974 Moon Report.

   The alternative futures, read into the record by the President, in the Moon Report were: "(1) closing the College immediately and establishing a working foundation to support scholarships for young people to attend a college of their choice; (2) merging with one of the major state-related institutions in Pennsylvania; becoming an experimental institution for one of these major institutions, probably handling juniors or seniors; a branch campus referring traditional programs; (3) giving it to the State of Pennsylvania, leaving intact all of its endowments and other assets as an inducement to accept it and run it for such purposes as the state might wish to make of it; (4) having the College act as a host institution inviting other institutions to offer work on the campus of a highly specialized /nature, such as career or technical education, while continuing to strengthen the College's liberal arts mission and uniqueness as a women's college . . . ; (5) having another institution of a specialized nature occupy the Wilson campus and/or the Penn Hall campus; (6) rapidly changing the total program emphasis of Wilson College, placing heavy emphasis upon career education and specialized courses of study reflecting at least some and possibly all of the major career areas now being undertaken in educational institutions around the country; (7) becoming co-educational." (pp. 857-859, Court Proceedings)

2. **The Middle States Accrediting Association for Schools and Colleges Evaluation** was submitted in April 1978. The Board member, Dr. McPherson, was asked by both Mr. Oler and Mr. Menaker to read portions of that report as quoted below:

"In short, it seems safe to say that the College's financial picture today may be viewed with guarded optimism. ... The team was also perplexed by what appeared to be a relative lack of interest and involvement in the self-study of all segments of the College. In any case, it is the opinion of the team that the quality of the program could be strengthened through greater clarity and more substantial agreement as to what the College really means by a liberal education. It is hoped that in sharpening its definition, the College will take cognizance of recent national trends and developments. Many institutions are, for instance, re-thinking the liberal arts concept in view of such national trends as declining student interest in certain areas; growing awareness of societal problems; changing career needs and the goals of students; and an increasing acceptance of the viewpoint that liberal and professional programs need not be mutually exclusive. It seemed to the team that Wilson's program would profit from a serious consideration of such current developments. ... The future is, of course, impossible to predict, and will depend largely upon success in increasing enrollments and sustaining a high level of gift income. It is encouraging to note, however, that the College, at this time, enjoys a somewhat greater degree of financial stability than has been true for the past few years." (pp. 684-686, Court Proceedings)

Board Chair, Martha Walker, was asked to read portions dealing with the administration. "The College is fortunate to have three major strengths in these areas. First, if the caliber of the Trustees whom the team met is indicative of the total Board, Wilson is governed by an active, capable, interested and knowledgeable Board of Trustees. The Trustees are apparently fully acquainted with the College's strengths and problems. They apparently are making an intensive (and somewhat successful) attempt to reduce the financial crisis. ... Secondly, the College has recently succeeded in attracting several young, capable and vigorous individuals to key administrative posts. In all respects, they seem to be an asset to the College. ... Thirdly, the College has apparently recovered from the unfortunate past turnover in top-level administrative posts which gave it three presidents and five Deans in five years. It is fortunate to have a hardworking, capable and respected President who is making a determined effort to have it succeed. She is, however, facing many problems, not the least of which is the fact that her office is dangerously over- extended because of a skeletal administrative staff. At the time of the team visit, there were several administrative vacancies. ... Admissions and Retention: This office is under capable, knowledgeable and creative leadership. It has a young, energetic, and enthusiastic staff which, although optimistic, appears to be fully cognizant of the formidable task it faces in trying to increase enrollments. It is a comparatively large staff for the size of the operation and is housed in adequate, comfortable and attractive offices which have 'front door' appeal for prospective students. ... All of this, of course, is solid evidence of administrative commitment to reversing the trend of declining enrollments. The seriousness of this trend is indicated by the fact that, in 1968-69, the College was at its peak enrollment of 720 students. This semester (spring 1978), there are 220 students enrolled. (pp. 1141-1143, Court Proceedings)

The Commission's report reaffirmed the accreditation at its meeting on June 22-23, 1978, and requested a report by April 1, 1981, with detailed attention to enrollment figures and trends; financial status; curricular re-examination and revision; administrative restructuring and delegation of authority; and institutional research studies on attrition, outcomes, and other pertinent areas. A full Periodic Review Report is due April 15, 1983."

YEARS PRIOR TO AND FOLLOWING THE WAGGONER APPOINTMENT

Paul Swain Havens had served Wilson College for 34 years, retiring in 1970. He was followed by Dr. Charles Cole (1970-1975), who had been Dean of Lafayette College. Stepping down in February 1975, Dr. Cole was followed by Interim President, Dr. Lawrence Dennis, who assumed the position in February 1975 until Dr. Waggoner took the presidency on August 2, 1975. There was an active search, but the committee received expressions of "not interested" from many candidates. Dr. Waggoner was named President by a unanimous vote of the Board. During the five years preceding her presidency, the College had been losing enrollment and incurring deficits which were covered by using the unrestricted

Chapter Two: The Alumnae vs. The Board of Trustees

endowment.

According to testimony of Martha Walker, there were resolutions/actions in Trustee minutes as a result of the recommendations of the Moon Report that indicated "that enrollment has declined in the last eight years by fifty percent, that substantial operating deficits have been incurred and that, therefore, with respect to enrollment and expenses, the Trustees declared a state of extreme financial exigency and further resolve that the College should make all reasonable efforts to reduce expenses, and take whatever other steps necessary to remedy the situation." (pp. 1079-1080, Court Proceedings) They needed to invade the restricted endowment and to effect some retrenchment of faculty. The Board also approved the One Plus One program and hire someone from the Academy of Educational Development (AED) to chair the recruitment campaign. The Board voted "to place a moratorium on the granting of tenure ... ; the purchase of equipment or library books and any expansion of staff or faculty without prior Board approval, and ... that the executive committee be established as an implementation committee to review the report of the AED and monitor the Board's implementation of the report. (p. 1080, Court Proceedings)

All deficits prior to 1978-1979 had been made up for by the unrestricted endowment. In years prior to 1975, testimony indicated that the College had used $4.3 million of its unrestricted endowment to cover deficits. (p. 907, Court Proceedings)

The Board attempted to sell the Penn Hall property but not the buildings and had an agreement with a real estate agent for one year that ended on August 15, 1975. No other attempts were made to sell the property.

In 1975 there were 49 full-time faculty and in 1979, 42.

Appointment of Dr. Waggoner

From testimony of Richard Hough, former Chair and current member of the Board, in answer to a question why Dr. Waggoner was hired:

"We interviewed a number of possible candidates, and the Board had considered very seriously the items in the Moon Report and particularly the question of whether we should move from the liberal arts education of women ... to something more career oriented, and the members of the Board and the faculty and in particular the alumnae members of the Board felt very strongly that Wilson should (remain) dedicated to the liberal education of women, and the Board had a strong personal commitment to the value of liberal education. So, one of the (challenges) the committee had was to find a new President who was likewise dedicated to the liberal education of women and would further those objectives; Dr. Waggoner met that qualification exceedingly well ... We were optimistic with a strong new President and conviction that there was a place in the scheme of things and an important place for a small women's liberal arts college. We felt we could do the job, and we didn't discuss the possibility of failure." (pp. 909-910, Court Proceedings)

In short, from this testimony, it was determined that the Board was ready to offer support—to help raise money and to know that enrollment was key, and that they needed a "substantially intensified program of recruitment." (p. 912, Court Proceedings)

On cross-examination of Mr. Hough, it was determined that they had never appraised the value of the Penn Hall buildings or property, and, that "if we had sold the property, we would have no school to operate, and there is a farm, but, as Dr. Waggoner testified, the equestrian program has had an important influence in being able to attract more students ..." (p. 914, Court Proceedings) The Board did investigate how they might sell the buildings but not the acreage.

Dr. Waggoner's Years, 1975-1978

When Dr. Waggoner took the position, she understood the condition of the College to be fragile, and that if she took the Presidency, she would talk to the Board about the difficulties.

Under cross-examination by Mr. Oler (pp. 835-836, Court Proceedings), it was established that Dr. Waggoner had had only three years of administrative experience as Dean at Smith College prior to the presidency of Wilson College. In 1973, she continued at Smith as a faculty member and was on leave doing research at Summit College in the philosophy of science until August 2, 1975, when she became President.

Enrollment

Peak enrollment in the fall of 1967 was 722; when Dr. Waggoner took office in 1975-76, the enrollment was around 385; for 1978-79, the enrollment was 214 students. As they looked to the fall of 1979, they estimated the enrollment was going to be around 200, with a freshman class of 50-60 and a similarly sized graduating class. Assuming attrition similar to 1978-1979, the size could go down to 180.

Dr. Waggoner: " ... we, in the fall of 1975, faced a very severe crisis in confidence in the institution. The 1974-1975 year had been a traumatic one ... There had been the very severe financial problems; the resignation of the President; the Academy of Educational Development coming in (the Moon Report); the word was out, if you like, to the public arena, that Wilson was in severe financial difficulty. In fact, we had, during that year, that summer and even continuing into the next year ... continual rumors, even newspaper publication of the closing of Wilson College." (p. 737, Court Proceedings) To counter this, they sent admissions staff to see as many guidance counselors as possible. Thirty-nine new students came in the fall of 1975; in 1975-76, the staff travelled more and had a small Student Search program, had college nights and college fairs, resulting in 60 new students for the fall of 1976. They changed publications and brought in the Academy for Education Development (AED) as consultants. (pp. 746-748, Court Proceedings) The admissions director resigned in the winter of the 1976-1977 academic year. She was replaced by a director in the spring of 1977 who had been a consultant to Wilson from AED. They revised the publications and set up a recruiting process that began in the junior year of high school. They used student search as well as high school visits, college nights, and college fairs to recruit the entering class for fall 1978.

Dr. Waggoner testified that they had a very small primary market (students who write to the College for information on their own initiative) and a small secondary market (students who were prompted to send in requests for information by an alumnae, a guidance counselor, another source). Often when they visited high schools, they saw no students—guidance counselors don't tend to recommend women's colleges—many come from co-ed schools and from public institutions.

... For recruiting the class that would enter in 1979, they reduced school visits and relied much more heavily on a test market fueled by names from Student Search (a test market). They tried to personalize and individualize the Student Search program and felt that a 14% reply to the Student Search mailing inquiry was impressive, but the percentage of applications was poor. The explanations for this were fewer women interested in women's colleges, in independent institutions, in being located in a rural community, in a small sized student body while high school graduating class sizes are getting larger.

The President questioned whether the College had the critical mass necessary for success— success in recruitment and success in providing an excellent curricular and co-curricular educational program. In addition to problems of recruiting, the attrition rate was high. Forty percent of the freshmen admitted in the fall 1977 did not return in the fall 1978. (p. 767, Court Proceedings) The College did put some effort into recruiting transfer students to help offset the attrition.

Condition of Physical Plant

In addition, there was quite a backlog of deferred maintenance, including the many old buildings being insufficiently insulated resulting in major heat loss. To meet the federal guidelines for handicapped accessibility would cost over $100,000.

Chapter Two: The Alumnae vs. The Board of Trustees

The high priority issues to be addressed in the physical plant that could yield longer savings included modifying the heat control system; renovating a Penn Hall building into a fine arts building that would be helpful in recruiting students; beginning a long-term program of repointing the buildings. Classes were rescheduled to handicapped accessible classrooms when needed.

Financial Situation

To address the financial situation in 1975 "we organized a very active program of obtaining funds from alumnae ... trying to increase the gifts and grants we could obtain for the institution. That ... was a very hard job to undertake successfully when there was much doubt about the viability of this institution. You cannot get grants for just bailing you out from meeting your deficit ..." (p. 739, Court Proceedings) They were able to increase the gifts and grants for the current operating costs and "almost doubled what had been raised the previous year." (p. 739, Court Proceedings)

"The deficit was made up by the College by [drawing on] its unrestricted endowment." (p 740, Court Proceedings) In addition, they consolidated staff positions and looked to reduce the custodial, grounds and maintenance staff. The financial situation was complicated by the federal guidelines on handicapped accessibility and the increasing costs of fuel.

In 1974-75, the College had raised $367,000; in 1975-1976, $618,000. In 1976-77, there was a bequest of $500,000. In 1977-1978, the College received a bequest of $1.1 million, giving a total of $1.5 million. Alumnae giving had been strong. The President felt that it was dropping off in 1978-79 because "I think people were worried, and I understand ... it was not only among alumnae, but also foundations and corporations; everyone was holding [up making commitments], worrying about what was going to happen to enrollment." (p. 761, Court Proceedings)

There was no salary increase for 1975-1976, but salary increases every year thereafter— approximately 6%. (p. 790, Court Proceedings)

<u>Turnover of Personnel</u>

When asked about administrative personnel, faculty testimony indicated that the turn-over in personnel seemed excessive. There were four Deans in three and one-half years during Dr. Waggoner's tenure (over a seven-year period counting one of the Deans who was hired in 1972 prior to Dr. Waggoner); two business officers; two alumnae affairs directors; two directors of development; two public information officers; and three admissions directors. (*These figures came from the Court Opinion and some from testimony*) Other testimony noted that the staff turnover was not normal in the admissions office.

<u>Relationship with the Town</u>

Although not a part of the court proceedings, **on March 1, 1976, on the Opinion Page of the *Public Opinion*, the following opinion piece, titled "The Problems of Wilson," appeared:**

> "Wilson College's problems are not over and may in fact be growing.
>
> From the interview with Dr. Margaret Waggoner, College President, in Friday's *Public Opinion*, it would seem that rumors about cutbacks in program, and faculty dismay are rife.
>
> The President admitted, for instance, that some faculty members have been telling sophomores to transfer elsewhere if they want to get a degree.
>
> This is pretty devastating news. It not only casts doubt upon the College's ability to retain the students it has, it also emphasized faculty disaffection and fear.
>
> Dr. Waggoner hedged about the number of new enrollees expected next September. Admittedly this is early to pin down

Chapter Two: The Alumnae vs. The Board of Trustees

enrollment, yet her roundabout comments on prospects, coupled with rumors of very small number confirmed for next year's freshmen class, add to questions.

The College President says if the College has 90 new enrollees next September, "it will be very nice indeed." Last year at this time it was claimed that a viable number freshmen was 100 or more.

The College newspaper, *Billboard*, has been carrying a number of items concerning prospects and rumors—including one that the January term is to be eliminated. The best Dr. Waggoner could come up with when questioned on this: "*Billboard* jumped the gun." She said that, on the contrary, a recommendation would go before the faculty to maintain the January term just as it was this year.

This implies that there had been a definite thought toward changing the term (eliminate it?) which the recommendation will counteract.

Departure of faculty members and administrative staff, some requested, some through attrition, some through doubts of the College's future, continues. Obviously, a trimming of the staff, academically and administratively, is good business if the quality of the College's offering and direction is not hurt. We can appreciate Dr. Waggoner's desire to have her own people with her—only in that way can the results be properly assessed.

The people of Chambersburg are as concerned as those immediately connected with the College as to its fate, not only for economic reasons but through genuine affection and pride in Wilson. This goodwill is being tapped only partially.

We believe recognition of the importance of Chambersburg to Wilson by the college administration as important as is recognition of the importance of Wilson to Chambersburg by the citizenry.

In this respect, we believe there has been a failure on the part of Dr. Waggoner not common to her immediate predecessors, and that this should be corrected quickly.

If it is the stated and adamant position of the Wilson administration that Wilson is a private college, and that its business is entirely its own and can have no relationship to the town, then townspeople will have to reevaluate their position.

We hope there is no tendency to withdraw behind the iron fence of the campus as the College's financial hurts deepen. If those beyond that fence can help and their help is welcome, we are sure it can be mustered. The community has helped substantially before without intruding on the College's prerogatives. **(end)**

The Announced Closing of the College

<u>The Decision to Close</u>

The two major issues were finances and enrollment. In order to have no deficit for the 1978-1979 fiscal year, they would need to raise in gifts and grants $1.3 million; as of the February 3rd meeting of the Board, they had raised $275,000. Best estimate as of the February 17th meeting when the Board voted to close the College was that the deficit would be $510,000. (p. 797, Court Proceedings)

In response to a question by Mr. Oler to Dr. McPherson, Mr. Oler said: "Would I also be correct in saying that the factor this year, 1979, in creating a crisis, of immediate urgency at Wilson was the extremely disappointing admissions report received on February 3,1979?" the witness said "Yes, although I would have to say that it would have been coupled in my own mind with the ... fiscal situation." (pp. 630-631, Court Proceedings)

Chapter Two: The Alumnae vs. The Board of Trustees

Further testimony from this Board member stated that the person felt that the President and the admissions staff were optimistic about the student search results of 70,000 names and 11,000 inquiries; the Board member stated: "Well, you are talking to an old hand and a pessimist, and I was not shocked because I know that students are making multiple applications and ... delight in receiving mail and being taken notice of and ... tend to send back the coupon, particularly if your college material came in early in the game, to get more information ... " (pp. 631-632, Court Proceedings)

Dr. McPherson had had notable experience in college administration as President of Bryn Mawr College, and she had also contributed to the Moon Report in 1974. She testified that " ... at that time, the College, its enrollment had shrunk. The administration had had considerable turnover. There was a conspicuous lack of leadership, and the financial situation of the College did not seem to be strong enough to sustain the enterprise given the shrinking enrollment ... there was an unhappy pattern evident in the institution that prevented it, in my view, from serving its purpose as a college for women. I think the students' morale and, in fact, the faculty's mood sustained my observation. I thought that the faculty, which was clearly devoted and hard-working and concerned for the institution, was nonetheless very traditionally trained, and was engaged in teaching a very standard curriculum. They had recently considered the possibility of increasing interdisciplinary work, but were finding it quite difficult to put that into effect at that time. I think that during that period of time, it was not customary for the Dean to offer much academic leadership, and it had been difficult for the faculty to attempt it alone ... to put some of the things that they wished to institute into place." (p. 612, Court Proceedings).

Testimony indicated that she had known of the fragile nature of the College from the time she went on the Board in 1976: "A definite problem with attracting and maintaining a sufficient number of students to support a rich enough educational program ... A small endowment; a small though loyal and hard-working alumnae body that did not seem to be an extraordinarily affluent alumnae body; an isolated geographical position which has become a liability ...; a difficult situation in realizing the benefits of a consortial relationship; its remoteness from any cultural center ..." (pp. 613-614, Court Proceedings)

Communicating the Decision

Testimony of the President concerning communicating the decision was, "I think it was clear from the statement by myself and others, that we were concerned not to speak of the possible closing of the College before a decision was in fact made because of our concern that if we had done so, we had no option, other than to close." (p. 1151, Court Proceedings.) She further testified that she had not been told by legal counsel that only the Court had the authority to decide whether this College should be closed or not. At the point at which the College filed *cy pres*, the Trustees had foreclosed the option of operating as an educational institution. The President did understand that it was up to the Court to decide whether the assets of the College could be put into a foundation. (p.1155, Court Proceedings)

None of the faculty testified to prior knowledge that the College would be closed, but they were aware that the College was, and had been, in a dangerous position for at least five years. Faculty felt they lived year to year—grateful for each year that the College opened. "We had been reassured in January that the budgetary figures for the following years were in good shape and there was no cause for alarm." (p.373, Court Proceedings) The reasons for this optimism that were cited were the article in the *Public Opinion* and a faculty meeting where the finances and admissions pictures were presented optimistically. "The President's presentation was intended to be—and I am quoting the President now— "a cause of reassurance and pride." (p. 388, Court Proceedings). A letter was sent dated March 7, 1979, to the faculty confirming the February 19th verbal notice.

Chapter Two: The Alumnae vs. The Board of Trustees

The testimony of Mrs. King, an alumna who had been a member of the Board of Trustees and who was a regular donor to the College, acknowledged that the she had been approached to give money, but that requests for money did not seem critical—"certainly not in the way you had the feeling you've got to do it or it is going to be closed." (p. 411, Court Proceedings) In 1975 "We [alumnae] did feel that when we made the change in the administration of the College, that we had really turned the corner and were on the road to success, because women's colleges were then coming back." (pp. 411-412, Court Proceedings).

President Waggoner, in the fall 1978, had indicated to alumnae that the College had turned the corner. They didn't doubt her sincerity but questioned why she felt the corner had been turned. I said, "how are things going, Margaret?" And she said, "well, we have turned the corner." (p. 413, Court Proceedings)

An important point made by the President was that the interview for the article in the *Public Opinion* had been in early December when there was still reason for optimism. It was not published until January 9, 1979.

The President, in her testimony, addressed the issue of persons being taken completely by surprise at the announcement of the decision. She noted that at all faculty meetings attended by officers of the Wilson College Student Government Association, "I have always reported at each meeting on where we are in our campaign for gifts and grants, and the goal for the year is surely known. So, faculty and students are, each month, made aware of where we are on the financial scene. (p. 803, Court Proceedings)

"At the February 3rd meeting … the Board … knew it was a major decision … they made that decision that they weren't ready to make a decision that day on the closing … they decided then to meet again in two weeks; they should not make that public because to make that public at that time would foreclose for them any options for actions, other than to make the decision to close.

Successful Graduates of the College

The first witness for the petitioners was Dr. Elizabeth Tidball, a professor in the Department of Physiology at the Medical Center of George Washington University. Dr. Tidball was something of an icon among women's colleges because of her research, beginning in 1969, regarding the success of women graduates of women's colleges. This research was widely published in higher education magazines and journals, and provided a strong case for the productivity of small private women's colleges.

The Court's interest—though challenged by Mr. Menaker—was that Dr. Tidball could testify as to the public trust and the public value of an institution such as Wilson as it now exists. (p. 25, Court Proceedings)

Her research involved identifying the success of women who were college graduates and went on to be cited for their career achievements in *Who's Who in American Women*. She also looked at women who had attained a research doctoral degree—mostly a Ph.D. In both these studies, graduates of women's colleges were found to be two or more times more likely to be cited for success defined in these two ways. Dr. Tidball credited the greater number of women achievers from women's colleges to the smaller size of the institution; to more women on the faculty than most co-educational institutions; and to the absence of, or very low numbers of, men on campus. She also found that the more money spent in academic budgets, the more likely the institution was to produce achievers. "However, for the same average amounts of money spent per year, between a group of very selective coeducational institutions and very selective women's colleges, the women's colleges still produced approximately twice as many achievers as did the coeducational institutions." (p. 33, Court Proceedings)

Yet another obvious finding was that there were many more opportunities for positions of leadership for women at women's colleges. All the resources allotted to campus activities go to women. Title IX will help at coeducational institutions, but women's colleges already have the equivalent.

"In terms of the Commonwealth of Pennsylvania, Wilson College has graduated students who have gone on to receive doctorates, such that it ranks third only behind Bryn Mawr and Swarthmore ... institutions with enrollments of under 2500 students ... graduates from 1920- 1974 ... Out of some approximately 3000 accredited institutions of high learning, Wilson ranks #124 in the nation for women graduates who have gone on to receive doctorates, regardless of the size of the institution ... 11th in physical sciences; 23rd in the life sciences; and 19th in the arts and humanities. That is placing it in the top 30 institutions in the country in terms of its productivity ... the number of graduates going on [to doctorates] ... women receiving their bachelor's degrees in the decade from 1960-1969 showed the same productivity as for the decade of the 1950s." (p. 49, Court Proceedings).

Mr. Menaker in his cross examination sought to bring out the point that Wilson of the past was not going to be Wilson of the future—with such a reduced student body in numbers, in SAT scores, in school grades. He also brought up the number of women's colleges that had closed— albeit mostly Roman Catholic, and none in the more prestigious category that Wilson is in.

Example of Colorado Women's College

Dr. Marjorie Bell Chambers, an expert witness, had held a number of positions, including the presidential appointment as Acting Chair of the National Advisory Committee for Women; National President of the American Association of University Women; Chair of the National Advisory Council on Women's Education programs; and President of Colorado Women's College from 1976-1978, when she resigned. Her major concern and interest was in women's equity in education, including implementing Title IX. The reason for her appearance was as an expert on expressing optimism for the future of women's institutions.

The court ruled to allow her testimony over Mr. Menaker's objection on the basis that Colorado Women's College's executive committee of the Board of Trustees voted to close the college on December 22nd—not to reopen on January 3rd in 1976. The court saw enough of a similar situation to admit the testimony.

Colorado Women's College was not closed on January 3rd, and the incoming class in the fall 1977 was 210—larger than for 1976, when it was only 151. In total the college had about 425 students. During her tenure, she revised the curriculum to make it more up-to-date for women's career aspirations within the traditional fields of the liberal arts. [It remains open today, 2018.]

Admissions

Two primary means of attracting students for the fall 1979 were the use of the Student Search Program through the College Entrance Examination Board and the One-Plus-One program (a program involving alumnae recruiting) as well as alumnae parties in their homes for prospective students. The Director of Admissions attended 4-5 national college fairs. There was a change in process from 1977-78 away from visiting high schools and attending college fairs to the mass mailings. The College was receiving fewer and fewer inquiries from the visitations.

The College had been losing enrollment since the late 1960s, and in the 1970s had had a fairly traditional recruiting program—high school visitations, college night programs, college fairs, some advertising. The One-Plus-One Program "was probably less successful than had been expected." (p. 651, Court Proceedings)

The testimony concerning from the Director of Admissions dealt mostly with process towards a goal of 150 new students for the fall 1979. The petitioners were wanting to prove that the process was badly flawed, and that there was much that could have been done that was not done. The respondents were concerned with making the point that they had done all they could to increase the enrollment, and that they had changed

Chapter Two: The Alumnae vs. The Board of Trustees

their processes for recruiting the 1979 incoming class since processes in past years had not produced many, if any, gains in enrollment.

The Director of Admissions had been at Wilson from March 1977 through March 1979, when the office closed down. One of his main efforts was to "generate inquiry pools sufficient enough to attract a class. I proposed that we step up the student search program and to try to personalize that program as much as possible ... I contacted Data Epsilon Management, a firm that has been helping colleges develop direct mail programs. I asked Luther Hoopes, a consultant in admissions for colleges around the country, to develop what we call a student prospectus, which is a 40-page brochure describing the programs at the College, activities, student life, a publication that describes in fairly good detail, life at Wilson College. Mr. Hoopes also redesigned the College catalog, and he produced a general brochure which we called a three- minute summary." In 1977-1978, admissions continued with the high school visits and college nights, but the results were very poor. (p. 952-956, Court Proceedings)

In the two years as Director of Admissions, he interviewed 250-300 students in person and they gave him reasons for not attending Wilson. "The fact that the College was a women's college, it was somewhat isolated in a rural setting, that the student body was, seemed to them to be abnormally small, that the curriculum of the College was very traditional without what they perceived to be sufficient preparation for entry into the job market upon graduation. It was not a career-oriented program ... business administration, nursing, dental hygiene, animal science, communications." (pp. 978-979, Court Proceedings)

A point was also made that the two campus visitation weekends held in the fall 1977 were not held in the fall 1978, in part because of the difficulty of getting students to host prospective students and a "negative attitude on campus about things in general." (p. 984, Court Proceedings)

In 1977-1978, they received 42,000 names from Student Search and sent out 42,000 letters resulting in 1,962 inquiries, 49 applications, and

36 enrollments or 25% of the total enrollment. That year there were 11 telephone inquiries resulting in 5 applications; college fairs—345 inquiries and 12 applications (3.5%); alumnae referrals—64 inquiries resulting in 7 applications—over 10%. (pp. 1011-1012, Court Proceedings) On cross examination, these numbers were used to make the point that more individual attention and personal contacts seemed to yield the best results. A survey questionnaire given to students who had applied in the fall of 1978 indicated that the top two factors influencing their applications were academic atmosphere and personalized atmosphere. On this same questionnaire, the overwhelming response of students applying was that there were very positive comments about the size of the student body. (p. 1018-1020, Court Proceedings)

One-Plus-One

The One-Plus-One program had 48 alumnae chairmen overseeing the work of 450 alumnae volunteers who received from the admissions office names and contact information as well as information about the College. They then made contact with prospective students in a variety of ways: visiting the student, calling the student, attending college nights, hosting teas in their homes. It was noted in testimony that materials from the College were sometimes late—too late for good recruiting.

In 1978-79, they had 25-35 programs in alumnae homes scheduled for names generated through the Student Search Program. In fall 1978, alumnae attended 25 college night programs in high schools; they did not do on-campus visitation weekends (that had been done in the fall 1977). " ... The number (of students) that attended were very, very small ... not productive in terms of generating applications." (pp. 979-980, Court Proceedings)

Testimony was taken from Susan Whitmore Brooks, '63, an alumna who headed a One-Plus- One program overseeing the work of 19 volunteers in the Baltimore area. One-Plus-One relied on inquiries coming from the admissions office and forwarded to the alumnae representatives

Chapter Two: The Alumnae vs. The Board of Trustees

according to geographic area for follow-up as soon as possible. Follow-up generally meant phone calls, but could also mean inviting a prospective student for a tea at home or another type of person-to- person contact.

According to testimony, on June 12, 1978, she contacted the Admissions Office and said that she was ready to receive the names of interested prospective students. She received no names until August when she received 20. None in September. Computer forms for the prospective students were not ready in September. In September, at the Alumnae Board meeting, they were told about the emphasis on student search and that they would no longer be doing high school visits or college days. The next time she received names of prospective students was in October when she received 102 names and then 60 in December; 25 in January and 25 in February 1979. These were students who had inquired between May 8 and August 10, 1978, with the bulk in May and June. Out of the first batch of 102, only 20 were still interested. In this area they had no meetings in their homes.

In general, over all the years of the program, the lists of names had come out late. The prospective students called in October were more likely to be interested. Six students from the Baltimore area enrolled, but it was hard to say what caused the enrollment.

There was an updated manual for One-Plus-One, finished late in 1978. Susan Brooks further testified that "The College ... had been in trouble for a long time, from the admission's standpoint, and my frustration has always been that there was insufficient manpower available, and somehow the coordination just hasn't been what it should have been." (P. 343, Court Proceedings) The Admissions Director explained that college day on campus which would have been in November was cancelled because he felt that high school students used it as an escape weekend at the College's expense.

An alumna, Phoebe Snavely Tobin, '62, testified that she did make calls in the Baltimore area and that she began receiving names in early

November, and she began making calls promptly. "We had a number of responses from students who said they had already decided to go to another college. Several did not even remember expressing an interest in Wilson." (pp. 353-354, Court Proceedings) She spoke with five or six out of ten prospective students. Most of the students had decided on other schools. "I had one student who went up to visit the school, but couldn't find anybody there to talk to, and the mother got on the phone and asked what had happened." (p. 356, Court Proceedings) Of the students she asked if they had heard from Wilson, none had received materials from the College. Another volunteer, Mrs. Carolyn Trembley Shaffer, noted in testimony that the girls she called in November and December were interested in nursing. Calls made in November found that half of the prospective students had already chosen their college. "Four girls out of the group I called in January were willing to come to Wilson on their spring break which was in April ..." (p. 362, Court Proceedings)

In October, the Director of Admissions met with this witness involved in One-Plus-One, and at that time he said, "... That at the present time, he was not in need of our help because of the student search and they had plenty of names. And when he needed our help, he would let us know ..." (p. 362, Court Proceedings)

<u>Student Search Program</u>

A summary of relevant portions of the admissions process concerning the student search for the class to be admitted in the fall 1979 follows:

- 70,000 names had been purchased in April 1978 from the College Entrance Examination Board using stringent criteria to obtain the names of students with high SAT scores and high rankings in their high school class. This also put Wilson in competition with the top schools.

- Letters were immediately sent by Data Epsilon, a company under contract to Wilson for bulk mailings, to these 70,000 students which included reply slips which students could send

Chapter Two: The Alumnae vs. The Board of Trustees

back to the College if they were interested in receiving more information. This generated 7,000 reply slips.

- A second mass mailing to 63,000 students who had not sent in the reply slips. This second mailing generated 4,000 reply slips.

- Those 11,000 students who had returned the reply slips received a bulk mailing using the College's System Six and including a two-page letter from the Director of Admissions, a brochure, the three-minute summary, and a postage return card. This was followed by a letter, a prospectus and application sent to all 11,000. Included was a reply card to be sent in if they wished to apply and receive a catalog and/or had any questions they wanted answered. Catalogs were sent only to students who applied to the College and some of these catalogs were one year old—1977-78—since the new catalogs were not available until September 1979. By August-September 1978, they had only a handful of applications for the fall 1979.

- Approximately 1,500 students sent in reply cards received by the College primarily in May, June, and July 1978— the student's second contact with the College. There is contradictory testimony as to whether the responses to these reply cards were ever actually mailed.

The Admissions Office addressed but did not fill out or send out postcards to 1500 prospective students who had sent in reply cards twice in the summer according to one person's testimony. Although this testimony was contradicted by the Director of Admissions who said that they had all had appropriate replies. The 1500 students did receive monthly updates encompassing a brochure and a form letter. Little individual attention was given to those who sent in two reply cards. Faculty were used in the recruitment effort to the extent that they wrote letters about their majors given to the Admissions Office. Selected individual questions from respective students were primarily answered by two faculty from the Athletics and Equestrian programs. In January 1979 there was a limited telephone campaign. From January 1st to February 19th, the Admissions Office received 163 reply cards.

Concerning the Student Search program, Dr. McPherson testified: "I think all colleges have become increasingly dependent on the Student Search ... and that is bound to, in the end, make it a less effective program. I think the literature would suggest that the Student Search service at least in its beginning years ... was more of an effective form of recruitment than ... the school service or the school nights ... I don't think, myself, that the College had any choice but to use it and use it hard, because it was the most efficient and effective way to reach the number of applicants that seemed to be required to attract a class of possible size to the institution." (pp. 622-623, Court Proceedings)

Several very important points came out in testimony: the importance of prompt responses to the names they received from the college search, and the fact that the first response came from a company contracted by Wilson and was somewhat impersonal; that the 1978-1979 material was not available until September and was not sent out in September; acknowledgment that students really interested in a small college like Wilson would expect very personalized responses to at least the 1,500 inquiries which would be the second inquiry to Wilson. If you don't reply promptly to the reply cards (inquiries), you lose the student's interest.

Road Visits

The Assistant Director of Admissions was given the responsibility of traveling in the fall 1978— largely to teas given in the homes of alumnae for prospective students. There were no other duties. Over Christmas time the Assistant Director was the only person in the office, and she stuffed envelopes and responded to new inquiries from students not currently in the system. She did not know about the 1500 reply cards until the beginning of January when the staff came back. They then began to respond to those, beginning with the prospective students who had replied most recently. She also made phone calls to people she had written to in December. No one instructed her to do this. There were applications that came in after the phone calls.

Recruitment Abroad

In 1973, Wilson had a Study Abroad program in Medellin, Colombia, in conjunction with the consortium (Franklin and Marshall, Dickinson and Gettysburg Colleges). Dr. Jose Diaz, one of our faculty members, was involved in that program and was also tasked with recruiting prospective students from Colombia and Venezuela. In 1975, he was appointed Resident Director of the Colombia program, and, with the Interim President of Wilson who knew the Minister of Education in Venezuela, it was arranged that the professor would travel to Caracas to meet with the Minister of Education. At just about the time, he was going to make that trip from Medellin to Caracas at a cost of $400, Dr. Waggoner was appointed President. The professor wanted her approval of the trip and she denied it. "Dr. Waggoner replied that I was not to continue this project of recruiting prospective students to Wilson College among qualified Venezuelan girls ..." In a follow-up conversation directly with Dr. Waggoner, the professor asked about the program to recruit qualified students from Venezuela, and she replied that "nothing had been done, because" in her words, "she was not going to turn Wilson into a school to teach English to foreigners." (p. 514-515, Court Proceedings) A further attempt to revive in 1977 still met with objection from the President. This seemed particularly regrettable since at that time the government of Venezuela was prepared to pay all the expenses for each student for four years of education.

Testimony of Dr. William Elliott

Dr. William Elliott was Vice-Provost for Enrollment Planning at Carnegie Mellon University since 1974 with all prior positions after his Ph.D. in the areas of admissions. He consulted with small colleges and with women's colleges on enrollment management. In short, he was considered an expert witness. His testimony, in essence, was that using the student search program as a primary means of recruiting had inherent weaknesses in that it largely just brought awareness of Wilson to prospective students. As a result, the percentage of inquiries generated from this approach is low, and there is no assurance that the students will enroll. There is also no easy way of assuring that the students generated through this program will have the necessary academic credentials Wilson was seeking. Students also are not necessarily in the geographic domain that the College most regularly attracts. The timing of responses to students' inquiries is critical since they apply to a number of schools. Applications are generally filled out during the Thanksgiving Weekend and arrive on college campuses shortly after December 1st.

He didn't understand why a college would ask a student to reply twice for a request for applications before they received a response. The 1500 replies would constitute a primary market and would be the most significant group with which to work to get an application pool. Most small struggling colleges don't rely on the mail exclusively but use the telephone. Also, using currently enrolled students to call and meet prospective students is very useful. This didn't happen at Wilson.

Dr. Elliott was a part of a team that looked at Bradford College. He got from Bradford all of the information that was requested by the team and he had five other reviewers looking at it. Then they went to campus and spent three days meeting faculty, students and the admissions staff. He wrote an extensive written report for the Board of Trustees. Adjustments were made and the College remained open. [Although this College subsequently closed in 2000, 21 years later.]

On cross-examination, one conclusion was that Wilson was not having success in the primary market, and they gave up what they had of a secondary market when they stopped visiting high schools.

Elliott considered the goal of 150 new students for the fall 1979 "a bit optimistic." From the statistics he saw, he would have expected 50-60 students to enroll. It was also noted that there would be a decline in high school graduates applying for colleges of about 40% over the next 17 years—especially in the mid-Atlantic and New England regions. Dr. Elliott felt that Wilson needed more staff with more experience; that the size of the College (215) was an impediment; that the College needed a curriculum that would be more in demand; tuition and fees are not an over-riding consideration; the College is admitting 82-83% of the students that apply—not abnormally high for a small private college.

Curriculum

Fundamentally, the testimony and focus on curriculum dealt with the seeming unwillingness of the Board or President to update the curriculum by incorporating a career orientation into the liberal arts to meet the needs of women entering careers that in the past had not been open to them. The attorney for the petitioners wanted to make the point that had this been done, it was likely that the College would not be facing closing and further, that there was still time to make a change to a more career-oriented focus to the liberal arts. The attorney for the respondents wanted to make the point that even had this been done, it would not have made a difference in enrollment and that it would, in the end, weaken the liberal arts nature of the College and make the College less attractive.

In testimony of Mrs. Walker reading from the Moon Report (November 1974): "The Trustees and President should ask the Dean and the faculty to give further consideration to curriculum revision. In our judgment, the job of revising the Wilson curriculum is not finished. While two years of time and a great deal of energy have been put into the recent revisions, they fall short of innovative or dramatic breakthroughs for even a small college which is educating women for complex career/family life styles of the future. We believe that the faculty and Dean have the capability, but there are also limitations that must be recognized." (p. 1122, Court Proceedings)

As a part of the testimony by Dr. McPherson, under re-examination by Mr. Oler for the petitioners, the following was quoted from the Moon Report: "We investigated a number of possibilities during the period of our study of future alternative courses which Wilson College might consider. These included … 'Rapidly change the total program emphasis of Wilson College, placing heavy emphasis upon career education and specialized courses of study affecting at least some, and possibly all, of the major career areas now being undertaken in educational institutions around the country." (p. 669, Court Proceedings) Additional suggestions, such as faculty retrenchment, were made in order to allow the College a chance to survive, but the other five alternative options, except for becoming co-educational, were far more draconian. The viability of a liberal arts curriculum in conjunction with courses and majors leading to specific careers was the main focus, however, of the testimonies. It was clear from the testimony of several of the witnesses that there had been alumnae with impressive credentials who volunteered time to work with the faculty and administration to look at curriculum, and their offers had been rebuffed. The main issue was whether to incorporate more career-oriented courses into the curriculum that would attract more students.

From the testimony around 1977, several ideas for new more career-oriented programs were mentioned, if not discussed: for example, medical technology integrating our science curriculum with the medical facilities in Chambersburg; a study of the environment; management; design; communications; landscape and architecture. The witness, Mrs. Jean Zehner, naming these ideas—among others mentioned at a Board meeting—said that she "was practically laughed out of the Board meeting, having been told that I wanted to start a trade school." (p. 274, Court Proceedings)

Chapter Two: The Alumnae vs. The Board of Trustees

No alternatives mentioned in the Moon Report suggested the status quo for Wilson.

Testimony suggested that there were good ways of integrating career-oriented courses and majors with the liberal arts and that there were grant moneys available for curriculum development. "There is no reason why career concentrations could not be introduced with restructuring of the faculty and have a strong liberal arts base and a strong liberal arts core." (p. 306, Court Proceedings)

There was flexibility to bring in new faculty since under 50% of the current faculty is tenured. Restructuring the curriculum would also mean eliminating some courses and changing others but still having a strong core in the liberal arts.

In a telling exchange between Mr. Oler and Dr. Waggoner concerning career orientation:

> Mr. Oler: "It is, in fact, is it not, that in 1975, you were a very strong advocate of not changing the traditional liberal arts program into an area of career orientation?"
>
> Dr. Waggoner: "I am committed, I guess is the word, to the importance, the value of the liberal education of women for the long term."
>
> Mr. Oler: "And may I read into that a disagreement and a fundamental disagreement with people who say that (there) should be substantially vocational or career type programs in traditional (liberal) arts institutions such as Wilson?"
>
> Dr. Waggoner: "I can answer that yes if I may explain the reason for my answer ... I tend to agree ... with Dr. Truman's testimony in which he said that when you have tried to do that to any large extent, it always becomes unsuccessful."
>
> Mr. Oler: "You were afraid in 1975 of the idea of Wilson becoming

a sort of vocational training school if it very much changed its curriculum?"

Dr. Waggoner: "... I did not think it should become a vocational school." (pp. 863- 865, Court Proceedings) Dr. Waggoner agreed with Mr. Oler's statement that there were a great many pressures in that direction in 1975.

Changes to the Curriculum

The President's testimony was that curricular changes and revisions during her four years were rather small. (p. 731, Court Proceedings) She tried to make changes, *e.g.*, in the English curriculum, but received no support from the faculty.

Faculty testifying also said that there had been no major changes in the curriculum. Professor James Applegate, a member of the Curriculum Committee, testified that "The kind of change that I would like to have seen, and would still like to see, would be one in which both the curriculum itself was changed and the way in which the curriculum is presented ... to emphasize the career potentialities that are in a liberal arts education in general ..." (p. 384, Court Proceedings)

No curriculum recommendations presented by the Dean had been turned down, but very few items were brought to the committee. They were put off the first half of the year (1977-78) from making recommendations by the Dean "on the grounds that a special committee for curriculum that had been set up for the Middle States Review was working on these things ... the report never did come to the committee." (p. 395, Court Proceedings)

Several proposals came to the curriculum committee, but the witness was not sure if they went on to the faculty—earth science and a revision to fine arts are examples. A proposal about reinvigorating the drama program was turned down by the committee.

A summary of faculty responses concerning questions about major changes in the curriculum in the last two-three years was that there were none.

The difficulties of providing a strong academic program with a relatively small number of faculty was noted since fewer faculty means relatively limited coverage of a field, and a small student body means a large number of very small classes and could mean that interaction among students was less educationally beneficial than would occur in a larger classroom situation.

Reorganization and Number of Courses

Prior to the President's arrival the faculty had begun the process of organization of 20+ departments into four divisions. Instead of calling them departments within the divisions, they were to be called disciplines. Many departments had only two members. The disciplinary coordination that needed to take place within the divisions did not occur as frequently as would have been preferred—both by the President and the Moon Report. When Dr. Waggoner arrived in 1975, she, with the Dean and faculty, completed a consolidation of the curriculum, but this consolidation was largely administrative—organizational with some 20 departments placed into four divisions. The College did provide for a variety of independent studies and majors that were new since 1975, and this did result in greater flexibility.

Other issues included the possibility of too many courses offered and that the curriculum was spread too thin—163 unique courses taught out of two departments for 300+ students, according to the 1974 Moon Report.

Financial Matters

Dean H. Kelsey, retired in 1978 as Vice-President for Business at Albright College where he had been for ten years, was admitted as an expert in financial matters. Mr. Kelsey testified that, if they received no more gift income, the deficit for the year would be around $1.1 million. In short, he gave some examples of ways financially to continue the College.

There was no question that under President Waggoner, the deficits were reduced, and there were several modest surpluses as a result of two major gifts—$500,000 in 1977 and $1,500,000 in FY1978. The College had very little debt and solid assets in buildings and equipment.

On cross-examination of President Waggoner, Mr. Oler made the following points concerning finances: (1) In 1976-77 and 1977-78, there were actual surpluses in the operating budget (albeit due to large gifts/bequests); (2) funds functioning as endowment as of early April 1979 were $98,000; (3) very little debt needing to be paid annually; a HUD loan of $450,000 at 2.75% interest; a capital lease program on two dormitories; and a science building grant of $565,000, a portion of which is repayable and negotiated with HEW. This latter would not have to be paid if they went out of business; other assets of the College included property; buildings insured for $16,000,000 and equipment $2,000,000, with no liens on that personal property. (pp. 838- 844, Court Proceedings)

Mr. Oler also pointed out that the alumnae had made $800,000 in conditional pledges should the College remain open (counter Dr. Waggoner's earlier point that if alumnae thought the college was closing, they would not give). In addition, there was $180,000 in the Presbyterian Major Mission fund that would come to the college should it remain open and $25,000 for renovating buildings for the handicapped. (pp. 846-854, Court Proceedings) There was also money in a will left to the College should it remain open.

In a fairly lengthy exchange, the President admitted that they had not calculated the costs or financial losses of closing the College other than $280,000 for unemployment insurance.

Faculty

Salaries/Pay Cuts

Under Dr. Waggoner there were no discussions of pay cuts in order to help the College. Under Dr. Cole (President from 1970-1974), there was a faculty retrenchment committee and an offer was made. During the time of the Moon Report (1974), there were faculty meetings and a retrenchment committee that studied how the College might reduce expenses. There was a recommendation that the faculty voluntarily engage in a pay reduction, but the Interim President (1974-1975) rejected the idea. There were, however, no salary increases.

Would the faculty help now? All the faculty members testifying said they agreed fully with one faculty member who testified: "At the present time, if there were the possibility of a renewed Wilson College, operating with a different administration and different Board of Directors, and if, on examination of the budgetary figures of the College, it was evidenced that such a pay cut would be a substantial help to the College, I would be quite willing to take it …" A follow-up questionnaire resulted in the faculty saying they would take a cut at least in the thousands of dollars.

In summary, there was no discussion of pay cuts under Dr. Waggoner, and there had been salary increases in 1976-77; 1977-78; and 1978-79. Faculty had not been asked to make a financial contribution in the past three years. Every faculty member who testified said that he would take a substantial cut in salary with the College under different management if the College could survive as a teaching institution.

Replacement of Faculty

There had been no attempts to replace faculty or other personnel necessary for 1979-1980 after the announcement of the closing. The importance of this question to the petitioners was that … "by announcing the closing … a number of things which make it more difficult for the College to go on have not been done." (p. 494, Court Proceedings) An interim person was appointed for the library until the actual closing of the College slated for June 30, 1979.

Flexibility of Faculty

The Moon Report had stated that the faculty was "mired in traditionalism and inflexible." (p. 398, Court Proceedings) The President agreed with the statement. (pp. 729-730, Court Proceedings) Faculty testimony felt that that statement was exaggerated, but with some validity, but as the faculty became aware of the problems the College was facing, there was a great deal less validity to the statement. (p. 399, Court Proceedings)

Use of Alumnae as Faculty

There were several alumnae called as witnesses to testify that they had offered to teach a course— one, for example, in children's literature, but had never received a reply to their offer.

Fundraising and Potential Trustees

The Presbyterian Church

In 1979, The Major Mission Fund of the Presbyterian Church (USA) had proposals from Wilson for two projects: $181,000 for human development and $14,764 for scholarship assistance for disadvantaged students. Wilson would receive the funds if it stayed open but not if it closed. This would be a new source of income for the College.

Save Wilson Committee

The Committee has two types of campaigns: one for gifts over a three-year pledge period with the first cards mailed out to all 6,500-7,000 alumnae on March 23, 1979, and the second one for special gifts mailed out April 26th to alumnae capable of major gifts. The total pledged for the three-year campaign as of May 7, 1979, was $804,009 from 1,840 pledges. The special gift fund had $18,200 from 60 pledges as of May 7, 1979, but with a later start. All of the pledges, as well as any money sent, were conditional upon the College remaining open as a college. They were going to be held in the Preservation of Wilson College Trust Fund, a nonprofit corporation.

In addition to fund-raising, the Save Wilson Committee was also looking for potential new Trustees should the court rule that the College could continue as a teaching institution. The court would not admit this as testimony or as evidence, but did admit as an exhibit a list of 25 persons with vitae and personal letters saying that they would "agree to be a Trustee of Wilson College, should the College continue to operate ..." (p. 448, Court Proceedings) These persons came forward on their own or had been contacted by a sub-committee of Save Wilson.

THE DECISION!

This decision was—and still is—a singular one in higher education legal history. It was and is the only time that trustees of a non-profit institution of higher education voted to close a college where alumnae took the board to court and won the case!

THE PETITIONERS' CASE

Let's begin, however, with the specifics of the petitioners when they asked the Court to take the case. Basically, these were their arguments, taken from their petition filed on March 27, 1979:

- No amendment to the articles of incorporation had been filed to authorize the termination of the College;
- No court order had been obtained authorizing a diversion of property committed to charitable purposes;
- No *cy pres* proceeding of any type had been instituted;
- Voting to close the College and making this action public caused irreparable harm to the institution, threatening its survival should the court conclude that the actions were improper;

- The Board of Trustees failed to implement the November 2, 1974, Moon Report;
- The Board of Trustees should be removed for having wasted and mismanaged the College

  by failing to:
  » take all the necessary and proper steps to correct the unfavorable financial and enrollment trends known to them as early as 1974;
  » adequately revise and restructure the curriculum to accommodate the needs and desires of the modern college woman;
  » adequately and competently recruit new enrollees and to respond in a timely manner, following up on written inquiries from prospective students;
  » adequately devise and implement a plan for faculty retrenchment;
  » sufficiently curtail expenditures in view of income;
  » reorganize and maintain a competent and effective administrative staff;
  » fully utilize alumnae in the recruitment of new students;
  » secure necessary and adequate funds to meet general operating expenses;
  » develop a highly visible policy of education consistent with the growing independence of and opportunities for women;
  » notify individual faculty members of the termination of their respective employment contracts, which created a liability for extended severance pay for certain faculty;

- » fully implement the recommendations of the Middle States Association Report in 1979-80, and, instead, terminate the College less than a year later, notwithstanding a degree of optimism expressed in the report regarding the financial picture;
- » fully implement a contract of enrollment with all currently enrolled students and accepted prospective students by implementing a resolution to permanently close the institution;

by violating and grossly deviating from the:

- » conditions and purpose of donations over the years by implementing a resolution to permanently close the institution;
- » original charter and amendments by taking substantial steps to close the College;
- » trust and thus grossly abusing the trust of the alumnae who will be permanently and irreparably damaged by the closing of the College;
- » the charitable purposes of the College and that abusing the public trust and damaging the public interest
- » generally failing to gather sufficient data and take the necessary action that reasonable people in similar circumstances would have taken to protect the trust corpus and perpetuate the charitable purposes of the trust. (pp. 9-12, Petition for removal of defendants as Trustees of Wilson College and other appropriate relief)

The burden of proof was, according to the court, to be on the Trustees.

THE JUDGMENT OF THE COURT

The Adjudication and *Decree Nisi* was passed down on May 25, 1979, and declared (in summary):

1. The closing of the College was enjoined and the college may not close without court approval.
2. Dr. Waggoner and Dr. McPherson were removed from the Board.
3. No funds from the College could be expended on behalf of the respondents, but, instead, the respondents shall pay their own costs.
4. The Court retained jurisdiction over the matter.

The conclusions of law that justified the Court's interest in the case and that permitted the Court jurisdiction were that the Board of Trustees needed prior court approval before they could determine the disposition of the assets of the College. Fundamentally, they needed the approval of the Court before they could publicize and begin the process of closing the College. They did not seek court approval in a timely manner. As a result, "neither on the facts or the law was the Board of Trustees justified in resolving on February 17, 1979, to close Wilson College as of June 30, 1979." (p. 82-83, Court Opinion) On May 4, 1979, the Trustees sought judicial approval to sell assets not donated for charitable purposes and to put those assets into the Wilson College Foundation. The hearing, however, was not to be held until July 2, 1979, after the College would have been closed.

The Court's Opinion is in four parts: Findings of Fact, Discussion, Conclusions of Law, and a *Decree Nisi*. I will offer a summary of the salient points which relate back to the testimony.

FINDINGS OF FACT

Decision to Close the College

All the petitioners were taken by surprise at the announcement of the closing. The alumnae testified that they had not been asked to help—in fact, they were told that their help was not needed. Faculty had not been asked to take salary cuts—in fact, they were given raises and in January 1979, and had asked for a 15% raise. An alumna who was a regular donor received a note on February 3 or 4, 1979, from the Development Office indicating her pledge was due. She sent it in, having no reason to believe that it would not be used for educating young women at the College. Another alumna donor was told in November that the College had turned the corner.

As of April 30, 1979, the Trustees admitted that their announcement to close the College did cause irreparable harm to the institution and that if they continued the actions taken to close the College, they would cause further harm, threatening the ability of the College to survive.

Admissions—Attrition—The Admissions Office

The Court gave these statistics: the largest entering class of 252 was in 1965 and that 138 graduated. Entering class enrollments/withdrawals: 1975, 92/52%; 1976, 39/15%; 1977, 62/42%; 1978, 55/4% as of December 1978. On February 1, 1979, there were 214 students including 12 full-time day and 19 part-time day students.

The drop in new enrollments in 1976 was attributed to the departure of a President and widespread concern about the future of the College. A new admissions officer was hired in September 1975 who used traditional methods including high school visits, college nights and fairs, personal staff contacts, and visits, advertising and alumnae involvement through the One-Plus-One program. That officer, for the fall of 1977, reversed the enrollment drop in 1976 and began planning for the next year. However, she resigned in the winter of 1976 due to job pressures.

A new admissions director was hired in the spring of 1977, and Dr. Waggoner told him to use whatever methods he thought would succeed in generating new enrollments. The most interesting point here is that "philosophically [he] had eliminated the traditional student recruitment technique from his considerations prior to becoming the Admissions Director of the College." (p. 18, Adjudication and *Decree Nisi*)

The practical result of this was to ignore past practice of two directors of admission who had emphasized the important of personal follow-up to student inquiries and a mix of student search and traditional techniques that were much more personal. The director followed through with a mix for the fall 1978 class yielding 185 applications and 63 enrollments.

For generating the class entering in fall 1979, however, the director chose to focus almost exclusively on student search, ordering 70,000 names with the hope of making the responses more personal. Notwithstanding his testimony that all 1,500 reply cards had proper responses, the follow-up to the ultimate number of 1,414 reply cards left a great deal to be desired. Findings of fact according to the Court were, in summary, that 778 cards received between June 8, 1978, and September 21, 1978, were not responded to by the admissions Office; 636 cards received between May 15, 1978, and June 7, 1978, received either just a prospectus (284), or a prospectus and a college application (76), or a prospectus, college applications and 1977-1978 catalogue (47). (p. 24, Adjudication and *Decree Nisi*)

Summarizing the analysis, the admissions office ignored 139 specific requests for applications; failed to answer specific questions on 436 rely cards; failed to respond to 7 inquiries concerning campus visits; and sent admission forms to 47 who didn't request them. (p. 25, Adjudication and *Decree Nisi*)

Such heavy reliance on Student Search utterly failed, even though they were encouraged in the fall when the College received the 70,000 names. The director, however, had not taken into consideration the risks

Chapter Two: The Alumnae vs. The Board of Trustees

involved in such a heavy reliance without considerable personal follow-up for which, regrettably, they did not have the human or financial resources to manage well.

Materials were sent late to the alumnae in the One-Plus-One program, and the interview forms sent to the alumnae in Baltimore on October 18, 1978, were from inquiries made in the Spring 1978—not timely! In an October meeting with alumnae in One-Plus-One, the Admissions Director said that their help was not needed. 150 high school students on their own asked the College Board to send the PSAT scores to Wilson, and the only follow-up was to acknowledge the receipt of the scores and ask for more information from the student. The plan of a faculty member to contact the Minister of Education in Venezuela was stopped.

Against a goal set of 150 enrollments, only 81 applications had been received by January 29, 1979, leading to the panic of the President and Board of Trustees and ultimately to the announcement of the closing.

In essence, the Court stated that "The Director of Admissions' projection of a 1979 freshmen class of 164 students based on an estimated 11,000 inquiries generated by the student search plan was not warranted on the basis of any facts submitted. It was misleading to the Board of Trustees and the President and represented mere puffery. The 87 minimum high school grade average, coupled with the 1180 minimum PSAT score, ... was unrealistically high, and undoubtedly excluded from consideration prospective students who would not have qualified at academically higher ranked colleges and universities, but would have been interested in matriculation at Wilson College ... all evidence [that] establishes [that] the Director of Admissions was not competent to perform the duties of his office, and [that] the student recruitment program of the College suffered accordingly ... [and that] the President of the College failed in her responsibility to adequately supervise the Director of Admissions in the discharge of his mission." (p. 32-33, Adjudication and *Decree Nisi*)

The Moon Report from the Academy of Educational Development

The Trustees admitted that they had failed to sufficiently implement the Moon Report, but they alleged that had no obligation to do so. Dr. McPherson, a current member of the Board of Trustees, had actually written a part of the report.

The Court paid a great deal of attention to this report, listing a number of its recommendations as well as Board motions to adopt some of them. "The Moon Report identified three crises which Wilson College must overcome to survive: identity, leadership and planning. The report indicates that the College must define its role as a women's college in the perspective of the future role of women in Western culture. Wilson must organize its leadership to overcome problems created by overstaffing, historical failure to delegate leadership burdens form the President to other key positions, and failure to utilize Trustees, alumnae, parents and student groups to accomplish tasks. In addition, the College must develop a viable plan of its future which is critical and objective and with contingency points built-in to permit flexibility when variable factors such as enrollment and inflation affect it." (p. 37, Adjudication and *Decree Nisi*)

Regarding the 15 major management recommendations from the Moon Report, the Court found that, "With the exception of the establishment of the One-Plus-One program involving alumnae in recruiting efforts, it does not appear that any serious, sustained or productive efforts were made by the Board or Administration to correct the major management limitations set forth in the Finding of Fact 134." (p. 40, Adjudication and *Decree Nisi*)

Regarding the eight specific recommendations concerning future academic management of the College, the Court found that, other than including women's studies courses in the curriculum, "it does not appear that the Board gave any further consideration to the said recommendations as might have been expected under its resolution in

Finding of Fact 124 (e)... or 137 (g) and (h)." (pp. 41-42, Adjudication and *Decree Nisi*)

The Court was equally critical of the very selective follow-through on the financial management recommendations, addressing only five out of fifteen. "There is no evidence that the Board or Administration took action or attempted to implement the other financial management recommendations." (p. 43, Adjudication and *Decree Nisi*) They failed to publicize a state of financial exigency, even though they declared it to exist at the November 2, 1974, Board meeting. Whereas President Waggoner did attempt to control costs, the Court could find no evidence of alternative financial and operating plans which should have covered a three-to-five year period; no evidence of an increase in tuition and no evidence of reductions in administrative staff. (pp. 44- 45, Adjudication and *Decree Nisi*)

The seven recommendations for managing external relations also appear to have been ignored.

Although the Executive Committee of the Board was to be the implementation committee to review the report, recommend additional action by the Board, monitor progress, and report monthly to the full Board, ... there was no evidence that that happened. (p. 46, Adjudication and *Decree Nisi*)

Curriculum

"Despite the commentary and recommendations of the Moon Report that the curriculum of the College be revitalized to reflect prevailing trends in women's education in the United States with more career orientation, the Board decided to retain the traditional liberal arts base. ... Presumably President Waggoner made known her philosophy concerning liberal arts education, *vis-à-vis* career oriented education or a combination of the two, to the Board search committee in 1975. Thus her employment as President of the College insured a maintenance of the basic curriculum." (p. 49, Adjudication and *Decree Nisi*)

Middle States Report

"The similarity in the deficiencies noted in the Middle Atlantic Association (sic) Report of April 1978, to findings in the Moon Report of 1974, evidences a continuing lack of change, modification or revision over a period in excess of three years." (p. 53, Adjudication and *Decree Nisi*)

The Panel of Experts, the Board, and the President

"Upon all the evidence, the panel concluded there was nothing more for the Board to do or change. The panel conducted its affairs in an informal manner, and no written report of any kind was even submitted.
With due regard to the expertise of the three panelists (*physically present at the meeting*) in their respective areas, it is inconceivable that they, with or without the help of President Waggoner, could have scanned, digested, and comprehended the mass of printed material presented to them and then conducted a meaningful examination of President Waggoner in six hours. We do not question the good intentions or the good motives of the panel of experts. However, comparing their six- hour meeting to the meticulous preliminary preparations, on campus investigations and interviews, team meetings, preliminary and final reports of the Moon Report consultants, and the Middle Atlantic Association evaluators, we find their oral report, as presented, utterly devoid of merit or value." (p. 57, Adjudication and *Decree Nisi*)

Ultimately the Court believed that "The Officers of the Board were not justified in relying on the oral report of Dr. Truman on a matter as monumentally serious as the closing of a 109-year-old college; nor were they justified in proceeding to draft a recommendation to the Board for such closing on such an inadequate study. ... They exceeded their express and implied authority by formulating a resolution to close the College, change the corporate name of the College to Wilson College Foundation, and to apply the assets of the College to the purposes of the foundation." (p. 58, Adjudication and *Decree Nisi*)

Chapter Two: The Alumnae vs. The Board of Trustees

The Court noted that, in total, Dr. Waggoner had had three years of administrative experience followed by two years of a study leave. Curriculum changes were small. She did attempt to strengthen the College financially, but her seeking of gifts and grants was without significant success. There was excessive turnover in her administration. In December 1978, she stated to the media that the College had "turned the corner" at a time when the admissions office knew that applications were falling behind expectations. She provided no evident leadership of the faculty, even when agreeing that they were traditional and inflexible, and there was significant lack of leadership in the faculty to change, revise or modernize the curriculum. (pp. 64 and 66, Adjudication and *Decree Nisi*)

IN CONCLUSION

The Judge based his decision in no small part on compelling evidence of: the alumnae's willingness to pledge money over a three-year period to keep the College open; the list of replacement Trustees who signified their willingness to serve; the Major Mission Fund of the Presbyterian Church (USA) of nearly $200,000; the willingness of at least four tenured faculty to take substantial salary cuts; the long-term indebtedness of only $1,250,000, a book value of the restricted endowment of $2,548,716, and the unrestricted endowment's market value of $1,300,000; the book value of campus buildings and equipment of nearly $10,000,000 was compelling. The full cost of closing had not yet been calculated by the Board, but it was not insignificant. "The College is not bankrupt or near that fiscal disaster point. The assets far exceed the established or presently known potential liabilities." (p. 70, Adjudication and *Decree Nisi*)

Judicial notice was also taken of the fact "that 37 members of the College faculty initiated an action *in assumpsit* against Wilson College on May 11, 1979, ... —118 claiming damages in the total amount of $666,906.71 ... alleging termination of their employment contracts and claims for severance pay." (p. 69, Adjudication and *Decree Nisi*)

The Court found that the damage done to the College by announcing the closing was incalculable but extremely serious—this in light of the fact that it was done without proper court authority.

> "Whether Wilson College can regain its viability as an ongoing educational institution cannot be determined at this time. Those members of the Board of Trustees who voted in favor of the resolution to conclude the operation of the College in its present form, establish a Foundation, and fund it with the remaining assets of the College acted precipitously without sufficient or valid information and consequently irresponsibly.
>
> The conduct of the officers of the Board is more subject to censure, for they failed to assure themselves of the expertise of the panel to address itself to the problems of a small college and its possible closing, the adequacy and accuracy of the information submitted to the panel, that the entire panel had been assembled and would devote the time required to consider issues involving the life or death of an institution. The action of the officers in exceeding the authority granted them by the Board in preparing the resolution for closing, creation of the foundation, and transfer of College assets to the foundation for presentation at the February 17, 1979, meeting was particularly censurable.
>
> The deletion from the final Board minutes of the February 17, 1979, meeting of the statements concerning the non-closing of the College, attributed to Dr. Truman by the Chairman, apparently without objection of any of the Board officers, is seriously suspect. President Waggoner misled the Board, the student body, alumnae, and the public as to the state of the College in the late months of 1978. This occurred either by design or by a total failure of the President to maintain any

supervision of the Director of Admissions. The failure of the President and Chairman to inform the Board, the student body, and the alumnae of the evident failure of the widely touted successful admissions program in early January 1979, was an unreasonable nondisclosure, improper, and irresponsible; and it directly contributed to the Board's panic reaction and sense of urgency to close at the February 3, 1979, meeting.

The extraordinary turnover rate of administrative staff, the well-documented incompetence of the present Director of Admissions, the failure to follow the clear recommendations of the Moon Report (excluding the liberal arts versus career course philosophical dispute) established the incompetency of President Waggoner as the chief executive of the College. The President's presentation to the Truman Panel on February 9, 1979, of a news release anticipating the February 17, 1979, Board action to close the College, establish a foundation and fund it with the remaining assets of the College is inexplicable, but of necessity creates the gravest doubts as to President Waggoner's motivation." (pp. 70-72, Adjudication and *Decree Nisi*)

The Court's Opinion goes on to state there was proper jurisdiction for the Court to act and that the laws that were not followed—approval of the Court before any property committed to charitable purposes can be diverted from that purpose; that the trustees of a nonprofit corporation must seek Orphan's Court approval before changing the nature of the institution. In addition, the public was deprived of the opportunity to comment on or protest the decision. (pp. 76-77, Adjudication and *Decree Nisi*)

It is important to note that there was NO evidence of fraudulent conduct of dishonest acts by any of the Trustees. The President was found to have grossly abused her authority and discretion and was removed from the Board by the Court; another Board member was removed from the Board for an existence of conflict of interest and failure to exercise special knowledge and expertise on behalf of the College.

"While we recognize, as we must, the distinct possibility that a time will come when the continuation of Wilson College as a teaching institution may become either impractical or impossible of fulfillment, the totality of the evidence did not persuade us that that time is now. The difficult days that lie ahead for Wilson College, its governing board, its alumnae, and its student body are obvious. However, we doubt that those future days are any more fraught with peril, any more risky, any more doomed to failure than the conditions and circumstances which confronted the incorporators 110 years ago.

The ... *petition inter alia* seeks the removal of all Trustees. ... Being mindful of the fact that the individual Trustees took their seats on the Board at various times over a period of many years and their tenure in office varied greatly, we are not prepared to attribute or even attempt to attribute collective Board action or inaction over an unidentified period of [time] to individual members of the Board ...

Speaking of Wilson alumnae, the Court feels it only appropriate to conclude this discussion by noting the singular appropriateness of Daniel Webster's famous statement in the Dartmouth College case: IT IS SIR, AS I HAVE SAID, A SMALL COLLEGE, AND YET THERE ARE THOSE WHO LOVE IT! (pp. 78-81, Adjudication and *Decree Nisi*)

This chapter can best be ended with a quote from the November 29, 1979, article by Sam Taylor in the *Lancaster New Era* entitled "Countian Breathes New Life into Wilson College As Its President." There is this sentence that summarizes it all:

Nothing equals the power of a woman, and the combined strength of an entire alumnae association prompted the winning court suit and resulted in more than a million dollars in cash and pledges to help keep the College open.

Professor James Applegate sharing the news of the court case triumph

Chapter Three
THE AFTERMATH AND PERSPECTIVES

THE AFTERMATH

The weekend of Commencement was one of shock and joy. It was also busy! The judgment of the court was rendered on Friday, May 25, 1979. On Saturday, May 26, 1979, the Board of Trustees met with eighteen members present out of twenty-five. The following comes from the minutes of that May 26, 1979, Board meeting.

May 26, 1979, Meeting of the Board of Trustees

The awarding of degrees and the procedure for granting Wilson College degrees in 1980 to students who would satisfactorily complete their work towards their degree at other institutions were approved.

The financial report was presented by President Waggoner: $500,000 left in the unrestricted endowment including funds functioning as endowment; a $700,000 deficit predicted by June 30, 1979, with $350,000 already transferred from the unrestricted endowment to offset the deficit; another $350,000 transferred to meet operating expenses and to offset the deficit, leaving approximately $200,000 in the unrestricted endowment. It was noted that a substantial number of faculty and staff had already obtained employment. No College funds had been used for the litigation.

The Chairman of the Board resigned, and a new Chairman was elected for a period not to exceed two weeks. The resignation of Margaret Waggoner tendered on April 28, 1979, was accepted with the understanding that she would receive her salary and continue to live in the house through August 31, 1979. An acting administrator of the College was approved until other arrangements could be made by the new Board. Fourteen Trustees in addition to the Chair resigned; eight Trustees remained, with two Trustees absent by virtue of being out of the country.

Appreciation was extended to the Chairman of the Board, Martha Walker, "for her efficient work as Chairman of the Board during an exceedingly difficult year, and [the Board] was especially grateful for her untiring and personal responses to letters and telephone calls from alumnae and other friends of the College during the controversy that arose after the February 17 decision to close the College." (p. 3, Minutes of the Board of Trustees, May 26, 1979)

From the Notes of Nan Clarkson about the Board Meeting, May 26, 1979:

> "... We Trustees whom the judge had elected not to remove were given the clear order to enjoin [stop] closure." This was an overwhelming awareness that hung over us as we filed into the Board room. My notes, taken in the meeting and later transcribed with fuller detail, show that there was a mood at first to fight the decision. There was a great deal of tension in that room. One Trustee had been a plaintiff in the court case and was with us; there were varying degrees of discomfort at the

Chapter Three: The Aftermath and Perspectives

presence of Margaret Waggoner and Mary Patterson McPherson, each having been removed by the judge from the Board. Many, who had thought this their last full meeting, found themselves saddled with an awesome new burden that was by no means welcome to all.

After a good deal of legal discussion with the Board's counsel, it became clear that to appeal, or contest, the court's decision would take forever. Tom Menaker, the lawyer for the Trustees: "My guess is Judge Eppinger wouldn't reverse Judge Keller—next step is the Supreme Court—probably two years, and this would effectively ruin any chance of saving the College. Among your alternatives is the resignation of those who oppose…" And so, after the necessary business involving the negotiations to be entered into about the *cy pres* document and discussion about fees, we got to the matter of who would resign. As we went around the table it seemed at first that all would leave. Then Lee Caldwell was the first to say, firmly, and with evident emotion, "I will not resign!" After her example, enough stayed to make a quorum, each one heroically: Betty Blackadar, Polly Austin, Woody Turner, Stanley Stillman, Catherine Sweeney, Sidney Palmer, Betsy Diely, Jean Zehner, Lee Caldwell and Nan Clarkson.

There are those to this day who wonder about the fact that Judge Keller left the old Trustees in place. I believe that he knew what he was doing. I like to believe that he knew that many would resign, but that those who remained would, with their special knowledge of the College and its crisis, augment their numbers with special recruits willing to join them in taking on perhaps the hardest challenge ever handed to a small college.

… I (Nan) was delegated to call Professor Donald Bletz to ask if he would take us on. As it happened, he was out walking a lame horse … But he called back and accepted our eager invitation, all details to be settled later, for which we were profoundly grateful. The second action of our little Board was to invite the Chairman of Save Wilson, Nancy Besch, who, as Alumnae President, had served on the Board of Trustees during the Cole Administration, to join us as Vice-Chairman. We would also invite the Save Wilson office to move up to the College. This action could speak louder than words of the united effort we would all make to continue the saving of our College ... **(end)**

May 27, 1979, Meeting of the Board of Trustees

Acting Chairman of the Board, Nan Hudnut Clarkson, '47, convened the meeting on Sunday, May 27, 1979, after Baccalaureate and before graduation. An additional Trustee resignation was accepted with regret and a Trustee who had resigned was re-elected. Nancy Besch, the Chairman of Save Wilson, was elected Vice-Chair of the Board and joined immediately. Eight additional members were proposed and elected to the board, but did not attend this meeting. At this meeting Dr. Donald Bletz was elected as Acting President for an indeterminate period of time and was directed "to take necessary steps to stabilize conditions on campus, to determine which of the faculty and staff would be in a position to return to the campus next term, and to take the necessary steps to maintain the College in readiness to re-open in the fall. (p. 2, Minutes of the Board of Trustees, May 27, 1979)

Mrs. Besch was asked to continue as Chairman of the Save Wilson Committee which would become a committee of the Board. They were invited to move the headquarters to the College and to continue their activities in conjunction with the other offices of the College.

This Board meeting never adjourned, and a special meeting to continue the work of the Board was called for June 8-9, 1979.

From Nan Clarkson's Personal Journal—May 25-27, 1979:

"... driving from State College to Chambersburg with Betty Blackadar,

Chapter Three: The Aftermath and Perspectives

I called the College to say we would be late. Find out staggering news: Judge Keller has just announced his decision: The College must stay open ... however, he did not elect to kick out the Board. He ordered us to immediately: - enjoin closure; remove Margaret Waggoner from the Board; remove Pat McPherson (President of Bryn Mawr College) from the Board for conflict of interest. Whew! Arrive in Chambersburg. College seemingly in chaos. No one at switchboard. Drive to Save Wilson headquarters.

Margaret Disert, Peg Gordy, Carol Tschop, Faith Wilson Flower, Marge Kirchhoff Rodenhaver, others, celebrating with champagne. We join the celebration, we are hugged—welcomed by all. Forgive and forget is the sisterly theme. We get a copy of the abbreviated orders in the 87-page decision handed down a few hours earlier. I take it over to the old jail ... stop to read it.

Awesome. Judge said no evidence that most Trustees individually had been out of line. Dinner at Cozy Corner. Met Sid Palmer at Snack Bar. ... Meeting of Trustees at 11:00 a.m. Extremely surprised to find Pat McPherson and Margaret Waggoner in attendance. Their presence was explained by the Chairman and legally by Tom Menaker our attorney. I myself feel very uncomfortable about their being there. Woody thought we might be in contempt of court. Jean Zehner will be in the Board meeting for a brief time and then go into a meeting of respondents which she, being a plaintiff, cannot attend. She is irate, obviously so. "Will there be another Board meeting?" she asks. "Perhaps," says the Chairman ... "We'll let you know. Don't go too far," was the final word.

Our lawyer opens saying about the decision, "I am shocked. I have lost a law case before, but I have never been shocked by a judge's decision. I can only assume it is political ... I am ... shocked." The Chairman ... had spent 6-8 hours in the hospital the night before—the news had upset her to such a degree that she went into false labor. It stopped, she went home. Now she is here, pale and subdued, looking ready to go for the real thing any second. Pat McPherson looks grim. Stanley Stillman indulges in one of his infrequent outbursts—cheeks pink, head lowered and charging, and this concerns Pat: "I think this conflict of interest charge should be fought to the highest level, Pat. It sets a dangerous precedent—utterly preposterous! I was shocked on your behalf, Pat!" Pat, eyes lowered, with a kind of grateful wounded dignity, said "Thank you, Stanley!"

Anyway, the big question was what to do. Should we appeal? If so, where? State Supreme Court? Higher Court of Appeals? The lawyers are, happily for them, in control. The language becomes dense with legalese. Through it one hears two voices using the words "fight it." Margaret Waggoner and Alice Beeman actually believe we may fight it. The other alternative: negotiate. Bill Alexander's is the quiet but convinced voice that says, "There is really no other way."

I believe that. What he is saying is that to appeal is to lose the only time available for "striking while irons are hot." It is delivering the College to sudden death when we have been ordered to keep it open. It is, however, openly apparent that Alice and Margaret and doubtless, Pat, had hoped for appeal …

We agree that the points to be negotiated involve tossing the judge's decision out of publication. Something about payment of fees. Something about the cy pres document. This decision will not become a part of "the law," but the transcript will always be available for those who seek it out. OK. Then we get to the matter of who will resign, resignations effective as soon as negotiation is completed and judge has signed the document of agreement. The Vice-Chairman of the Board and the Chairman of the Board resign as do Mimi Wood, Jane Stewart, Sid Palmer, and Bill Alexander. Lee Caldwell will not resign—said firmly, emotionally. She has driven from Rochester, setting out at 5:00 a.m. Another waivers and concludes by saying, "Well, I go off the Board end of June anyway." So she doesn't resign as we're told we'll need either a quorum of nine or more to vote in new members Polly Austin, Woody Turner, Stanley Stillman, Betsy Diely, Jean Zehner and I do not resign.

Chapter Three: The Aftermath and Perspectives

Polly Austin nominates me as Acting Chairman, and I am elected unanimously and am a reluctant bride. Now when things are close to desperate, I am given the role temporarily and because there is no one else. The attorneys are getting along with the negotiations.

Lunch in the private dining room. I sit with the Vice-Chairman (who has resigned) and his wife. He is absolutely brotherly loving with me.

In the afternoon the remaining Trustees meet in Norland Parlor. We decide to call Don Bletz and ask if he'll be acting CEO. Done. We go through proposed Board names and elect Nancy Besch. Plan meeting of "new" Board for June 8th—reunion weekend. New problem surfaces. Lawyers Menaker and Oler come back with their contract for Jean Zehner (who was a plaintiff and a member of the Board) to sign. After much discussion and negotiation, the "consent agreement" is presented. Jean's husband refuses to let her sign. His point is that in this agreement all but Jean are protected from suit in the event that someone sues us for something we do. "She's liable for up to a million dollars," he raves. Would your husband allow you to sign? Of course not. We say that chances of such a suit are almost zero. "We'll take no chances," he storms. The plaintiffs' lawyers cast their eyes to heaven. They admit that he has a point that needs resolving. They put it something like this: "We agree there's almost no iota of a chance of anyone's suing, but, if they did, she's not covered. We would not bring it up, but once the point is raised, it's got to be resolved." This held us up for hours, right up to two minutes before the commencement procession. Through the late afternoon, by phone all evening, in and out of conferences Sunday—lawyers summoned from here and there—a real hornet's nest. For this uneasy, tense period, the fate of Wilson hung on one signature.

Dinner at Mimi Woods'—a stunning house, back on a country road and high above Chambersburg. Mimi and Chase gave us a perfectly elegant dinner, and the mood was a little wild and relieved to be rid of the tensions of the day...

To bed at 2:00 a.m.—*Nancy Besch and Eudora Roseman came by room 301 to tell me they'd spent an hour with the Zehner's at Margaret Disert's house ...*

Sunday meeting at 8:30 a.m.—*We meet with Don Bletz. We elect Board members on a contingency basis—until an agreement is signed.*

I go to Baccalaureate and sit by myself, feel emptied of self, and ask help for living through the day so as to bring a measure of reconciliation. After the service, things bogged down again. We continue meeting. Lunch. Escape to room to work briefly on remarks for Commencement, a progress report ... Tom Menaker slumped down in a chair, glowering. Things at an impasse. Jean comes in, asks me to come out. I go out to the Norland entry where Lisle Zehner and I are alone talking, and he demanded and I, by necessity, promised a new choice of lawyer for the College ......I went back in and two minutes later, Jean signed. Rejoicing. I say "Jean, get in your robe." Welcome Nenah Fry. We line up. I march with the Dean.

Commencement: 2:30 Laird Hall. The procession moves through waves of spectators like the Israelites marching down the corridor of the Red Sea. Excitement, drama, deliverance. The place is crowded, people standing along the walls. Klieg lights, the whir of television cameras ... my welcome:

> *Class of 1979 ... parents, relatives, honored guests ... faculty, Trustees, alumnae. Some of you may wonder who I am so let me introduce myself. I am Elisabeth Ann Hudnut Clarkson, Class of 1947, Acting Chairman of the Wilson College Board of Trustees.*

Before the word "Trustees" was out, my words were cut off by what the newspaper, the Harrisburg Patriot, *called "thunderous applause." They were not clapping for me so much as they were cheering the news that the guard had changed and my new office was tangible evidence. I went on to give a progress report concerning these facts: the newly constituted Board would meet June 8th; Jan Buys would be acting CEO until June*

2nd (stony silence); Don Bletz would become Acting President on June 2nd (wild cheering); seniors gave a standing ovation; Mrs. Nancy Besch was elected to the Trustees and would continue as Chairman of the Save Wilson Committee which would, ASAP, move to new quarters on the Wilson campus. Every sentence or so was punctuated by applause. The mood was thrilling. It was perhaps the most dramatic moment I've ever lived through—at least at center stage. The funny thing was that I felt drained of personal ego and had asked, rather, in the silence of the chapel to be given strength to do things right, to be used for a good cause. My goal for this brief term in office was to be a reconciling force. And it seems that it was given to me to be just such a person in that time and place. I mean that without pride—it was a great moment in my life, but never before have my gifts been used to the hilt as then. My years of tutelage in public speaking from the past-masters of my family were strengthened by the leadership strategies I've learned from Will: people don't want rhetoric so much as they want to know how we're doing, where we're going, open communication, candor.

After Nenah's great talk—Nenah Fry, Dean of Wells College—I said the great bit it was my duty to say, "By the authority vested in me by the Commonwealth of Pennsylvania and the Wilson College Board of Trustees ... "

After commencement, meetings with the Board, with Jan Buys, with lawyers Menaker and McQuaide (freshly back from the consent agreement signing with Judge Keller in Waynesboro) ...

Back home, and a week followed of phone calls beginning at 7:30 a.m. Phone calls from reporters—Chambersburg, Washington, etc., Presbyterian Church, bankers, Jean Zehner; lawyers; Jan Buys each day at 5:00; Don Bletz, Nancy Besch; and the whole Save Wilson group. The bank wants to be let off the hook as treasurer. Why? I find out and suggest they let us take the initiative in this matter. The Presbyterian Church feels that they have been short-changed by Wilson, that even though they've given us little, it represents more to them of their budget than we know and for that, we gave nothing. My impression of the scene at Wilson is of a whirlwind. Is Don Bletz the quiet center of the whirlwind or is he confused, tangential? How is he coordinating all offers of help?

Several Board members want me to stay on. Do I want to? Not really. Yet, for all the responsibility and work, it is easy for me to see that there are not many others who could do more than I can. (Vol. 8, Personal Journal)

Press Release from the College, May 31, 1979

Dr. Donald Bletz, a retired U.S. Army colonel with a long history of experience in both the military and civilian educational system, has been appointed Acting President of Wilson College.

Dr. Bletz, 53, was named Acting President by the new Wilson College Board of Trustees following a May 25th Court ruling reversing the old Board of Trustees decision to close the 110-year-old school.

"Wilson College has a long and enviable tradition of providing educational excellence, but that history is now in jeopardy," Dr. Bletz said. "During the coming weeks, the new Board of Trustees and I intend to assess the financial and student recruitment problems which Wilson now faces and then chart a realistic course of action to solve those problems."

Dr. Bletz is an associate professor of Political Science on the Wilson College Faculty and served as half-time assistant to the College President from January 1976 until December 1977. He has also served as an adjunct professor at Dickinson College, Southern Illinois University and was a Fellow at the Harvard University Center for International Affairs. Dr. Bletz received his Ph.D. in International Studies from the American University, Washington D.C., where he was also awarded a Masters' Degree in International Relations. He was a history major at the University of Omaha, where he received his Bachelors' Degree in 1963.

Dr. Bletz retired from the U.S. Army with the rank of full colonel in 1975. His military educational services included periods spent as Chairman of the Department of National and International Security Studies at the U.S. Army War College and an instructor at the War College on a variety of subjects ... **(end)**

May 29, 1979, CONSENT DECREE REPLACING THE *DECREE NISI*

The Board could have chosen to appeal the decision of the Court, but the reality of that action would have been that it could have taken months or even several years during which time they would have been required to keep the College open. Instead the lawyers for both sides negotiated an agreement that was signed on May 29, 1979 and replaced the Adjudication and *Decree Nisi* issued by the Court on May 25, 1979.

In an article written by Nan Clarkson for the Wilson Alumnae Quarterly, Winter 1980 entitled "A Critical Look at a Crucial Year," Nan reflects on this meeting:

" ... we met not as a Board, but as defendants in the suit. We had to decide what we would do about this. I think there were a few who would have been pleased to fight the decision. ... The important thing is that the majority took a very fair stand; they knew it would finish the College if we were to appeal; the case might take years to come before the higher courts. Judge Keller himself half expected us to appeal, and felt the Trustees behaved well in deciding against this. That would have been the death of the College right there. However, in negotiating, we had to give on certain matters that irked some of the alumnae—and I can understand that,—but what we gained was the settlement that allowed us the chance to combine forces with Save Wilson and try to make good this reprieve. ... I was elected Acting Chairman by the old Board and I accepted it with a heavy heart, with a really awesome feeling of commitment to it. It was an opportunity to work in a way I felt prepared to do, by all those years of observing. It was also a chance to help work out some of the wrongs, help open up the atmosphere. **(end)**

In essence, the negotiated agreement listed the names of 15 respondent Trustees who had resigned. The agreement noted that the Board of Trustees would convene for the purpose of filling vacant positions; that the pending *cy pres* petition would be withdrawn; that the College would continue as a teaching institution and that no decision to close the College could be implemented without prior court approval. Finally, a majority of the remaining members of the Board were authorized to constitute a quorum for transacting business at the first Board meeting following approval of the stipulation and agreement.

Perhaps of greatest importance was that the resigning respondent Trustees were not held liable for the consequences of their respective resignations from the Board and that "the remaining members of the Board will, at their first meeting following approval of this Consent Decree by the Court, approve the College's payment of $7,500, and no more, toward the expenses of defending this case on behalf of the Respondents. The record costs of this action will be paid by the Respondents." (p. 2, Consent Decree)

Summarized from the Minutes of the June 9, 1979, Meeting of the Board of Trustees

Dr. Donald Bletz had been chosen to serve as Acting President. (It turned out that he was a "providential choice"—using the words of Nan Clarkson—because he was the choice of Save Wilson and also of the Trustees who had voted in April not to close the College.) He told the Board that he would serve for no more than two years, so that set the time frame for a successful completion for a nationwide search for President. What was very clear in the minutes and in actual fact was that the Board would work very closely with the College administration as they reorganized.

Officers of the Board were elected: Nan Hudnut Clarkson, '47, Chairwoman of the Board; Nancy Adams Besch, '48, of Camp Hill, Pennsylvania and Chairwoman of Save Wilson, Vice-Chairwoman; Woodruff Turner, an attorney from Pittsburgh, Secretary; Ella Dorman Pethick, a retired stockbroker from Cranford, N.J., Treasurer; and Robert Brown, President of the Waynesboro Construction Company of Waynesboro, Pennsylvania, Assistant Secretary.

At this Board meeting, the Board heard reports from the administrative officers of the College and on the efforts to recruit the freshmen class for the fall of 1979—a few short months away.

Their next meeting was scheduled for July 7th.

From Nan Clarkson's Personal Journal, June 7, 1979

Thursday, June 7, 1979, flew to Wilson ... moved into Norland Hall, Room 204. Off to dinner in the Cozy Inn with Don Bletz. We set the agenda for the Saturday meetings. He is a lovely man. One cannot help wondering whether he has the force or the energy or the decisiveness to do the job. He has a fine face and an aura of kindness. You know you can trust him. But can you trust him to move mountains? Quiet night. Back to the high-ceiling dingy grandeur of the McClure room.

Friday, June 8, 1979—breakfast in the small dining room. Dick Zimmerman, Sam Sollenberger, Sid Palmer, Charlie Davison, and Donald Bletz. We talk about the treasurer matter. Valley Bank has been treasurer and wants off the hook. Rightly so—it's been ambiguous and full of possible conflicts. But the PR situation just now is touchy: half their shareholders want to save Wilson; half want to make sure the bank isn't putting good money after bad in Wilson. A headline would do neither them nor us any good—"Valley Bank Pulls Out" would look as if there's something terminal about the College finances (true) and they don't want to look like ogres. So my approach was to suggest that we take the initiative—we elect our own treasurer. Talked about the position of the business manager. He is not to be treasurer, but rather assistant treasurer.

Dave Dunkle of the Public Opinion interviewed me on the front porch of Norland He a late 1960s-type young man, shaggy and wholesome looking, a cool questioner, who enjoyed fitting my pieces of the puzzle into his own vast picture ...

Went into alumnae meetings—met with the Board. I felt it was a very fruitful exchange, but later on found out that some of them were really put off by my mention of the difficulties we were having with the plaintiff Trustee. I saw it as frankness and figured they knew all about it (her charge that we conspired about Margaret's resignation). They saw it as a personal vendetta. Funny thing is, I believe it was a bit of both. I must be very careful about such situations.

2:30: A businessman came to campus: Bob Shively, Dick Zimmerman, Sid, Nancy Besch, Don, and I met, and we were fully informed about the interest the Mormons take in Wilson. Of course, for the people of Chambersburg, having the Mormons at Wilson would be close to perfect. They'd be setting up a college with close to 10,000 students (750 to begin) and a student body too good to be true (no booze, no cigarettes, no dancing, no cards, no troublemakers—just a wholesome mob of proselytizers until they start converting the young of Chambersburg!).

This poses an ideological problem—one not easily discussed openly among the hordes of returning alumnae. Those who fancy they have just saved Wilson would have the scalp of any who dare mention "selling out" to the Mormons. It would be considered traitorous to the Save Wilson cause to even entertain the thought of "what if." What if we don't make it? There can be few buyers in the whole world who want to buy the entire campus. The Mormons would pay the 11-12 million we feel it's worth ..."

Chapter Three: The Aftermath and Perspectives

A Telegram from the President of the United States

A telegram was sent by President Jimmy Carter to the members of the Alumnae Association of Wilson College on the occasion of their 100th anniversary:

> I send warm greetings to members of the Alumni Association of Wilson College as you observe the centennial year of the Association and the one hundred and tenth anniversary of the school.
>
> I can think of no more appropriate way to celebrate the successful completion of your campaign to "Save Wilson College." Together, you and your school have struggled for survival and have won. Through your arduous efforts, this fine institution will be able to continue to provide young women with an outstanding academic experience. Your perseverance in the face of seemingly overwhelming odds should serve as an inspiration to other small private schools across the country.
>
> You have my best wishes as you begin your second century and your school enters a new era of development. JIMMY CARTER

"TRUSTEES, ALUMNAE LOOK TO WILSON'S FUTURE," by Dave Dunkle, *Public Opinion*, Monday, June 11, 1979 (Reprint permission granted) It is quoted in full:

> It was a weekend of celebration, conciliation and concentration at Wilson College as nearly 800 alumnae gathered on campus.
>
> The celebration was two-fold: for the 100th anniversary of the Wilson College Alumnae Association and for the May 26 court decision by Franklin County Judge John W. Keller that reversed the Board of Trustees' proposed closing of the College this year.
>
> The conciliation was between alumnae and Trustees. The Board, although reconstituted with mostly new members, was on

the other side of the courtroom from the alumnae during the hearing, the two groups got together Saturday morning in an attempt to wash away any remaining bitterness.

The concentration was directed toward the College itself—which still suffers from many problems, including a lack of students and money. Alumnae met in workshop sessions Saturday afternoon to discuss student recruitment, fund-raising, and curriculum revisions aimed at getting the weakened institution back on its feet.

Acting Trustees' Chairperson Elisabeth (Nan) Clarkson addressed the assembled alumnae Saturday, explaining the Board's motives in making the closing decision and asking alumnae to forget the past and work with the Trustees to ensure Wilson's survival. Of the closing, Clarkson said: "The Board made a decision, according to Judge Keller, that it had no right to make. For my part, I have to say that we acted in good faith at that time.

Truly, we might have done some things differently, but that's hindsight," she said. "We misread the wishes and energy of our alumnae. Never did we suspect the reaction we would receive on this campus."

Clarkson, who originally voted in favor of the closing, remained on the Board when most resigned following the Keller decision. She said Keller did not grant the Save Wilson Committee's request to remove the entire Board.

"No matter how misguided we may have been, he (Keller) specifically left us in charge of opening the College, she said in explaining her decision to remain a Trustee."

Clarkson cautioned the alumnae against looking for "scapegoats," saying "there is a little scapegoat in all of us." She said the Board has been over-criticized for its role in the closing, pointing out that alumnae support has dwindled in recent years and that the percentage of alumnae contributing money to the College "had never been over 39 percent." She said the "creative rage" sparked by the way the announcement was made might not have existed had the Board acted differently.

"There might have been a great deal of hand-wringing if we had announced the closing beforehand, but it might not have produced the creative rage of the Save Wilson Committee." Clarkson said. "Now, the time has come to put away 'we' and 'they.' It has to be 'us' working together if Wilson College is going to be what we know it can be."

Following Clarkson's remarks, Acting College President Dr. Donald Bletz walked to the podium and told the audience: "What you have accomplished is unique—you have set a precedent. Most of all, you have given the College new life."

Bletz, a political science professor until he was named Acting President following the resignation of Dr. Margaret Waggoner, was also named to the Board of Trustees over the weekend, one of 12 new Trustees appointed that weekend, including former Pennsylvania Secretary of Education Caryl Kline.

"At these times, I understand, the President is supposed to report on the state of the College," Bletz said. "The state of the College, ladies and gentlemen, is precarious.

"We have to set aside our differences because we will not succeed if we don't work together," he added. "I think we can succeed; in fact, I'm sure we can succeed."

Newly elected Trustee Nancy Besch, who also chaired the Save Wilson Committee, received a standing ovation when she approached the stage. Besch was a tireless worker in the fight to keep the College from closing, and to her fell the task of helping to unify old and new members of the Board of Trustees. "These continuing Board members are very sincere in their efforts to see that this College continues, ..." Besch said.

She also praised Judge Keller, as did nearly every speaker, calling him "a compassionate man ... who really cared about what was happening. Now we've got to prove to him that he was right in making this decision." **(end)**

June 1979, The Wilson College Alumnae Newsletter No. 5. I quote it in the main:

MESSAGE FROM THE PRESIDENT

The last three and a half weeks have been hectic, at times chaotic but always gratifying. What you have accomplished to reverse the closing of Wilson College, to attract students and to prepare for the fall term, is truly remarkable. Your letters, telephone calls and personal communications have helped me a great deal as we have worked to insure

Wilson's future ... Your guidance and concerns are often echoed by the leading educators of this country who have written and telephoned their advice and offers of help. There is no secret that our two most pressing needs are new students and financial support. This newsletter will bring you up to date on both of these critical areas. I would just like to add that because of recent events the College has become the focus of national attention. Many in the academic world and in the media are watching as we continue our Save Wilson campaign. Your help in recruiting new and transfer students and your continued financial support is needed now, more than ever.

Working together, all of us can insure that Wilson's second

century will improve on the traditional educational excellence of the past.

Don Bletz, Ph.D. Acting President

NEW BOARD OF TRUSTEES TO OVERSEE COLLEGE REORGANIZATION

The new Wilson College Board of Trustees began a major reorganization of the College's administration, fundraising efforts, and student recruitment during its first day-long meeting on Saturday, June 9th. At the end of a full day of deliberations during which new Board officers were elected, the Board voted not to adjourn but to recess until July 7th, "to permit a continuing, day-to-day concentration on the many problems facing Wilson," said new Chairwoman of the Board of Trustees Nan Hudnut Clarkson, '47, Buffalo, N.Y.

During the Saturday of Reunion Weekend the new Board of Trustees recessed twice, first to be presented to the Alumnae Association and later in the afternoon to hear a major address by Dr Elizabeth Tidball, associate professor at George Washington University, on the need for women's education.

Throughout the day, Board members heard reports on various aspects of college operation including admissions, finances, curriculum, faculty retention, and the state of the College's physical plant.

"Board members will be on the Wilson campus throughout the summer, working with the College administration in various areas to strengthen the institution and to demonstrate the new Board's commitment to Wilson College," Mrs. Clarkson added...

Other members of the Board of Trustees include: Robert G. Crist, Camp Hill, Pennsylvania, partner in the firm of Crist & Crist; Jane Troutman Ensminger, Class of '52, Lawrenceville, New

Jersey, President-elect, Wilson College Alumnae Association; Phyllis Gansz, Class of '50, Middleburg, Virginia, Academic Dean, Foxcroft School; Caryl Kline, Pittsburgh, Pennsylvania, former Pennsylvania Secretary of Education; Sidney M. Palmer, Chambersburg, Pennsylvania, Executive Vice-President of Valley Bank and Trust Co.; Dr. Eleathea Caldwell, Class of '62, Scottsville, New York, Assistant Professor of Plastic Surgery at the University of Rochester School of Medicine and Dentistry; Stanley W. Stillman, New York, New York, Time, Inc.; Jean Colgan Zehner, Class of '41, Pittsburgh, Pennsylvania, Vice-President for Consumer Affairs of the May Department Stores Co.; George C. Mason, Philadelphia, Pennsylvania, Managing Director, W.H. Newbold's Son & Co., Inc.; Catherine Sweeney, Coconut Grove, Florida, botanist and topical ecology expert; Mary H. Laprade, North Hampton, Massachusetts, Director of Clark Science Center, Smith College; Mary Work, Class of '29, Harrisburg, Pennsylvania, member of Board of Medical College of Pennsylvania; Edgar A. Yale, Lancaster, Pennsylvania, recently retired Group Vice-President, Armstrong Cork Co; Betty Blackadar, Class of '42, State College, Pennsylvania, Gloria Scott, Atlanta, Georgia, Vice-President, Clark College.

Dr. Don Bletz, Acting President of the College, also serves on the Board of Trustees.

REUNION WEEKEND AND ALUMNAE CENTENNIAL BIRTHDAY CELEBRATION

Laird Hall is still alive with the sights and sounds of the 100th Anniversary Party for the Wilson College Alumnae Association, held on Friday June 8, 1979.

Applause, singing, laughter and conversations still echo, as a reminder of a happy, jubilant occasion for the 800 alumnae and friends who returned to the Wilson campus.

Chapter Three: The Aftermath and Perspectives

Following the opening prayer Friday night by The Reverend Dr. Edward Elson, former member and President of the Board of Trustees, and Chaplain of the U.S. Senate, the alumnae were welcomed by Betsy Diely, President of the Alumnae Association.

There followed a skit on the history of the Alumnae Association ably produced by Charlotte Weaver Gelzer, '72, and Louise Colgan Allen, '48. Narration was done by Charlotte Weaver Gelzer and Book Leitch with music provided by Carol Tschop, '72. The singing tradition was revived with a "sing" ... The group moved on to the birthday party later Friday evening, complete with cake topped with a figure of "Aunt Sally," ice cream, and a champagne punch. The birthday cake was decorated with 100 candles in honor of the anniversary. Candles were blown out by representatives of each class, during which the decorations holding up the top tier of the three-tiered cake were accidentally set ablaze. Betsy Diely and her daughter then cut the cake. Feelings of joy, excitement and commitment to the task ahead permeated many conversations ...

The Annual Meeting of the Alumnae Association was held Saturday morning, beginning with many introductions and reports. New and continuing members of the Board of Trustees were also introduced as was the Acting President. Jane Troutman Ensminger, '52, was inducted as the new President of the Alumnae Association. Dr. Tidball gave the address at the luncheon. She praised the Wilson alumnae for doing something "virtually unprecedented in keeping the College from closing." The weekend ended with a chapel service Sunday morning with an alumnae choir; Judith Ann Brown,'70, as organist; Dr. Lucetta Mowry, '34, as speaker.

ADMISSIONS WORK ENCOURAGING—YOUR HELP NEEDED

Trying to squeeze an entire recruiting year into three months is not an easy task, yet this is what the Admissions Office staff and volunteers are doing this summer. The office reopened on Wednesday, May 30 ... Our first major promotion was the immediate sending of a Western Union mailgram to approximately 510 prospective and current students, announcing our rebirth and encouraging their participation in our renewal efforts. The staff followed the mailgram with a letter and reply card to the 1,500 names of the neglected prospective students. Our most recent contact with the students was an attractive invitation to the Summer College Days program to be held July 13-15 on campus. We are anxiously awaiting responses to these last two mailings. In the meantime, we are encouraged by many phone calls from well-wishers and alumnae who are offering their talents and help in this tremendous project.

Admissions volunteers are keeping close tabs on the number of inquiries which come in to the Office and the number which go out. Answers to mailgrams and new inquiries are being carefully monitored by the experienced hand of Book Leitch (former Director of Admissions) and students are following up each inquiry with a personalized note, telephone calls and pertinent materials. In the last three weeks, the Office has sent out 1934 communications, including 338 letters, 55 phone calls, and 510 Mailgrams. We have received 78 positive responses to our Mailgram from both new students and returning students. As of June 18, 1979, 10 new students have indicated that they plan to come to Wilson in the fall, and 67 returning students have indicated that they will come back.

In percentages, 48.8 percent of the student body have indicated they will return this fall, 4.0 percent have indicated they will not be returning to Wilson, 10.4 percent are undecided but have

Chapter Three: The Aftermath and Perspectives

requested information, and 36.8 percent have not responded. The Admissions Office is responding to the undecided students and those students who have not answered the Mailgram with personal telephone calls from other returning students, faculty or alumnae. As part of our campaign to keep our former students while winning new and transfer students the College has decided to provide a credit of up to $100.00 for those new, returning, and transfer students who may have already sent a deposit to another educational institution ...

In our condensed summer recruiting effort, alumnae can help in several ways. The amount of assistance you will be able to give, of course, depends on your geographic location and your ability to donate a certain amount of your time. (1) Prospective student referrals and media clipping. Because our inquiry pool is small, at this point each alumna can aid the Admissions Office tremendously by sending us the names of students she knows who are still undecided about College next year, both freshmen and transfer, or the names of senior high school students who are just beginning to think about college. Each name we receive is vitally important, and we will see that she receives a prompt response from the office. (2) The Admissions staff will be able to utilize a certain amount of volunteer office help. This involves such duties as typing, stuffing envelopes, answering letters and making direct telephone contact with prospective students. We are amazed by how quickly major mailings are completed when there are enough hands. (3) Organization. Alumnae can help the recruiting efforts for the fall by using this summer to organize their ranks. We plan to set up an Executive Committee of alumnae to oversee the operation which will include national chairpersons to be in charge of certain areas, *i.e.*, College Days, telephone contacts, high school visitations and college fairs, etc. These positions will be set by the Admissions Office from suggestions made by alumnae Secondly, the local One-Plus-One members need to be an integral part of the club, not a separate entity. The summer will be an excellent time for local One-Plus-One area chairpersons to pull together their assistants and plan strategy for the important fall months. Come September, we'll be prepared to move ahead. (4) Summer College Days. One important activity in the summer program will be the Summer College Days on July 13-15.

Within this program, alumnae efforts can be utilized in several ways. (a) Transportation to and from Wilson for prospective students from your local area. (b) Phone calls to area students to encourage participation in the program. (c) Participation by alumnae on the alumnae panel which will focus on the careers and lifestyles of successful Wilson graduates from many different fields. The Admissions staff will be in touch with area chairpersons by the first week in July to give specifics on these various programs. Your continued input and suggestions are essential to all of these efforts.

VOLUNTEERS NEEDED

All College offices will be relying on volunteer efforts this summer. Your help and expertise are welcomed and greatly needed.

The Volunteer Services Office is open, staffed by Ellen Harrison, Assistant to the Dean for Career Planning and Placement, and Connie Crawford, secretary. The office is located in Edgar Hall.

This office is coordinating the volunteer efforts of students, parents, faculty, alumnae, and friends who are needed to help do the many odd jobs necessary to prepare the College for classes in September.

Housing will be available for volunteers in McElwain-Davison (please bring your own sheets and towels). Three meals a day are available, Monday through Saturday at the Campus Center Snack Bar for students and other volunteers returning to campus to work.

The office is especially seeking people to do various "housekeeping" chores like cleaning, waxing, yard work, minor electrical work, fixing doors, hinges, painting, etc. Also needed are workers to type, file, answer mail, handle the phones, and help in the library in particular; a nurse is needed at the Health Center to care for all the volunteers.

Locally, the Faculty Dames (Faculty Wives) are active and are planning an Ice Cream Social to take place during the Wilson College Days weekend, July 13-15. They plan to have a Barber Shop Quartet and band to entertain the prospective students.

FINANCIAL REPORT—WILSON NEEDS YOUR DOLLARS—NOW!

It is through your timely efforts that Wilson College is now experiencing a rebirth; in her curriculum, in admissions and recruitment efforts, in the competence demanded from those who lead her, indeed, in her very commitment to the kind and quality of education necessary for the contemporary young woman. In keeping with this renewed spirit of

dedication is the belief of the Administration and the Trustees that all alumnae and friends of Wilson need to be continually apprised of the financial situation facing the College today.

You should know that there is a serious cash flow problem on campus right now. Moneys are needed immediately for the operation of the offices on campus, salaries, supplies, maintenance, and, particularly to cover expenses incurred through the implementation of a large recruitment effort aimed at providing us with a student population this fall and in future academic years. Our situation, to quote Dr. Bletz, is "precarious." Precarious, most definitely, but not hopeless.

The fact that so many of you supported the struggle to keep Wilson alive indicates your high esteem for the College and your commitment to its tradition of academic excellence. We call upon you to demonstrate once again that wonderful sense of community so unique to Wilson alumnae.

Those of you who have yet to send a check or write a pledge, get busy! Those of you who have previously dug into your pocket for a contribution, dig deeper, give more. This will be an ongoing effort, this fundraising business, and the part that alumnae must play in this effort is critical ...

As of June 18, 1979, $260,541.73 has been contributed to the Annual Fund for 1978-79. That is only 59% of our goal of $345,000.

COLLEGE OFFICES OPEN AND WORKING

Wilson College is open for business and all offices are staffed and working.

Plans for Summer College Days as well as Mailgram efforts to prospective freshmen and returning students are being coordinated by Dolly Swisher, '73, Acting Director of Admissions, and her staff, Debbie Cramer and Kathy Haines,'76. Gloria Weagley is in charge of System 6, and Annabelle Foster is full-time secretary.

Jeannette Lehman, '48, former director of the annual fund (1968-1974) is in charge of the Development Office. The office is presently involved in reversing the closing information which was sent out to matching gift companies and foundations.

Chapter Three: The Aftermath and Perspectives

... Dr. Theony Condos, Professor of Classics and Assistant to the Dean for Student Advising, has been invited to become Acting Dean of the College. Miss Condos has worked very closely with the Dean's Office through her work with the faculty where she chaired the Curriculum Committee ...

As of July 1, Mr. James Hyatt, retired from the Heinz Co., will become the Business Manager.

... Mr. Dick Brunner returned to the College as Director of Information and Publications. Carol Tschop, '72, ... is Assistant Director ... Joan Edwards, '58, has offered to continue her volunteer efforts as needed.

Other personnel include Mary Emmons and Barbara Sabo in the Communications and Post Offices; Shirley Moul in the bookstore; Elizabeth Boyd as Library Director; Alice Leighty as Registrar with Adeline Thompson as her assistant; Bonnie Rosenbaum as Assistant Director of the Alumnae Office. **(end)**

Student Role

The students played a major role in saving the college which resulted in the president and a number of trustees resigning. Gretchen Van Ness headed the Wilson College Student Government Association and in an article titled "Saving Her College", by Beth Polio, in the Rochester New York paper, August 23, 1979 she is quoted as saying "I'm still sorting it out," says Gretchen Van Ness. "It was such an incredible experience ... It's much more than we expected ... It was a great vote of confidence ... The events made us very aware of our importance as a women's school and the need for our type of education," she said. "We were really forced to take a look at ourselves, to settle our priorities and see where things had to be changed. Not many schools are forced to examine those issues." Gretchen and approximately 200 students worked diligently on behalf of saving the college.

Chairman of the Board, Nan Clarkson, wrote an unpublished piece from her perspective as a Trustee focusing on 1979-1981. A portion of these notes were quoted above as they related directly to the May 26, 1979, Board meeting. Another portion is quoted as follows:

> The gallant story of Wilson's near-death experience and rise to new life and usefulness will always be told in the "Save Wilson" version, for history is written in its defining moments: it is the victorious image of the College gathered at the steps of Warfield as Jim Applegate reads out the astounding news of Judge Keller's decision. We alumnae take pride in the drama of that moment when, indeed, the court case brought by the Save Wilson forces against the Trustees, who had voted to close the College, was decided in their favor. It had been three months of incredible organizing, communicating, hiring legal help, raising money and galvanizing all the College constituencies in their effort to avert the closing of the College. In their passion for their cause, loyalties were reawakened—for, while many alumnae had kept an active tie with Wilson, many more had grown weary in support. Feelings ran high: after Save Wilson decided to take the Trustees to court, the sisterhood of alumnae was often sorely tested.
>
> It is not my purpose here to retell the thrilling story of the court victory. As an alumna who loves the College deeply, I know it well, and have recounted it often. My perspective is, rather, as one of the Trustees who indeed voted to close Wilson in that fateful February of 1979, albeit tearfully, but also one who remained in May, to be chosen to lead the new Board as it set about the awesome work of reconstruction. Three months of closing down—canceling insurance and other contracts, transferring students and faculty, and breaking ties of all sorts, had weakened a College that had for the past years been slowly losing ground.
>
> To be sure, as Judge Keller pointed out in his patiently reasoned

Chapter Three: The Aftermath and Perspectives

points of law, we still had several millions in endowment (not available for operating funds), and there had been hanky-panky over significantly missing records in the admissions office, and, yes, the administration had marketed the notion of a foundation for women's education as a noble higher use for our endowment. Worse, perhaps, the Board had too easily been swayed by a panel of experts, whom we discovered after had never actually met to discuss our situation; they advised closing. And, in sorry fact, the administration saw fit to delete a very important admonition that the experts gave to the Board, in the case of the "doctored minutes." This was passed along to the Save Wilson lawyers by a loyal alumnae Trustee—and though the admonition to the effect that Wilson could possible carry on if we were all willing to put in a huge long-term effort may not have been positively received, the fact that the President's office deleted it from the final draft of the minutes speaks volumes. At least one Trustee compared drafts and thought the deletion an evidence of skullduggery. The judge evidently agreed!

In a way, mine is a unique perspective. In 1979, I had experienced nine years of institutional effort to cope with declining registrations and dwindling financial support— trying to understand the forces beyond our control that had an impact on our numbers, and making a real effort to inform myself and make a worthy contribution. This was not easy, given the patriarchal make-up of that era's Board, and what at least women had begun to see as weak leadership in the administration. Because I see these years as leading so clearly to the crisis of 1979, it may be useful to give my own, possibly flawed but observant overview.

I have always kept the kind of journal that Scott Fitzgerald called a "writer's material." One of the tasks I have set myself in these reflective later years is taping some of them for my children and in doing this, I have been especially interested in the record of my experiences on the Wilson Board. These began for me in May of 1970 with a phone call. I had from Paul Swain Havens' voice far away but so recognizable, saying "Nan, this is my last call from this office as President, and I want you to know that you have just been elected to take your uncle's place on the Board!" It was a singular moment, memorable to this day. My uncle, Bill Hudnut, had just resigned—he and "Prexie" had been great friends at Princeton, and this had landed me at Wilson—but the thought of joining this august group, especially as his successor and with Dr. Havens no longer President, almost took my breath away,—but of course I accepted. And felt honored.

The seeds on 1979 were surely planted already. Magnificent as his years had been, even Paul Havens himself felt that he had stayed on past his greatest strengths—and the building of the science center had taken its toll. The Search Committee for the next president had only one acceptance to their offers, and refusing to re-open the search, they offered the presidency to Charles Cole, a historian and a good man, who simply had neither leadership ability or the confidence in himself to guide the College through the difficult times it would have with the new issues that marked changing times.

Let me give you a vignette from those times: Saturday, May 21, 1971. Dr. Elson (Chairman) says it was the most difficult meeting he had ever conducted. To me it was absolutely fascinating. Parietals were the issue (*i.e.*, visiting privileges for men in student rooms—they may now visit from 2:00 p.m. to midnight; the students want privileges 24 hours a day). Charley Cole had pretty well laid his demands on the line—no 24-hour parietals!

The Executive Committee had softened this statement. The "Victorian Caucus" (I call it) headed by Mr. Templeton and ardently supported by Mr. Gabler and the Reverend Stauning

Chapter Three: The Aftermath and Perspectives

came out early for the original tough statement. Mr. Templeton, a financial wizard and President of Princeton Seminary's Board, gives hints that beneath his placid exterior beats a reactionary heart. He said "Wilson might gather strength—might even solve its enrollment problem—by taking a Christian stand—proclaiming its chastity, so to speak." To which Lucetta Mowry, distinguished Wellesley professor and Biblical scholar, formerly not all in our camp, replied very firmly, "To be known as Chastity College nowadays would be the kiss of death." Then Polly Austin, in her inimitable way, suggested that we as Ts should not be voting on a matter that concerns only the students and the College family. Immediate rebuttal by grim Mr. Stauning. Charley Cole was not happy. During the Cole years, the Board gained strength in its numbers of women members— Polly Austin, Betty Blackadar, Sarah Keyser, Mary Wheeler King, Lucetta Mowry and me; later we gained Nancy Besch, alumnae President, and Catherine Sweeney. As we were a minority in a somewhat patriarchal male majority, we joined in a kind of informal caucus that, in time, overcame strong resistance to bringing an outside consultant, Rex Moon, to evaluate the administration. The Moon Report, with its careful analysis of the serious problems in our College administration was instrumental in Dr. Coles' resignation. But his Presidency had added a burden of faculty discontent, campus politics, student transfer and further financial insecurity to a trip that was already heading toward 1979.

In Margaret Waggoner, we had every right to be optimistic, for her resume was impressive, with staff leadership roles at both Vassar and Smith and scholarly credentials to win the most critical faculty. Even so, she was the only one of the excellent candidates brought to our Search Committee in New York, who, when offered the presidency was willing to take it on; as with Charles Cole, we had no choice beyond starting the search all over again. By this time, I knew full well the difficulties Wilson offered—the reasons why the others turned us down—and I was grateful for her courage in accepting the challenge of our presidency!

Because our focus is on 1979, I will simply say that it was not long until we became aware of new concerns. Staff members began to come and go with alarming regularity and there were rumors of a tense work atmosphere. Our ties with the Presbyterian church were cut off by Margaret, with little, if any, consultation. The all black doors to the Norland parlors were locked, and—one of the most egregious of these emblematic acts (to my mind) was her move to replace our *Alma Mater*... with one of her own composition. This would have been funny if it hadn't shown such a kind of embarrassing insensitivity.

Trustees, of course, have much more to worry about than locked doors, but things like these piled up on top of the turnover of staff, student complaints, and a critical, insecure faculty. The atmosphere around the College began to reflect the lack of trust that emanated from the President's office. Trustees were discouraged from meetings with faculty friends, and because any criticism was seen as disloyal, many of us felt somehow silenced. I certainly was, by the President herself. Many of us felt distanced from any real action and I remember almost no executive sessions, in which feelings about the administration could be freely expressed. With all this, it was possible for the unthinkable to happen, and it did.

... That the College mishandled the news of this traumatic decision, sending the letters by slow mail—proved to be an economy that only fanned the fury and strengthened the solidarity of Save Wilson. **(end)**

Chapter Three: The Aftermath and Perspectives

PERSPECTIVES ON THE OUTCOME OF THE COURT CASE

The perspectives of the College community, the Trustees, the alumnae, the national press and the higher education community were wide-ranging and were written about over a ten-year period. There were those who felt that the Trustees were correct and should have prevailed; that continuing the College would mean that it would be sufficiently different as to not live up to its distinguished academic reputation and its past; that moving more concretely into continuing education for adults and revising the liberal arts curriculum to include more career-oriented paths of interest to women would be a diminution of the College to a very large extent. There were articles focusing on the role of the Board. What follows is a sampling of the major writings that cover differing points of view.

"How College Was Saved," in the June 5, 1979, issue of *The New York Times* was written by Fred M. Hechinger in the section "About Education." (Reprint permission granted) The article is quoted in full here:

> When the Wilson College Alumnae Association marks its 100th anniversary this weekend, it will also celebrate an unprecedented event in American higher education— the resurrection of a college proclaimed dead less than four months ago by its own Trustees. The saving of the small 110-year-old liberal arts college for women in Chambersburg, Pennsylvania, was accomplished by an extraordinary show of loyalty by hundreds of alumnae and by a local judge who performed an unusually thorough autopsy on the alleged corpse only to rescind its death.
>
> Beyond the jubilation of the "Save Wilson Committee," which not only went to court to prevent the closing, but also raised more than a million dollars in cash and pledges to pay for keeping it open, the Wilson College case has important implications for other hard-pressed small colleges.

On February 19, the Trustees of Wilson College announced that the institution would cease operation at the end of the academic year and that its remaining assets would be used to create a Wilson College Foundation to aid the higher education of women.

The Trustees' action was backed by a dismal record of decline. The modest endowment had been invaded to close budget gaps for six years running. Since the College had its largest entering freshmen class—252 students—in 1965, the pool of first-year students had shrunk to 92 in 1975, 39 in 1976, 62 in 1977, and 55 in 1978.

Although faculty and facilities were adequate to handle 650 students, enrollment was down to 214. Forty-two full-time and eight part-time faculty members meant an intolerably costly student-teacher ratio of 5 to 1, against a normal 12 to 1 ratio at comparable colleges. Moreover, those who supported the closure decision said, the College was in a relatively remote, though physically attractive and serene area, and thus too distant from datable men to attract enough women students.

Difficult as it might have seemed to argue against the Trustees' contention that the situation was beyond repair, the 10 alumnae, students and faculty members who went to court maintained that the closing was unjustified, that the College's plight was caused not by inevitable conditions but by an inept, rigid and unimaginative leadership.

Judge John W. Keller of Franklin County ordered a week ago (May 25, 1979) that the College remain open. He also ordered the removal of two Trustees—Dr. Margaret Waggoner, who had resigned as the College's President and Dr. Mary Patterson McPherson, whose position as President of Bryn Mawr College, also in Pennsylvania, he considered a possible conflict of interest.

Chapter Three: The Aftermath and Perspectives

Fourteen other Trustees resigned.

In the closing section of his 87-page opinion, Judge Keller recalled the "singular appropriateness" of the historic Dartmouth College case in 1818 when Daniel Webster said: "It is, sir, a small college, and yet there are those who love it."

What errors by Wilson's leadership made the judge conclude that wiser heads might yet save the College?

Despite the 1974 recommendations of a groups of consultants ("Survival for Wilson College: Time for Stewardship and Sacrifice" published by the Academy for Educational Development), the College continued to do business as usual. The consultants had urged these basic reforms:

> *A redefinition of the role of a women's college to make it responsive to the demands of the women's movement and the changed lives and aspirations of young women.
>
> *The addition of career-oriented courses to a strong basic liberal education program
>
> *Effective recruiting and a more realistic admissions policy
>
> *A balanced retrenchment to bring students and faculty into alignment.
>
> *Better communication among administration, faculty, and students as the basis for tackling difficult decisions.

In early 1978, the official college accrediting team that visited Wilson found the situation to be worse than it had been four years earlier.

Wilson's administration had sneered at the suggestion of career-oriented programs, calling them fit only for "a trade school." No persuasive prospectus for a modern woman's education had been devised. Recruiting had deteriorated as admissions directors came and went; many inquiries by potential applicants were ignored or answered in an impersonal fashion. The faculty, uninformed about the crisis, asked for a steep raise one day before the fatal Trustees' meeting.

More prestigious experts were convened. They were given reams of documents and, after six hours' deliberations, supported the shut-down. Judge Keller, unimpressed by academic celebrities, called that whirlwind study "utterly devoid of merit or value."

Wilson College, the judge concluded, is not bankrupt. He did not find any malfeasance among Trustees and administration—only ineptness and inaction—but he made it clear that he considered the role of college trustees far more than merely honorific. He spoke caustically about self-perpetuating boards.

The judge cited Hood College, a small women's school in Frederick, Maryland, that at one point had "suffered the same problems." In 1973, he said, Hood's enrollment was down to 500 but the board and new administration revitalized admissions, reorganized the curriculum and created a new understanding among faculty, administration, students, and alumnae. Today, he said, Hood's enrollment stands about 1,000, and academic standards are high.

Technically, Judge Keller made a point that may set academic-judicial precedent: A private college chartered as a teaching institution cannot, without approval, shed its teaching function, If the time should even come, as it may, that Wilson cannot make it, the judge said, let it come back and persuade me.

That time, he said, is not now. He acknowledged difficulties ahead, particularly since Wilson must quickly insure a September class, a Herculean task now that everybody has been told to go away and study elsewhere.

But some key "Save Wilson" alumnae are filling the Board vacancies, and acting President Donald Bletz says, "We're open for business." If Wilson remains precarious, Judge Keller said, he doubts "that those future days are any more fraught with peril … than the conditions and circumstances which confronted the incorporators 110 years ago. **(end)**

Did the College Close? NO!

A real hurdle to overcome was the perception that, indeed, the College had closed. In fact, of course, the college had not died. In truth, it had never closed but that was not the general perception given the local, regional and national news coverage the trial had attracted.

Alice L Beeman, the author of the Beeman Case Study and Secretary to the Board of Trustees 1978-79, wrote a letter to the editor titled, "Why Pennsylvania's Wilson College Had to Die," published in *The New York Times* on June 29, 1979, in response to Dr. Hechinger's article of June 5, 1979. She contended, in part, Basically, however, I believe the bitterness over "saving" Wilson has obscured more fundamental questions: Can liberal education be saved, not just at Wilson but at scores of private colleges? And should Wilson survive? Given the conditions of our times that affect all colleges—inflation, declining birthrates, emphasis on career training—should it try to continue?… It can continue only if it drastically changes its character and its historic mission …"

This was countered by Jane Troutman Ensminger, President of the Alumnae Association and on the Board of Trustees, who wrote a letter to the editor titled "Wilson College has Not Died," published on August 18, 1979, in *The New York Times*. She declared "Far from being dead, Wilson College has received a *mandate* to continue. While we have no monopoly on the aim to educate women to be responsible and responsive to the needs and problems posed by our times, a great many people recognize that Wilson College has made a significant contribution to higher education in the past and will continue to do so in the future."

It is worthy of note that in the book *Trustees, Trusteeship and the Public Good: Issues of Accountability for Hospitals, Museums, Universities and Libraries,* **Quorum Books, 1987, pp. 66-74 by James C. Baughman,** Baughman quotes Hechinger saying that "he felt Hechinger 'hit the nail on the head' when Hechinger wrote that, 'Perhaps the real reason why the Wilson College case alarmed so many College Trustees is that Judge Keller said what Board members preferred not to hear. He told the Wilson Board bluntly that it had not done its job. It had failed, he said, to inform itself about the institution's management." (p. 69)

Several other major points in the Baughman article were that: a) no one – even trustees – is above the law and the board does not alone govern the institution. " ... the Trustees of Wilson College have a fiduciary responsibility to the College to fulfill the mandate of its charter, *viz*, that it be a teaching institution...the Trustees could determine that the corporation should discontinue its chartered non-profit activities; but it had no right to set a termination date for those non-profit activities or take any steps toward the implementation of that termination decision until court approval had been secured." (p. 71)

It is not unusual for a board to place too much power, confidence and responsibility in and on its chief executive officer. They need to be aware of this and should always consult the staff but "never replace their own judgment with staff consultations and recommendations because the essential function of trusteeship is to render disinterested judgments on the college's programs ..." (p. 74)

In summary, Baughman would say that there are limits so trustee power and the court will step in and involve itself in the internal matters if the trustees act against the public good.

The **Pennsylvania Association of Colleges and Universities (PACU)** helped to fund the Beeman Case Study and requested of their lawyers an explanation of the settlement of Wilson College lawsuit which was sent to all member presidents. Basically, since there was no appeal,

Chapter Three: The Aftermath and Perspectives

the settlement was that a majority of the old Board of Trustees would resign and that new Trustees could then be appointed "who would attempt to keep the College going as long as the funds hold out or until Judge Keller gives permission to close it ... " In return, none of the old Trustees would be financially liable for their actions as Trustees, nor for any consequences following their resignation from the Board. Since the consent decree replaced the *decree nisi*, this case would not serve as a legal precedent for resolving future cases. (20 July 1979 letter from McNees Wallace and Nurick to PACU)

The position of the higher education community was stated in the **American Council on Education's President's Letter, August 6, 1979. Permission granted by Sarah Zogby by phone to reprint 02/06/20)**

> Implications of the Wilson Case ...
>
> I am concerned about the implications of the Wilson College case. Since there will be no appeal, we cannot file an *amicus* brief. But the Association of Governing Boards will take the lead in establishing some principles by which the higher education community may get on record some points that perhaps can be useful to the next judge and the next governing board faced with a similar issue. Without trying to prejudge all that we will want to say, I think there are some obvious points that we want to make, for example, that contrary to the reported statement of the judge, there is not necessarily any conflict of interest in having the President of one institution sit on the Board of another. **(end)**

In the September 1979 issue of *Change Magazine*, there was an editorial titled "Judicial Overkill." (Reprint permission granted) I have summarized some parts and quoted other parts.

The editorial argues that the courts are intruding into academic institutions far more pervasively in the last 20 years and in ways that are beyond the courts' competence. The Wilson College case was seen by the editorial as a flagrant case of overkill. "There are a number of lessons to be learned from this episode, not only in terms of the competency of courts to decide complex academic and managerial issues, but also in terms of the arcane habits of academic, which contribute rather than avoid conditions that encourage such judicial overriding ..." (p. 53)

The point was made that the recommendations of several reports (Moon and Middle States) regarding admissions procedures, curricular updates, and coeducation were not accepted by the Board. Improvements that were made were not enough to stem continuing declines in enrollment. The panel of experts chosen to advise the Board in February 1979, "advised that Wilson was now committed to a highly precarious course..." (p. 53)

What makes Judge Keller's opinion fascinating is not so much its legal significance, which one can easily overestimate, but the sheer bizarreness of its argument. Other facts intrude: Wilson's 125 employees make up a major industry for small-town Chambersburg, and Judge Keller was about to stand for popular retention election, which Pennsylvania commonwealth law requires of its judges every 10 years. The judge's *decree nisi* consists of a schoolmasterish potpourri of managerial nit-picking and some outright ludicrous assumptions. Over 60 paragraphs alone are devoted to a detailed recitation of the functioning or malfunctioning of Wilson's admissions office, including a count of admissions reply cards. Judge Keller ordered Wilson's President, Margaret Waggoner, removed from her office and from the Board ..." He removed the President of Bryn Mawr, "a topflight academic," from the Board also, even though "Wilson, it should be said, is about as competitive with Bryn Mawr as is the Franklin County Court with the United States Supreme Court ...There is, of course, no telling whether Wilson's troubles could have been avoided in the first place. There is evidence to suggest that Wilson's recent administration was possibly excessively rigid and less than open, that its admissions procedures were quite inadequate to the harsh competitiveness of the times, and that the faculty were severely torn by

Chapter Three: The Aftermath and Perspectives

the pressures to balance budgets and a student attrition rate of 40%. None of these can make institutional stability or bring forth a spirit of collaboration and creative planning. But President Waggoner did balance her budget.

What is important to understand is that precisely such circumstances now prevail at hundreds of other institutions. Even if every liberal arts college administration were as competent as Judge Keller somehow demands it to be, if student recruitment were the envy of Madison Avenue, and each faculty member a collegiate Mr. Chips, the tide of constantly rising deficits and the consequent life-and-death struggle would perhaps not be avoidable.

The right question to be asked in the Wilson College case is this: Is it not the option of a private educational institution to determine its own mission, even if this in the end proves not be sufficiently marketable? And is it in fact in the best ecological interests of higher education to have every marginal institution stay alive at any cost?

There are also certain functional facts of life to be faced: The first is that when the question of terminating college operations becomes the crucial issue, confidentiality, if not secrecy, may in fact be the prudent course for a formative period of time, a notion wholly contrary to academic custom. Publicized failure inevitably spawns still more failure. Secondly, organizations cannot wait until all the money runs out before deciding on bankruptcy. Finally, while it is true that Daniel Webster revered "a small college and yet there are those who love it," Mr. Webster does not have to put up the money to save the Wilsons of this world. (p. 54) **(end)**

In the October 1979 issue of *Change Magazine* (pp. 4-5), there were four Letters to the Editor regarding the above-mentioned editorial on Judicial Overkill. A summary of the points made includes agreement/gratitude for stating uncertainty that the Waggoner administration was as rigid and closed as had been claimed by the plaintiffs; a belief that that many of the conclusions drawn by judge were unsupported; hope that other presidents "will not be subject to the calumny and abuse that (Margaret Waggoner) had to suffer" (p.5); a question about where those opposing boards of trustees' actions can go except to the courts.

The Association of Governing Boards published three articles on Wilson in their July/August 1980, issue of *AGB Reports*. (Reprint permission granted)

AGB Reports, **July/August 1980, pp. 3-5, Joseph C. Gies, Editor of Publications for the Association of Governing Boards, wrote "The Wilson College Case."**

In summary, Gies notes that the court opinion in the Wilson College case "stirred a furor throughout the higher education community ... When three and half months earlier (February 3, 1979) the Wilson Board had pronounced the death of the College, few if any Trustees had imagined that they might be judicially questioned." (p.3) Gies reflects that one of the mistakes the Trustees had made might have been confidentiality, even though they feared creating an alarm that would adversely affect enrollment and fundraising.

However, when the decision was announced, the shock to the College community and to the alumnae was evident.

> "In the course of the conflict between those who wanted to keep the College open— alumnae, students, friends of the College—and the President and Trustees who had decided, however reluctantly, to close it, emotions ran high, and some bitterness is still evident a year later. Yet it is to the credit of all those involved in this difficult problem that a high degree of civility and mutual good sense was maintained." (p. 4)

Elisabeth Hudnut Clarkson ... recalls a vivid and touching moment. The Board held a meeting in March 1979, in New

Chapter Three: The Aftermath and Perspectives

York, at which after hearing a presentation by the Save Wilson Committee, it reaffirmed its decision on closure. Mrs. Clarkson had a plane to catch and left the meeting early "Coming out of the revolving door, I saw the busload of students and a few alumnae standing in the cold, singing the *Alma Mater*. I could hardly bear to look at them, they were so brave and so hopeful, and of course I knew that the news was bad. Gretchen Van Ness broke ranks and came and gave me a hug. She saw my tears, and she knew what had happened. The look of compassion on Gretchen's face remains with me to this day." (p. 4)

At the April Board meeting, seven members of the Board objected to the closing and voted "no" but the majority prevailed ... (when she learned of Judge Keller's decision on Commencement weekend, she and her friend and fellow Board member, Betty Blackadar, went at once to the Save Wilson headquarters—"and I shall never forget that when we walked in there wasn't a person in the room who didn't come forth to welcome us." (p. 4)

This new Board and the new President it appointed found themselves confronted, amid all their other problems, with a severe public relations handicap: the instant negative reaction of their peers in Pennsylvania and around the country to the shock of Judge Keller's decision, almost universally perceived as government intrusion. (p. 4)

The numerous adverse comments in the education press were reinforced by what seemed a quasi-official document, "Wilson College: A Case Study," prepared for the Pennsylvania Association of Colleges and Universities and the Lilly Endowment by Alice Beeman, an officer of the old Board. Many of those engaged in the continuing effort to save Wilson feel that the Beeman report is not a sufficiently full or objective account and that it has misled some of its readers. (pp. 4-5) **(end)**

Article #2 in *AGB Reports*, August/September 1980 (pp. 12-15) was written by G. Philip Anderson and Kent M. Weeks, partners in a law firm specializing in higher education, wrote the article titled "The Lessons of Wilson." I am summarizing this article as follows:

Although certain aspects of the Wilson case are governed by Pennsylvania law and judicial procedure, the decision is instructive for colleges chartered in other states. The Pennsylvania Nonprofit Corporation Law provides that trustees must act with good faith and with the highest fidelity. Moreover, the statute, as interpreted by the courts, required court approval before any property committed to charitable purposes could be diverted from the original purpose for which the property was donated. Another section of the statute provided for the removal of directors. (p. 12)

The Moon Report commissioned by and delivered to the Board of Trustees in November, 1974 had a number of recommendations. One which was not adopted by the Board was that "Members of the Board should be asked to recommit themselves as Trustees and should be expected to devote their time, talents and money to help Wilson College through this difficult period. If the Trustees are unable or unwilling to make such a commitment, they should be given the opportunity to resign from the Board so that others willing to exercise such stewardship of the resources of the College may take their places." (p. 13) In 1977, the accrediting team found basically the same deficiencies (poor management, lacking leadership and planning, and needing to restructure the educational program) as had been noted in the Moon Report.

Chapter Three: The Aftermath and Perspectives

This article goes on to describe the actions of the court which appear elsewhere in this book. The writers determined several points to be applicable to independent colleges. "The bottom line may well be the existence of a viable alternative. A judge may be reluctant to allow an institution to close if there is evidence that alumnae, friends, faculty and prospective Trustees wish the College to continue. Most important is the court's finding that the Board had been misled and that it did not receive the fullest possible analysis of alternatives from the panel of experts who hurriedly surveyed the situation. In essence, the Board did not have full information when it acted. What the judge seems to be saying is that Trustees must insist on full information, and that in performing their duties Trustees must bring their particular expertise to a Board." (p 15)

The two lawyers writing this article did not see an inherent conflict of interest with Bryn Mawr's President sitting on the Board.

"Trustees should take an active role in the development of objectives, planning and financing of an institution. If recommendations by committees or consultants are to be rejected, officers and trustees should state why they are being rejected; if recommendations are accepted, then implementation and follow-up procedures should be developed.

Perhaps the most important conclusion to be gleaned from this opinion is that trustees should make sure that they are fully informed so that they will not be caught in a similar legal trap. (p. 15) **(end)**

Finally, the third article in *AGB Reports*, August/September 1980 (pp. 6-11), Elisabeth Hudnut Clarkson wrote an article titled "Ten Misconceptions about the Wilson College Case. "In summary, these are the ten misconceptions:

271

1. **That the Wilson case became precedent in law.** *In short, it did not!* While the defendants felt very certain that they would win the case and did not, they were faced with a dilemma—continue to run the College under court order while appealing the decision or negotiate a consent decree that would and did replace the *Decree Nisi* of the court. They chose the latter course and negotiated a settlement that guaranteed that a majority—but not all—of the Board would resign, leaving room for new Trustees, and that the defendant Trustees would incur no financial liability. It did have major significance, however, in the relationship between colleges and universities and the law.

2. **"The College is not bankrupt** or near that fiscal disaster point. The assets far exceed the established or presently known potential liabilities." (p. 7)

3. **That Judge Keller was the villain of the case.** *This was not true.* "Largely because there is widespread and justifiable fear of legal interference in academic domains, many have assumed John Keller is a poor judge, or that his motives were questionable. In fact, he has a firmly established reputation of wisdom and integrity. He is frank to say that the Wilson College case was the most difficult one he ever expects to have." (p.7) Some felt that since he was up for retention election in 1979, that that swayed his opinion; however, with 39,000 registered voters, the 125 people on the payroll would hardly sway the election. It is a reality that most people did not bet on Save Wilson's winning but evidence "... of administrative ineptitude or insensitivity, disaster in the admissions department, ... a record of poor human relations, plus an instance of altered Board minutes with a whiff of cloak-and-dagger about it ..." led several of the defendant Trustees to feel that there were "shrewd questions from a thoughtful judge." (p.8)

4. That the old Wilson Board acted wisely. *In retrospect, no.* Although it seemed a prudent decision on the part of the Board at the time and it seemed particularly wise to have a unanimous vote, in retrospect, alumnae members of the Board including the writer of this article did wonder why they acted so quickly. These are Clarkson's conclusions:

   a. We acted too quickly; "panicked," as the judge put it ... we voted to close with only two weeks deliberation and with amazingly little debate.

   b. We authorized the choice of a panel of "experts"—delegating all of our authority in this vital matter to our officers and the President of the College. The "experts" were to review every possible shred of information to see if they thought there was any mode of "salvation" for the College which we had missed. The panel never once met as a whole, and they never met with us as a Board.

   c. We accepted the recommendations of officers and administration based on findings of the "experts" with almost no struggle, as if the will to live had been crushed. Far more reprehensible, we accepted a proposal for the creation of a Foundation which would administer the remaining assets of the College. This was, in effect, a change in our charter purpose. One new member, a lawyer, questioned the legality of the Foundation—but I noted that none of us debated the matter very seriously.

   d. While we articulated a corporate wish to conduct the closing down of the College with all due "dignity" and "compassion," we did not lay out guidelines for ground rules, even though many of us realized that implementation was left to an administration that was at loggerheads with almost every campus constituency.

e. Most importantly, the Board at Wilson, like boards at so many colleges, had taken neither the time nor the interest in conducting an annual evaluation of the chief executive, the President. Furthermore, in my opinion, this had resulted in an extraordinary abdication of Board powers to the office of the Presidency. (pp. 8-9)

5. **That the plaintiffs were maverick dissidents.** *"...over 3000 of Wilson's 6000 alumnae responded in overwhelming ways—with time, money, and offers of every sort of help."* **(p. 9)** The Save Wilson Committee asked of the court only two things: to keep the College open and to remove the entire Board and substitute a Board of their choosing. The judge granted the first but not the second. He removed only the President and one other Trustee for whom he declared a conflict of interest.

6. **That the new Wilson Board is parochial.** *The new Board is made up of 10 members of the old Board (including the writer of this article) and 17 new members.* **Mrs. Clarkson's reaction to this is as follows:**

   a. We have been called "parochial," apparently in the sense of our having a fairly high quota of alumnae. (Even many of the men on the Board have Wilson ties.) All I can say to this is that perhaps, at times of crisis and survival, there's no one like "family" to do the work that has to be done.

   b. It's the strongest Board in my memory of ten years' service as a Wilson Trustee. We have a variety of people from diverse areas and professions, most specifically chosen for some special contribution. We are in need of a few multimillionaires who believe in small women's colleges!

   c. ... we have, at least in this first new year, invited all Board members to executive committee meetings. It has been a year of survival management, but we are deeply aware

Chapter Three: The Aftermath and Perspectives

of the need for Board development, long-range planning, and the help that is available to us through collegial organization. (pp. 9-10)

7. **That Judge Keller was all wrong about the President of Bryn Mawr.** *Not totally.* Whereas, there really was no conflict of interest, his point about not using her expert knowledge, " ... it is distinctly possible that she might have been a great deal more critical and outspoken in an area where the Trustees were, I believe, seriously underinformed . . . Mary Patterson McPherson was singled out for a criticism that might have been leveled at all of us ..." (p. 10)

8. **That the Beeman Report tells the whole story.** *It does not.* "Miss Beeman gives the facts of the case, but she does not give all the facts, by any means." (p 10) One example is that she quotes a line from the Middle States Association giving unqualified praise to the college but does not list their concerns about the administrative style of the President. She mentions that letters about the closing were sent to all constituencies but does not mention that the letter to the alumnae was sent third class. She describes the work of the Admissions' Director, but does mention that a predecessor in that office had had no recruiting or admissions experience which cost the College dearly. She "mentions the departure of an excellent and popular Dean in a way that leaves the reader with the impression that the Dean's sole reason for leaving was to take a better position. Even most of the Trustees know that the Dean would not have been job-hunting had it not been for the deterioration of collegial relationships." (p. 11) The report seems to many who are at Wilson "less a case study than a defense of the decision to close the College, of the administration in general and of the President in particular." (p. 11)

9. **That Wilson College is now "saved."** *It is not saved but it was granted another chance.*

10. **That Wilson and many other small struggling colleges do not deserve to live.** *"Well, colleges like people, do not want to die. And while they still have a mission and purpose, as we believe Wilson does, while they still have some wonderful alternatives to provide... while there's all this life, who can blame us for hope?" (p. 11)* **(end)**

The Alice L. Beeman Case Study

In August 1979, Alice L. Beeman, who had served as Secretary of the Board of Trustees, wrote a case study of the events leading up to and culminating in the court decision. This study was funded by the Lilly Endowment with a grant given to The Pennsylvania Association of Colleges and Universities. Nan Clarkson was asked to comment on this study.

Ms. Clarkson was on the Board and search committee that selected Dr. Waggoner for the Presidency. She takes a point of view counter to that of Ms. Beeman. Ms. Beeman admitted to a strong bias that the College should have been closed. Miss Beeman wrote: 'I became a member of the Board of Trustees of Wilson College in July 1977; I served as a member of its Committee on Public Relations and Development for one year and as Chairman of that committee for one year; I was Secretary of the Board of Trustees in 1978-79. I voted consistently in favor of the decision to close the College, and it is still my conviction that closing was the wise and responsible decision. This account thus does not pretend to objectivity, but I believe that it presents the facts. Wilson College: A Case Study, Alice L. Beeman, (p.2). **The case study in full can be found in the archives at Wilson College.**

Nan Clarkson's comments on the Alice l. Beeman Case Study summarized with quotes from Ms. Clarkson's comments dated September 20, 1979, that pertain to trusteeship:

Chapter Three: The Aftermath and Perspectives

1. Beeman contends that years of decline had been tolerated by the Board and that, over the years, the Board should have been more willing to make tough decisions. Judge Keller felt that faced with the admissions report—far below expectations—the Board panicked, asked too few questions, and voted to close the College after just two weeks of study. Clarkson notes that, "At the root of both extremes—delayed action and overreaction—there is the contributing cause of insufficient information supplied to Trustees."

2. Clarkson refers to Beeman's reported "suspicion among some alumnae that the whole idea of the Wilson College Foundation was a 'plot' to provide a lifetime sinecure for the past President." Clarkson does not believe this, but does believe "that the Trustees in their February 17th meeting, reeling from the pain of the closing decision, were perhaps unduly pressured by the officers to adopt this conception." She notes that this is a real problem for all boards who have trustees coming from all over the country for three or four meetings a year. Boards do rely on Executive Committees and, in this case, the officers sitting on the Executive Committee. Questions of balance of power can be legitimately raised when the President and the Chairman of the Board select the committee chairmen who serve on the executive committee.

3. Addressing the controversial decision of the court to ask one of the Trustees who served concurrently as President of another women's college to resign, it was a consensus point of view that there was no conflict of interest. What could be argued is if there was a failure to exercise considerable expertise. As a part of the Board member's testimony, she noted that it was inappropriate to interfere in the operations of the College, "but should she have been raising sharp and insistent questions in Trustee meetings about enrollment figures and dusty

curriculum . . .?" Should others have done the same? "Yes, 'failure' to exercise 'expertise' on behalf of the institution we serve is a charge which most Board members must read with a shock of recognition. (This Board member) bore the brunt of an indictment which many of us deserved."

4. The judge questioned the wisdom of self-perpetuating boards and the implication of this is the importance of "new blood" on all boards.

5. As Clarkson sees the heart of the case—both from the Beeman Case Study and the court opinion—the most important work of the Trustees is in the selection of the President, but "the Board must then assess the effectiveness of that person from time to time, to provide support and constructive criticism ... all too often we abdicate this responsibility ..."

Acting on that assessment and then actually terminating the President, if called for, is typically very difficult for a Board. The Moon Report resulted in the President in 1974 resigning. "Between Judge Keller's stringent criticism of President Waggoner's administration and Miss Beeman's strong advocacy of the same, there is a tale of Board responsibilities not adequately carried out, of opportunities unrealized, and of a distinguished teaching career (Waggoner's) diverted and hurt. The Board of Trustees bears a blame here that was not adequately assessed." **(end)**

In the October 11, 1979, letter from Dorothy Weeks to Dr. Laura Bornholdt, Vice- President for Education of the Lilly Endowment, which helped fund the Beeman study, Dr. Weeks makes these comments on the Beeman Study:

" ... Since I have known Wilson College for so long, approximately 50 years, and so well, and Frances Wick, Professor of Physics at Vassar, a Wilson alumna and Trustee as well as a close friend of

Chapter Three: The Aftermath and Perspectives

Louise McDowell's, the Wilson College case study impresses me as the tip of the iceberg. To thoroughly understand where the Wilson College case differs from those "fly-by-night" institutions that have to close, Wilson College in 1930 would have been ranked in about the twelve top women's colleges in this country. Wheaton College in Norton, Massachusetts, and Wilson compared almost equally in assets and endowments. Wilson College had quality, tradition, high standards and endowment. Its demise did not start with President Cole. It was slow, insidious changes, almost imperceptible, which as they mounted led to the Trustees' decision of February 9, 1979.

An analysis of the Trustees' meetings from 1936 to 1970, similar to the analysis that Alice Beeman has done for the later years, would be interesting. There are many facets to the Wilson College case. By 1950, most of the women on the faculty appointed by President Warfield had retired. The number of men on the faculty was steadily increasing. The salary scale had almost become topsy-turvy. A young man appointed assistant professor in philosophy, who had not quite completed his doctorate, found on his arrival that his salary was only $400 less than the senior member of the faculty. So many unexplainable situations occurred which were never aired and which did not foster a good campus spirit.

Trustees are persons who hold responsible positions. They need to be well informed on the essential points of the operation of the College. Often what may appear unimportant may be very important. Do they receive the complete story? Should a college president nominate his friends for the Board of Trustees? From my knowledge of Wilson College and the various situations that have been called to my attention, I would conclude that the President has had too much power that has not been shared with faculty and administration, that has not been checked by the Board of Trustees, that there has been a lack of openness as to the financial picture. For a college to succeed there must be great teamwork, and each group should be encouraged to participate and contribute to the final decisions. Although to a slight degree some of this has existed at Wilson, the degree was very slight. It seems especially so to me since I have been so close to my *Alma Mater* and know the power of Wellesley's faculty and the lack of it at Wilson.

No one mentions the real conflict of interest with Dr. Mary Patterson McPherson, President of Bryn Mawr College. In the Moon Report, part of which was contributed by Dr. McPherson, it mentions, after giving advice and listing steps to be taken to keep Wilson as a teaching institution, other suggestions if Wilson is not to be maintained as a teaching institution. The establishment of a Wilson College Foundation, granting scholarships to girls for a liberal arts education, is its first suggestion. Therefore, such scholarships could be used by students to attend Bryn Mawr. Two weeks after February 19th, the day of the announcement of closing Wilson, on March 5th, Margaret Waggoner sent out a letter to those of us who had a bequest in our wills for Wilson College. She asked us to change this bequest to the Foundation. This implied that Margaret Waggoner was to administer it. Of course the many unpleasant things that were said should not have been, but certainly in this case there were acts to provoke them.

There is no question that Dr. Cole inherited great problems and, of course, so did Margaret Waggoner. Too often an executive committee of the Board is the only one fully informed and makes the decision. Margaret Waggoner was beginning to build a Board with her friends. Alice Beeman and McPherson were already serving. She was only following the example set by Paul Havens. The Wilson College case is an extremely complex one.

How deeply it should be studied depends upon the questions to be answered." **(end)**

ATTORNEYS DIFFER ON DECISION'S IMPACT, by Bob LoMendola, in the Wilson College Special Section, *Public Opinion*, Friday, August 31, 1979. (Reprint permission granted)

In summary: Both attorneys agreed that the "landmark decision in Chambersburg will no likely be a landmark anywhere else." (p.9) This is because it was drawn very narrowly and not appealed. "But the decision is important in that it tested a state ruling dealing with court intervention in the workings of private organizations." (p. 9)

What is interesting is that this suit really is unique. The non-profit corporation code is relatively new stating that "an orphan's court has the right to look into the internal workings of a non-profit organization under certain circumstances." (p. 9)

The attorney for the Trustees felt that boards of trustees should be able to make decisions about their organizations since they have knowledge collectively beyond what a judge can know. He also felt that the advice of the panel of experts was overlooked by the judge and noted strongly that removing a person from the Board who was a president of another Pennsylvania college for women for a conflict of interest was strongly against higher education common practice. He believed that the public opinion of the President's style and decisions were "often unfair … she didn't panic or try to panic the Board with a bleak presentation 14 days before the Board announced the closing.

It was her obligation to present the facts to the Board in February … I don't think she colored it; I don't think she sought the decision or felt any great pride in being the last President of the College."

What neither side questioned was that this case will be studied by colleges and universities and may have the effect of having trustees being very careful before they decide on closing a college.

In many ways the lawyers for the petitioners took a risk—a studied one, for sure—but not one that covered previously proven ground. They took the case only after determining that they had the right to appear in court. Once the judge took the case, the lawyer for the respondents felt that the main issue was whether or not Wilson could survive as a teaching institution.

All the attorneys agreed "that the facts in the case were brought out and well-presented but disagreed on what they added up to. The Save Wilson attorneys concentrated on weaknesses in recruiting methods and the fact that there were both financial and spiritual assets left untapped to keep the College going. Tom Menaker (attorney for the Trustees) argued for the Trustees that the better plan would be to sell the property valued at $20 million, add in the tied up scholarship donations of about $3 million and start a scholarship fund." (p.9) **(end)**

FIGHT TO SAVE COLLEGE MADE HEADLINES, by J. Kenneth Beaver, Editorial Page Editor for *Public Opinion*, Friday, August 31, 1979, p. 2 of special section on Wilson College. (Reprint permission granted)

It took the threat of death to make Wilson College a celebrated cause. Only as the last tremors seemed to afflict the small liberal arts women's college did it make the headlines.

Then education writers, editorialists, and news writers for *The New York Times*, the Associated Press and far-flung Pennsylvania papers discovered Wilson.

Chapter Three: The Aftermath and Perspectives

On second thought, it wasn't so much the threat of death as the brave, audacious fight to save it from death that spread the fame of Wilson.

Many a small liberal arts college has died in recent years with scarcely a ripple in the news—but that was because they died.

It was the resurrection of Wilson through the courage of her students, alumnae, faculty members, and a scattering of Trustees that captured the interest of news writers.

One of the proudest documentary exhibits compiled by the Save Wilson Committee is the bound volume of all the editorial and news column comments, pro and con, the death and resurrection of Wilson aroused.

Tops in snob appeal, perhaps, was the column by *New York Times* education writer Fred M. Hechinger. He detailed the slow progress of the seemingly fatal afflictions of Wilson, the pronouncement of death by the Trustees, the frenzied effort by Wilson supporters to halt the final rites, the court decision that Wilson was not so much dead as being done to death, and the fulfilling work of resuscitation.

The Board of Trustees read Wilson's pulse, checked her "vital" signs—deficit financing, declining enrollment, rising maintenance and instructional costs, adverse student/faculty ratio, and the failure of high hopes for an upsurge in student registration. And they said the College was finished and set the date for its funeral for this past June.

Students first, then alumnae, and then the faculty read the same signs and admitted they were serious, but they balanced them against evidences of mismanagement, ineptness, inefficiency, misconstruction of events. They adopted a "can do" attitude as against what they saw as the Trustees "can't do" posture. This probably was best exemplified in two letters to *The New York Times* elicited by Hechinger's article on "How College Was Saved."

One letter was signed by Alice L. Beeman, Secretary of the "old" Wilson College Board of Trustees. She expressed herself as dismayed by the Judge's order to keep Wilson open. She summed up the reasons for closing Wilson, and then asked: "Should Wilson survive?"

She answered that it could only survive if it drastically changed its character and its historic mission, turned to "vocationalism" (a derogatory term, particularly in the misleading connotations she managed to give it), and suggested it was better to strengthen a smaller number of excellent colleges rather than squander resources on keeping one open, no matter its qualifications.

In contrast, the other letter, signed by Jane Troutman Ensminger, member of the new Wilson Board of Trustees and President of the Alumnae Association, took a more up-beat approach.

"Far from being dead," she wrote, "Wilson College has received a mandate to continue." She cited the reorganization of the Board, appointment of a new staff, including an Acting President from the faculty, the reopening of the admissions office under new leadership and with a new motivation, and the beginnings of curriculum revision to meet the needs of the times and of modern women.

The example of Wilson, even if its resuscitation should fail finally, will have repercussions throughout the small, private college world. The struggle has pitted the traditional against the innovative; status quo against changing needs.

A part of this comes through in an article which appeared in The Chronicle of Higher Education under the headline, "Pennsylvania Judge Bars Closing of Private College."

Chapter Three: The Aftermath and Perspectives

In recapitulating the Judge's opinion that Wilson should remain open, the article pointed out that, "The order marked the first time a judge had found a conflict of interest was created when the president of one college served on the board of another," and "It was also the first time that a judge had ruled that the trustees of a private college must first come to court if they want to close the college."

And it noted again some of the negativism which appeared in the Beeman letter mentioned earlier when it quoted one of the former Trustees as saying that Wilson "is geographically remote; it is a single-sex institution; and it has a traditional curriculum, and Pennsylvania has more institutions than are necessary."

"Perhaps," the present staff and Trustees of Wilson say, "but it is not necessarily true that Wilson is one of the excess institutions to be dispensed with." (p. 2) **(end)**

Wilson College received local, regional and national press on the court judgment to remain open. Wilson's announced closing happened during a time when there were a number of liberal arts colleges and liberal arts college for women were closing, merging, or developing strategies for change. No other college had such a group of determined alumnae that actually took the Board of Trustees to court, designed strategies for remaining open and raised money to do so. To the group of really committed alumnae, closing was simply not an option. The strength of the feeling of the alumnae certainly took the board and administration by surprise. The court judgment resulted in alumnae, friends, and higher education community eager to see what would happen next. Not everyone—by a long shot—felt that the college could survive in the short run—not to mention the long run. A new administration and new members on the board were surrounded and supported by many volunteers—volunteers to teach, to do the gardening, to do office work, and to do painting and renovation of buildings. It was an impressive effort. There was little time to reach out to prospective students and to get the word out that the college was open.

Newspapers all over the region ran the following article taken from the Associated Press (Chambersburg) using various headlines. Here is the article in full as it appeared on June 7, 1979, in the *Wilmington, Delaware Journal* with the headline "'Silver & Blue' is Sung Again as College Refuses to Die." (Reprint permission granted by the Associated Press)

"Silver and Blue, we love you," Josephine Benincaso sang after a judge reversed a trustees' decision to close Wilson College, a 110-year old liberal arts school for women. And two days later Miss Benincaso, 22, accepted her diploma without tears, happy her class wouldn't be Wilson's last after all.

"Women's colleges right now are on the upswing," said the Italian-born New Yorker who will return to Italy for medical school. 'We survived when other failed, and we aren't going to fail now.'

It is a hope shared by Dr. Donald Bletz, a part-time political science professor who became Wilson's Acting President after Franklin County Court Judge John W. Keller ordered Wilson to stay open last month.

"Our goal is to rebuild,' Bletz said in the office vacated by Dr. Margaret Waggoner, the President for four years who quit after the court's ruling. "The College has been around 110 years, and there's no reason we can't be around for another 110 years. We don't think the situation is hopeless."

Bletz said the faculty—those who didn't get new jobs after Wilson announced in February that it would close—is supportive, reorganizing, and considering curriculum changes.

"We are a liberal arts college, but we find little incompatibility with a certain amount of career orientation," Bletz said. "We do

Chapter Three: The Aftermath and Perspectives

not intend to become a trade school or a vocational school. We are planning to remain a women's college."

The unexpected decision to shutter Wilson and turn its assets into a scholarship foundation for college-bound women was fought by alumni, students, and faculty who sought an injunction to block the closing.

"They didn't believe anyone would protest," said Gretchen Van Ness, 20, of Rochester, New York, the president of the student government association. "I think they were shocked that students and alumnae fought so hard to keep it open."

Dr. Harry Buck, professor of religion studies since 1959, blamed the move to close on an administration that forgot it was the 1970s and ran the school like it was still the 1950s. The school had been criticized earlier for not offering career-oriented courses.

And, said Dr. R.G. Townsend, an economics professor: "We could have adjusted to the times … but we didn't."

Dr. Waggoner told a reporter a day before the court ruling, "the college was in very serious trouble when I came here …

"Our goal is to tough it out in the coming year," Bletz said. "We will be open no matter how many students we get … We will have a program, and a good program, for those students who'll be there."

Mrs. Walker, in assessing enrollment, said informal surveys of the first year class indicated "we would have a College smaller than last year," and added, "We didn't think it was morally right to bring freshmen to campus when we weren't sure we'd be open another year, or maybe be in bankruptcy. I think we had become too small to be attractive to prospective students."

Mrs. Walker also pointed to reports that in the next ten years there will be one-third fewer high school students. "When you see the Harvards and Yales and Princetons and Bryn Mawrs worrying, ... what's in the cards for Wilson?" she asked.

Wilson isn't bankrupt, but it's dipped heavily into endowments to pay operating expenses for the 300-acre campus, with its 32 buildings, in this predominantly farm area near the Maryland border.

"From 1968-69 through 1975-76, the College operated at an annual deficit, the largest being $862,546 in 1974-75," the Trustees said in a statement seeking to justify the decision to close.

Mrs. Walker said, "If President Waggoner hadn't made cuts in the budget, this place would have folded two years ago."

The 32-year-old lawyer added: "I love the place ... I'm heartbroken. I certainly didn't want to be part of any closing." **(end)**

Personal Memo from Martha Walker, '69, to Mary-Linda Armacost

November 7, 2018
John Stewart Library
Wilson College
Second Floor front stacks

I sit at the same table in the library I studied at in 1968, 50 years ago. My old carrel is gone, replaced by quiet study rooms and comfortable chairs by the windows across from the Science Center.

I came here for inspiration in order to honor a promise to Dr. Mary Linda Merriam Armacost, the author of this book, that I would review her drafts and that I would help her make sure "it portrays the different points of view honestly."

Chapter Three: The Aftermath and Perspectives

I set aside today from my busy schedule of being a family law attorney in Chambersburg, Pennsylvania, to write something her readers would find interesting. Writing should be easy for me, as after all, I have been an attorney for 46 years, and writing emails, letters, memos and briefs has been part of my daily existence.

I should be able to fall back in my mind to that Winter-Spring 1979 and recall the events and emotion of that time period. I spent hours several weeks ago in the Wilson College alumnae archives reading 10 years of Wilson College Board of Trustee minutes to refresh myself. I should be able to express myself coherently on the memorable events of 1979. But … this is very hard work. I want to say certain things and yet what more is there to say? I want to both remember and forget. I want to share my emotions and thoughts; yet I want to hold all of that in reserve.

I am as conflicted about the first six months of 1979 now as I was then. While I can write with the benefit of 40 years of hindsight, I find it hard even now to critique and analyze my decisions back then.

In retrospect, I had no business serving as the Chair of the Wilson College Board of Trustees from January 1, 1979, to May 26, 1979. I was 32 years old. I was a young lawyer trying to establish a practice in Franklin County, where from 1972-1977, I was the first and only female attorney admitted to the Bar. I was a young mother of a 2½ year old daughter and pregnant with my son, who was born on June 8, 1979. I was establishing a home with my then husband of six years. I was just starting my first years as the first woman and youngest director of the F&M Trust Company, a local Chambersburg bank. I was a relatively new Trustee having been elected to the Board in 1972 to be the so called "young alumnae Trustee."

I was inexperienced in leadership of a board of directors, other than my experience chairing the WCGA Senate my senior year (1969) and vice-chairing the Student Bar Association my senior year of Dickinson School of Law in 1972.

I was already over-committed in the community as a Board member of the Franklin County United Way, on my church council and still officiating college basketball and field hockey games on weekends.

In looking in the rear-view mirror of life, I now know I should have said "no thanks" to my selection as Board Chair by my fellow Trustees in November 1978.

My Wilson College pre-1979 experiences had not been preparatory for this job. Although I had served the Admissions Office in a One-Plus-One role in 1975; although I had taught a law course at the College in the January term of 1973; although I had been a member of several Board committees such as Educational Policy, Buildings & Grounds and Student Services; although I was on the search team to find a new President (Margaret Waggoner began on August 1, 1975), I still was woefully unprepared to lead a non-profit Board of Trustees of my *Alma Mater*.

Ask me now, 49 years from my graduation in 1969, and I will say that I can chair most any board. I've served on over 30 non-profit boards in Franklin County and I have chaired at least 10 of them. I have served on five CEO, Headmaster, or Executive Director search committees, and I now know and understand what effective leadership of any organization looks and feels like.

But back then, in 1979, I was a naïve, immature attorney and Trustee, who accepted a job I wasn't ready or able to do. I'm sorry I did so.

So that's my excuse and apology of sorts. I seek no sympathy.

Chapter Three: The Aftermath and Perspectives

I'm just saying that's how I was then. I wish I had not been the Chairman of the Board in 1979.

To this day, several months before the 40th anniversary of the vote to close Wilson College and the Court's decision and the alumnae's "Save Wilson" efforts, I remain unclear in my head as to whether the Boards' vote to close Wilson College was right or wrong.

As a lifelong advocate, used to outlining my client's positions, I can still argue for and against that decision.

<u>Why was it right at the time</u>?

1) Wilson College would have never arisen from ashes without a closure vote that ignited the passions of the Save Wilson Alumnae and opened their pocketbooks to raise sorely needed operating funds.

2) The College would have limped along with low enrollment and unbalanced budgets for years without some dramatic event to resuscitate it.

3) The President was newly elected and the Board was determined to support her. Had the Board not voted to close the College, I believe the Board would have supported Margaret Waggoner, having just gone through a succession of Presidents (Havens, Cole, Dennis, Waggoner) in five years.

<u>Why was it wrong</u>?

1) The Board should have delayed its decision and implemented plans to work with the "Save Wilson" alumnae to see what changes could have been made to raise funds and enrollment.

2) The Board should have sought additional expertise other than the four member panel Margaret Waggoner assembled hastily to evaluate Wilson's situation beforevoting.

3) The Board should have evaluated itself as to whether the "horses" were in place to take Wilson to a renewed existence. Unfortunately, while individual Board members were bright and accomplished, they were mostly older and had held too long of terms on the Board (as self-perpetuating Trustees), and were too fearful of the unknown future. Mostly conservative and in their 50's to 60's, most were ill equipped to take on the challenge of reworking what needed to be restructured at the College, (*e.g.* Development, Admissions, Curriculum). The Board did not have the patience or vision to see the way through the morass of Wilson's difficulties. I see this now in hindsight. I also see in hindsight that the previous Boards under President Havens and Cole were not taking steps to ensure the College's future. The Boards were receiving reports but not taking action to deal with what were already signs for concern regarding national enrollment trends and census figures. The Board was balancing budgets with endowment funds, deferring maintenance, turning over administration positions, delaying curricular changes, avoiding the co-ed question, etc. The Board minutes reflect much discussion on many of these issues, but no action. The Cole Presidency (1970-February 1975) must be blamed for failure to put forward actionable programs to deal with the future concerns then facing all of higher education, not just Wilson College.

4) Margaret Waggoner had a difficult, strained relationship with many of the faculty. She had changed several players and positions in the administration (which any new President would be expected to do), but her choices did not inspire hope or loyalty. The Board, having recently appointed her after an extensive national search, felt constrained to support her recommendations regarding closing the College.

Chapter Three: The Aftermath and Perspectives

5) The critique made by my Chambersburg dear friend and former alumna, Carol Tschop (deceased in 2014), was that the "Board vastly misunderstood the potential result of their secrecy and arrogant disregard in communicating the College's difficulties to its most loyal consistency." I disagree with this. The Board had a certain stubbornness and gravitas to it but was not arrogant. Nothing was secret. Meetings and minutes were open to the alumnae, except executive sessions, and at various times letters and alumnae magazine reports detailed the enrollment and financial woes. I do agree that Margaret Waggoner was not a transparent and communicative leader and she operated high-handedly on the campus, which the Board mostly learned about after the threatened closing. She also was wary of conveying the seriousness of the situation for fear of quelling prospective student enrollments and suppressing donor gifts. So yes, in this failure to convey the urgency and gravity of the situation, both the President and the Board failed its alumnae base.

The several things that are very clear to me from those terrible months: the stress of being on a Board that I could not lead appropriately; the turmoil of my conflicted emotions about voting to close a College I loved; the anguish of disagreeing with a President I had been part of recruiting; the pain of telling my classmates and fellow alumnae of the decision and the Board's reasons. These horrible memories are vivid. I'm still upset to this very day that I was a part of a Board that gave up. Yet, had the Board not given up, Wilson College would not be here today. Of course, it is now altered in its student body, and now co-ed (a necessary decision in my mind); now changed in its courses and majors (*e.g.*, nursing programs, vet-tech and business and accounting majors, equestrian studies); different with its

293

community engagement and involvement (now an important contributor to Chambersburg's economy, outreach and culture).

I believe Wilson College had to fail in order to rebuild. I wish in retrospect I had been on the other side, being a leader in the Save Wilson efforts, but I wasn't. I was chairing a Board that made a fateful decision. That decision, however, became the genesis of Wilson College's revival and survival.

I'm happy that Wilson College continues as a place of higher learning that still embraces and promotes the attributes I loved when I was there. It's still Wilson College and the lights burn brightly on the campus when I drive by. I want nothing more than for her to grow and thrive and never again have to face a decision to close its doors.

In conclusion, I bring nothing to this book that illuminates the Board's closure decision. Others have eloquently written on this subject with far better analysis than I. I particularly concur with Elisabeth Hudnut Clarkson's article in the Aug/Sept AGB reports, titled "Ten Misconceptions About the Wilson College Case." Her points provide an excellent summary from her prospective as a Trustee prior to and post-closing that most of the then Trustees will probably endorse, as I do fully.

She does not state the conclusion that I have come to realize after 40 years: that had the Board had different leadership, not so young and inexperienced as myself, and had the Trustees been not so entrenched and conservative as the majority of the Board, maybe Wilson College history would have been different. Maybe the Board would have changed its constitution and processes, maybe the Board would have evaluated Margaret Waggoner after her two-year anniversary, maybe the Board would have deliberated and debated more and embraced "Save Wilson" women and ideas, and maybe previous Boards would have been change agents when cracks were then occurring . . . there is a lot of blame to go around in trying to figure out why Wilson College Trustees voted to close.

I share a profound sense of responsibility which still haunts me 40 years later. **(end)**

Nan Clarkson dictated the following statement to Mary-Linda Armacost on March 3, 2019:

At the time that Marty Walker was persuaded by Immediate Past Chairman, Richard Hough, to take on the Chairmanship of the Wilson College Board of Trustees, she had fairly clear knowledge, as did most of the members of the Board, that we were in a period of change. Marty was perhaps our youngest member, brave enough with Dick's help and encouragement, to confront whatever was coming. Still, it was not a quiet time in her life. She was a young mother of one, expecting another in June 1979; and she was an active member of a law firm in Chambersburg.

She had always been the very model of 'the young Wilson woman'— attractive, bright, athletic, representing us in our college town exactly as we appreciated being represented.

At the time that Marty accepted the Chairmanship of the Wilson Board, she was arguably the person who fit the role best for the Board and its College. For we were in the not yet fully realized throes of a history that was moving inexorably in the direction of unknowable change.

Marty Walker, following her experiences, led the Board in a way that suited its traditional liberal arts history and the wishes of the Board.

Resigning from the Board with grace after the court case and its ruling, she left a clear and well-tempered group of ten remaining Trustees to deal with the steps that followed. The fact that after she resigned, she maintained a good relationship with all constituencies of the College spoke so well of her character.

Chapter Four
BEGINNING AGAIN 110 YEARS LATER: 1979-1981

President Donald Bletz

June 1979-June 1981 saw Wilson in the national, regional and local news, including being featured on the PBS network show entitled "Pennsylvania." There was considerable interest in the survival of the College. Would it or wouldn't it? The College never actually closed, but it was amazing to realize how many people and organizations thought that it had. Major amounts of money (at least $1,000,000) that had been on offer to Wilson did not materialize due to the fact that the organization or person was angry over not having been contacted in a timely manner about the proposed closing or angry at the court decision. Some moneyed people in Chambersburg withdrew their support. About half the faculty departed for other jobs and most of the students were looking for other schools. Twenty-two (22) strongly loyal faculty remained and adjuncts were recruited—many volunteered! The Board had to be reconstituted and most of the administration had ties to the College but little academic administrative experience. Those who remained, however, were determined, committed, and hard-working in face of the odds for survival. The 1979-80 school year opened with 125 full-time equivalent students with 110 in residence.

Dr. Donald Bletz became Acting President of Wilson College at the Board meeting on May 27, 1979 and was named President at the Board meeting in November 1979. The Bletz years (1979-1981) were full of challenges, to say the least. His attitude was crucial to success. The following was sent to the author by his son, Michael.

COLONEL (USA Ret.) DONALD F. BLETZ PhD

Donald (Don) Ferree Bletz was born in Mountville, Lancaster County, PA on July 28, 1925, son of the late Paul Hamilton Bletz Jr. and Ellen Lucille Hoover Bletz. Donald is the widower of Patricia Ann Thomas Bletz who died on July 29, 2012 at Carlisle, PA. They were married for over sixty-three years. He was always proud of his German ancestry and of his French Huguenot middle name which came from his maternal grandfather, Ferree Hess Hoover of Lancaster County and goes back to Marie Wartenbuer (Fierre) Ferree who settled in Lancaster County under a grant from William Penn.

Don enlisted in the Army on June 10, 1943, the same day that he graduated from high school in Columbia, PA, and served with the 89th Infantry Division in Europe as a sergeant. Commissioned a 2nd Lieutenant of Infantry at the Infantry Officer's Candidate School at Fort Benning, GA in 1946 he soon found himself back in Europe, northern Italy this time, in the 88th Infantry Division on the Yugoslav border, early in the Cold War. He later served in the United States contingent of the Allied Forces in the Free Territory of Trieste (TRUST), also a relic of the Cold War where he served in the Allied Military Government and later commanded Co. A, 351st Infantry. Back in the United States he served in the 11th Airborne Division at Fort Campbell, KY, in Korea in the 2nd Infantry Division, and in the International Affairs Division of MACV Headquarters in Saigon, and later, the 173rd Airborne Brigade, also in Vietnam. Don is very proud of his years of active military service.

His Army schooling included the Infantry School Career courses, the Command and General Staff College at Fort Leavenworth, KS, the Armed Forces Staff College in Norfolk, VA, the National War College in Washington, DC and, what he always considered an exceptionally unique experience; he was the Army Fellow at the Harvard University Center for International Affairs in the 1970-71 academic year. His non-military schooling included a bachelor's degree from the University of Omaha and a Master of Arts and Doctor of Philosophy from the American University in Washington, DC. His Army career included several faculty assignments including the Infantry School, The Command and General Staff College, and the Army War College at Carlisle Barracks. It was this teaching experience that led him to seek an academic career after military retirement. He is the author of one book and several articles on political military affairs.

Upon retirement from the Army in 1975 Don and his wife Pat lived in Cumberland County in the village of Centerville for 27 years and then in Carlisle since 2002. Since 2011 he has lived at Cumberland Crossings Retirement Community. His desire to pursue an academic career was realized when he joined the faculty of Wilson College in Chambersburg, PA the day after he left the Army. He served there for 20 years, teaching political science and management. During two of those years he served as interim college president during a crisis period. His pride in his service at Wilson College equals that of his Army service. Don continues his interest in politics, particularly international politics and follows world affairs and domestic politics closely.

The Wilson College Special Section of the *Public Opinion*, Friday, August 31, 1979, in the article entitled Bletz "We are really very optimistic," portrays Dr. Bletz as knowing his own ability as well as the magnitude of the challenge. "The loss of students, faculty, and perhaps most importantly, the loss of time at a critical juncture in the College's history, all have combined to cast a shadow over the future of Wilson College. Dr. Bletz felt that the spring of 1980 would be the most telling— the time when they would "have to think very seriously about where we stand." Under his administration there was no conflict between the liberal arts and career-oriented courses. The faculty was amenable to career-oriented studies within the context of the liberal arts curriculum.

Also in the Wilson College Special Section of the *Public Opinion*, August 31, 1979, was an article from the faculty perspective: "Faculty are optimistic about the future," by Marty Rolfe. (Reprint permission granted). It is quoted in part here:

> Faculty members at Wilson are cautiously optimistic about the College's chances for survival and pleased at the role they'll be playing in helping to keep it alive.
>
> "Morale is very high" among the 21 full-time faculty members who will be teaching this year, says the administrator who works most closely with them, acting Dean Theony Condos. About 20 faculty supplement a teaching staff reduced to about half of last year's level after Trustees announced in February that the College would close. But of the 18 faculty members who have left Wilson, 11 have requested leaves of absence and may return next year. Those who remain won't say they're certain the College is out of danger, but don't regret their decisions to stay and see what happens ...
>
> The faculty actually received a slight increase in pay this year ... "The administration is showing good faith, Professor Harry

Buck said. These are hard days, and I think they reached as far as they could in granting raises ..."

Although some voice their opinions more strongly and bitterly than others, faculty members agree the College's troubles stemmed from an unresponsive, sometimes secretive administration and Board of Trustees. Most say their advice on curriculum matters was never sought and ignored when offered...

Faculty members unanimously praise the selection of Acting President Dr. Donald Bletz and Acting Dean Condos. They say authority is being delegated more and the faculty have a greater voice in the College's future, particularly in curriculum changes where four new programs have been introduced already. Professor Buck describes the new administration as "people who seem to have vision ... There is a creative thinking now that wasn't encouraged before. We've done in the last two months what we should have been doing in the last five years," said Professor (Donald) Henry, who is coordinator of the division of Natural Sciences and Mathematics. He said the Faculty Committee on Cooperation with the Board of Trustees has met once with the new Board and he personally is "pleased with their openness. The attitude is so positive. You can feel it," said Professor Diaz... **(end)**

An article about Dr. Bletz published in the *Lancaster New Era*, written by Sam Taylor on November 29, 1979, captures the man and the state of the College. Here are just several quotations from that article. The full article can be found in the Wilson College archives.

"A Lancaster native has tackled one of the biggest jobs that can be found in education, the resurrection of an old and time-honored college. In fact, Donald Bletz, PhD., can almost be compared to a doctor who is called in after the patient has been declared legally dead, but somehow has been roused and is still suffering from erratic pulse and in need of life support systems. However, Bletz is convinced that the vital signs are strong and healthy and he can be one of the chief factors in returning Wilson College to full strength ..."

"There's a very practical streak in Bletz, and it comes out in one of the programs he has adopted to increase the revenue of the College. Twenty-five years ago, his move would have been tantamount to a duchess taking in washing—today it didn't cause a ripple. He has rented out part of the College to a professional training group. Vale National, which trains insurance adjustors for most of the major insurance companies in the U.S., is not only leasing dormitory, classroom and storage space in parts of the College which would otherwise be standing empty and inviting deterioration, it is also helping to pay the grocery bill by leasing food service from the College."

"Why did Wilson, which once occupied a pre-eminent position among the nation's women's colleges, go into a near-fatal decline? Bletz is quite candid in his answer. "There have been all sorts of theories, but the bald fact is that Wilson failed to keep abreast of changing educational requirements and interest. The curriculum continued to be very conservative and very traditional in the liberal arts at a time when career orientation for the changing role of women demanded a reorganization which did not come.

"Bletz says there has been a resurgence of town and gown relationship since the threat of Wilson's demise suddenly alerted Chambersburg residents to the plight of the school, which had been so much a part of Philadelphia Avenue that everybody thought it would stay there forever. "Our relationship with the town and with the local paper and radio stations has been renewed in a very meaningful way," he continued. "There has been a tremendous expression of interest in the College from the community and individuals, and material evidences of support, and this interest has been returned by the College."

"Bletz says there is not too much difference between administering a college and operating a military command. "The main principles are the same," he points out, "they just have to be applied in a different way."

The Pittsburgh Post-Gazette had an article by Jane Shaw on August 25, 1979, which set the stage for the Bletz years. (Reprint permission granted). It is quoted in full:

"My first duty was to call the telephone company and tell them, don't disconnect the phones." It was that basic.

Don Bletz, acting president of Wilson College, was discussing his first days in that office. He was appointed immediately following Judge John W. Keller's May 25th decision that the 110-year-old college remain open as a teaching institution, reversing the Wilson college board of trustees' action on Feb, 17 to close the college.

The phones have been busy ever since—outgoing calls to prospective students, incoming calls from students, alumnae and townspeople volunteering, and calls in both directions to arrange for faculty, financing, and the future.

The atmosphere on the campus as the college prepares for the beginning of classes Sept. 5th is invigorating. Enthusiasm is high and optimism prevails.

"We were able to reconstruct our administrative staff and have attracted some fine people," said Bletz, a retired U.S. Army colonel and an associate professor of political science at Wilson. "And the board is now reconstituted with 24 members and five vacancies."

The board has approved a $2.3 million budget for 1979-1980, with 25.8 percent to come from tuition and fees of $3,385 a year.

Wilson had 176 resident students graduation weekend when the judge's decision was announced. Sixty graduated. Of the remaining 116, 80 have indicated they will return. The school also expects at least 23 freshmen and four transfer students.

"We will have a very viable but small student body," Bletz said.

Wilson had 42 full-time faculty members last year. This year there will be 21. Half the faculty had already accepted other teaching appointments when the judge's decision was announced. All those who left were given a year's leave of absence by Wilson, enabling them to return next year if they wish. Eighteen part-time professors will be added to complete the faculty for this year.

"I'm really quite pleased with the faculty. The academic program will be a strong one, and I'm looking forward to a good academic year," Bletz said. "We will be able to provide courses for any student who needs something. We will have no unmanageable faculty gap in academic programs."

In fact, Wilson is expanding its academic offerings. Three majors and two programs have been added to the curriculum. The majors are economics and business administration, dance and communications and media. The new programs are equitation, or horsemanship, and athletic coaching.

"All five are career-oriented," Bletz said. "There is often a concern expressed about the lack of compatibility of liberal arts education with career orientation. I do not share that concern."

A new emphasis has been developed for continuing education. This program is headed by Marilyn R. Mumford, a Wilson graduate and professor of English at Bucknell University, who

Chapter Four: Beginning Again 110 Years Later: 1979-1981

took a one-year leave of absence to come to Wilson as special assistant to the president to "see what I could do to help."

The continuing education program for adults is being advertised daily in the local newspaper. It is open to men, but they cannot receive a degree. As an incentive, the first four courses are being offered at half price—$210 for three credits.

"There has been a considerable resurgence in interest," Mrs. Mumford said. "And the gas shortage is helping, as are the new programs. Adults who might have gone to Harrisburg or Shippensburg are considering us."

She predicted the program will have between 34 and 70 students.

Although the College is not bankrupt, has had a balanced budget and has a $4.8 million endowment, it needs other financial help.

"One concern has been that we are here occupying a very large campus with some empty buildings, and we have been keeping up these buildings with no income," Bletz observed.

The school is negotiating with Vale National in Blairsville, an insurance school, to have it use an unoccupied dormitory and some office and classroom space.

Maintenance of the 300-acre campus and 32 buildings is costly. But this summer, the college has had an unexpected source of help: volunteers. Nearly 100 students, alumnae, their children and husbands, parents and townspeople have come to the campus to paint, weed, serve in the snack bar, and do clerical work.

Dolly Swisher, an alumna and acting director of admissions, said many of the 36 students not returning to Wilson had made arrangements to go to another college. Some said they were taking the year off and might return. Others are foreign students

305

who had arranged to attend other colleges and had received good scholarships.

After the decision to keep Wilson open, Miss Swisher said, the admission office faced the monumental task of getting the information to students and prospective students. The next step was to respond to the 1,500 inquiry cards that had never been answered and gather names of interested students from alumnae.

"For this summer, we have been a little more flexible in admission standards and have taken some students that might have been considered marginal in the past, but we have not taken any that we thought couldn't do the work," she said.

"Under the acting director of development, Jeanette Lehman, we have initiated efforts for foundation, corporate and government grants, and the annual giving fund for alumnae will be not disrupted," Bletz said. "And we are examining the possibilities of borrowing, should it be necessary."

Last year, alumnae contributed $225,749 to the annual giving fund. The Save Wilson College Fund, organized and administered by alumnae after the closing was announced, raised $1.1 million in cash and pledges in a matter of months. Pledges are still coming in.

"I think the strength and vigor of the alumnae of Wilson College are remarkable," Bletz said. "What they have accomplished—to have reversed the decision to close—it's that strength shown by alumnae that is very important to all of us. I feel it's one of the primary reasons all of us feel the task can be accomplished.

"All of the present administrative staff feel that there's a good possibility that we will succeed in what we are under-taking or

Chapter Four: Beginning Again 110 Years Later: 1979-1981

they wouldn't be here. All of us are aware of the enormity of the task. We are realistic, but we don't feel it's impossible." **(end)**

***The New York Times*, September 23, 1979, published an article on Wilson written by Gene I. Maeroff. (Reprint permission granted). Mr. Maeroff had spent three days on campus interviewing 32 administrators, alumnae, students and faculty. This article gives a good sense of the challenges faced by the administration. It is quoted in full.**

Each application for admission is cause for celebration at Wilson College, so the arrival yesterday of the first deposit for next year's freshmen class sent the admissions director racing to the President's office with the good news. Considering that the school was pronounced dead by its Trustees last February, this preoccupation with vital signs is not surprising.

Only because a group of stubborn alumnae intervened and got a county court to block the proposed June 30 closing was the institution able to open this month for its 111th year.

But, by the time of the judge's ruling on May 25, Wilson College had gone through the spring without signing up a freshman class, many enrolled students had made arrangements to transfer, and almost half the faculty had lined up new jobs.

Thus, 80 returning upperclassmen have been joined here this fall by only 30 freshmen, hurriedly recruited over the summer, producing an enrollment of only 110 and making those on the spacious, 300-acre campus feel like a family that has chartered the Queen Elizabeth II for an ocean voyage.

More and more colleges are expected to find themselves in similar straits in the 1980s as the number of high school graduates declines and it grows more difficult to maintain enrollments in higher education.

Whether to Cling to Life

The crucial question that such institutions will face, as was discovered at Wilson, is whether to close with dignity before utter disaster takes hold or cling to life as long as possible.

The experience of this small liberal arts institution for women has brought the issue into sharp focus, creating a situation in which sincere backers of the College have found themselves in conflict over the proper course of action.

"We didn't feel it was responsible to continue operating right on down to the last cent," said Martha B. Walker, the former Chairman of Wilson's Board of Trustees, who is a 1969 graduate and a lawyer in this southern Pennsylvania town. "Is it morally right to bring young women into such a situation?"

Nevertheless, those opposed to the closing maintained that the administration and the Trustees had not exhausted all the possibilities for regenerating the College and that, in fact, it was in trouble not because its mission was no longer tenable but because it had been poorly run. They turned to the court on the basis of a Pennsylvania law that apparently gives the state the right of approval in the termination of a nonprofit corporation or charitable trust.

Judge Refuses Closing

Judge John W. Keller of Franklin County refused to authorize the closing, ruling that "the totality of the evidence did not persuade us that that time is now."

Such a decision, one of the few times a court has stepped in to stop a college from shutting its doors, has stirred a wide controversy, making educators around the country wonder who has the final authority to decide when a college should close.

Chapter Four: Beginning Again 110 Years Later: 1979-1981

The matter of timing that Judge Keller cited remains crucial at Wilson College despite the high morale engendered by the verdict. Key members of the restructured administration and faculty acknowledged that, without a substantial enrollment gain, the institution would simply be too small to offer a well-rounded academic and social experience.

"We will have to ask ourselves at various points whether it is fair to continue this effort," said Donald F. Bletz, a political science professor who is the College's Acting President.

As it was, Wilson had been caught in a slide since 1967, when the enrollment was 722, and in six of the last seven years, it has lost half its students before graduation. Even the lush playing fields, a stable and equitation program that allows horses to be boarded on campus, the challenging liberal arts courses in which tests are given on the honor system, have failed to dissuade students from leaving.

All Applicants Get Parts

An illustration of the kind of problem gripping the school was seen one night this week when there was a casting call for the freshmen play and only six students showed up.

Luckily, *When Men Are Scarce*, has only six parts.

The field hockey team has not been so fortunate. Only eight students appeared at tryouts, and they are still attempting to persuade others to join them so they will have enough players for scrimmages, the regular schedule having been cancelled.

"It's tough on all of us because we're each getting involved in more activities than normal to keep them all going until we get more students," said Kathy Safran, a senior from Pittsburgh who is captain of the hockey team.

In the classroom, where the average number of students per teacher has shrunk to 6 to 1, there is "more personalized attention than ever," according to Ann Brickles, a junior from the Philadelphia suburb of Exton, who is majoring in biology and psychology.

21 Teachers for 21 Majors

But the range of offering has almost become a joke, with the catalogue listing 21 majors at a time when the full-time faculty has dwindled to exactly 21 members. Theony Condos, a classicist, who has moved up from the faculty to be acting Dean, thinks that the College must rapidly raise its enrollment to at least 300.

"There comes a point," she said, "where if the number of students gets too low, the academic community loses momentum and falls apart. There must be a critical mass for bouncing ideas around. Even if we raised $100 million this year but came up with a class of 40 freshmen, it wouldn't make us a viable institution in this respect."

Yet, the uncertainty of its future has not given Wilson the air of an institution on borrowed time. The slate-roofed buildings are well maintained and the verdant campus is trim. This appearance is bolstered by the abounding loyalty of the students.

"I'm paying my own way through College, and I'm not sorry I came," said Betty A. Giostra, a freshmen from Paterson, New Jersey, who enrolled after the court blocked the closing. "I'd recommend this place to anyone." **(end)**

Quoting from the writings of Joan Foresman Edwards:

In the six-month period following the announcement that Wilson would close this June, the 1974 Moon Report has been a key factor in the total effort to breathe new life into the institution ... it epitomizes the spirit observed on the campus by

Chapter Four: Beginning Again 110 Years Later: 1979-1981

this volunteer during the summer.

Following a brief period of joyful celebration, the Board of Trustees, the newly appointed Acting President, and Save Wilson committee people were faced with the incredible realities of the situation. The challenge we inherited is well stated in Judge Keller's court decision, Section 264: "The February 19, 1979, notice of the Board's decision damaged the College as to: (a) the maintenance of the present student body; (b) the availability of any incoming 1979 freshmen class; (c) the status of the present faculty, the administrative staff and maintenance staff; (d) potential liability, *e.g.*, the Commonwealth unemployment compensation claim, the HUD mortgage claim, the faculty severance pay suit; (e) its ongoing academic integrity; (f) its financial integrity; (g) its potential credibility as a functioning educational institution.

Acting President Donald Bletz leapt into action on May 29, meeting with every constituency to ensure that the College would begin to function.

Our volunteer staff at Save Wilson Headquarters and the mutual respect of alumnae and administration continues as it must in any small private institution like Wilson. The lack of such respect was a major factor during the Waggoner administration, and ironically, probably precipitated the instant "creative rage" that ultimately saved the College. The presence of alumnae in every office and on the Board, and their highly visible presence on the campus all summer, demonstrate beyond question that Wilson alumnae are an unusually devoted group. We knew that the real work would begin if we won the court battle, and the evidence is strong that there will always be the kind of commitment needed—whether it be time, money, or reaffirming Wilson's credibility and visibility.

The five areas of concern as pointed out by Judge Keller, and which happen to be the most frequently asked questions of any alumna of Wilson these days, are responded to as follows:

- The student body count is obviously the number one concern. It is heartening to most of us to realize that about 100 students will be on campus this fall including about 70% returning students. Recruitment efforts by alumnae and a skeletal admission staff resulted in approximately 32 prospective students attending Summer College days in mid-July. The atmosphere on campus that weekend was very upbeat—not unlike the weekend many years ago when I was first introduced to the "Wilson Way." According to Dolly Swisher, the presence of alumnae weeding, mowing and painting impressed the parents who attended; and I'm sure the fact that dozens of the Wilson students who entertained the prospective students had been living and working on campus without pay had to make a deep impression. Apparently the small population is not going to deter those present Wilson women from obtaining a Wilson degree. In a few short weeks we persuaded 19 new students to attend Wilson, so we feel confident that under our new Director of Admissions and with new emphasis on alumnae recruitment, enrollment will rise to very acceptable levels.

- ... Attrition of faculty and staff was perhaps the biggest shock to me when we arrived on campus May 30th. Half of the faculty were committed to other jobs; administrative staff, practically non-existent. Offices were vacant and the switchboard was closed. It took weeks, but gradually every office was functioning, staffed by Save Wilson volunteers and the handful of secretaries who displayed infinite patience with us. Administrative posts changed frequently and everybody—paid and volunteer—worked at several jobs simultaneously. One secretary joked about playing "musical offices." Student volunteers arrived within a week, and it became necessary to establish an office of Volunteer Services, which had the highly challenging job of not only coordinating the work but also dealing with problems of feeding and housing people. Out of chaos and experimentation grew a functional system—perhaps not an ideal one but the only way that Wilson could have gotten the job done this summer given the real lack of financial and personnel resources.

- Potential liabilities did not really occur.

- Wilson's academic integrity and credibility do not seem to be major concerns at this time, in my opinion. I believe that Wilson's academic standing never faltered in spite of her other problems. The immediate actions of the faculty under former Dean Van Marter resulted in three new majors and an expansion of the existing programs in the first month and was an amazing demonstration of their commitment to modernizing Wilson's curriculum. The speed with which an adequate faculty has been assembled using 21 full-time and 19 part-time professors is very encouraging to me. The range of courses being offered this fall certainly does not suggest that Wilson is not a functioning educational institution. Indeed, our new offerings have stimulated an impressive number of inquiries from adults in the community, showing that continuing education students will probably be seen in larger numbers than ever before.

- Financial integrity is still an unknown quantity. ... A consultant for development at Wilson told me recently that he firmly believes that Wilson can overcome its present crisis. Our record alumnae giving figure for 1978-79 included gifts from 42.4% of our alumnae. This kind of demonstrated faith in the institution will impress foundations. A long-term plan for development is being formulated by a committee of the Board of Trustees in consultation with experts in the field. A consultant is on campus several days a week to direct the efforts of the staff and volunteers. The search for a well-qualified director continues.

I spoke at the beginning of stewardship and sacrifice. For everyone involved at Wilson College this summer, paid or volunteer, these words apply. **(end)**

THE BLETZ TEAM MADE CHANGES

There were 125 full-time equivalent students in 1979-1980; 180 in 1980-1981; 222 in the fall of 1981-82. Of the 38 full-time faculty, 19 remained in the fall of 1979. 29 part-time faculty were utilized in 1979-1980, with 7 of those volunteering their services. Full-time faculty in 1980-1981 increased to 30, with part-time at 19. (Taken from Middle States Association report, May 1983.)

Admissions: The Save Wilson Committee had done an extensive study of the admissions process and had written a plan which was largely followed. The College went back to a very personal approach with outreach, inviting students to campus and limited use of purchasing names from Student Search. Hallmarks were use of the alumnae with training and organization; more attention to local recruitment; personalized follow-ups to responses from prospective students; use of current students; and reorganization of the admissions staff. It was recognized that they needed a long range plan, ... and heeded the advice of an expert in the field of educational marketing and produced a study of the market. The staff was enlarged and headed by Frank Kamus, a seasoned professional hired as admissions director on August 15, 1979. An admissions evaluation team, headed by Dr. William Elliot of Carnegie-Mellon University, completed a study of Wilson's admissions program.

As of December 7, 1979, the College had received 2,760 inquiries for 1980, with 41 applications and six students enrolled for January 1980. Staff and alumnae had visited 333 schools and had attended 106 college nights/days/fairs. (Wilson Newsletter, December 1979)

Curriculum: There is little doubt that the curriculum changes during 1979-1981 were a key component for the College to survive. Additions included majors in: Communications Studies; Economics and Business Administration with new courses in Business Law, Accounting, Finance and Management; Dance; Journalism; a Veterinary Medical Technology associate degree and a degree in Equitation Management, with certificates in Equitation and in Athletic Coaching.

Curriculum change seemed to be the key to enrollment and thus to the financial picture of Wilson. At the July 7th meeting of the Board of Trustees, the following framework was approved by the Board:

> "The Trustees of Wilson College believe in the compatibility between a liberal education and a career-orientation and endorse the development of a program. This program for the education of women stresses access to the skills, background, and experience necessary for establishing a career upon graduation beyond the baccalaureate degree; and strengthens her personally and intellectually, so that she may well concentrate on the special responsibilities she chooses to carry in life. A career orientation occurring within a strong liberal arts context fosters each student's capacity for meeting the changing demands of career and society." (Board minutes, p. 8, July 7, 1979)

From the notes of Dr. Bletz sent in a personal email to the author on 10/14/18:

> Near the end of my term, the Board had approved equitation as a degree subject and Veterinary Medical Technology as an associate degree. We had stables and horses on campus. A few students who owned horses brought them with them and boarded them at Wilson. There was no program to use the stables or horses for any purpose other than recreational riding.
>
> Colonel Alfred (Bud) Kitts, a friend and colleague on the faculty of the Army War College, had put together a riding program at the War College in which some of us participated, including Pat and me. Bud Kitts was an internationally known equestrian. At the 1936 Olympics in Germany, Bud's father was a member of the US Equestrian team, and Bud, as a youngster, went with his father. Those were the Olympics where Jesse Owens won many high awards in competition with Hitler's Aryan race. This made Hitler very angry and he left the arena. We wondered at Wilson if this asset could not be put to use other than for those who brought their horses with them. Could it possibly be put to some use as part of an academic program? Bud was invited to come to Wilson for a visit and to tell us what we might be able to do with those assets. He reported that we could do something positive with them. Bud was not a fool, nor was he a liberal arts enthusiast, but he saw some potential in an equitation program beyond just recreational riding. Bud and Dean Theony Condos went to Lake Erie College in Ohio to observe their apparently successful equestrian program. Even the classicist, Theony, saw potential there.
>
> The faculty and Trustees were not initially very enthusiastic, but finally approved an equestrian four year major. Eventually, sometime later, Bud came aboard on the faculty and took charge

of the equestrian program, and it became a success. Bud and I worked out a scheme where I took credit for the idea and he took credit for building the program. One of our students, Lindsay Baird, was a graduate of the equestrian program and went from Wilson to law school and has been an attorney in Carlisle ever since.

Richard Fulton, the husband of Trustee and graduate, Susan Breakefield Fulton, '61, was instrumental in the establishment of the Veterinary Medical Technology (VMT) program ... The size of our farm and the horses already provided the large animals for VMT studies. Dave Grove, a biology professor, working with a local retired veterinarian, put together a basic curriculum for a two-year associate degree program which was later changed to a four year program.

I do know that both the Equestrian and the VMT programs have been very successful, as were the other programs that were added at that time. **(end)**

The restructured curriculum included an interdisciplinary major elected from 12 that were offered; four courses promoting language skills in English and another language; and three all- college conference courses focusing on contemporary issues and emphasizing global dimensions of the issues selected.

Staffing: Dr. Bletz revamped his staff in 1979. Dr. Theony Condos, Dean; Dr. Marilyn Mumford, Assistant to the President; Richard Brunner, Director of Public Information; James Hyatt, Business Manager; Carol Tschop, first as acting in October 1979 then as permanent Director of Development in May 1980; Kathi Torpy, Director of Alumnae Affairs. The academic year 1979-1980 shows 21 full-time faculty and 19 part-time faculty.

Volunteer Program: One of the great and wonderful events was the extensive work of volunteers led by Ethaline Cortelyou, fondly know as

Cort. Cort had no ties to the College but she had seen the article in *The New York Times* and, for room and board, had become the head of the volunteer brigade for several years into the Merriam administration. She was an extraordinary woman, a radiochemist and scientific writer who worked on the Manhattan project and was born in 1909. On January 14, 1980, Cort was nominated for Outstanding Citizen Award in 1979, sponsored by the *Pittsburg Post-Gazette* and the American Institute for Public Service, Washington, D.C.

In the summer of 1979 fifteen students returned and lived on campus to volunteer their efforts typing, running the switchboard, and pruning the shrubbery among other activities. Thirty other volunteers—mainly alumnae—commute to the College to work-day-long jobs. The need for volunteers was great—filing, mailing, running office machinery, writing materials. Scout troops and church youth groups were contacted for help. Volunteer help continued for a number of years.

Church Relationship: The relationship with the Presbyterian Church of the USA was reinstated and the Reverend George H. Pike, a Presbyterian minister, was named a Trustee. The church made a gift to Wilson of $20,000 in the fall of 1979.

Lease Agreements for the utilization of unused buildings: A lease agreement was signed with Vale National for the purpose of training insurance adjustors. Later on an agreement was signed with the Pennsylvania Judiciary for the training of judges.

Fund-raising: The annual fund goal for 1979-1980 was set by the Board at $1 million. By December 7, 1979, $430,555.74 had been raised. On November 13, 1979, Lili Kraus, a world-renowned pianist and recipient of an honorary degree from Wilson, gave a benefit concert with all the proceeds coming to Wilson. For all the faculty had been through, the faculty wives organized a campaign and on December 17, 1979, gave a gift of $1,400 for scholarships!

Chapter Four: Beginning Again 110 Years Later: 1979-1981

Chairman of the Board, Nan Clarkson, wrote an unpublished piece from her perspective as a Trustee, focusing on 1979-1981. Portions were quoted in Chapter Three. Here is the final portion that relates to this time period and trustee activity.

"Some Trustee Activity, 1979-1981: The Wilson College Campus was humming all summer. Alumnae volunteers came to work on every area from the landscape to the kitchen—some of them staying for long periods of time. This had to be coordinated by alumnae and Trustees and administration working together. The new Board had to monitor the infrastructure. What we had, the morning after the court decision, was a College that was "saved" in name only—a College that was seriously without funds. Basic questions of how to make the weekly payroll and pay the water and electric bills loomed large. We had been winding down for months; all of our insurance had been canceled—and goodness knows how many other contracts and necessary suppliers had been cut off. We had an administration that was as newly constituted as the Trustees, and it was a period when we all had to help each other overtime.

Once Don Bletz was in place in the President's Office, he and I immediately began to solidify confidence in the College's financial basis. The local bankers were nervous— several had even offered to fly up to Buffalo to talk over their concerns as to the differences among their own constituencies over the wisdom of the court's decision. We had to reassure them, putting our integrity and credit, as well as our hope, on the line that court order or no, Wilson was a viable institution despite our heavy indebtedness, our light cash flow and our present vulnerability. We were committed to a healthy survival, and we needed the banks of Chambersburg to support a great community asset in her time of trial.

We were in immediate contact with our investment firm in New York, then Weiss Peck and Greer, good friends who had following our story with great interest in *The New York Times*. They not only agreed to waive their investment fee for a year, but also invited our whole Board to lunch at their handsome board room high above Wall Street for a comprehensive look at our financial portfolio. It was support like this which added pleasure and confidence to the load we were carrying.

Much work had to be done to repair ties to the Chambersburg and Cumberland Valley communities, many of which had been deliberately ignored or broken in the years before the announced closing. And it was a concerted effort by our Board to restore the full relationship with the Presbyterian Church, which had also been severed by the previous administration. That whole first summer was a time when the new Board provided support and leadership when, to our surprise, few in the academic community wished us well and when our administration, new to college management, was finding its way. Key decisions were being made each day, it seemed—and new initiatives put into place to ensure that Wilson would stabilize and survive on a day-to-day basis long enough to grow strong.

And at summer's end? The College that had been programmed to die opened its 111th year with 110 students.

I wish I could record a year of no complaints, no hassles, no tugs of war between faculty and staff, no discord with concerned alumnae—as if the trauma of 1979 made grateful Polly-annas of us all. Not so, of course. And our extreme poverty was often to blame.

Every nerve was strained, so to speak, to keep us financially afloat. We were often close to broke. Sidney Palmer (trustee treasurer) and Don Bletz and I were in weekly contact—and it was sad but

Chapter Four: Beginning Again 110 Years Later: 1979-1981

true to remember that from the first we had a contingency plan which was to go into effect in the event of a crisis that would necessitate our going to, as we called it, Plan B.

One particularly difficult time was in the second year when so much was going well for us, but there simply wasn't enough money to get through the year—our second year, I believe. We had to raise over $150,000 to pay our bills or go to Plan B. Every possibility had been pursued to no avail. It was then that we knew we had to sell our Fine Arts collection. This was more of an "accumulation" than a "collection," strictly speaking.

And it consisted of a disparate number of treasures, ranging from furniture, to objects d'art, to a number of rare and prized oriental rugs, given to the College by a major benefactor, one Hagop Bogigian, a friend of our President Warfield and Theodore Roosevelt's appointee to raise the Red Cross funds for Armenian Relief.

Fortunately, we had access to Christies, the reputable auction house in New York, and a team of their arts experts came to campus to appraise our treasures; they were of the opinion that their sale could yield the amount we needed. The Board of Trustees approved this necessary measure but the faculty was up in arms. Before it became a real conflict, we entertained the faculty at the President's House where the debate was aired and peace restored. But this was just one of the many instances of the constant challenge. We had to help all the constituencies understand the magnitude of our problems. And, happy to say, the money was raised and once again Wilson was saved.

We made an intensive effort to win the support of the Association of Governing Boards, visited the Lilly Foundation in Indianapolis to appeal for faculty support, and some of us came to Chambersburg to take part in the crucial Middle States

Report, a report we had every cause to worry about. When it was published, we were happy to see that it cited the hard work and dedication of Wilson's Board of Trustees as a great strength." **(end)**

A CRITICAL LOOK AT A CRUCIAL YEAR: What Happened—What's Ahead, by Elisabeth (Nan) Clarkson, '47, in the Winter 1980 edition of the Wilson Alumnae Quarterly. I am excerpting (without the questions asked) key points concerning the transition since she served as a member of the Trustees prior to May 25, 1979, and then as Acting Chairman and then Chairman of the "new" Board from May 26, 1979, through June 30, 1982. Nan took copious notes throughout this momentous time and had the wisdom and thoughtfulness that is useful to our understanding of some of the feelings of some of the Trustees as well as to the challenges that lay ahead of the Board and its Acting President.

"It's been a long way from February 1979 to February 1980, and probably the most valuable thing I can contribute is a comparison of our situation—as I see it—then and now."

Feelings about the vote: "Given the information of last year at this time and the past mode of decision-making and that same cast of characters, we made a prudent decision. How do I feel about it now? Guilty about a lot of things. Guilty that we panicked in the face of what seemed like overwhelming odds; that we by and large accepted Alice Beeman's proposal to set up a foundation; that we had allowed a situation to come about in which the officers (however unintentionally) had pre-empted too much power of decision-making. ... We delegated too much responsibility to a few to avoid too many meetings of the whole Board. Very few of the Trustees were secure in their decision ... it was a terrible ambivalence that I felt. And every other alumnae on that Board felt it."

Chapter Four: Beginning Again 110 Years Later: 1979-1981

Starting in June: "... we were still starting in June (with all the disadvantages) with more esprit de corps, more enthusiasm and public image than we had had in years. Wilson was news. Wilson was a metaphor of rebirth. Wilson was controversial. Wilson was a place where a young woman could come with pride, expecting to participate in some of the social action of saving a college as well as getting an education ..."

Predicting the future with variable cloudiness: "... compared to the last ten years, Wilson College is a happier place than it has ever been. People do significantly better work when morale is high, when they feel that they can speak up and be heard, when conflict can be confronted and dealt with, when valid information is available to all those who must make vital decisions. ... Our President's leadership style is so open and participative ... we are becoming a strong Board. We have a nucleus of our making Wilson College a priority and they're eager for action, for signs of success. ... Some members of the Board have even played roles that were more administrative than policy-making ... I see the present Board making its wishes known to the administration and I see the Board trying its best to be responsive to the needs of the College ... An example: By November, we found out that the euphoria of September was well over. Vale National Insurance Center was a thorn in the side of many; there was real difficulty with the kitchen personnel; a grave lack of funds for student projects, owing to the small number of student activity fees, was affecting morale ... Luckily, this situation was made known to me and to Dr. Bletz ... We met, grievances were aired, the President brought recommendations to the Board, and certain immediate steps were taken at the November (Board) meetings ... We had a press conference for student leaders after the Board meeting ... These same students then came along with us to an informal supper for faculty and Trustees at the President's House.

Dedication to Openness: What is new is mostly a dedication to openness. Things like meetings are open to any members of the Board who wish to attend. We also rejoined collegial organizations that can help us to become a far more effective Board in the future, if Wilson is to be granted a long-term future … We have been given the precious gift of time. But what if, by a certain time … we have no evidence of an adequate student body? … The signs are good—except for fall (1980) enrollment.

Deep Divisions: There were many times when I was reminded of the deep divisions. This bothers me a lot, because it has always seemed to me that all must be forgiven and understood (rather than forgotten) if we are really to save Wilson. We must be a united force, we are sister alumnae and we must forget the business of being judgmental. I, for one, will never rest easily until the day when those alumnae who were among the "old" Trustees who resigned—so many had given in a really sacrificial way to Wilson—feel free to come back again and feel welcome on the campus. People of good will must be free to confront the same facts and disagree about them. And people of good will on both sides must have it in their hearts to reconcile—to move ahead." **(end)**

Excerpted from Nan Clarkson's Personal Journal

October 31, 1979: Through the painter who picked me up at the airport, I hear that the new head of maintenance, is not able to exert leadership, that the electrician doesn't know a hill of beans about his job, that the front of the Penn Hall buildings, pillars and porticos are getting a coat of paint for cosmetic purposes.

Staying in Norland Hall, room 201, a handsome and serene reward— quieter than the McClure Room, with views that break my heart. The "pickle train" whistling in the night. There's a Halloween party on down at Sharpe House, and the sound of ghosts and goblins comes across on

Chapter Four: Beginning Again 110 Years Later: 1979-1981

the balmy smoky October wind. It's so lovely to be here.

Thursday morning—9:00 a.m. in the President's office. With Gretchen Van Ness, W.C.G.A. President, "Save Wilson" heroine, an absolutely trustworthy, exemplary Wilson woman, currently suffering from a number of post-revolutionary complaints. It is essential to hear her out, for caught early enough, we may apply the palliatives that will perhaps forestall attrition in February. She speaks for the articulate minority (majority?) who feel disenfranchised by the overwhelming presence of the Vale people, infuriated by the abrasiveness of the Food Services Manager and by the food he serves. One meal we had potatoes and macaroni; another time, when we said we'd rather have a salad bar at lunch than meat at every breakfast, he said—"well, that's tough, because the Vale folks want meat, and lady, you wouldn't be here without them!" But the delay in getting things fixed (like the film projector, six weeks on the blitz, or the toaster, ailing all term). These woes are real enough. Deeper than that is the confrontation with the long hard pull. It must have hurt to hear her saying how remote the President was from students—how "nothing has changed"—when we know so well that much has changed and that the President is pulled in all directions. Frustrating to hear this student perception.

Gretchen's eyes show candor, friendliness and intelligence ... During last year her natural qualities of leadership had ample opportunity to flower. It could be called "forced bloom." Gloria Scott (a Trustee and President of a women's college) was later to say of Gretchen and the other strong Wilson women, "when you've been part of a revolution, you somehow feel you own that revolution ... and maybe this place. It's very difficult to adjust to peace and quiet." There is danger in getting used to high drama. They are now in the period of consolidation and the hardship of poverty, smallness and isolation are all perhaps magnified—the focus now is on admissions and money raising and there's no high drama for them in that. Well, it was a good meeting. We left Gretchen with the feeling that she had been heard, I think. For two hours, Don and I had an informative meeting—he telling me everything that we may expect to hear on campus—me telling him the things I'd "picked up" on my radar – e.g., "no one knows who reports to whom." I suspect this largely means they don't know whether they are supposed to do what Mardi Mumford and Kendrick Smith ask them to and what priority these requests should get. We have an excellent "reporting relationship," I think.

Lunch with campus feminists, very few, to judge by the fact that we could only fill the small dining room. Over club sandwiches, Mardi Mumford described the xeroxed sheets she had given everyone and other announcements. We discussed the need for a really good women's studies program. Displeasure with certain professors (who evidently manage to convey chauvinist proclivities in their classrooms) was noted, compared and deplored. ... They had been invited to lunch to talk with me. One would never have suspected this. Don Bletz was there.

It seems to me that Wilson needs to liberate itself and become educated in the field on women's history, literature, etc. But this should not happen as the result of a cult of followers of one person, or post-revolutionaries. To make feminist activity exclusive is to invite failure at Wilson, I think. The sun came out and I walked around campus, into the library, over the brick walks with their worn herring bone patters, under the giant tress, their leaves still gold and burnished pink as the sun flared. Dave Dunkle (the **Public Opinion**) came to talk with me and we sat on a bench outside Norland, talking over the philosophical aspects of Wilson's life and future. "Trouble is, the College isn't news any more," he said ruefully. I like him so very much, and we enjoy talking to each other. But, apart from this, he has been very good to the College. He wrote the lion's share of the 12- page supplement they published in August 1979.

December 3, 4, 5, 1979: *Executive committee meetings. Also invited to a faculty meeting. Dinner with Carol Tschop, getting things set up. At last, the goals of individuals are integrated with the goals of the institution. The mood is expectant. Only the students look tired, look not expectant.*

Chapter Four: Beginning Again 110 Years Later: 1979-1981

One student signed, sealed and delivered for September 1980. This sends a chill down my spine.

January 27, 1980: *Back to the womb. Back to Wilson—back to the* Alma Mater *arms "who blessed me on my way." My shabby and well-loved Victorian grandeur—a week in the McClure room. Bathed, much welcomed, well wined and dined at the President's House before Opening Convocation, it's so comforting to sit here, to know there's a week of good work to do, sociability too, an atmosphere I cherish: no housework and a great deal of the kind of tasks I find stimulating—research in the admissions department and meetings galore.*

But I am also fearful. This is too big a job for me. This College is by no means "saved," and it seems to me that our top administrative staff is woefully inadequate to our needs.

Discouraging to see only a handful of students at convocation tonight— and only 44 guests. Nancy Besch is furious that there wasn't more publicity. We gave Sylvia Rambo (just appointed a federal judge in this area) an honorary degree. The dinner party Pat and Don gave at the President's house was just delightful. But oh, the chapel was so empty. Met Judge Keller on this night.

Judge John Keller—the "folk hero of your local press who is actually the fulfillment of our worst fantasies"—a quote from the Association of Governing Boards (AGB) President representing the educational establishment. I sat next to Judge Keller at dinner and we were rude— albeit unintentionally so—to those nearby, for we were as a couple in love, so much had we to exchange and to question of the other. Some of the aspects that were still mysteries to him, were known to me—on the other hand, he was boyishly eager to test me on points of law—do you remember the letter of February 19th?" he'd say, for example,— "well, remember such and such a clause?" ... he and his wife were terribly upset by the article in Change. *"It was their suggesting that Keller was unethical that got me," she said, still sending sparks. "Why, he's the most ethical man I* *know." He has a tired, lovely look to him—"I believe that this will prove to have been the most absorbing and interesting case of my life," he said. He also said he wanted to sue <u>Change</u> magazine! All during dinner we kept coming back to a quiet, continuing replay of the case—then someone would interrupt or we'd make an effort to be nice to the others around us and then we couldn't wait to return to the pursuit of that history, that delving ...*

... I have enjoyed this thing of Chairman, but it's bad for ego, image, etc. I'd rather be the Board maverick. ... As it is I must be exemplary ...

Vis-à-vis my work at Wilson—it is a work I love, in which I have a true sense of my ability to effect things. Whether we succeed or fail in keeping the College open, no one will regret having given so much to this truly wonderful year when, for the first time in a decade, relationships may be candid and friendly—when all the constituencies are open to change and to each other ...

There has been a large amount of Wilson work. Never before have I felt so thoroughly involved, or so able to work effectively. They are putting pressure on me for continuing another year as Chairman of the Board. Because of this, I felt secure enough—and also enough time has now elapsed to allow this—to appoint Betty Blackadar to go about the essential task of information gathering in the delicate realm of contingency planning. It does not seem to me that caring or prudent leadership can avoid this task, for it is possible that future discussions will demand knowledge of this sort ...

Betty is such a tower of strength. She brings organizing capability, the thorough mind of a classics scholar, and the dogged, tireless persistence of a long-distance runner to everything she does at Wilson. This year alone she has given hours of truly substantive help to admissions, development and the Board nominating committee. She has instituted a procedure for nominating that enables her committee to make wise choices and encourages all constituencies to get pertinent information to

Chapter Four: Beginning Again 110 Years Later: 1979-1981

the committee. Now, in this highly sensitive area, she is taking on a real workload, highly creative—for it is uncharted—and the information she comes up with is essential for many purposes—to chart our course, to judge our performance, merely to be fully aware as we work—and quite possible, God forbid, to close with compassion.

Don Bletz is a singularly dear man. A less likely army colonel I cannot imagine. For the period since July he has been invaluable, as big brother to the College, healer of multiple wounds, consolidator, communicator most bounteous, and genial attractive public persona—a man seemingly perfect for the job. And it was with these thoughts that we made him President through June 1981. Now, having made it through the winter we see May looming: the time when the Board will expect certain results to provide them with material to make their decision. We really have to have new students to make our continuation viable and at present we have only five.

So the women are organizing. Mardi, Theony, Carmen Jordan-Cox, Kathy Torpy, and Carol Tschop. They will try to light fires under the admissions program. They sense the crisis and the need and the brief time we have to make a showing. And I would suspect they will show! We can have raised money closer to our goal than ever in history—we can have high morale and a miraculously recovered College community—all that, and yet, if we have not enough young women who want to come to receive what we offer, we will have to close.

Saving Wilson may come to mean saving all that is best in Wilson's heritage and communications' network and finding a new life for her old campus that is no longer a women's college.

... Received a letter from a frequent Wilson complainer—an alumna. I wrote back to say that we're doing everything we can to stay alive—part of this effort is a mandated modernization of the curriculum to allow for the faculty we have, the facilities and the students we hope to attract. I said that this is a terribly difficult time in the life of the College. We have

to change in order to live, Middle States told us this. Our alumnae have told us this. But most important, prospective students have been telling us this by not enrolling. We have taken on some new things—we have not given up the old. Let's hope for the best. (taken from personal journal, Vol. 8)

June 1, 1981, there is an article in the *Chronicle of Higher Education*, Vol XXII, No. 15, titled "2 Years After Trustees Decided to Close It, Wilson College Graduates Another Class," by Lawrence Biemiller quoted in part here, omitting the retelling of the lawsuit. (Reprint permission granted)

In 1869, Miss Sarah Wilson provided $30,000 to help two Presbyterian ministers open a liberal-arts college for woman in this small town in the Cumberland Valley. For a century, the College grew and prospered. But in February of 1979, with enrollment standing at only 214 and the unrestricted endowment drained by a decade of deficits, the Trustees of Wilson College voted to close the institution and devote its remaining assets to an educational foundation for women.

Last week, the women of Wilson College's class of 1981—30 women who had protested the Trustees' decision and joined an alumnae lawsuit to keep Wilson open, who had bravely returned the next fall to a College that was scarcely alive, who then recruited freshmen and painted buildings and volunteered for a hundred other tasks to help nurse it back to health— were graduated in the shade of the enormous old trees on the College's front lawn ...

"We had nothing," recalls Donald F. Bletz, a professor of political science who became Acting President and later President. "Every principal staff officer on this campus had gone or would be gone within a month. People in higher education were laughing at us." The Admissions Office had been closed since February, grant applications had been withdrawn, and half the faculty had found other jobs.

"The faculty met all summer long," says Joyce E. Donatelli, assistant professor of physical education. "We became frantically busy with the scheduling of classes, wiht figuring out who among us were left, what courses we could offer and when and how."

The 1979 fall semester began with 125 students, 21 full-time faculty members, and a number of adjunct professors, some of them volunteers. Meanwhile the faculty was at work on a revision of the curriculum. Not only was the old curriculum, which included 22 majors, viewed as overly traditional, but the Middle States Association of Colleges and Schools had criticized it as being too ambitious for an institution of Wilson's size.

According to Theony Condos, an associate professor of classics who became Dean of the College that fall, the new curriculum looked "not toward career training— vocationalism—but toward a little more focusing of our academic programs in particular career directions. This seemed not to contradict our liberal-arts philosophy. The result is a curriculum centered on 11 "major fields of study," all of which are interdisciplinary.

The behavioral studies program, for instance, allows students to specialize in either psychology or sociology, but requires them also to take courses in anthropology, biology, computer science, mathematics, psychology, sociology and philosophy or religion.

Wilson students are also required to take three "all-college conference courses" during their four years. These focus on a different topic each semester—"Energy and the Survival of Life," and "Women's Self-perception in the Arts" have been offered recently—and are taught by teams of faculty members.

Language Requirement Kept

The interdisciplinary programs and the conference courses are both popular with faculty members. "They draw the faculty together into an integrated teaching and learning community," says Raymond K. Anderson, associate professor of religion studies.

"They're tremendously stimulating. The two times that I've led conference courses, I think I've learned more than any of my students."

The College has retained its foreign-language requirement and non-major programs in athletic coaching, physical education, and equine studies. It is adding an associate degree program in veterinary medical technology. Wilson students, who say they work harder than students at comparable colleges, and that, because of the College's small size, they dare neither cut classes nor attend unprepared, are pleased with the quality of their education. "When I go home and talk to my friends, I get the feeling that I'm much more articulate than they are, and that I have a better understanding of what's going on around me," says Sue Ann Morin, one of last week's graduates.

"The scale of things here enables us to be very flexible," says Eugene L. Beecher, an assistant professor of elementary education who came to Wilson this year from Rhode Island College. "We can take advantage of situations as they arise," he says. "When we were in the middle of a public-school strike, we could pile into my nine-passenger vehicle and shoot off to talk to some of the teachers or go to a school board meeting. It's almost like guerrilla education."

... total enrollment this coming fall is expected to be about 250... **(end)**

Chapter Four: Beginning Again 110 Years Later: 1979-1981

In the journal, *Fund Raising Management*, March 1981, pp. 14-23, there was an article that featured a dialogue between Wilson's Director of Development, Carol Tschop, and the writer, John McLaughlin. The title was "Fight For Survival: Wilson College Triumphs." (out of print) It is paraphrased and/or quoted in part here with topics, as opposed to the questions. A substantial part of the article deals with the actions of the Save Wilson Committee and the lawsuit and the aftermath covered elsewhere of this book. The focus here is on fundraising.

> "Faced with a financial crisis in 1979, a high degree of support from devoted alumnae saved Wilson College from closing. The successful "Save Wilson" campaign at the all- women's college in Chambersburg, Pennsylvania, raised a remarkable $1.1 million in three months."
>
> **History of fundraising at Wilson:** The Alumnae Association was nearly 60 years old while the first annual fund campaign was begun in 1930. The first full-time director came as Vice-President for Development in the 1950's. The College—begun as a four-year liberal arts college for women—had always had strong support from the Presbyterian Church. In 1981, there were 6,800 living alumnae.
>
> **Major reasons behind bringing the College to the brink of financial disaster:** Declining enrollment and dwindling finances; fewer women attracted to a women's college and Wilson's purist liberal curriculum; tremendous turnover in staff—two Presidents and one Interim President in 10 years, from 1975 on, a new Dean every year, two or three Admissions Directors, a couple of development people; a very centralized power structure, no long range plan, and several studies done by professionals with suggested actions that were not implemented. A substantial unrestricted endowment that was drawn on during

333

the 1970s kept the College going as long as it did in the face of yearly operating deficits.

Fundraising: "We raised $1.1 million in pledges over a three-year period with almost $200,000 from the Presbyterian Church, ... but then last year (1979-80), after we had won the court decision and we had to come up with a figure, we came up with a $1 million fund raising goal. Last year we exceeded that goal by some $370.00."

Fundraising was all done by volunteers. Quoting from Carol Tschop: "I think the key to the effort was that we had a cause. Most people who go to Wilson feel that it is a very special college. It's a very fine college. It's got a great history, and it inspires a lot of affection and nostalgia by its graduates. So there is—there was—a cause here. There is a very loyal constituency, and there was a crisis. What ended up happening is that everybody kind of rallied around the flag when the College was threatened ... the phonathon was entirely staffed by volunteers ... think we contacted between 1,000 and 2,000 people with 80-90% reached by telephone." (p. 17)

Problems faced by the development office after the court decision: "We had no staff. We were very fortunate that one of our volunteers had worked at the 'Save Wilson' headquarters as former director of the annual fund. She agreed to come back and run the office on a volunteer basis for the month of June. She did so, with the help of one other volunteer. The only actual employee left within the development office was a secretary who was going to leave the following month for a new job. So we had a month to process these checks and close out the 1978-79 fundraising record, then to get some kind of a campaign on board here. We were also blessed with a very capable consultant who came in and began to put together the kind of organization and plan

Chapter Four: Beginning Again 110 Years Later: 1979-1981

that we would need. He came on in mid-summer, Ken Smith. Ken put together the kind of volunteer structure that identified priorities for us and helped us get the previous year wrapped up. He helped us direct our thinking toward how we were going to raise the $1 million goal he had outlined—the kinds of efforts we should be making in terms of foundations, corporations, and government funds. Then we had to put a staff together, because you just can't run something like this with volunteers forever. It had worked very well. When we did come in here, we had just a handful of checks. People were so thrilled by the fact that we had won the court decision that they immediately started to pay their first year pledge. Three hundred thousand of the million was the 1979-1980 share of the preservation fund payments. We are now in the second year of the preservation fund. Out of the goal of about $1,200,000 that we have for 1980-81 academic year, we have about the same amount as this year's share ...

"Right now (1980-81), we have a very unusual kind of circumstance because the enrollment is still so small. During the 1980-81 academic year, 24% of the operating budget comes from tuition-related income which is terribly, terribly small. Normally it is in the vicinity of 70-80 percent. The remaining 76% has to come from the endowment income, the unrestricted endowment that we have left, leasing the campus facilities, which we are doing, and fundraising ...

"We are having greater success this year than last. But I think it is important that you know that when we came on board last summer, we discovered that every foundation and corporation within the file had received a letter saying that the College was closing. There were many times when we felt that this might be a whole lot easier if were we were starting from scratch because we had the negative impact to overcome. People are justifiably skeptical about how much we will be able to do. Can we reverse ten years in two or three?

"We have had a great deal of success to date. Certainly, the alumnae commitment is probably the most important thing. But I think there is the fact that people thought the little guy fought the big guys and won. We are trying to continue the success that we had last year. The alumnae became very tuned in to what was going on, on campus. And what happened is that they bought themselves a college. I think that our job in some instances is very easy because everybody knows our needs. They know that the money has to come in so that we can pay the fuel bills, salaries, maintenance costs, and tuitions ...

"This year more so than last we have had a more sympathetic ear from foundations and corporations. Last year, I think a lot of people were saying what we are trying to do is admirable, but it is too late. There were people that didn't think we could make it into last fall, and we did. There were people who didn't think that we could make it into last February (1980) for the second semester, and we did. There were people that didn't think we could make it through the summer and into this year, and we did. We are growing stronger. The longer we are able to hang on and grow and increase enrollment and have success with our fund raising, the more we modify the curriculum so that it is more responsive to the needs of women today.

"There has been a lot of support from the Chambersburg community, not only financially, but also in advice and in making us feel as though we are a revered part of the Chambersburg community. There had always been an austere environment that encased the College. It was as though we were an Ivory Tower that was removed from the rest of Franklin County.

"One of the things we wanted to do was combat that, so last

Chapter Four: Beginning Again 110 Years Later: 1979-1981

year we had a series of luncheons for various people within the community such as doctors, lawyers, newspaper people, people in social service agencies, people involved in the arts, and lecturers groups. We told about what we wanted to do, and asked them for their input. How did they feel Chambersburg and Franklin County perceived Wilson? How could we better serve the community? Out of that is coming some curriculum changes such as arts and lecture classes and extension programs that will help make us a much more active member of the Franklin County community."

"The goal for 1980-81 is $1,200,000, and half has been met—exactly where we were last year. There are two professionals in the office—one in charge of the annual fund, and the other for friends, parents, etc. There is also a gal helping Carol with research on corporate major gift prospects and on proposals.

"There is a College newsletter which includes an appeal; letters; appeals such as the 'Aunt Sally' mailing. This year we have a plan including a phonathon to increase the percentage of alumnae who give. In 1979-80, the percentage was 50.3; this year they want 55% and will have class agents calling those not having given by March. There is a need to broaden the support base and enlarge the planned giving…" **(end)**

Dr. Bletz on October 9, 2018, sent a personal email to Dr. Armacost:

I had agreed to serve two years as Acting President at which time the College should have found a "real" President by a regular, proper search. I was asked by Harry Buck, a faculty member of the search committee if I wanted to be considered for further duty as President. I replied, "No, but I would be happy to stay at Wilson on the faculty if that were possible." We worked out a scheme of provisional tenure to encourage young faculty to stay with us. This idea is borrowed from Juniata College in Huntington,

Pennsylvania. I never accepted tenure after returning to the faculty for that very reason.

As ex-officio member of the Board of Trustees I had the pleasure of voting for Mary- Linda Merriam. Her name was forwarded to the committee for consideration. I retired from the faculty in 1995, after 20 years at Wilson. I hope I served Wilson well during those years. My wife, Pat, was not impressed that I had accepted the role of President. Pat and I had had several very long separations—Korea and Vietnam, but she pitched in and helped very much. When I was succeeded by Mary-Linda, I told her I would stay out of her way if I returned to the faculty, but would be happy to help if I could. Wilson got a "proper" President at last! **(end)**

Excerpted Notes from Nan Clarkson's Personal Journal

***June 11, 1980:** Huge cumulus clouds, suffused with pearly pink looked like baroque gates to heaven—huge and close ... I am exhilarated by being needed and widely used at Wilson, and the prospects are excellent as we convene to approve a re- structured budget—a staying-in-business budget as opposed to the suicidal $900,000 deficit projected in May ...*

***July 11-12, 1980:** The finance committee went from 1:00-5:00 p.m. It was harrowing work for me, but full of education in how to deal with budgets. We went through the 1979-80 budget section by section and often line by line, both stated and actual, with the motive of finding the discrepancies, explaining them, and learning from them ... This was the process, all quite new to me. But I knew that if I were to chair the meeting the next day—a meeting which it would be impossible to overstate the importance of—I must know at least everything that this dress rehearsal would teach me. Finally we have a cash-flow projection. Finally we have a person (in Alan) who can answer our questions with a degree of perception and authority. Apart from the addressing of the revised* *budget, we decided to recommend further reductions, moving the deficit down past the $500,000 figure to about 4.5 million. Next day, I thought Susan Fulton put this so well— "Well," Susan answered, "we have to remember that we're not running a business here—not exactly, we have got to keep in mind that our purpose is to save a college—we all came on, never mind at what point, to do that thing, to save Wilson College. And it helps to think in terms of how much are we willing to invest? What is it worth—in our funds, in the assets of the institution—to save it? We have to assess our prudence in that way.'*

Brave Susan. I must remark that in my considered opinion, my railroading of Susan Breakefield Fulton onto the Wilson Board (and it was just that, done with fairly heavy hand) was one of my best gifts to Wilson. She has, in just a half year plus, done so much for the College. She has come for days on end to train admissions staff, to introduce consultants of her recruiting; she has attended extra sessions in Congressman Shuster's office in Washington, to help persuade HUD to release funds to us; she attends every meeting and she contributes substantially. She had real expertise in marketing to contribute, as a V.P. of Metromedia—and it is all the more impressive and effective for her emotional ties to her College. There is a strong familial dimension to her advocacy. And having a husband who is legal counsel to over 20 education-related agencies, she brings an additional expert field to us that we use in diverse ways. She's a joy to work with.

We worked so hard, all afternoon. Sidney kept us in good humor and there was a real feeling of camaraderie as we did our job. Dinner at the President's house—drinks first in the garden. It was at this time that Don Bletz and I had a chance to get caught up, and was able to prepare me for the substance of the meeting with the faculty next day: they are evidently furious about the Bradshaw Report. It was helpful to be warned ahead of time of the hornet's nest that I would enter, particularly in the exhausted state that is predictable after hours of trustee meetings.

After dinner we had a movie on trusteeship by AGB. For we who have survived a trial by fire in this activity, it seemed ... bland? But the discussion that followed was not. Here Ed Yale made his first moves to a "fish or cut bait" advocacy for tomorrow; here we sat around and talked—not very productively, but in a way that helps us to know and trust each other when we are sitting around that very public Board the next few days with the eyes of every campus constituency upon us from the sidelines—students, staff, faculty (thus our commitment to openness). It helps when you know a person's behavior patterns, where they're coming from. Despite this, it was worthwhile preparation.

Executive Committee breakfast at 7:00 a.m. at a table set with orange juice and enormous bun-like sweet rolls.

The Nominating Committee met on the porch. We voted to give honorary degrees to Jane Grant, Bill Putch and Jean Stapleton, and Louise Nevelson.

On Sunday morning Mardi Mumford called me to inform me that the 14-year-old son of the summer session kitchen director had been killed in our freight elevator on Friday. He'd been fooling around and had been warned against it several times. What a tragic event for the campus, especially for the Vale contingent since they were Vale people.

The budget, which we had asked to be cut was, indeed, cut from $900,000 to $400,000 of which $155,000 was shaved off projected expenses and the rest was upping projected forms of revenue. When Sidney announced the end of the Finance Committee meeting report, everyone clapped. It had been a new experience—a very business-like confrontation of a budget that was a going-out-of-business budget to one that, while still beyond our means, is a staying-in-business budget. The meeting seemed to herald a new professionalism on the part of the staff—a new recognition of the need for limits, goals and objectives. Also the news is good. There were 82 new students then—there are 87 now, and the staff knows that this Board means business.

Chapter Four: Beginning Again 110 Years Later: 1979-1981

The item of business that provoked the most discussion of a general nature, other than Ed Yale's search for parameters—for a point at which we say we gotta close down—was the proposal of selling some of these assets for the purpose of operating exigencies. This is the area when some of the Trustees who were alumnae and others come to combative life representing the alumnae, the donors—the fancied owners of these possessions.

Questions of ethics, questions of what alumnae will stand for! What wasn't brought up was the fact, I think, that actually the Trustees are the legal owners. You'd think that the Bogigian oriental rugs were the sacred symbols of the College, the way they talked.

Teaching collections of antiquities make more sense to be defensive about—but if we could get a half-year's operating cost from their sale, and if only two or three students are advanced enough in the fields of classics and archeology to use them—could not these students travel to any one of the many great museums to study similar artifacts? Well, the Chair was instructed to appoint an ad hoc *committee to have things appraised and to bring a report to the Board.*

After the Board meeting I met with the Faculty Co-op Committee—Nancy Besch and Woody Turner joined me too. We were 40 minutes late in meeting with them. Jane Morris tried to pre-empt me on the way in; "I've been waiting longer than they to see you!" I was weary; put my poor old sprained and still swollen ankle up on a chair and settled down to receive the trouble I had been warned was coming. They first spoke of the anger that had been generated by the Bradshaw Report; its secrecy, in a new atmosphere of openness. I explained how that came about: its delivery to Buffalo; it's not having been sent ahead to Don Bletz; its time-frame and the rationale for its existence as well as its benefits from my personal point of view.

Then they spoke of their feelings that the Bradshaw Report was a "set up" for Mardi to become President of the College without a wide search: her path being paved by the provost position. Well, it was a good meeting. At least they know that there was no collusion, with Trustees trying to prime Mardi for the Presidency. I let them know that their suspicions were, to say the least, disappointing to me, proclaiming a low trust level which I thought had been rather different. Nancy Besch spoke strongly to Mardi's self-sacrifice and her only "wanting was best for Wilson." And I was able to say that my personal goal and her goals for the institution were in perfect synchrony—and that this was a situation which produced the best work effort. I also said that in all probability she would be a candidate, and a strong one—but that she would have to go through the experience of the search committee, just like any other. We all agreed that the meeting was a good one.

August 23, 1980: *Yesterday morning I was called by Mardi Mumford to be told that Paul Swain Havens had died at 7:30 a.m. . . . He was the reason for going to Wilson. ... My letter to Mrs. Havens tried to tell her how much he meant to me—that stuffy English-type Princetonian, with his squinting twinkle and his pipe and his tweeds. "For generations of Wilson women he provided the role model for the ultimate gentleman and scholar—the person we could most revere and respect. And always his dignity and intellectuality were made more human for your smile and warmth at his side. And, more than you know, both of you have provided so much of the inspiration for working towards the new life for Wilson."*

Well, and so, yes, perhaps he stayed too long. But he still was a great man and his best years were Wilson's best, and we were able to be so proud of him. And for me, one of the deepest satisfactions of mine has been knowing that he saw and valued my metamorphosis from a flighty, bubbling, rather dippy student butterfly to a Chairman of Wilson's Board of Trustees.

September 1980: *Opening Convocation at Wilson. A thrilling sight to see the 96 new students rise when Don addressed them; Nenah Fry received an honorary degree. My talk ... was well-received ... Cautiously I feel we are off to a happy year.*

Chapter Four: Beginning Again 110 Years Later: 1979-1981

I worked with Pat Polete to see the fine arts collection so that it might be appraised and put up for auction for much needed funds for the College. Generations of Wilson women have given things to the College. One feels the College imposed no standards on the givers but played the role of grateful, indiscriminate recipient of this eclectic and not entirely glorious windfall. First, we must have it appraised to see if we are indeed sitting on a golden egg.

Board meeting: Executive committee. I felt paralyzed. Things moved slowly as in a dream. I couldn't feel bright or clairvoyant. Financial picture not as great as enrollment picture. Most important was the search committee report. Long time spent on this. All seemed appalled that we don't close applications until December 8th. Must speed up Ed Yale. Don's organization chart and long range planning took most time. Jim Applegate brought up the totally inappropriate matter of the office of the provost. This forced me to reply. Tacky. We have heavy work to do this fall—this year.

October 29-November 2, 1980: *I drove. Mr. Brian Cole of Christies was with us for a day. A tall, ebullient, pink-cheeked and Clarkson-eyed Englishman who pronounced our fine arts possessions, "not of an order for a study collection, but extremely collectible." The President's House gave us a whole new dimension to being at Wilson. We were able to take food down, and, though the house was missing such necessities as paring knives and salad tossers, we made do with the delight of children playing house.*

Notable other memories: good frank discussion on Friday night re the collections' sale, report of Christie's visit, what we can or cannot pay a president—an excellent executive session on Saturday late afternoon in which Don remained and several very interesting issues were aired— (1) Don's wish to give his staff some measure of job security for next year; (2) reflections on his organization; and (3) trustee dismay at the ornery qualities of the faculty, evident at the Co-op Committee where Vern

Buckles and Jim Applegate spoke for the group, asking for salary raises (while denying that they were): "we just feel you should see this chart that shows how low Wilson's scale is" and criticizing the development office—inexperienced, unprofessional. We felt there was an absence of the collegial feeling of last year, a forgetfulness that though jobs may not pay well at Wilson, nonetheless, the College is there and open. And we resoundingly supported Carol Tschop and the Development Office. Trustee Gloria Scott prefers that these matters be prepared for ahead of time to prevent such discussions, with their often inevitable brush with conflict. I feel, on the contrary, that, for this, airing of opposite views is healthy—for conflict is there and is more effectively dealt with in the open in executive session.

The Saturday night cocktail buffet's drama was the announcement, done in tandem by Trustee Ellie Allen and me, about our sale of Wilson's unused assets. The faculty responded well. The emeriti were anguished.

December 7, 1980: *Well, here we are again looking out on all the beauty here—the boxwood borders on the garden walk, the winding willow edges of the Conococheague, all silver in the winter sun. The haze of the Penn Hall farm lands beyond the fringe of Wilson trees. The President's House is so cozy with gleaming floors—silver service polished, beds made by Shelvey, dinner being brought in by the food service—a campus that unfolds beyond the windows, tended and lovely as an estate in England. How can we be unhealthy? We look so well.*

Christmas Vespers: *The chapel beautiful—scotch pines trimmed in red and white plus many candles made our gold and white chapel magical. The choir (only 12 last year) had over twice that many members. Professor Charlie Farris outdid himself, and the choirmaster was a gifted and enthusiastic conductor.*

January 1981: *It was a difficult meeting at the Lilly Endowment. The welcome was not warm. The VP for education at the Lilly Endowment,* *was with us... I was on my own from the beginning to explain why we were meeting. They did not ask questions; they merely sat there, awaiting my message with a kind of silent expectancy devoid of kindness. Well, I got my thoughts across: they know that the Beeman Report has caused us much difficulty. They also know that we are by no means a lost cause. And they informed me of two important things: one, that grants are no more given to private institutions; two, that there are a number of excellent workshops available to colleges which we might apply for. The bulk of their funding is in workshops and faculty development programs that help colleges to help themselves.*

By the interview's end, they did praise certain Wilson graduates and professors, but they never once wished Wilson College well.

February 17-18, 1981: *Went to Wilson to meet with the Middle States visiting evaluation team: Virginia Radley, President of SUNY Oswego; Patti Peterson, President of Wells, and the VP for Finance of Wellesley. It mattered, our going. Very moving moments— Virginia Radley complimented my article in AGB and Patti Peterson, in leaving, shook hands and said, "they're very lucky to have you as Chairman and, believe me, I know!" I was very deeply touched by these unexpected strokes. They complimented our faculty on the new curriculum and said too bad it took a crisis to produce it!*

April 29, 1981: *Drove to Chambersburg today. A gray wet day ... How pleasant to walk into the President's House and feel very at home—it smells so fragrant—the campus is so beautiful, with blossoms everywhere. Dinner for honors students at the President's House tonight. After dinner I went over to the Women in Management Workshop at the Science Center. It was a fascinating panel discussion—three men and three women. It was extremely stimulating—many viewpoints. Have the big room with the large screened porch and lovely big bath, comfort and a feeling of real pleasure to be here in this well-loved place for a few days of May Day and work.*

May 2, 1981: *May Day at Wilson: I often wonder in this women's world whether I could have managed life as a spinster. Last night I spent time with Helen Nutting—a brilliant history professor, known for her wit and her wise, caustic evaluation of people and events. She lives in a New England house across from campus. Her dog, Jeremy, is a renowned Wilson character. Those here in a college community live in a kind of extended family where Helen Nutting certainly is valued.*

Highlights: Letter to Trustees done for me in the President's Office. I have only to sign and send; lunch with Theony—a very frank, warm talk. Meeting with Theony and Mardi re Lilly Endowment. Moving toward a problem statement: how to plan for the future when the values and premises upon which Wilson was conceived and flourished traditionally are no longer either valued or deemed important? Meeting with Charlie Davison, Phil Cosentine, and Don Bletz at their law offices. We are being sued by a former staff member. Unpleasant. Supper here with Helen and then a superb concert by the choir and a play by the Kittochtinny Players. Living in an academic community is the best way to live on your own. Gorgeous May Day.

May 4, 1981: *The end of a busy, fruitful few days here at Wilson. Perhaps the most important thing was the meeting this morning with the President of Valley Bank, Sam Sollenberger, brought out to us by Sidney Palmer. We met with Don, Alan Sheely, Jim Hyatt. We borrowed $150,000 a few weeks ago. Now the business office wishes to get authorization for another $200,000 if we should need it—if, as Sam called it, "the worst case" should materialize; if the Christie's sale should return us $113,000 or less, rather than the $150,000 we've budgeted it for; if HUD funds are held up beyond our payroll date. Another worst case, Sam asked—what if you only have 100 new students instead of 130 in the fall? Don—after Alan had said this would mean $130,000 loss in budget—said, but we could find that we had a windfall too—a will—a gift. Then, reaching for Sam's respect, I said that money could not substituted for a student deficit. Truly we need that 250 students for more than the budget; we*

Chapter Four: Beginning Again 110 Years Later: 1979-1981

need it to create a stimulating student body; we need it to convince donors that we are indeed able to grow according to plan; we need it to become a true Wilson again. It is possible that Don and Sidney did not like this frankness. So in answer to what if? I'd say the Board will view any student deficit very seriously and meet as soon as possible. I truly hope we won't be faced with that problem. So now the bankers go back to their bank and decide whether we can borrow from them if we need to. I hope we won't need to. Don and I met at length over a number of things.

Yesterday's supper was a lovely time. It was warm, and the long shadows of late afternoon picked out, shaped, sunny circles on the President's House lawn and students sat there in groups—all colorful ... Nancy Besch, Pat and Don, and I stood on the veranda greeting each group who arrived through the boxwood hedges—in the dining room was a great buffet. I gave Mary Linda's (President Elect) greeting and my own remarks, ending with a note from May Day and Robert Frost's poem— Wilson was a path less traveled and I ended, "you have made all the difference."

Jack Apperson, commander of DESCOM with 42,000 people under him, is the two-star general living in the President's House—he commands DESCOM and has 42,000 people reporting to him. The campus rolls away gently under the gentle gaslights that mark the brick walks and the turn off to Penn Hall—great trees move their branches over these glowing centers—quiet is broken only by the occasional traffic slowing at the turn and the train across the valley. The experience of living here has been very happy for me. Our genteel poverty is a fact of life here.

June 7, 1981: *It happens like this—life becomes so stretched over a period that there is no time to record it—and soon it is lost to memory but for a few highlights. Since last writing the days have flown—there was the auction at Christies and its meeting time with Mary-Linda, a the merry luncheon with guests at the Metropolitan Club ... There was the May Board meeting, commencement, the trustee dinner for Don and Pat, with* *funny songs and perfect late afternoon sunlight in the President's house garden.*

In a personal email and telephone conversation between Dr. Bletz and the author on January 31, 2019, Don noted that Nan Clarkson was absolutely critical to the success that they enjoyed in the two years he served. He was and is grateful for all that she did.

The Search Process

From the Personal Journal of Nan Clarkson:

__The Search Committee__ work has been immensely involving. At first the various factions were defensive and always ready to bristle—the faculty snapped, the students looked bored, the Trustees snapped back. Not so now. We've spent so much time together. The system has been great. We had a great deal of fun. Sidney offered us his house, and it was a spacious setting for our interviewing. We'll remember hilarity over the cold of the dining room and the warmth of the living room—the candidate who said "where are you from honey" to the Chairman of the Board ... the other who called the students "kids" or Wilson "a girl's school" ... the one who bragged about his football team ... Nancy and me with flowers in our teeth ... going over folders at midnight (punchy with tiredness) in our nightgowns ... the sheer excitement of discovering a real winner ... Grant Palmer listening in ... the cat in the cupboard with the cornflakes ... Buzz Livas supporting psychological testing as another tool ... and after I called one of our candidates a turkey, Nancy pulling out a sign saying, "how can I soar with eagles if I have to work with turkeys?"

In retrospect my impressions of my meeting with Mary-Linda Merriam: "That will be our future President." She came on too strong at breakfast. The morning person probably doesn't realize how jarring it is to the night person, not comfortably awake at an early meeting, to be assaulted by excess enthusiasm, vigor, and radiant charm before appropriate amounts of coffee have been consumed. She seemed to me nervously eager, talking a blue streak, just too gung-ho. At the time I didn't know that she is an alumna daughter and that makes a difference vis-à-vis *her action, which was warmly expressed. In my early a.m. scrooge mood, it seemed excessive. But, when that young woman spoke of her wish to lead our College, laid out her plan, goals,* modus operandi—*it was clear that she had done her homework, was bright, articulate, purposeful—enough of a work-horse to be a wonderful role model to our often casual troops—and that she had deep emotional motivation to take us on and turn us around. It will take a very strong "other" to prevent her being my first choice for the Wilson presidency.*

January 15-18: *Presidential search continued. Wilson's meetings with the search committee went back and forth from the College private dining room to Sidney's house to the President's house. Interviewed four people—all of interest. An English woman, utterly fascinating—an actress "on stage," but with a mind and a capability to do the job that kept her listeners from dismissing her for all of her "poses." Another was a solid woman, salt of the earth, quite well-qualified. One was just excellent in so many respects, but he scared us by his admission that though he can work with people, this is not his overarching skill. A man of immense personal energy and confidence but a driver, a do- it-my-way person ... his wife looked utterly worn out by him. We could not risk him! A fourth from the Yale Divinity School—head of development—was a dark horse. Easy-going, pipe, nice wife, excellent credentials—turns out to be a finalist. I really do prefer Mary-Linda Merriam. This week Don said, after meeting the other candidate, "yeah, sure, I liked him but you know he seemed a fella a lot like me." The inference being that it's our chance to bring in someone new, different, more exciting. We learn a lot just from listening to what each candidate says must be done. I've taken heavy notes and, after the new President is chosen, must remember to get these together and list good ideas for him/her. Both finalists are going to spend days at Wilson and at Westport being evaluated by Dr. Jim Gillespie, an industrialist psychologist.*

March 14, 1981: *Today we elected a President at Wilson: Mary-Linda Merriam. She was my choice, though not without the realization that she was not the first choice of most of the faculty or staff. "She'll ruffle feathers," said her opponents. "It will be change that ruffles feathers," said Sidney, "not Mary-Linda." She has* *a better sense of Wilson College, I think. And she has the skills and capabilities to gain grass roots support for her efforts to bring about the needed change. It was an exhausting four hours debate. At the end, all had had their chance to speak. We took a roll call note, Woody Turner, our secretary, reading out our names alphabetically. At that point my hands shook and my knees shivered. The vote was not even close. Why had I been so distraught? Because at the end it was apparent to me that the other candidate would be wrong for Wilson now. The myth of impartiality had been shattered in the two candidates' presentations. It felt certain that MLM had what it will take to save Wilson if indeed leadership can do it and that the other did not.*

There was a time to remember in the other finalist's presentation: his wife, was there— uninvited by me, she simply came in and sat down. At the end of the question period, Ed Yale asked her how she envisioned her role as the wife of Wilson's President. This woman is a teacher who will have to give up her role as an independent women—she said something like this,—"Oh, I'll enjoy life on the campus—I would hope the girls will drop in—I can be a kind of counselor. I bake cookies—we have always been a team. I'd like getting to know people here—would see my role as being active in civic organizations here—travel? Why, whatever he has to do, of course." It was the creed of the dutiful wife, and it would be that supportive role model so common to the '40s and '50s, and so archaic in 1981, which she would bring to a presidency. Why were we few feminists so discomforted by this, with eyes cast down in embarrassment. And most others glowed with approval—the perfect wife! The litany of loving support. This was my own role—why was it distasteful to me in this situation? I'm still puzzling whether it was a personal distaste— best I think, it was that her very presence, let alone her statement, was a political act: it was calculated as a strength—as an evidence of something that is true, but shouldn't be "used" (in my value system) today—i.e., that with the other finalist we were getting two for the price of one.

Mary-Linda, in contrast, when questioned about her life as a single woman and what that would mean for Wilson answered, "I'd be a different kind of role model." A working woman. A woman who can achieve a presidency. An awesome example ... Lorraine Havens was the ultimate President's wife model. The Havens', even the memory of them standing on the garden walk between the box hedges—he reserved and presidential, she elegant, wise, and twinkling with a humor that saved her husband.

My Recollections

The Search Committee was composed of trustees, faculty, administration, students, and alumnae—in all, I recall 20 to 30 members, plus numerous other interviewers. The fact that over 100 applicants for a college that had received nationwide publicity for nearly closing is a real testimony to the reputation of Wilson. Mother loved Wilson College, although she had never been to a reunion and had not be an active alumna. Her lifelong best friends were with her at Wilson and I grew up with Wilson aunts. When I received the letter inviting me to apply for the Presidency, I was Assistant to the President, Dr. John Silber, at Boston University. I remember going to him and asking what I should do. He said, "apply because it will be good experience; you are young (36 at the time of the letter), and someday you will be a president." I hadn't really planned on being a college president, but I applied. It was an amazing process that included not only the interviews with the Search Committee and other groups on-site, but also what turned into a five- hour interview with trustee Dr. Buzz Livas, who lived in New Hampshire. After I became a finalist, they wanted a paper with my goals and plans for the College. I remember well writing the 22 pages with an emphasis on continuing education to broaden our market. More importantly and very unusually for that time, they asked for a day-long testing and interviewing process with Dr. James Gillespie, an industrial psychologist who did this work for corporations, including Graphics Control, whose CEO was the husband of the Chairman of the Board of Wilson, Nan Clarkson.

My response to their request to be tested was quick—I would be happy to do that under two conditions: I receive a copy of what he writes and sends to the Board, and that the document is shared only with Board members. The Chair of the Search Committee agreed to these conditions. In truth, after Mother and I read it, Mother's response was that she couldn't have done better herself in describing me! I had made a critical error in the mathematical testing and to this day I wish I could retake that test! Isn't it funny how out of all the positive comments and test scores, we often focus mostly on the negative!

The other memory I have is that Mother and Father had driven to Chambersburg to meet me after the Saturday morning interview. We drove to the Nittany Lion Inn in State College where we were going to spend the night before I flew home to Boston. I had been told that I would be contacted by 5:00 p.m. that Saturday with the outcome—positive or negative. We sat in our room and waited—5:00 p.m., 5:15 p.m., 5:30 p.m., 5:45 p.m., 5:55 p.m.! Finally, at 5:55 p.m., I said to my parents, "let's go eat our dinner, and we can get the message when we get back!" I was certain I was not going to get the job. As we were going out the front door of the Nittany Lion Inn, I heard my name being called loudly! I went to the desk and they said that they had a phone call for me which I could take in the lobby. The Chair of the Search Committee said, "Where were you!" "Well," I said, "you said you would call at 5:00 p.m., so we were just going out to dinner." He was taken aback! He told me I had gotten the job, and I thanked him. When I hung up, I remember feeling terror! I had really wanted to "win," but would have liked to call the other candidate and hand the actual job over to him! When I called Dr. Silber the next morning at 8:00 a.m., I said to him that I wasn't feeling joy, only terror. He said, "Mary-Linda, that is the appropriate response!"

What overcame the feeling of terror was both my own desire to succeed, the overwhelming and constant support of my parents, and the fabulous network of colleagues in administration I had built up over the past four years since the American Council on Education Fellows program in 1977-78!

In retrospect, what is now very clear to me, is that the determination, competence and sheer will of the Chairwoman of the Board, Nan Clarkson, and of a group of the Save Wilson Committee, led by Nancy Besch, who then became Vice-Chairperson of the Board, resulted in a thorough search process. The use of the industrial psychologist was far from usual practice in higher education searches at the time but the data were really useful to the Board. I believe that they felt *that they had one last chance to get it right. I will be forever grateful that I was the one chosen!*

In the *Tribune Review* (Greensburg, Pennsylvania), Monday, March 16, 1981, the following article appeared written by staff writer Paul Teske. (Reprint permission granted)

Jeannette Woman to Head Wilson College

Jeannette native Dr. Mary-Linda Sorber Merriam is looking forward to the "challenging experience" of assuming this summer the Presidency of Wilson College, the South Central Pennsylvania liberal arts college for women which survived a decision to close in 1979. "I'm very, very excited. It certainly is a challenge, but I really feel Wilson College has a real place in education," Dr. Merriam told the *Tribune Review* Sunday afternoon in a telephone interview.

She was reached at University Park, where she was visiting Penn State University friends the day after her appointment as Wilson President-Elect was announced in Chambersburg. Effective July 1, she will be heading the College from which her mother, Madeline Sorber, graduated in 1930. Her father, Everett S.C. Sorber, is a Greensburg attorney. The Sorbers reside at 119 North First St., Jeannette. At 37, Dr. Merriam will be one of the youngest college presidents in the nation and the 14th President of Wilson.

She will succeed Dr. Donald Bletz, who has been serving as Wilson's chief executive since May 1979. Wilson's Board of Trustees selected Dr. Merriam following her nomination by an 11-member search committee that screened more than 100 applicants during a nationwide search, the College said.

"In choosing Dr. Merriam as its new President, the Wilson Board of Trustees has made a clear choice for a strong, energetic and imaginative professional—a young woman who will provide the College with dynamic leadership in the years ahead," said Elisabeth Hudnut Clarkson, Chairwoman of the Board. "A person of impressive skills and personal capabilities, she had sound experience in small college administration and has apprenticed for 15 months with Boston University President John R. Silber, one of the best known and most articulate spokesmen for independent higher education in the country. This intensive experience of decision-making and problem-solving provides us with a remarkable capability to deal with Wilson's plan for growth."

That growth is continuing this year after a group of alumnae organized a "Save Wilson" campaign and waged a victorious legal battle to overturn the administration's decision to close the College two years ago because of decreased enrollment and increased operating costs. "Wilson is now in its 112th year," commented Dr. Merriam. "It has history, it has tradition, and I am very confident it will continue to grow."

Wilson had 110 students at the start of the 1979-80 academic year. With the largest freshman class since 1973, enrollment expanded to 196 last September. "It all looks very promising," said Dr. Merriam, in referring to the renewed interest of potential Wilson students and increases in financial contributions. She said 116 have applied for admission, compared to 51 at this time last year, and inquiries have soared from 3,300 to 6,500. Wilson is progressing on a five-year plan that calls for 500 students with 40 full-time faculty members. The College is still operating at a deficit, but Dr. Merriam said officials "have plans to reduce the deficit. I have confidence, I know that everything possible will be done. All the signs are good. There is positive movement."

As President, Dr. Merriam said her goal "will be to build a strong

Chapter Four: Beginning Again 110 Years Later: 1979-1981

linkage among the College, the community, the church, and the alumnae who have done so much." Dr. Merriam said she feels she has been "very lucky, very fortunate" in the experience she has gained in her career. "In the last few years I have felt that I wanted to return to a smaller College, and I have prepared by getting involved in various aspects of administration."

She had seven years of administrative experience at Emerson College in Boston, attaining the post of (acting) Vice-President for administration. She was appointed Assistant to the President of Boston University in November 1979. In that capacity, she was legislative liaison with state lawmakers on all matters relating to higher education, represented the university with or in place of Dr. Silber, and was responsible for other administration assignments. She also has experience in labor relations. After graduating with honors from Jeannette Senior High School, Dr. Merriam earned her B.A., M.A., and Ph.D. degrees in speech communication at the Pennsylvania State University. Early in her professional career, she was named research associate at Penn State's Individual and Family Consultation Center. She also has studied at Grove City College; at the Center for the Study of Languages in Neuchatel, Switzerland; and at Harvard University's Institute for Educational Management.

She holds memberships in several professional and civic organization including the American Association for Higher Education; the Academy for Academic Personnel Administration; the National Academy of Television Arts and Sciences, the Boston New England chapter; and the Boston Zoological Society.

She has been chosen for membership in Phi Kappa Phi, the national scholastic honor society; Pi Kappa Delta, the national forensic honor society and Rho Tau Sigma, the national broadcasting honorary society. She was an American Council on

Education fellow in academic administration in 1977-78, and was named in *Outstanding Young Women of America* in 1978.

Wilson now joins several other leading women's colleges in choosing a woman as President. **(end)**

CHANGING OF THE GUARD

In the 1980-81 Annual Report titled "The Turning Point," this was the message from Dr. Bletz:

The 1980-81 academic year saw a continuation of the rebuilding process begun in May 1979. Through this past year, we have worked hard to pursue the five-year objectives approved by the Board in 1979. These objectives have provided an essential focus for our planning in student recruitment, curriculum and faculty development, utilization of physical assets, and fund-raising. We have worked hard to turn our unused resources into income-producing assets and to maximize the effectiveness of the unique facilities we possess—such as the farm and the stables.

The academic philosophy at Wilson College remains rooted in the liberal arts tradition, but we have acted to bring the implementation of that philosophy into line with the present needs and desires of young women. For example, the most attractive programs at the College today did not exist in the spring of 1979.

Under the direction of Mrs. Elisabeth Clarkson, '47, Chairwoman of the Board of Trustees, we have been working hard to develop further our very active and devoted Board. Considerable work has been directed to the continued restoration of our ties with the Presbyterian Church, and our own religious activities on campus have been enhanced, most notably by the new "minister in residence" program. Our ability to deal with the unexpected has been enhanced as our administrative staff grew in experience and expertise. Indeed, I would probably describe the 1980-1981 academic year as one in which we moved from crisis management to a much more deliberate and, I trust, effective managerial style based on planning and thought.

To say that, at the close of the 1980-81 academic year, Wilson College's problems have been resolved and there is a clear road ahead would not be true. It is fair to say, however, that the pieces have been put back together and that there is real hope for the future, provided the entire Wilson College team of students, faculty, staff, Trustees, friends, and especially alumnae, maintain the spirit generated in the spring of 1979.

I look forward to continuing at Wilson College as a member of the faculty in the coming year. Dr. Merriam, our new President, has been in office three months as this report goes to press, and her talents as a leader have been clearly demonstrated. I look forward to service with her in our respective new capacities. (Wilson College Annual Report, 1980- 81, p. 3)

Chapter Five
SECURING THE FUTURE: 1981-1990

President Mary-Linda Sorber Merriam

I had the privilege of serving as President for ten years from 1981-1991. This chapter concludes with the October 1989 celebration, when well over 1,000 alumnae, friends and college community gathered in Laird Hall to celebrate the 10th Anniversary of the near closing and at that time declared Wilson to be saved. It does, also, include follow-up articles printed in 1990.

This chapter in Wilson's history would never had been as successful as it was without the devoted, competent hard work of Marian McAtee, Assistant to the President and liaison with the Board of Trustees; Dr. Patricia Cormier, Dean of the College; Karen Jewell, Continuing Studies; Carol Tschop, Vice-President of Advancement; Susan Waring, Dean of Students; Margaret Taylor, Director of Public Affairs; Kathy A. Torpy, Director of Alumnae Affairs; Kathy Lehman, Director of Conferences; Susan Matusek, Head of Library; Alan McKee, Head of Security and Dennis Wenger, Business Manager/Controller. While I single these people out for their leadership and extraordinary service, we are all in the debt of every single faculty and staff member from 1981- 1991. Without their willingness to do without pay increases, their exceedingly hard work and cooperation, and the flexibility in agreeing to and meeting the many changes we underwent, the College simply would not have survived. Enough cannot be said, also, about Ethaline Cortelyou who had no connection with the college but had read the story in the *New York Times*. She came to and lived at Wilson for at least three or four years and was the head of volunteer services. Many alumnae came regularly to campus to help in our beautification and to do other jobs that needed doing. She coordinated their efforts. Wilson College would not have had a future had it not been for all of these good souls!

As Dr. Bletz noted in his final message to the alumnae, quoted at the end of Chapter Four, there were plenty of challenges yet to be faced. Those with the financial means who felt the College should have closed withdrew their support. Some major foundations which had supported the College no longer wanted to do so since they were uncertain of its future. Many in the Chambersburg, foundation, and higher education communities felt we would be closed within two years. In addition, the College was under a "show cause" order by the Middle States Accrediting Association, which, if not removed, would have meant no financial aid for a student body in which 80-90% were dependent upon federal and/or state aid. In essence, it would have meant the closing of the College. Dr. Bletz had to borrow $470,000 of the restricted endowment in September 1980, during the reorganization period, with the promise of repayment. There were three pending lawsuits to be dismissed or settled. Above all, the need to broaden the market in order to get more students was the major order of the day.

As a team we set out to secure the future being guided by several broad objectives: ...

> **Building Trust:** In order to secure the future for the College, the only option—in my mind and in the minds of my senior

staff—was to build trust by providing accurate data and sharing all information that was not confidential, such as personnel information. The Board had to stand behind the President, but not blindly. Annual evaluations did occur and the Board was to be free to ask any questions of anyone and request any and all data. In the same vein, I had to trust the work of my senior administration and conduct annual evaluations. All problems and mistakes needed to be shared and, where appropriate, solved as a group. No one needed to be concerned about his/her job if they told the truth and accepted responsibility for the error. A valued and loved trustee once said, "Mary-Linda, I will always tell you the truth as I know it." There is such wisdom in that statement, since that is all each of us can do. What I know may not be the ultimate truth, but it is the truth as I know it with the information available to me at the time.

To the end of building trust and educating alumnae on the state of the college, I visited 22 alumnae clubs in the first year and shared the financial information in detail. Each year for the next three or four, an aggressive schedule of alumnae club meetings was met.

We had to face squarely the fact that many thought we had closed or, worse, would close soon. I needed to look forward—not back—no reliving of the past—just strategizing for the future. While relentlessly and truthfully optimistic, the challenges that lay ahead of us could not be understated.

Broadening the Market for Students: We needed to broaden the market for students while at the same time making whatever changes needed to be made to attract residential students. However, without reaching out to the adult market in a concerted way, the chances of increasing the enrollment of only residential women sufficiently and quickly enough seemed unrealistic.

Gaining Greater Visibility: Margie Taylor, Director of Public Relations, did a phenomenal job of keeping us in the media and in assuring that we connected with the audiences necessary for our survival. She and Carol Tschop agreed that as president I needed to be as visible as possible. To that end and over a period of time, they and the Board supported my serving on many boards locally, regionally and nationally. Many of our faculty and staff were actively involved in the community and professionally.

Establishing Financial Stability: In order to reorganize and keep the College running in those first two years, it was necessary for the Bletz administration to borrow $470,000 from the restricted endowment. We had to plan on repayment of those funds and to eliminate operating deficits. That was accomplished beginning in 1982-83. It was very important not to have operating deficits if we hoped to attract money from major donors, foundations and corporations. The physical assets of the College needed to be fully utilized in ways that increased revenue. Buildings that were closed needed to be opened.

Eliminating "Show Cause": We were able to have the "show cause" by the Middle States Accrediting Association rescinded on December 1, 1981, with the understanding that a periodic review report would be submitted on May 1, 1983, and a full report would be forthcoming at our ten-year visit in 1988.

In the Wilson Newsletter for July 1981, No. 16, titled The Legacy of Leadership, there is the following letter to alumnae and friends written by President Merriam:

> I cannot express easily the excitement and the challenge I feel of having been selected to serve as the fourteenth President of Wilson College. What an honor! To be given an opportunity to lead is a gift. To be given an opportunity to lead a college so

Chapter Five: Securing the Future: 1981-1989

beloved by those associated with her over the years is a gift to be treasured. Personally, the dedication of my grandfather to an education for women and the outstanding experience Mother (Madeleine Case, Class of '30) had at Wilson enriches my feeling of having been blessed.

Henry Heald, former President of the Ford Foundation, noted that alumnae are a college's living endowment. How fortunate Wilson College is to be endowed so generously, so lovingly, so courageously and so devotedly. Wilson daughters—whether in favor of the closing or against—displayed grit and determination.

I would like to take this opportunity to extend my admiration and gratitude to Dr. Donald Bletz and his able administration. His support and organizational abilities have assured a good transition. Without the wisdom, hard work and diligence of the faculty, Trustees and administration, we would not have nearly the legacy we now enjoy and upon which we must build.

The challenge lying ahead of us is awesome—as it is for all of independent and public higher education institutions. Wilson brings to her students a quality education in a highly personalized way. Of critical importance to us is a clear definition of our mission. We must continually define those elements essential to the education of women of all ages. We must both adapt to the changing times and exert positive leadership in changing the times. We must do this without losing sight of the essence of Wilson College. That essence includes commitment to the highest possible standards for a liberal education for women, the active involvement of the students in the governance of the College and the opportunity for all members of the College community—students, faculty, administration, Trustees, alumnae—to engage jointly in personal growth—moral, spiritual, physical and intellectual.

We need to expand our vision and to increase our enrollment. We will do this both through maintaining the excellence of our education and through the labor of every constituency of the College, recruiting students and sharing with them their own experience of Wilson. I join with all of you as together we seek new and common ground upon which to expand the vision and renew the dream of Aunt Sarah Wilson.

Dr. Mary-Linda Merriam, President Wilson College **(end)**

From Nan Clarkson's Personal Journal:

July 1981: Mary-Linda Merriam feels good about her first ten days. Just finished my first phone call with her. What bliss to hear a professional on the other end—she thinks (enrollment of) 230 is the best we can expect.

My first concern—my first slight altercation was over the subject of the inauguration. I was informed that the Alumnae Council would be held then too as well as Parent's Weekend. I questioned loosely, and probably defensively, the wisdom of intentionally crowding the campus so heavily. However, the goal seems to be to have a large crowd at the inauguration. In any event, Mary-Linda is a very positive person to have a difference with: she assumes a stance that is not black and white—offers new solutions, stands ready to listen, back and fill, retrench while still pushing ahead. It is not going to be all easy. But it will be a new way of operating, all to the good.

July 27, 1981: The first day back home. Well. Phone call tonight with Mary-Linda Merriam gives me hope. Yes, really—hope. She is firing a staff member—what courage! She is beginning chapel service on Wednesdays at noon—not compulsory but your President will be there! She is beginning courses for religious education professionals— she is excellent. We talked about our ways of dealing with our potential conflicts. I was so struck with the sincerity in her words: "I will be honest with you; I will never keep things from you—sometimes I'm in a hurry and forget to inform you but almost never!" She begs me to be utterly frank at any criticism I might have, and of course I say to her— "the same!" I cannot bear the thought of Wilson going under. Not just because of the College, no matter how one loves it, Rather the thought of all those who would love to see us fold. It may seem terribly unreal and visionary, but I dare to believe we might survive. Even more so after a phone call on July 31st at 5:00 p.m. Earlier that morning (the day she was to ask the staff member to resign), I sent her 1½ dozen roses saying "we never promised you a rose garden, but we do promise you loyalty, support, and appreciation. Signed, your Board of Trustees." She loved it on this tough day. But more, she did it, and our apprehensions exceeded the horrors of the task. She managed in a way that left them friends and the staff member a consultant to the Office of the President.

August 20-22, 1981: *Drove to Wilson ... and arrived at dinner time. Quick impression of the President's House with MLM installed: a new femininity, Victorian knickknacks, a huge four-poster in the master bedroom with white flounces and a pink, pale satin comforter at the foot. Pale Kerman oriental rugs on the floors but "my" room the very same. Sidney took us to dinner at the Cozy Inn—crab cakes and Greek salad— and back home to work until about 11:30 on our finances. Work with Marian McAtee, Assistant to the President and the Board of Trustees, getting committees set up. Visits to major administrative officers—lunch with MLM and Carol Tschop, Director of Development.*

Meeting with Sam Banks, President of Dickinson College, and Charles Glassick, President of Gettysburg, regarding the Central Pennsylvania Consortium. We bargained our ladylike way out of the consortium— we won our objective, saving our $16,000 membership fee for the price of withdrawing gracefully. In our current state of low SAT scores and lowering standards, sad but true, we are an embarrassment to them. Mary-Linda and I used all our wits to gain a fine solution to a painful problem. Friday afternoon later—meeting with MLM and Charles Smith, financial VP of Boston University, who is now our financial consultant—a gift from Dr. Silber—and a better man in this area and a more humane, personable one I haven't met. It is a new level of expertise for Wilson.

Dinner at Sidney's by the pool. Lovely. A little lavish for our small group, but warm relationships abound.

Executive Committee Saturday a.m. Cannot begin to describe in detail. Financial facts horrendous. Mood very low—worse than winter 1979. Deficits in both money and students abound. Woody Turner asks, "with all this, are we wise to continue?" MLM leaned forward and looked straight at him and said, "I just don't know. But there seems to be enough to justify a try." Then wave after wave of thoughtful analysis and projection—reports of wise things set in motion, actions taken. It's the effect of an expertise that we have never seen before brought to bear upon our circumstances. Little by little, I actually felt a lightening, or let's say a modicum of legitimate hope. Ed Yale could make a joke. Bob Brown could smile. Amazing. At the end of the meeting, we stood and clapped. It was a personal triumph for Mary-Linda.

5:00-6:00 p.m.: I watched MLM and Charles Smith (Vice-President for finance at Boston University) go through our audit—we're broke ... our net worth is $12 million.

October 1-2, The Inauguration: A well-packed, well-organized drive to Wilson. Howard Johnson's, room 114. Mary-Linda and I have dinner, work at a booth in the dining room at Howard Johnson's.

—Write speech. Attend inaugural forums. Meet with Professor Florence Bloom, Carol Tschop, Professor Helen Nutting, and Dean Theony Condos. The gist of the meeting with Dean Condos is that we have received one of about 38 invitations to the Lilly conference—25 will be chosen. Now is the time to settle what our final problem question is to be. My feelings or intuitions say they would like to ask us. So, our question must be good. I believe it should center on the woman's issue—more specifically, how best can Wilson move toward being a college _for_ women rather than primarily a college _of_ women. Went to Juanita's Side Door for dinner, owned by

Chapter Five: Securing the Future: 1981-1989

Susan Breakefield Fulton's mother ... Mary-Linda comes and "mingles." Dinner is good, dessert superb ... Back at motel a real hassle—no rooms for two Trustees who were late arrivals. I go to desk, "sound off,"—get in touch with Marian McAtee in the President's Office, and she gets room for one at the President's House and rooms for the other at Mardi's house. Back to room, which looks mighty cozy. Will (Clarkson) has a cold. It is so good to have him here for this great occasion in my life.

Times gone by—a magnificent inauguration It should be recorded for me to remember that the inauguration of Mary-Linda Merriam was also a moment of high ego satisfaction for me. Perhaps in my role of wife it is utterly unsuitable for me to rejoice in such a public moment. But I take pride in remembering words well read—a telegram from the President—a homily by the Governor, and my own small talk. It was well done, and that is a huge satisfaction.

Jack Keller was there—the Presbyterian Church pledged us its protection— Mary-Linda was <u>good</u>—I spoke from the book of Esther "who knoweth but thou wert brought to the kingdom for such a time as this?"

THE ALUMNAE

The changing role of alumnae can perhaps best be stated by quoting parts of the keynote address to the Alumnae Association by Joan Foresman Edwards, President in October 1985:

"... Our theme this year is Wilson College Today. You are well aware of the heightened level of activity on campus in recent history. During these years of transition, it has been difficult for alumnae to keep abreast of all the changes at the College. Led by my predecessors in this office, Jane Ensminger and Julia Billings, the Alumnae Board of Directors has attained the highest level of commitment in Association history. Never before has the alumnae presence been so strongly felt or so sorely needed at the College. The former Alumnae Council was renamed Alumnae Leadership Conference, not only to place emphasis on this leadership role, but also to identify and train new leaders. I think that President Julia Billings said it best in her 1984 annual report to the Alumnae Association: "It is clear that the role of the alumnae has changed dramatically in this half decade. We are becoming working partners with all who share the responsibility for the good health of Wilson." The key words are "working partners."

The reason we have assembled here this weekend is to explore that special partnership between Wilson and her alumnae and to reaffirm our responsibility to our beloved College ... I would like to cite some examples of direct alumnae involvement in the many new programs begun by the administration during the past six years (1979-1985): The Alumnae Student Compact (TASC) scholarships; Continuing Studies Division; Equestrian Studies Program; Conference program; community outreach programs including establishment of the Wilson Affairs Committee of the local Chamber of Commerce; the Institute for Retired Persons and the Wilson School of Gymnastics; re- establishment of our ties with the Presbyterian Church; successful pursuit of financial support from government and foundations; attainment of ranking in the top five women's colleges in the nation and 12th among all colleges and universities for participation by alumnae in annual giving (58.6%); establishment of Volunteer Services; campus restoration; student recruitment; the Aunt Sarah program; the development of an Alumnae Career Network.

I have just listed thirteen innovative programs initiated by or strongly dependent on alumnae involvement. All are vital to Wilson College Today. I cannot resist adding one more initiative to the list—namely the group of alumnae in Western Pennsylvania who found President Mary-Linda Merriam for us. I can't really say what role, if any, her alumnae mother and friends played in

Chapter Five: Securing the Future: 1981-1989

persuading her to accept the challenge, but we all know that it is difficult to say no to Wilson Women!

Although listing accomplishments gives much deserved credit and provides the opportunity to say thank you to all of you, my real purpose in describing this amazing women's network is to point out that we have attracted the attention of the outside world in a positive way which has a direct relationship to how the College is perceived.

1) ... in 1984, Wilson Alumnae won an Exceptional Achievement Award for Volunteerism in a competition sponsored by the Council for the Advancement and Support of Education.

2) That the Ingersoll Group—a top admissions consulting firm—spent a year on our campus and have affirmed that yes, Wilson can continue to attract students, and they have given us the tools to do it ... the workshop on admissions today will give you answers to the questions of why we do not have 500 undergraduates yet and why there is so much emphasis on non- traditional students ...

3) You will be hearing more about Ketchum, Inc. (fundraising firm in Pittsburgh), who have studied this College for a year and, as outsiders, have caught the spirit of the Wilson alumnae which resulted in their recommendation to move forward with plans for a capital campaign.

4) Another exciting coup for Wilson is that we will be included in the new book titled <u>The Best Buys in Higher Education Today</u>, by Ted Fiske, Education Editor of the New York Times. The book refers to Wilson alumnae as saviors and most likely the reason that the College will continue.

The purpose of the association in the By-Laws is "To advance the interest of Wilson College by assisting in the recruitment of students, the raising of funds for the College, promoting alumnae involvement in academic and student affairs, and participating in college policy development."

… Six years ago, we believed in Wilson College enough to save her. For the past six years, we have believed in Wilson College enough to preserve her. It is my sincere hope that we will all believe enough in the Future of Wilson College to ensure the next 116 years … **(end)**

The alumnae were active in both recruiting and retaining students. They were also very active in the formation of the Alumnae Restoration Committee which took the lead in restoring in 1984, Laird Hall, the Patterson Room, and the Admissions Offices. In 1984, the Alumnae Association's Save Wilson Committee won the well-deserved Exceptional Achievement Award of Volunteer Involvement from the Council for Advancement and Support of Education (CASE).

COLLEGE ADVANCEMENT

The reality of 1979-1991 was that without extraordinary unrestricted giving (including unrestricted bequests used for the operating budget when absolutely necessary) from alumnae, trustees, friends, and foundation and corporation gifts and grants, this College would not have survived. **Carol A. Tschop** and her teams over the years, deserve every bit of credit for our success. We had no mega donors—only small and medium ones. Maintaining the level of giving that the College reached and upon which it was dependent was no small accomplishment. Carol was director of development from the beginning; in 1985, the Office of College Advancement was created to include, initially, public relations, alumnae and development; admissions was added in 1987. Carol became the Director of the Office of College Advancement in 1985 and Vice-

Chapter Five: Securing the Future: 1981-1989

President for Admissions and College Advancement in 1988.

The Eden Hall Foundation in Pittsburgh played a major role early on by providing challenge grants for the annual fund. A major challenge in 1987 of $100,000 was fully met by the alumnae. They were one of the first foundations to help us when so many were afraid the college would not survive.

Jean Stapleton, a co-star of "All in the Family," and husband William Putch, of the Totem Pole Playhouse, brought fame to the College in 1987 by donating the William Putch-Totem Pole Playhouse and her own Jean Stapleton Collection, including her Emmy, to the archives. They also gave fundraisers for the College. Ms. Stapleton performed a one-woman show—*The Italian Lesson*—in 1989, raising $9,000.

Percentage of Alumnae	Participation	Total Gift and Grant Income w/o Cap. Camp.
1978-79	**28%**	**$ 839,110**
1979-80	50.3%	$1,371,799
1980-81	47.3%	$1,286,712
1981-82	47%	$1,487,333
1982-83	56.4%	$1,542,651
1983-84	53.6%	$1,460,861
1984-85	54.7%	$1,429,167
1985-86	58.6%	$1,196,334
1986-87	53.5%	$1,140,663
1987-88	54.2%	$1,100,000 (est.)
1988-89	46.3%	$1,069,990
1989-90	59.2%	$1,025,000 (est.)

In *Fund Raising Management*, December 1983, Carol A. Tschop wrote an article titled "Make Crisis Work For You: Wilson College Case History." (out of print) It is quoted here:

The editors wrote: "Back from the brink of officially announcing its closing in 1979, Wilson College in four short years is now in the black and among the top women's schools in its percentage of alumnae giving. One of the prime movers in this dramatic turnaround describes the dynamics of revitalization."

"Monday, February 19, 1979, was notable among the residents of many eastern states for the "Blizzard of 1979," an unrelenting storm which blanketed the region with nearly 20 inches of snow. Alumnae, students, and faculty of Wilson College, a small private liberal arts college for women in Chambersburg, Pennsylvania, remember the day for an equally dramatic reason. On this date, the Board of Trustees announced that, because of dwindling finances and rapidly shrinking enrollment, 110-year-old Wilson College would forever close its doors as a teaching institution.

At the time, no one could have imagined that this decision would unleash its own blizzard: a controversy resulting in a court hearing that reversed the Trustees' ruling ...

Almost five years later, Wilson College is not only open, but renewed, growing and optimistic. Although it would be an exaggeration to state that Wilson has achieved financial prosperity, or that all its dormitories are filled to overflowing, it is true that a remarkable turnaround has been effected in almost every facet of College operation.

Nearly a decade of deficit financing has been replaced with two consecutive years of balanced operating budgets (1983-84 will be third year of operating in the black).

Enrollment has grown from a total population (both full-time and part-time) of 145 in September 1979 to 313 this fall ...

A new core curriculum, combining a strengthened humanities/ liberal arts focus with coursework in management and technology is being readied for implementation in the fall of 1984. Capital improvements to the physical plant in the form of a $100,000 indoor equitation arena and a small animal holding facility, have enabled the College to inaugurate popular academic programs in equestrian studies and veterinary medical technology. An active conference program is responsible for generating much-needed operating income from previously unused campus facilities. A new Division of Continuing Studies has expanded the mission of Wilson College to include men as well as women students, most from the Chambersburg area, in its evening degree programs.

Fund Raising Program Grows

These improvements, which naturally reflect the dedicated efforts of many individuals working with the confines of radically curtailed budgets, were supported significantly by another tangible indication of Wilson's growing stability—its fundraising program.

Since 1979, income through gifts and grants has provided fully one-third of the College's yearly $4 million operating budget.

The alumnae and friends of Wilson College have consistently met this challenge with compelling results, among them:

- The annual alumnae fund has more than doubled since 1978-79, the year of the proposed closing. Alumnae contributions in 1978-79 totaled $225,700 and the percentage of participation was 28 percent. In 1982-83, gifts from alumnae totaled $575,600 and the percentage of participation reached 56.4 percent, a record for Wilson and one which ranks the College among the top five women's colleges nationally for alumnae participation in annual giving.
- Matching corporate contributions have increased from $57,000 in 1979-80 to nearly $100,000 in 1982-83.

- Foundation support has increased from $118,000 in 1979-80 to $276,000 in 1982-83.

- The College received notification of the largest federal grant in its history, a three-year award for over three hundred thousand dollars.

The growth of Wilson's fundraising program has evolved during a time of increasing financial difficulty for many small independent colleges. Despite the fluctuating economic climate and lingering public skepticism surrounding the near-closing and Wilson's chances for survival, the College has been able to inspire the confidence and financial support of increasing numbers of people. Wilson is recovering successfully from a crisis of great magnitude and is emerging a stronger and more vital institution.

It has been estimated that during the next decade hundreds of small colleges across the country may be forced to close their doors because of financial hardship coupled with a decline in the enrollment of traditional college-age students. Many of these colleges no doubt have much in common with Wilson—less than optimum enrollment, small endowment, fewer than 10,000 alumnae, limited financial resources and unavoidably high labor costs.

We at Wilson suggest that, although these conditions may indeed limit one's options, they can be used to advantage in building or rebuilding a strong fundraising program which will help to bolster an institution's stability.

Identifying a Strategy Base

Although the summer of 1979 presented many challenges for Wilson's new administration, three positive factors formed the basis of our fund raising and promotional strategy.

Chapter Five: Securing the Future: 1981-1989

1. The Cause: Wilson College, a small private liberal arts college for women, founded in 1869, has for most of its history enjoyed a modest but excellent regional reputation as an institution of high academic quality. By tradition and design, Wilson has always been a small college (its population normally ranging from 300-500 students), believing that a personal environment helps students to pursue and acquire a high level of academic performance and to develop leadership skills in an atmosphere directed to meet the needs of women. Numerous graduates have achieved distinction in careers not usually open to women; others have embraced more traditional occupations or volunteer community service with equal competence and zeal.

2. The Crisis: In the 1970s, Wilson almost succumbed to its own tradition and reputation, unable either to respond quickly to the demands of students for a career-oriented education or to recognize the opportunities for redirection and growth stimulated by the changing climate in higher education. Fewer students enrolled, administrative turnover was high, and the faculty were demoralized. By 1979, the problems appeared insurmountable and the demise of the college seemed almost certain.

3. The Constituency: A line from the Wilson College *Alma Mater* reads, "We are small but we are mighty." The truth of this statement was clearly illustrated in 1979, when alumnae mustered students, faculty, parents, friends, and the local community to begin the rebuilding effort. Most colleges feel justifiably proud of their alumni and consider them a living endowment of the institution. In Wilson's case, alumnae commitment was felt in many unusual

ways. Wilson graduates and their families volunteered as unpaid staff members, helping out in offices, on the maintenance and grounds crews and in reactivating idle Wilson College Clubs throughout the country. They responded to the need for operating capital by doubling alumnae giving in one year. They instituted a three-year Preservation Pledge Campaign totaling more than $1.2 million and actively helped to reorganize volunteer class agents who assisted in fundraising. Donations of furniture, equipment, automobiles, and many other items helped to refurbish the campus without draining the budget. Several alumnae who had been instrumental in guiding the "Save Wilson" committee to a successful conclusion became members of the Alumnae Association Board of Directors and of the Board of Trustees and are continuing their involvement in College activities.

Designing the Program

Clearly, Wilson College alumnae were the key to rebuilding an effective fund- raising program, not only through their own contributions, but also in generating other external support by their example. How could Wilson maintain and increase this level of commitment while distancing the College from the immediacy and drama of a crisis mentality? This challenge became the focus of the development and public relations program.

Fortunately, this focus became clear early on in our efforts to design a sound promotional program. Our development consultant ... insisted that the new administration begin its planning by producing a case statement for the College. He helped us identify and analyze the historical strengths and weaknesses of the College, understand the implications of each, and subsequently use our findings to plot a course for the future.

Attendant with this research of internal data was our identification of the external factors which could adversely affect Wilson's chance of survival and growth.

Finally, we had to offer convincing and defensible reasons why individuals other than die-hard Wilson romantics should invest in us.

This exercise was, I believe, the single most important task undertaken by the Wilson community during the early days of the new administration. The case statement enabled us to base our strategies upon concrete information and not just gut instinct. We learned to define ourselves as a college and to separate commonly held perceptions from fact. We began to understand the impact that Wilson College had on the public it served, and why alumnae so fiercely supported the College in times of adversity. Once we could articulate what Wilson College was about, and why it was important, planning our case for support was infinitely easier.

Formulating the Themes

There were essentially two recurring themes which were emphasized to alumnae and the general public. First, the traditional strengths of the College, those which produced the tremendous outpouring or affection and financial support, were to be cherished and preserved. Wilson's mission was not only noble but necessary in an increasingly complex and confusing society.

Secondly, we sought to minimize the damaging effects of the near-closing by taking an "open for business as usual" approach.

After all, in spite of the uniqueness of its situation, Wilson was really just one among many small colleges struggling to cope with common problems of shifting enrollment patterns, limited financial and human resources, declining fiscal stability and an unclear image of itself. The problems, numerous and worrisome all, were not insurmountable.

To begin with, Wilson's record of alumnae giving had certainly been respectable through the (in 1979) 28-year history of the annual alumnae fund. The percentage of participation had averaged 35 percent between 1951 and 1979. In addition the major building blocks of a successful annual giving program were firmly in place and had become part of the Wilson tradition.

Reactivating class gift competitions, class agent solicitations and the pursuit of leadership gifts was not as difficult as we had feared because of the thorough and important work of our predecessors. The new development staff re-established their model, then set about trying to refine and enlarge it to meet the growing demands of the College. We began by raising the gifts of our already committed alumnae and using their example to stimulate foundation and grant support.

Implementing the Strategies

In 1967, the Wilson College Society had been inaugurated to honor leadership gifts to the College at three circle levels: $100-249, $250-499, and $500 and above.

During Wilson's Centennial year in 1969, a fourth circle was added to commemorate gifts of $1,000 and above. The gift levels had remained unchanged since that time.

Two factors led us to believe that it was appropriate to upgrade the society levels. First, the amount of alumnae support had been extraordinary. Many individuals doubled or even tripled

Chapter Five: Securing the Future: 1981-1989

their annual gift because they realized Wilson's immediate need. Secondly, in 1978-79, the national average alumni contribution to private four-year colleges exceeded $100 for the first time ($105.01).

Since 1979, three changes in the Wilson College Society have helped to promote new interest in our development program and have generated increased gift income:

*A $5,000 circle level was instituted in 1980-81 and attracted 26 charter members its first year. Membership reaching 30 in 1982-83 and is expected to increase again this year.

*All remaining circle levels were upgraded so that society membership now begins with a contribution of at least $200.

*Last year (1981-82), the Wilson College Charter Club was initiated to acknowledge those whose gift is at least equal to the age of the College ... The Charter Club provides the means for its members to belong to a recognized gift club while steadily increasing the level of their contribution at an affordable rate.

Although one year's performance may not fully predict the success or failure of the Charter Club, the results have been encouraging. Fully half of the more than 1,000 donors who had normally given $100 per year joined the Charter Club.

Many increased their gift by more than $13; others aspired to dual membership in a circle as well as the Charter Club. Still others whose gifts had never reached $100 were attracted to the concept and increased their gift accordingly.

The new gift levels were promoted by means of an inexpensive but effective two- color brochure and reinforced by subsequent ads in regular alumnae publications. The yearly annual fund appeal format was revised from that of general letters to printed "theme" brochures with photographs. These appeals emphasized Wilson's traditions, the strong sense of community among students, faculty, and alumnae, the quality of a Wilson Education as evidenced by alumnae career achievements, and the present and future needs of the College.

The most pressing need, financially at least, was for operating income, and this, too, was presented clearly and often. Alumnae realized that money for salaries, fuel bills, and other daily expenses had to take precedence over more attractive and lasting gift opportunities. They responded in record numbers and many suggested cost-saving methods of streamlining the fundraising program, One such method goes against a basic tenet of successful fund raising, but it has worked well for Wilson's unique situation.

We added a space on the return wallet-flap envelope of each appeal for the donor to indicate, "To save the College postage, please do not acknowledge. My canceled check will be my receipt." Last year, approximately 90% of Wilson's 3,730 alumnae donors checked this box and saved the College nearly $800 in postage. We published a general thank-you in our November 1983 *Alumnae Quarterly* so that alumnae were made aware of how much we appreciate their helping us to stretch our budget.

In addition to their willingness to contribute unrestricted annual gifts, alumnae actively supported an innovative student aid program called "TASC," designed by Dr. Marilyn Mumford, '56, who served Wilson as provost from 1979-81, while on leave from Bucknell University.

First introduced in 1979, the TASC plan stands for The Alumnae Student Contract because it was conceived originally as a means by which groups of alumnae could pool their financial resources to underwrite some of the expenses of a student who would otherwise not be able to attend Wilson. Later the program was expanded to include as sponsors not only alumnae but also service clubs, church organizations, professional societies, women's groups, and private foundations.

The unique feature of the program is that each TASC scholar who receives aid agrees to become a sponsor herself for four years after she graduates, thus investing in a younger woman the same faith her sponsors invested in her ...

Because we are a small shop on a limited budget (approximately 3.5 percent of the College budget), we've adopted one cost-saving technique that allows us to remain responsive to requests for information but relieves the sometime overwhelming paper flow. The members of our professional staff have 5"x7" note cards printed with their name, title and the College logo. These cards are used to handle short routine correspondence............
and are hand-written. This idea, actually used initially by our President, has saved countless hours ... as well as 7 cents in postage. This year other campus offices have adopted this inexpensive and personal means of communication ... Many alumnae have complimented us on this procedure, remarking how nice it is to receive a personal note instead of "official" correspondence.

Investing in the Future

The tremendous amount of alumnae support has not been lost on current Wilson students who have a much greater awareness of and are more involved with the annual fund than their predecessors. The alumnae and development offices have instituted inexpensive and enjoyable activities for the senior class to introduce them to the joys and responsibilities of "alumnaehood." At the conclusion of festivities (for seniors), class members are asked to sign a pledge card promising

$100 to Wilson by the time of their fifth reunion—an average of $20 a year ... the class of 1983 boasted 81% participation in last year's annual fund ...

Conclusion

The most recent long-range plan of Wilson College, written in (the fall of) 1981 and reaffirmed last spring, was guided by seven planning assumptions, one of which is quoted here: "For the College to be sustained and strengthened, Trustees and executive leadership must be pragmatic, creative and dynamic; the faculty and professional staff must be competent, resourceful and flexible; the students and external constituencies must be informed, motivated and responsive. All must work in concert to ensure the educational and financial viability of the College."

Those of us involved in the development and public relations program have worked hard to make that planning assumption a daily practice in our own operation and in our relationships with other campus offices.

The administration's strong leadership, its team approach to management, and its attention to planning and detail have been essential factors in our effort to meet the financial needs of the College. Although the visibility and importance of our program was greatly increased in 1979 and remains a top priority of the College, all of us in fundraising realize that to continue to be successful, we must go beyond simply raising money or putting on a good face to the public.

We must work closely and supportively with faculty, students, other administrators, and alumnae. We must seek to serve in better ways the various functions of the College, particularly the academic program, for in do doing we improve our ability to promote the College and to generate increased support.

Chapter Five: Securing the Future: 1981-1989

I have been told on several occasions that the near-closing of the College might well have been one of the best things that ever happened to Wilson. Although I wouldn't go that far, I do believe that the crisis mobilized the Wilson community more quickly and effectively than would have been the case without such dramatic circumstances. We have been able to sustain the momentum through concerted positive action.

It is our hope that other small colleges can avoid the problems which led to Wilson's predicament in 1979. But, should they arise, they can be solved. Wilson is living proof. (pp. 22-27) **(end)**

From Mary-Linda Merriam Armacost's Personal Recollections

Perhaps my most vivid memory was Christmas 1983. We were $25,000 short of being able to make payroll. I had attended a recent meeting of the Pennsylvania Association of Colleges and Universities and had met the Exxon Foundation's CEO. Unbeknownst to me, they gave periodic presidential discretion grants. That Christmas the foundation sent us $25,000! We met payroll!

I was on the road quite a bit—visiting over 20 Alumnae Clubs each year for the first few years in order to present our financial situation and our need for their active involvement in fund raising, recruiting and mentoring our students. Both Carol and I felt that it was important that I be out and about asking for money and also very visible in organizations. It was amazing to me how many people both in Chambersburg and throughout the country equated the health of Wilson with my state of mind, which I might say was eternally optimistic.

Carol and I had many laughs—some rueful. There was the time she stood at the graveside and gave our deepest sympathies—only to discover that it was the wrong funeral and no one there had a clue who she or what Wilson College was. Then the time that she was visiting an alumna to ask for money and when she used their bathroom, she got locked in and couldn't get out. Too embarrassed to call for help, she climbed out the bathroom window and presented herself again at the front door!

We made some mistakes—like the time she sent me to Florida to meet with an alumna whom she had researched and felt had substantial funds. When I got there, it seemed without question that not only was the person in no position to give anything much less a major gift, but also that I had best buy the bagels for our breakfast.

I was on the road so much visiting alumnae, friends, foundations and serving on national, state and local community boards that gave maximum visibility to the College that after about five years of my Presidency, at a faculty meeting, a faculty member said that all I cared about was money; I didn't care about them. I felt very sad about that remark, but the budget was so dependent on fund raising and the need for visibility for the College, that I certainly couldn't argue with the fact that I was off campus a good bit. The saving grace was the extraordinarily competent senior administrative team that kept College operations going!

Title III grant, Strengthening Developing Institutions

In June of 1982, Wilson College was chosen to receive federal grant funds under the U.S. Department of Education's Title III program. Nearly 1,000 institutions applied for this grant and it was awarded to a very few. Over a period of three years the College received $327,000 with $144,000 allocated for 1982-83. The purposes were to plan and implement programs to enrich the curriculum, to strengthen the admissions operation and to expand the career planning and academic advisement areas. This grant was critical to the programs needed to start the Division of Continuing Studies.

(I received the phone call while I was interviewing Dr. Patricia Cormier, an American Council on Education Fellow from the University of Pennsylvania. I wanted her to choose Wilson for her placement as Assistant to the President. As she tells it, it was the phone call where I was literally jumping up and down that convinced her to come to Wilson College.)

National Endowment for the Humanities Challenge Grant - 1984

This was awarded to us with the challenge to match the $45,000 three to one, generating $180,000 for the implementation of the new core curriculum in the humanities.

The Capital Campaign of 1984-86

It had been more than 20 years since the College had had a capital campaign. The campaign's theme was "Standing as One," and it was co-chaired by Eleanor Martin Allen, '49, and W. Bennett Connor, Jr., both Trustees. Mrs. J. R. McLain King, '23 (honored with the Distinguished Alumnae Award in 1984 and an honorary degree in 1974 and a College Trustee for 24 years), and The Reverend Dr. Edward L.R. Elson, Trustee Emeritus (Chaplain of the Senate for many years and on the Board of Trustees of Wilson College during the Havens Presidency), served as honorary Co-Chairmen of the campaign. Chairman of the Family Gifts Division: Nancy A. Besch, '48, Chair of the Board of Trustees; Chairman of the Trustee Gifts: Candace L. Straight, '69; Leadership Gifts Chairmen: Jane Everhard Murray, '67, and Peter Mazur, member of the Board; Chairmen of Major Gifts: Charles S. Tidball, member of the Board, Sue A. Tompkins, '59, member of the Alumnae Association Board, and Jane Troutman Ensminger, '52, former Trustee and Past Alumnae Association President.

The goals, which were exceeded, were for Physical Plant ($1,529,810); Academic/instructional ($200,000); and Endowment ($2,000,000).

The Capital Campaign permitted the College to address new roofs and boilers, up-dated electrical systems and much painting. A contract with VIRON, an energy management company, provided the College with heating controls and energy conservation measures which will be financed over the next ten years. The campaign also funded large animal and small animal facilities and rooms for surgery for the Medical Veterinary Technology program; and 56 personal computers and a large DEC PDP 11/44 computer with 13 terminals.

From the Wilson College Newsletter, Winter 1986, written by Carol A. Tschop:

> The Capital Campaign received an early and enthusiastic endorsement from Wilson's faculty and staff when the Family Gifts Division began solicitation last fall. All members of the full-time faculty, administration, and staff were informed of the purposes of the campaign and were asked to make their own pledge by the time the Board of Trustees convened on campus last November (1985). The response was overwhelming. One hundred per cent of the faculty and eighty-five percent of the staff committed their support to the campaign, yielding cash, pledges and planned gifts totaling nearly
>
> $325,000. These results set new employee campaign records among non-profit organizations nationwide. Vice-President and Dean Patricia P. Cormier chaired the faculty gifts campaign. Staff solicitation was led by Director of College Advancement, Carol A. Tschop, '72.
>
> "I came to Wilson College three years ago because of the people I met here and their exemplary commitment to this fine College," Dean Cormier said. "Their response to the Capital Campaign is a dramatic illustration of the depth of that commitment." Ms. Tschop added, "Until now, Wilson has been noted primarily for its alumnae giving. The success of our faculty and staff solicitation for the Capital Campaign adds a new dimension to our program. We're very, very proud of this accomplishment." **(end)**

My Personal Recollection

> *A vivid memory, when we were selecting capital campaign counsel, is of Carol Tshop and I meeting with Bob Carter and another senior member of Ketchum, Inc. It was a Saturday morning and we couldn't afford to heat Norland Hall on the weekends, so we sat in our coats, holding cups of hot drinks for the entire meeting. Ketchum felt we couldn't raise*

more than $2 million—we were already exceeding $1,000,000 a year in annual giving— among the highest in the nation—but Carol and I said in one voice, "No, $4 million is the goal." **The campaign yielded $4.3 million.**

THE DIVISION OF CONTINUING STUDIES

Dr. Nancy Ricks, Assistant to the President for Continuing Education, Conferences and Extension Programs, led a task force including faculty in a three-month study including interviews with community employers and leaders, reviews of employee and community interest surveys, a compilation of current data on demographic trends, a review of educational programs at neighboring institutions and other women's colleges, and an analysis of market potential. The Board, at its May 1982 meeting, approved the creation of a Division of Continuing Studies, separate from the undergraduate program, and approved the associate degree in supervision and management as the first degree to be offered within the division. The structure was intentionally separate from the undergraduate program since both men and women could earn degrees. The goal also was to limit the number of associate degrees in the women's college to one in medical veterinary technology, which also had a four-year option.

This was not without controversy. One new faculty member organized the students in the spring and they wore buttons saying "Question Authority!" Students were worried about the effect the Division would have on the Women's College. At the faculty meeting in early May, the faculty voted down the Division. At the meeting at the end of May, after all but the graduating seniors had departed, the Division passed with only two negative votes and one abstention. This meant that the President and the Faculty could and did recommend the division and the new associate degree program to the Board—a united front!

Continuing to grow the Division meant staying up with the needs of the area. Over time there were new associate degree opportunities added. In 1986, the Adult Learning Program to complete a baccalaureate degree was developed; and the Teacher Intern Program, in 1985, was designed to earn teacher accreditation after having obtained a baccalaureate degree. All programs were well received and popular. Associate degree programs were expanded to include Accounting, Management, Liberal Studies, Management Information Systems, and, of course, Medical Veterinary Technology also in the Women's College. Certificate programs were offered in Entrepreneurship, Small Business Management, and Business Communications. Scholarship assistance became available.

To extend the regional reach of the College, we established a relationship with Harrisburg Community College and offered courses on their campus. Over the years we offered courses in five locations regionally: Harrisburg, Carlisle, Newville, Camp Hill, and Gettysburg.

At the start, 70% of the students in the Division were men; in 1990, 75% enrolled in credit courses through the division were women.

ENROLLMENT

Growing the enrollment in the residential women's college was always a major challenge. In the fall of 1981, the College employed Stein & Associates of Atlanta to conduct a marketing study and to develop new admissions publications which subsequently won awards for them and the College. The trends for enrollment in women's colleges nationwide were decreasing over the decade. In 1985, the decrease for women's colleges nationally was 12%; Wilson, 12.6%. We had lost our admissions director in November 1981, and in 1982, a new admissions director was employed. In 1984, The Ingersoll Group Inc. of Colorado was retained as admissions consultants.

In 1986 through November of 1987, Elms and Associates were under contract to run the admissions office.

Chapter Five: Securing the Future: 1981-1989

My recollection: The enrollment in the women's college was always a major and worrying concern. A bit of levity (and despair) came when one of the consultants working with us was housed in Norland in the McClure Room. One night she swore a ghost appeared to her. The next morning she left the College! Well, who knows!

Financial aid was a critical factor in recruiting students, and in September 1981, 84% of the student body required aid, with 67% receiving aid from the College funds. The threats to cutting financial aid on the federal and state levels were real since, even though not yet enacted, parents were more fearful of looking at private colleges facing cuts in financial aid. The Editorial in the *Public Opinion*, titled "Education cuts pose high risk," reads in part:

> Wilson College President, Dr. Mary-Linda Merriam, carried an important message yesterday to a U.S. Senate subcommittee on education, which is considering changes in financial aid for college students. Although subsidized student aid is generally considered safe for another year, some deep cuts are expected in the federal education budget for 1986. Merriam, in testimony before the subcommittee on Education, Arts and Humanities, recommended the government continue financial aid programs for needy students—but not to the exclusion of middle-income students whose families can demonstrate need for such aid. **(end)**

Between 1979-80 and 1990-91, the women's college enrollment grew from 146 headcount to 191 while the total enrollment grew from 146 headcount to 874. It is fair to say, however, that small colleges were at some peril – especially those with enrollments under 1000, small endowments, and in rural areas. To quote from the **March 5, 1982, Wall Street Journal article by Burt Schorr, titled "Small Colleges Struggle to Survive in Face of Aid Cuts, Population Shifts"**

"… in the next few years, many of those [colleges] with 800 or fewer—about one-third of the total—could find themselves in [bad] straits or out of business entirely. A fact of life for all college administrators in the 1980s, along with inflation, is the steadily declining number of college-age Americans. In the northeastern and midwestern states where many of the independents are located, the drop could total 30% or more by the end of the decade."

YEAR	WOMEN'S COLLEGE TOTAL		CONTINUING STUDIES		TOTAL	
	HDCT	FTE	HDCT	FTE	HDCT	FTE
1979-80	146	125	0	0	146	125
1980-81	196	180	0	0	196	180
1981-82	237	222	0	0	237	222
1982-83	215	213	50	17	265	230
1983-84	208	206	105	35	313	241
1984-85	198	195	120	39.5	318	234
1985-86	188	182	145	50	333	232
1986-87	177	173	236	85	444	275
1987-88	190	188	349	130	539	318
1988-89	177	174	525	173	702	347
1989-90	176	175	616	218	792	393
1990-91	191	190	683	242	874	432

Please note that FTE means full-time equivalent enrollment and HDCT equals headcount.

A real public relations bonanza for the College occurred when we were listed in the college guide titled "The Best Buys in College Education," by Edward B. Fiske, education editor of *The New York Times,* **released in October 1985 by Times Books. This is a guide to colleges that offer high quality education at a reasonable cost.**

CURRICULUM

Dr. Patricia Cormier came to the College as Assistant to the President in 1982-83; she became Acting Dean in 1983-84 and from 1984-1988 served

Chapter Five: Securing the Future: 1981-1989

as Vice-President and Dean of the College. It is hard to overestimate how much she was loved and respected. She was responsible for leading the faculty in the curriculum design and implementation from 1982-83 until her resignation to take a position in Philadelphia in 1988. Lynn Kelley served for one year as Dean followed by Professor James Applegate, who guided the College with distinction from 1989 through the change in Presidency in 1991.

In a March 10, 1985, article in **the *New York Times* titled, "Wave of Curriculum Change Sweeping American Colleges," Dean Dr. Patricia Cormier** is quoted as saying: ... Other reasons cited for the changes range from internal faculty policies to marketing and recruiting needs at a time when the number of 18-year-olds is declining. Dr. Patricia P. Cormier, Dean of Academic Affairs at Wilson College in Pennsylvania, which has a stiff new general education program that takes up half of a student's program, said, "We need to be able to say exactly what a Wilson College graduate knows and can do."

The major needs were to strongly combine the core liberal arts with relevant majors and to reduce the number of majors that could be supported. Adding new majors that met student demand was critical. In total, the reorganization of the curriculum resulted in 13 majors plus a self-designed option. The core curriculum, developed in 1983 and implemented in 1984, had three cores: the inner core challenged students to understand key factors in the development of human culture through courses in ancient and medieval cultures, history and philosophy of science and technology, comparative contemporary cultures and the preservation of planet earth. The middle core ensures competencies in English, use of computers, quantitative skills and a foreign language. The outer core required electives not related to the student's major.

Veterinary Medical Technology was begun in 1979 and accredited in 1984; a four-year baccalaureate degree program was developed in 1984—at that time, the only four-year veterinary medical technology program in Pennsylvania.

With the initiative of Dr. Bletz in 1979-80, and his recruiting Col. Alfred Kitts, the College was able, in 1982-83, to replace the newly designed two-year equestran degree with a four-year bachelor's degree with two areas of concentration: Equine Management Track for those interested in the horse industry; the Equestrian Riding track for those interested in riding and the teaching of riding. The Olive Delp Overly, '42, Indoor Equitation Arena made year-round teaching and competition possible.

Cooperative agreements with the College of Allied Health Sciences of Thomas Jefferson University in a 2 plus 2 program—two years at Wilson and 2 years at TJU—and with Georgia Institute of Technology in engineering gave additional opportunities to our students.

Business and Economics, also begun in 1979, expanded, and communications was added.

Again, building on a Bletz initiative encouraged by Dr. Mumford, we extended our invitation for students from Chambersburg's Sister City, Gotemba, Japan. In addition, through President Merriam's mother's connection, we established a sister college relationship with Aichi Shukutoku University in Nagoya, Japan, in 1989, and welcomed 32 young Japanese women into a five-week program in English as a Second Language.

STUDENT AFFAIRS

Susan Waring, Director of Career Planning and then Dean of Students, contributed so much to the College. She set up a mentoring program and matched alumnae with students for half-day sessions in the spring and fall to help them identify academic requirements for specific careers and worked tirelessly with alumnae involving them in many ways in the lives of students. Wilson College was one of the founders, in the early 1900s, of the Honor Principle. While students held to it academically, the social part of the Honor Principle was much more difficult and very important. Susan Waring and her team, and those who followed her, worked diligently to see that the honor principle was respected. The area of career planning was constantly enlarged since it played a critical role in recruiting students and it preparing them for placements when they graduated.

It was Susan's idea and hard work that allowed us to establish the premiere child-care center that later set the stage for President's Jensen's program on Women with Children.

BOARD LEADERSHIP

There was no question that the Board took charge of the College from 1979-1981 in ways that would not have happened under ordinary circumstances. Part of my challenge was rebalancing the roles of the Board and the administration. Building trust through honesty, sharing of information, access to the campus, and a clearer definition of roles was essential. There is no question, however, that the new President was concerned about fund raising and about the role of the Board in that endeavor. The Board Chair had real concerns about the role of the President in influencing Board actions. Those concerns were not unfounded. As a first-year president, it was unusual and according to some articles—very dangerous—for a new president to meddle too much in changing the composition of the Board. I was guilty of that given the concern for raising the funds that we desperately needed and given the budget cuts that we had to make. Nan questioned my suggestions about the number of Trustees and who should or should not be invited to return; following up on financial gifts promised from Trustees; and an idea about having the executive committee be chaired by someone other than the Chair of the Board. And I quote from her journal: *"Building a strong Board should be a priority for both of us. And it is probably true that a tension between the President (who is, surely, responsible for the College to an extent) and the Board (which is ultimately and legally responsible) is inevitable and creative. Within limits, healthy."*

I can't think of a better Chair for that first year than Nan Clarkson. We were able to speak candidly with one another and give and take on all of the decisions. Under very difficult circumstances, we worked hand in glove towards the end goal of making sure that Wilson College was indeed saved! Nancy Besch, who followed her as Chairman, was also fantastic to work with as was Ellie Allen. As President, I was truly blessed by three superb Chairmen during my ten years: Nan Clarkson (1981-82), Nancy Besch (1982-88), and Eleanor Martin Allen (1988-91). They questioned, argued and challenged me and when we arrived at decisions or courses of action, they were in total support.

From Nan Clarkson's Personal Journal—her last six months as Chair of the Board

> *January 22, 1982: ... to be Chairman of Wilson's Board of Trustees has been a total immersion for the last 2¾ years. Now it is nearly over, for Nancy Besch will take my place in June—my final year on the Board will be far more relaxed. It is the responsibility that has been so heavy. I have worked so hard toward its survival. We've raised money; we got ourselves an excellent President; we achieved the Lilly Endowment invitation to the workshop; we got our Middle States accreditation—all these are such strong achievements. But every year is a terrible struggle. Right now, I see distressing signs—student morale that is low and vocal; faculty coolness to the President; enrollment figures behind last year (even though annual giving is ahead so far). We've given it everything. If we "make it" then my spirit will glow. But if we cannot (and most of me, reading all the figures, all the national forecasts in a depressed economy and educational trends away from our type of place, says we probably cannot) then I pray, truly to finish my term of office before that decision must be made. Cowardly, perhaps, but realistically knowing that a closing would be better received if Nancy is Chairman than if I, an "old Trustee," was in charge. Even though I am well aware that my leadership has been key to much that we have achieved. And, oh, how I have loved these years.*

Chapter Five: Securing the Future: 1981-1989

February 5, 1982: *It has been a remarkable time. Oh, how I love "my Board." Each one so different, so utterly indefensible in a piercing light—so un-trustee-like, but how effective—how able to be the force behind this struggling College. Long remember the admissions committee, with it's new, mustachioed, plain-speaking, serious-eyed consultant. Long remember the Nominating Committee—an hour at least on revising the minutes of the Philadelphia meeting—wisely so. Long remember Mary-Linda's and my supper meeting last night—in which I candidly told her my angst at more than three matters in the Nominating minutes. All my worries were erased when it became apparent that Mary-Linda was more worried than I about my concerns—and that she has a genuine desire to work together well. Given that underlying motivations we can move mountains.*

Nan: "I thought it was a good meeting." MLM (very earnest) "We've never had one that wasn't!

The Board meeting went <u>very</u> well. At least the business part in the morning. Mary-Linda presented her report and her case for continuing education with more emphasis on men's enrollment. With government aids of all sorts to students, we simply must find new sources of students to recruit. The Board accepted in concept. Sidney began his financial report saying it was the first time he had real confidence in what he was reporting! All the committee reports were upbeat. The new head of student government is impressive.

After the tea with students, we went over to Sidney Palmer's for dinner with my casserole and Jan Livas' ham and salad. We all then went to see the play in Laird which was the best I've seen at Wilson and attracted a huge audience.

Such a busy day—flashes of memory: Susan Breakefield Fulton's locomotive laugh; Mary-Linda's lovely garnet velvet jacket over pale rose slacks; Woody Turner's immobility during the faculty bylaws discussion fiasco; Stanley Stillman's useful explanation of a situation that was

Greek to me; the embarrassment and sadness about Don May's and Bob Crist's leaving the Board; the fine new member—Nancy Morrell.

Mary-Linda came back to my room and we talked until 1:30 a.m. We covered matters such as the need for us to deal with her contract in the May meeting and the importance of contingency planning for September 1982. There was our President looking half her age in a pink satin quilted robe and gown and at some point in the conversation thinking of possible closing saying, "they won't put us in jail, will they?"

We left her this morning, sleeping in her big four foster bed in her big President's house with all the big problems of saving Wilson College. I drove the many hours home wondering if we can "make it" through the next year.

February 9, 1982: *in writing my thanks to so many at Wilson, etc., I decided to write to Leslie Smith, the vivid young actress who is a freshman at Wilson and thinking of leaving to go to a place more centered in theatre studies. I wrote about Alison's career ... At Wilson you have the opportunity to be a very big fish in a little pond—to produce, direct, star and even initiate productions—to add zest to theatre life at Wilson—to be a wonderful leader. It would be wonderful for Wilson if you'd think of giving us at least one more year!"*

April 15-16, 1982: *Washington, D.C. Flew down on Thursday and had an appointment with Bob Gale, AGB President—a call on Wilson's behalf and a very nice visit. At the Sulgrave Club, an hour with Mary-Linda. She gave me the latest news of the College, but mostly we worked on her evaluation, preparing for her contract, etc. Exec committee meeting at Jack Myer's office from 10:00-3:00 p.m. About 15 present; Agenda: Presidential evaluation, budget preliminaries, and talk about assessing our institutional health in the fall. Mary-Linda is optimistic.*

Wilson College Board Meeting, Reunion and Commencement Weekend: *It began with dinner with Mary-Linda ... it was clear to me that Mary-Linda had laid herself on the line for continuing education, that my last*

Chapter Five: Securing the Future: 1981-1989

meeting as Chair of the Board had several challenges stronger than any yet encountered— (1) to finish the ratification of the bylaws, and (2) to see that our Board supported its President. That Thursday afternoon, the faculty had voted all but 2 negative and 1 abstention, to support the continuing education division implementation. Only the students held out, overwhelmingly against it, thinking that it will change the nature of the College. And they're right. But without it and the extra students we trust it will bring us, we simply cannot survive. Mary-Linda believes this clearly, and though I have real doubts (differing class price scales, etc.) and concerns (will our own students get short-changed?), I see that we must give it a try.

Well, Friday morning Charles Smith, the V. P. from Boston University, came and had breakfast with me and drove me out to the College. We had a fine buildings and grounds meeting. Lunch with students in the dining room; after it I went and sat down with a new professor who has evidently politicked a good deal vis-à-vis *the continuing education matter. He is a very slight young man with good features, pocked skin and pale blue eyes, cold and luminous, with a kind of hostility even when he smiles. He's one of the four to go to the Lilly workshop. Wise or not, I decided to talk about the controversial subject of continuing education with him. He feigned neutrality. My intention was to assure him that the Trustees, too, were concerned and would inevitably back the President, notwithstanding. We would monitor it closely, for we were as much as he was concerned for Wilson. It was a curiously unsatisfying encounter. He's full of ego and has become a hero to students, stirring up their political feelings against this issue. He may have done real harm.*

The afternoon was full of meetings—nominating and then finance and then the long- drawn-out and contentious ed policy committee in which the continuing ed division proposal was discussed at length. With a student leader taking a strong adversary position. At one point, when another student said that some might not return if continuing education was voted in, I said with some heat, something to the effect that it would

397

be a sad thing if Wilson women would thus punish their College, thereby assuring its demise— also something about disagreeing but then accepting differing views. Even as I spoke up I could sense that Mary-Linda wished I would shut up. Her dismay showed. That means, probably, that she does not believe that feelings are legitimate to be expressed in dignified meetings. One's demeanor, especially if one is Chairperson of the Board, should be grave, thoughtful, cool. Above all, non-disclosing. Later, checked with Nancy about my brief impassioned comments. "It needed to be said," she agreed. After a while I left the meeting. After all, my Trustees were all gathered over at Sidney's house, and we were even by then one hour late. Plus my reuniting classmates were dining all over town and I wanted to finish with Trustees and see them.

It was pouring rain when a group of five arrived, raincoats over heads and I rushed out to meet them, thinking it the lagging ed policy members. Not so. It was the Kennedy family—all five arrived for the weekend when Louisa would be being presented an honorary degree. As the family had its roots deep in Chambersburg history, they were absolutely enchanted to be there and we had soon drawn them into our group. Tom Stewart had Princeton connections with them and I privately felt very self-congratulatory, for it was I who discovered their Chambersburg connections in a New Yorker *article about the hostages—an interview with the senior Kennedys that mentioned Mike's Riddle great grandfather who founded the railway between Chambersburg and Harrisburg and for whom Riddle Hall was named. Louisa, his wife, is now a trustee, too, so it's been a fortuitous connection.* (Note: Louisa Kennedy was the national spokesperson during the Iranian crisis. Her husband Moorhead (Mike) Kennedy was the highest-ranking hostage.)

Finally, the ed policy people arrived, and after they were given a quick drink, we sat down to dinner.

And then something happened which I'll never forget. They surprised me. Everyone sat down and Nancy Besch took over—I was surrounded

Chapter Five: Securing the Future: 1981-1989

by beaming faces—and Nancy, recounting the memories of my role in these past three years in a beaming, affectionate recollection. Why, my knees shook, it was such an unexpected and touching thing. They then presented me with four Chambersburg prints on the bottom of which the artist had sketched a small, personalized medallion. The one of Norland Hall had, of all things, my likeness in the medallion. Of course, I replied— all I remember saying was that, apart from marriage and family, this had been the most significant involvement of my life, and thank you. Nancy Besch, Betty Bikle and Ellie Pethick had been the spirits behind this, and I was just overwhelmed with gratitude. That was my first and undoubtedly only moment of being so honored. My only regret was that Will wasn't there.

Afterwards I walked back to the campus and, as the alumnae program was over, went looking for my class. My whole reunion had moved to the snack bar where they were having a step sing and 1947 was leading it.

Saturday, May 29: *I banged the gavel opening my last meeting as Chairwoman of the Wilson Board. By lunchtime, we had finished our business, and the continuing education division was approved. At 12:30 we went as a full Board to the Alumnae luncheon. I sat with my class. When class gifts were given, three TASC scholarship were given by the class of 1947 in honor of Nan Hudnut Clarkson for all her contributions to Wilson. Once again, I was truly, deeply honored.*

The Trustees reconvened at 3:00 p.m. Draft #4 of the by-laws was voted in after discussion of each section. The afternoon was very hot and outside there were many distractions—groups of alumnae, whose chatter could be heard through the open windows, and once, George Mason called out, "hey, look," and there was the daisy chain forming, laying out its "W" formation on the lawn in the courtyard, then shouldering it to process down to the banks of the Conococheague where the seniors awaited them for the lovely traditional ceremony of songs and dances. Flies buzzed, people got up to get ice water, they sighed heavily and looked put upon, but section by section of the new bylaws we ploughed through. As Chair, I urged on, encouraged, pushed and cajoled—Woody Turner provided the perfect counterpoint, and at 5:38 p.m., we completed the task which has been my major preoccupation and was now my swan song.

Will arrived and we went to the President's House for a very special party. All the platform party for the commencement ceremonies were there including the Kennedys and the Keller's—Judge Keller was the speaker. The Trustees and class of 1947 made for a huge crowd. And this was my time of true regret—so many to see, so little time—such crowded space. But it was a lovely party—elegant, lovely food tables out on the terraces in the balmy night. A kind of social culmination to my years of being Chairman and indeed obtained for us by that fact. Afterwards Will and I went over to the front of Riddle where my class gathered and sang.

Sunday, May 30: *It was time to robe and line up for the academic procession. Will had been lunching with the Kennedys. He sat with the Sorbers right behind the faculty. We processed in, not knowing exactly what to expect. Would the faculty glare, would the students refuse to shake my hand, would the senior President use her speech to lobby against continuing ed? All fears groundless. The senior President spoke with dignity and love for her* Alma Mater; *the faculty smiled; Helen Nutting cocked an owlish marshal's eye at me and whispered, "hiya, honey." (This is an in-joke from our search committee days) and as for not shaking my hand—all shook my hand warmly and Mary Conboy was one of the ones who gave me a big hug. Wonders never cease.*

I presented the second annual trustee award to Betty Blackadar and she received a standing ovation. No one could have deserved it more. I think she really felt the love and gratitude and honor that flowed up to her from students and faculty and her class and the whole crowd. The thought of Betty not being on the Board is beyond me. It's been ten years at least, maybe more, counting her year in Germany. No one could more embody a Wilson woman; no one has given more to Alma Mater.

Judge Keller gave a fine address. He called the seniors "survivors," and spoke wonderfully and realistically about these past three years and what is to come. These were the young women, he said, who stayed with us when the College reopened; he spoke of the hardships they've experienced and their contribution to Wilson. For those who expected more erudition or more elegance, I suppose there was disappointment. Will was one of these. For me, it was Jack—a fine man—speaking his heart about an amazing chapter in his life and using the survivor image to send out with the class of '82.

On Wednesday, June 30th, Wilson got the Title III grant which is an incredible boon, especially in this coming year."

THE CHURCH RELATIONSHIP

We had a pastor-in-residence and a simple Wednesday noon worship service right from the very beginning. The arrangements for a pastor/seminary student serving our students varied over the years. Many Presbyterian churches sent their young people on mission trips to work on projects for the college. The Synod of the Trinity re-established Wilson as its meeting place for its two-week Synod School. Founded by two Presbyterian ministers, the church relationship was very important to the College. The college joined and subsequently I was on the Executive Committee and then became the President of the Association of Presbyterian Colleges and Universities (APCU) with 70 institutions and 74,000 students in 26 states. I had the honor of chairing the committee that recommended to the General Assembly that they have a Commission on Higher Education, which was subsequently established in 1989.

In the Synod of the Trinity newsletter July/August 1986, it was noted that I was the first woman President of APCU, and I note that "my goal during my tenure as President (of APCU) is to further the relationship between the Presbyterian Church (USA) and the 70-members of APCU by working with the national church to place appropriate emphasis on higher education in the new structure as the church reorganizes." Presbyterian churches in the tri-state region were generous in having me preach—extending the reach of Wilson College.

COMMUNITY INVOLVEMENT

In 1984, the Pennsylvania Governor's Private Sector Initiatives Task Force awarded Wilson the Keystone Award of Merit for its outreach programs.

- **The Wilson Child Care Center, opened in 1985,** was entirely the initiative of Dean Susan Waring. It served the local community and ran year-round. Serving 50 pre-schoolers, it was widely regarded as the best program in the region.

- **The Institute for Retired Persons**, began by Dr. Hal Schaffer, served over 200 people.

- **Non-credit courses and programs through the Division of Continuing Studies** reached a peak enrollment in 1990-1991 of 898 persons from the local community.

- **Summer Enrichment and Exploration Day School (SEEDS),** begun in the summer of 1989, served more than 220 local children in its second year—summer of 1990.

- **Cumberland Valley School of Music** used our college facilities.

- **Conference facilities**—over time from the summer of 1982 and in July of 1983, Synod School returned to Wilson and again became the traditional home for the synod schools—two week-long events every summer. We also welcomed in 1983 the Mormon Youth Conference, the Presbyterian Senior Citizens from New York City, the Rudolf Steiner Institute, and a United States Department of Agriculture meeting. That summer alone, over 1000 people visited the campus.

Chapter Five: Securing the Future: 1981-1989

For the majority of 1981-1991 years, Kathy Lehman did yeoman's work in the growing numbers of people who came on campus for weddings, meetings, and conferences. By 1987 the College was hosting approximately 8,000 persons annually. Those from out-of-town contributed to the local economy.

Many faculty and staff were very involved in community affairs and we welcomed community organizations and events to the campus. As President, I was involved locally and regionally as a member of the Board of Scotland School for Veterans' Children; the Chambersburg Hospital as a member and as Vice-Chair; member, Vice-Chair and Chair of the Board of Directors, WITF, Inc.; the Blue Ribbon Committee, Borough of Chambersburg and Chair of the sub-committee on meeting the needs of the low-income; President of the Chambersburg Area Council for the Arts; Board of Directors of Sprint/United Telephone; Board of Directors, Cumberland Valley Foreign Policy Study Group.

In the July 17, 1986, issue of the *Public Opinion*, there was an article by Keesha E. Lawson titled "Wilson generates economic, cultural benefits to area." (Reprint permission granted) It is quoted in large part as follows:

> Chambersburg businessman Robert Sollenberger is proud of his chance to do some work for his favorite movie star, Jimmy Stewart ... A picture of Dr. Mary-Linda Merriam, Wilson's President, presenting the plaque to Stewart, hangs in Sollenberger's store ... "Wilson College is definitely an attribute to the area," says Tammy Sollenberger. That attribute, according to Wilson officials, goes beyond educational and cultural contributions to Franklin County and surrounding areas. Wilson is, they say, an important economic part of the community, adding $4.9 million to the community in the 1984-85 academic year ...
>
> Wilson's financial impact involves large and small businesses, including South Penn Motor Club, Kline's PhotoShop, The

Little Shop, and The Art Center, as well as the Borough of Chambersburg ...

According to Wilson's figures, the College's 1984-85 budget was $4.3 million. "Most, if not all, of that money goes into the local economy. It's the money Wilson spends to keep its doors open," said Merriam.

Expenditures by conferees and other groups boosted local spending to $4.9 million. The figure was derived by adding actual purchases plus estimates of spending by conference groups and students.

Spending by Vale National Training Institute and Pennsylvania Minor Judiciary Board increase the amount spent to $4.9 million circulated in the local economy from outside sources in 1984-85.

Wilson's payroll was $2.2 million last year, exclusive of fringe benefits. Nearly all that money stayed within the Franklin County retail zone because very few employees live outside a 25-mile radius of Chambersburg.

College students spend an average of $600 per year beyond tuition. Wilson's enrollment in 1984-85 was 318 students. Their spending added an additional $120,000 to retail revenues.

Employee payroll, local purchases and student spending resulted in more than $3.8 million going into the local economy.

The College is also having its first capital campaign in 20 years, "Standing As One: A Campaign for the Future of Wilson College." Its goal is to raise $4 million ...

Wilson is the 11th largest employer in the borough, according to statistics supplied by the Chambersburg Area Chamber of Commerce. College employees paid more than $24,000 in local borough taxes (exclusive of real estate) while the College paid $289,500 in borough utility bills. **(end)**

In the *News-Chronicle*, Shippensburg, Pennsylvania, Monday, October 19, 1987, by Jeanne Toney, "Wilson College continues to offer many community services" (Reprint permission granted)

"Wilson College in Chambersburg experienced a time of troubles and doubt in the 1970s ... Today President Mary-Linda Merriam gives tremendous credit to the acting administration that followed the court decision. Interim President Donald Bletz, Dean Theony Condos, and Dr. Marilyn Mumford were in charge, after President Margaret Waggoner's resignation. They provided two years of consolidation, hiring new faculty, getting students back, raising money ($1.3 million in pledges) and keeping the College together. Also, a presidential search was carried out during that period and resulted in Dr. Merriam's appointment as President.

The 1960s were years of growth in the nation's colleges, followed by a downturn. In the 1970s, most colleges began to take seriously the problem of gaining more students and more revenues. At Wilson, a new approach came only after the school had gone through its period of self-analysis, court action, and administrative turnover, some 110 years after its beginning in 1869.

"In 1981, we began aggressively to market Wilson so that we could more fully utilize the campus," the President said. The campus is heavily utilized at the present time, and facilities which are not used are rented out to corporate tenants.

In 1982, the faculty voted to establish the division of continuing students which today has 349 men and women in degree-granting programs. "The faculty," says Carol Tschop, Director of College Advancement, "firmly believes in the rigor and overwhelming value of a good solid liberal arts education as a foundation. With levels of modern technology, we needed to institute more practical courses and skills" to supplement the liberal arts program. Today all Wilson baccalaureates must meet proficiencies in foreign language, a specialized major, and an interdisciplinary program that combines flexibility with study of current issues and traditional knowledge.

New major programs were introduced to balance the heavily weighted liberal arts program. These include veterinary medical technology, business and economics, communications, and equitation.

Bringing the liberal arts curriculum "into the 20th century" has enhanced recruitment in the 1980s. Vice-President and Dean of the College, Dr. Patricia Cormier, says there are 190 women living on campus this year. That's an increase from the low almost 10 years ago. In 1965, there were 252 entering freshman; this fell to 55 freshmen in 1978. In one year, 1979-1980 there were 28 freshmen and a total full-time enrollment of 107. The next year that increased to 152 total full-time students.

As college attendance declined in recent years, especially in the women's colleges, Wilson has been able to counter that trend. "Overall, the College has survived because it has achieved a reputation as one of the best buys in education," says Dean Cormier. It is listed in a nationwide compilation of educational "best buys." But survival is due also to the efforts of an administration that redefined College goals and made difficult decisions …

Minority students are actively recruited—"we have a mission," they say—and regularly Wilson contacts potential students in San Antonio, Baltimore, and Washington D.C. Foreign students are recruited through the Institute for International Education, and this year they come from India, Sri Lanka, and from Gotemba, Chambersburg's sister city in Japan.

Wilson has an alumnae/student mentor program which opens prospective employment doors to Wilson graduates. And for the second year, Wilson has sponsored a business/college day for students with declared majors. They intern for a day with community business. Explains Margaret Taylor, director of public affairs, 'they learn about the practical aspects of career choices and come away with a clearer picture of what is involved for them personally.'" **(end)**

PHYSICAL PLANT

Under the Bletz administration Rosencrans and Disert, two unused dormitories, were rented out and remained rented out throughout my administration to Vale National and Minor Judiciary, both offering educational programs. In addition, the College rented space to the Wilson School of Gymnastics and the Penn Laurel Girl Scout Council, Inc.

The capital campaign yielded over $1 million to upgrade the physical plant including new electrical systems, boilers and roofs.

Alumnae Hall, largely unused since 1974, was razed and resulted in additional, vitally needed parking space for students enrolled in the Division of Continuing Studies and for visitors. Warfield Hall, the primary classroom building for years, was closed in 1979 and reopened in 1983.

As agreement of sale was signed in 1987 for 32 acres and four buildings on the former campus of Penn Hall Preparatory School were sold for a retirement center with an option to buy an additional 37 acres. This left the College with more than 120 acres of the original 200 acres of the Penn Hall property for its programs. The equestrian program was moved across the creek.

FISCAL DISCIPLINE

Fiscal discipline was the order of the day and involved balancing the operating budget using some unrestricted bequests where absolutely necessary; utilizing physical assets to generate revenue, maintaining a very high level of fund-raising of over $1,000,000 a year, and increasing enrollment. In 1980-81 the percentage of the revenue that came from tuition and fees was 22% (student headcount 196) and from contributions, 34%; in 1988-89, tuition and fees accounted for 35.8% and contributions, 24% (students headcount 702). Financial aid had to be kept under control; the $470,000 owed to the restricted endowment had to be repaid and the plant fund deficit had to be eliminated. It was all accomplished. Above all, the College could not permit itself to go into debt.

ACCREDITATION

In 1988, after an exhaustive review of all the College's operations, the Middle States Association of Colleges and Schools granted continuing approval for full accreditation to Wilson College. Surveys of alumnae who attended Wilson in the post-1979 era showed they were more satisfied with their education than are students from a national sample of colleges who answered the same survey questions.

Chapter Five: Securing the Future: 1981-1989

!!!!1989!!!!

1989 WAS A YEAR OF CELEBRATION CULMINATING IN OCTOBER WHEN 1,500 ALUMNAE, FACULTY, STUDENTS, FRIENDS, TRUSTEES, STAFF CONGREGATED IN LAIRD HALL TO ACKNOWLEDGE THE SAVING OF WILSON COLLEGE!

The 1979 graduation was marked by tears of joy and exhilaration. The Homecoming for Alumnae, October 13, 14, 15, 1989, was also an unbelievable experience for all of us privileged to be there. As at the graduation, where there was a sense of wonder and gratitude— we had made it! The end game in both cases had been far from assured.

Wilson College: TEN Years of Accomplishment, 1979-1989, published by the Office of College Advancement, March 1989

Letter from Mary-Linda Merriam, President

"Last May 18th, the Wilson community gathered on Prentis Green to celebrate ten years of accomplishment. We planted a pine and a maple tree. And between them buried a time capsule to be opened on the College's 200th birthday in 2069. The festivities were a joyous symbol of the new life given to Wilson ten years ago, and a reminder of the sacrifice and stewardship which has brought us to this occasion.

It has been a rewarding ten years for those of us privileged to have played a role. As we look back, we do so knowing that the past serves to motivate the future. We have ample challenges ahead with no lack of problems to solve. I am convinced that the strengths of the past will be those of the future—hard work, loyalty and commitment of alumnae, faculty, Trustees, friends, staff, and administration working together to continue to make available a liberal arts education of high quality, shared in a very individualized and personalized manner.

Small is special. This is what places Wilson among a select few colleges in the country. The success of our graduates shows that mentoring system of education that fully engages students is a dynamic process. This past year 99% of our students applying to graduate or professional schools were accepted!

Let us reflect upon some of our accomplishments of the past ten years:

- The College for Women has remained stable in numbers but has increased in the quality of the student body as measured by SAT scores and rank in class. As of this writing, the SAT averages of the entering freshmen class are 1022—nearly 100 points higher than eight years ago.

- The growth of the Division of Continuing Studies has brought diversity and numbers to the academic program of the College. Begun in 1982, with 50 women and men registered in credit courses, the division enrolled 525 students last fall. In addition, each term another 250-300 students take non-credit courses. Total part-time and full- time enrollment in credit courses has grown from 125 in 1979 to 702 in 1988.

- An outstanding record of giving among our alumnae, ranging from 50-58% in eight of our last ten years, has kept us among the top women's colleges in the United States. Alumnae have generated $5.8 million over the last ten years for our Annual Fund, and have established other initiatives, including the Aunt Sally student pen pal program, the alumnae Student Contract loan program (TASC), and new alumnae committees on undergraduate student relations, admissions and development. The Restoration Committee is accomplishing much-needed redecorating on the campus. In 1987, devoted Penn Hall alumnae banded together under our *aegis* to form the Penn Hall Alumnae Association.

- The reorganization of the curriculum brought about the foundation of a core liberal arts program for every student, comprising one-half of the graduation requirements, and including two years of a foreign language. The number of majors was reduced in line with recommendations from the Middle States Accrediting Association. New majors were added in Veterinary Medical Technology, Equestrian Studies, Business and Economics and communications. Associate degree programs were added in the Division of Continuing Studies in Management and Supervision, Computer Information Systems, and Accounting. The Middle States Association of Schools and Colleges fully re-accredited Wilson College in 1988, when it came on campus for the ten-year visit.

- Ground floor Prentis has been renovated to accommodate an excellent Child Care Center serving 65-70 children throughout the year. This program is becoming increasingly utilized as a part of our educational curricula.

- The creation of the Museum of Natural History attracts several thousand school children a year to campus and is a point of pride for us all.

- The effective utilization of our campus now contributes over $600,000 a year to our budget of $5.8 million. An active conference and special events program brings 7,000-8,000 people a year to campus.

- The College is on a firm financial footing with a record of balanced operating budgets for the last eight years. We have eliminated a $562,000 operating deficit. The sale of

37 acres and four buildings on the Penn Hall property allowed us to eliminate a plant fund deficit of $393,000 and to establish a Plant Fund Endowment of $450,000. Complete repayment of the $470,000 loan from the restricted scholarship endowment and the consequent lifting of the lien placed on the Wilson campus have been accomplished. Our endowment now stands at $5.6 million.

- As a result of the 1984 Capital Campaign the College addressed such pressing needs as new roofs, boilers, updated electrical systems, and much painting. Facilities for a Medical Veterinary Technology program—a large animal facility, a small animal facility and rooms for surgery – were added. We have 56 personal computers and a large DEC PDP 11/44 computer with 13 terminals. A contract with VIRON, an energy management company, provided the College with heating controls and energy conservation measures which will be financed over the next ten years.

OUR FUTURE

Our future is now, and it is exciting. We must raise more money in our Annual Fund each year to give in financial aid—our goal for 1989-90 is a record $1,025,000. We must increase the levels of faculty salaries. We still must upgrade our physical plant, and are currently making plans for relocating and expanding our equestrian center onto the farm.

Also, on the horizon are plans to renovate McElwain-Davison and the Dining Hall Platform to accommodate a Student Commons area with rooms dedicated to student activities. New furniture for the dormitories is badly needed.

Just as you have played a vital part in the past ten years of accomplishment, we trust you will be actively involved in our future. I look forward to working with you as we meet the newest and latest challenges.

Mary-Linda Merriam, President **(end)**

U.S. News **Ranks Wilson Among the Best,** Wilson Alumnae Quarterly**, Fall 1989, Vol. 62, No. 4**

Wilson College is ranked fifth in the Northeast among regional liberal arts college, according to *U.S. News & World Report's* special report "America's Best Colleges."

The liberal arts colleges were ranked by the magazine in five key areas: (1) quality of the student body as measured by each school's selectivity; (2) faculty quality; (3) reputation for academic excellence; (4) financials resources; and (5) ability to retain and graduate students.

"We measure our success as a college by the success of our students and graduates. Wilson's listing in 'America's Best Colleges' affirms what our alumnae tell us," said Mary-Linda Merriam, President.

"Our faculty emphasize teaching. They are committed to helping students stretch their abilities to think and reason and communicate. Faculty-student interaction is a key ingredient in the learning process at Wilson," Merriam said.

"At the recent educational conference called by President [George H. W.] Bush, the point was made that smaller schools often provide better learning environments for students.

There is value in being small, and students are the beneficiaries," Merriam said.

Of Wilson's graduating class, over 90 percent of the students who applied to graduate schools were accepted.

This College is among the most productive in the nation for graduating women who go on to earn the Ph.D. in the natural sciences.

Wilson was founded shortly after the Civil War as Pennsylvania's first college for women. Today it has two divisions: the College for Women, for residential students, and the Division of Continuing Studies, which offers programs for adults. **(end)**

Alumnae Quarterly, Fall 1990, Vol. 63, No. 4

U.S. News Ranks Wilson Among the Best for the Second Year In a Row!

Wilson College is ranked among America's best colleges for the second consecutive year, according to the latest *U. S. News & World Report* special report released recently. Once again Wilson College is named in the top ten regional liberal arts colleges in the North in the special edition of "America's Best Colleges." Wilson ranked eighth overall among 73 regional liberal arts colleges in the North. It ranked fourth in the area of student selectivity and ninth in faculty resources.

Wilson Ranks in Top Ten Nationally in Annual Alumnae Participation

Wilson College ranked eighth nationally for alumnae participation in annual giving in a survey recently released by Centre College in Kentucky.

With 59.2 percent participation for 1989-90, Wilson was the top ranking Pennsylvania and women's college in the survey ...

"Women's college no anachronism: Wilson survival underscores enduring nature of its specialized role," written by Dr. Mary-Linda

Chapter Five: Securing the Future: 1981-1989

Merriam, *The Patriot News*, Harrisburg, PA, Thursday, June 15, 1989, quoted in full. (Reprint permission granted)

TEN YEARS AGO, Wilson College nearly died. Some had thought the small, first-rate Liberal arts college for women—then 110 years old—simply wasn't going to make it in the age of co-ed mega-universities.

Wilson never closed, however. The College lives because so many alumnae, friends, foundations, and corporations declared that Wilson had a role to play in the system of higher education in this country. Their support gave us time to pay our debts and turn red ink to black. And that we have done.

That's why, beginning this spring and continuing through October, the Wilson College family is celebrating ten years of remarkable accomplishment.

Now, I don't believe in surviving for the sake of the past. I want to know who we are today and what we can become as we seek to fill a need in our society.

There is little question that when Wilson began, in 1869, there was a desperate need for liberal arts education for women at the baccalaureate level equal to that available to men. Wilson was the first college for women chartered in Pennsylvania, and the fourth or fifth in the nation, that began as a full-fledged baccalaureate-degree granting college as opposed to a female seminary.

Education, other than at a finishing school, simply was not available to women. Gratefully that is not the case today. Nearly every one of the nation's 3000 institutions of higher education admits women. Do we still need women's colleges? I would say so, most emphatically. On the basis of research done in this decade, there is compelling evidence that women's colleges do the very best job of preparing women for careers.

In two major studies done by Elizabeth Tidball, of George Washington University, women's colleges were the most productive in educating women for Ph.D.s in the sciences. Graduates of women's colleges were, she found, six times more likely to receive doctorates in the sciences and five times as likely in the natural sciences. They were twice as likely to go to medical schools. Why? While we have no certain answers to that question, we do know that the personal, intimate nature of the education assures individualized attention.

We know women's colleges tend to have more women on the faculty who act as role models. We know that the environment encourages women in non-traditional fields, such as the sciences, far more effectively. A 1968 study by the Women's College Coalition surveyed graduates of women's colleges from the classes of 1967 to 1977. Of the 1967 women's college graduates working in 1985, 28% were earning more than $35,000 per year, compared to only 8% for all who graduated.

The profile of a women's college graduate, according to the survey, reveals a person who is employed full time, has a graduate degree, is married, has or plans to have children, earns between $20,000 to $30,000 a year, has achieved recognition in her career and is involved with her college. If she were to choose, she would go to a women's college again.

Wilson College is proud to remain a women's college on the undergraduate residential level. The leadership opportunities and the small classes are proven when we note that 96% of our graduates who so choose are accepted into professional or graduate schools. The success rate is superior. It is no wonder that our alumnae defended and stood by their college 10 years ago. They knew the liberal arts education they received was a rare gift indeed in today's world. **(end)**

***The Chronicle of Higher Education*, March 21, 1990, "The Renaissance of Wilson College, a Financial and Academic Success" by Julie L. Nicklin quoted in full. (Reprint permission granted)**

"Wilson College occupies a unique place in the history of American higher education. It is believed to be the only college ever ordered to remain open by a court of law. Nearly 11 years ago Wilson's Trustees voted to close the institution's doors forever. Enrollment at the small—some would say tiny—liberal arts college for women had declined from a high of 722 to 236. More than half of the nearly $10 million endowment had been used to pay for day-to-day operations. Prospects were so bleak that half of the 44 faculty members had found other jobs, and the admissions and fundraising offices were shut down. And an accreditation team criticized its curriculum as "too traditional."

But not everyone associated with Wilson was preparing eulogies. A group of alumnae was preparing a lawsuit to keep the College open after a rigid and unimaginative administration, they charged, let it fall apart. Franklin County Judge John W. Keller, citing more than 100 facts in the longest court decision he says he has ever written, ruled in favor of the alumnae.

The Endowment

That's where the story of Wilson College's success begins. Today, Wilson's full-time enrollment is 176, with more than 600 additional part-time students enrolled in evening courses. More aggressive fundraising has increased annual giving to $1 million. The general endowment has grown to $6.2 million, a $1.1 million physical plant endowment has been created and the College's operating budget has been balanced for the past eight years.

Perhaps most important, the College's programs have been transformed to meet the changing interests and ages of its students. "As painful as the near-closing of the College was, the experience has had a 'positive effect' on the institution," says Mary- Linda Merriam, Wilson's President. "It was a very mixed blessing."

Ms. Merriam has been guiding Wilson's rebirth since becoming President in 1981. Before she came, the new Trustees had begun a major overhaul of the College's curriculum, which eventually reduced the number of programs from 22 to 13. Unpopular majors were thrown out and new ones—business administration, equestrian studies, and veterinary medical technology—were added.

In what some say was an unconventional move, Ms. Merriam proposed that Wilson also create a division of continuing studies through which both men and women could earn an associate degree in such disciplines as accounting and business communications. The idea met some resistance from alumnae who thought their reasons for saving Wilson— preserving women's education, in particular—were being undermined because men would be admitted and their beloved Wilson would be turned into a community college.

But College officials and alumnae now agree that Wilson has become a blend of two complementary parts—the women's college and the division of continuing studies. The program was dependent upon male students, who made up the majority of the 50 who enrolled in 1982, the program's first year. But now women constitute 75 per cent of the 616 students enrolled.

The Women's College Coalition applauds the steps Wilson has taken to preserve itself as a women's institution. Two other women's colleges, Chatham and Mills, are currently considering proposals to become coeducational to overcome their financial difficulties.

"Wilson exemplifies what can be done when an institution that is committed to women makes a decision that they want to thrive, prosper and succeed," says Peter Mirijanian, the group's associate director. "Wilson's continuing studies division," he adds, "lays the groundwork for the College's continued success. Studies show that by 2000, more than half of the nation's college students will be in their mid-to-late 20s."

Wilson was founded by Presbyterian ministers in 1869 as the first degree-granting college for women in Pennsylvania. Now more than half of Wilson's students graduate in the physical and life sciences. A 1988 College Board survey of students nationwide showed that Wilson graduates were happier with their education than many of their counterparts elsewhere.

Ask some students here why and they'll tell you: The strong concentration on academics, the small size that allows students to know each other well, the supportive faculty—and the decreased pressure on appearance because men aren't always around. Their only complaint is the dining-hall food.

Ice Cream and Flagellum

"My professors are my best friends," says Cassandra Semple, a biology major. "Nowhere else would you have professors take you out to dinner or ice cream or answer the phone at 10:00 o'clock at night to explain 'flagellum.'"

Although Wilson officials have discussed admitting men full-time, they have no present plans to do so, Ms. Merriam says, "because the qualities of an all-women's institution are too valuable to lose.

"Wilson's supportive environment offers more leadership opportunities and role models than a coeducational college," she says, a fact that she believes accounts for the nearly 96 per cent of its graduates who are accepted when they apply to professional or graduate schools.

In Wilson's future, Ms. Merriam envisions 1,000 students enrolled in the continuing studies program and nearly 300 in the women's college. Approximately 60 per cent of the 6,000 Wilson alumnae throughout the United States and abroad actively support the campus, Ms. Merriam says. Alumnae donations account for half of the annual fund, many alumnae place students in internships and jobs, and an "Aunt Sarah" program—named for Sarah Wilson, who donated funds to start the College—matches a "secret pal" alumna with a new student.

One of the forces behind the College's success is Carol Tschop, a 1972 Wilson alumna, who was a member of the Save Wilson Committee in 1979. Ms. Tschop, who is now Wilson's Vice-President for Admissions and College Advancement, makes her message to prospective students clear: "We're back," she says. "We're new and improved, and better than ever." (p. A3) **(end)**

Wilson ranked 8th among Northeast liberal arts colleges, Sunday *Patriot-News*, Harrisburg, Pennsylvania. Sunday, October 7, 1990, by Wythe Keever. (Reprint permission granted) Quoted in part:

Wilson College in Chambersburg—for the second consecutive year—has been ranked among the best liberal arts colleges in the Northeast by *U.S. News & World Report*. The magazine's special edition, "America's Best Colleges," which will be available at newsstands tomorrow, ranked Wilson eighth among 73 regional liberal arts colleges in the northeastern U.S. Harvard was listed as the nation's best university by the magazine, the school has received that honor several times since *U.S. News & World Report* started its ranking in 1983.

"We measure our success as a College by the success of our students and graduates," said Mary-Linda Merriam, Wilson President. "Wilson's listing in 'America's Best Colleges' affirms what our alumnae tell us." **(end)**

In an article entitled "Wilson College survives against odds," *Intelligencer Journal*, **Lancaster, Pennsylvania, May 24, 1989,** there were several points worth noting. In one quote I said, and still believe to this day that "I never felt we would not make it. I never thought for a moment we would not succeed," said Mary-Linda Merriam, President of Wilson since 1981. In point of fact, the college's resilience and restructuring mirrored the experience of other small liberal arts colleges facing financial hardships in the last two decades and into this very day in 2020. "It's a wonderful example of an institution overcoming adversity with ... leadership and commitment to an ideal," said Allan Splete, President of the Council of Independent Colleges. Some 270 colleges, most with enrollments of less than 5,000, belong to the Washington-based organization. "It's very difficult to kill a liberal arts college," said Richard F. Rosser, President of the National Association of Independent Colleges and Universities in Washington. "That's one of the reasons they've survived all these years."

Letter from President Merriam to the Alumnae and Friends of the College, November 15, 1990: (in part)

Dear Alumnae(i) and Friends of Wilson College,

With a mixture of sadness and excitement, I am writing to tell you that I have accepted a new presidency. On Wednesday, November 14th, the Board of Trustees of Moore College of Art and Design voted to offer me the Presidency, effective on July 1, 1991 ...

Are you as amazed as I am that on June 30, 1991, I will have been your President for ten years? These ten years have been the most joyous and challenging years of my life. When I came to Wilson, there were many doubts expressed and unexpressed about our life span as a liberal arts college for women. Today, ten years later, because of your strength and undaunted love for Wilson, doubts have become thoughts of the past. You have made higher education history!

In so many ways our College is in a strong position as it is based for a new Presidency:

- With James Applegate as Acting Dean, the new President will be able to choose a Dean.

- Several years will elapse before the launching of the next major endowment campaign. This will give the new President time to settle in.

- 1990 was the second consecutive year that Wilson has been listed in the top ten regional liberal arts colleges published in *U.S. News and World Report*.

- Enrollment in headcount is at an all-time high of 943, with the SAT scores for our entering freshmen class averaging 1019—higher than many of our competitors in the ranks of other women's colleges.

- Wilson is first among the women's colleges and eighth in the nation among all colleges and universities for percentage of alumnae giving—59.2%.

- We have paid back the $470,000 to the restricted endowment (borrowed during the years of reorganization (1979-81); reduced the plant fund deficit, and eliminated the cumulative operating deficit of $56,992. Total debt service primarily on Rosencrans, Disert and Prentis is

Chapter Five: Securing the Future: 1981-1989

> $116,000 a year on an annual operating budget of over $6 million.
>
> I am endlessly grateful to each of you for ten marvelous years ... Wilson College will always be a part of my life—as the daughter of a Wilson alumna and as an honorary alumna.
>
> With affection,
>
> Mary-Linda Merriam **(end)**

In 1990, I had begun to feel that it was time to think about new leadership for the college. I had been privileged to have spectacular teamwork among trustees, alumnae, faculty, administrators, and staff. With a multitude of small donors and careful financial management and some great good luck, we had established a base upon which the next President could attract major donors to move the College forward—especially by building the endowment. That happened!

The one area which we were not able to meet our own goals was the enrollment of traditionally aged women who would be in residence. It was time to have someone else try their hand at that challenge.

Sharing with the Executive Committee of the Board of Trustees in 1990 that I would begin seeking another college presidency, I was committed to giving them as much notice as possible so that they could begin a search for a new President for Wilson. An offer from Moore College of Art and Design came in the fall 1990, and in the spring 1991, Wilson named a new President.

I made the decision to leave Wilson at the end of ten years with the knowledge that there was a sufficiently strong foundation for the College to move ahead in all areas. Certainly, there were still going to be challenges—some issues we had left unresolved.

With new presidents come inevitable changes and the need to distinguish oneself from one's predecessor. Dr. Bletz did all he could to insure that his staff would be saved. Regrettably, they were not all able to stay since we had an operating deficit of $500,000 that had to be managed in 1981-82, and not all of his staff had the skill sets I needed. On my end, a budget I thought was balanced for Dr. Gwen Jensen's first year was not. She, too, had staffing changes.

What I didn't realize was that making a decision with your head was not the same as making it with your heart. I grieved leaving that College for many months. I well remember Dr. Jensen, the President-Elect, saying, "well, of course, you will be at the inauguration" and my saying, "no— only if you want a person on the stage weeping her heart out." It was as if I were turning over my baby to another mother! Strange, but true! My life had been completely consumed by the College for ten years. Letting go was difficult beyond my wildest imagination.

I recovered in time—10 years later—for Dr. Edmundson's inauguration and Dr. Jensen and I attended it; all three of us "wore bells" for Dr. Mistick's!

The College has moved forward. Indeed, each of us stood on the shoulders of those who had preceded us. We all had good shoulders upon which to stand! I am eternally grateful to each and every trustee, alumna, administrator, staff member, faculty member and student who played a part in continuing the legacy of Wilson College. Indeed, sustaining and growing this college took a village!

EPILOGUE

A dear friend and supporter of Wilson College in Chambersburg once said to me, "You know, Mary-Linda, in this life you are either going from glory to glory or one darn thing to another!" Wilson College has gone from glory to glory while facing into and meeting the challenges of "one darn thing to another"!

Following Dr. Bletz's two-year term, the college has been fortunate to have had a series of presidents with long tenures: Merriam (Armacost), Jensen, and Edmundson each ten years; Mistick, eight years. A small college needs continuity in order to solidify advances. It was also important for each of us to build upon successes, address the weaknesses left for us, and meet the new challenges that inevitably come along. That has happened.

A fair summary of the challenges faced by each of us would be twofold: (1) placing and/or maintaining the College on a solid financial footing; and (2) growing the enrollment. In short, sustainability!

Each president supplied the information that follows.

GWENDOLYN EVANS JENSEN – 1991-2001

Dr. Jensen came to Wilson from having been Provost and Dean of Marietta College in Ohio. Prior to her position at Marietta, which also included being Professor of History, she was Vice-President for Academic Affairs and Professor of History at Western State College of Colorado for three years; and for seven years, Dean of the Graduate School and

Professor of History at the University of New Haven. She had served in consultant-evaluator and a member of the Review Committee on the North Central Accrediting Association and as Chair of the Deans' Task Force of the Council of Independent Colleges. Dr. Jensen earned the Ph.D. in History from the University of Connecticut; the M.A. in history from Trinity College, Hartford; and a B.A. in English from the University of Hartford. She also attended Connecticut College for Women and Cedar Crest College.

Major accomplishments:

- Through the beneficence of a major donor along with many others, and an emphasis on planned giving, the endowment grew from close to $6 million in 1991 to around $34 million in 2001.

- Creation of the Hankey Center for the Education of Women located in the former President's House. The Center is also the home of the C. Elizabeth Boyd Archives.

- Renovation of Sharpe House, now the President's House.

- Becoming a part of the NCAA, Division III, with the development of the athletic program, adding basketball, gymnastics and soccer.

- Continued the development of the equestrian program and the medical veterinary technology program with the building of a large arena and a new VMT facility.

- Reinstated electing members to Phi Beta Kappa annually.

- Created the Center for Sustainable Living and the Fulton Farm and added an environmental major and minor by utilizing the farm and the College's strengths in the sciences.

- Began an endowment for a faculty chair in philosophy and included a faculty chair in music in the capital campaign.

- Restored the organ and established the Van Loy annual organ concert.

- The Disert scholarships were reconfigured to support student research.

- Established the Women with Children program—now called the Single Parent Scholars Program—made possible by an Eden Hall Foundation gift for dorm renovation and the locally acclaimed Child Care Center that had been established in 1986.

- Created the Lenfest Commons by renovating McElwain and Davison Halls to create a vibrant student center.

LORNA DUPHINEY EDMUNDSON – 2001-2011

President Edmundson came to Wilson with thirty years of experience in higher education. She served as President of the Association of Vermont Independent Colleges and Trinity College of Vermont. Dr. Edmundson was a J. William Fulbright Research scholar to Japan and spent a year as a Visiting Scholar in Teaching and Academic leadership at Columbia University. She held senior leadership posts at the American University in Paris; Columbia University's Teachers College School of General Studies and Columbia College; Marymount and Colby-Sawyer Colleges. Dr. Edmundson graduated from Columbia University's Teachers College; Columbia Graduate School of Business's Executive program in Accounting and Finance; Boston College and Rhode Island College. She also studied at the University of Paris.

Major accomplishments:

- Increased the endowment from $34 million in 2001 to over $70 million in 2011 through the Wilson with Confidence Capital Campaign.

- Established the Strategic Innovation Fund which supported more than 30 proposals from faculty and staff designed to improve the teaching/learning environment.

- Named #1 as a Best Buy for students and cited for eight consecutive years as Top Tier/Best Value College in the north by *U.S. News and World Report.*

- Reduced employee attrition from 27% to 8.25%—beating the 15% industry-wide benchmark.

- Introduced Wilson's first Masters' Degree program in Education and strengthened the Women with Children program. Launched new interdisciplinary majors in Equine Studies, Journalism, and Environmental Science and Sustainability (first begun as a disciplinary major in 1990s.)

- Founded the Women's Institute for Math, Science and Technology, with funds from the Richard Lansbury Foundation.

- Established the National Center for Women and Children and hosted the first national Conference on Women and Children.

- Established a close working relationship between the Fulton Center for Sustainability, begun in the 1990s, and the new Harry R. Brooks Complex for Science, Math and Technology, emphasizing cooperative teaching and learning relationships among the faculty and students.

- Established the Global Citizenship Initiative with start-up funding from the Henry Luce and Heinz Foundations. Initiated faculty study tours to Asia and became the only small college to win an award from the Henry Luce Foundation. Created agreements/programs for global/cross cultural exchange in Japan, South Korea, Saudi Arabia, Armenia, Hong Kong, China, and Ireland with students coming to campus from 17 countries.

- Renovated and opened the new Lenfest Student Commons and Hankey Center archival facility with funds raised by President Jensen.

- Renovated the Fulton Farm barn and farmhouse.

- Significantly reduced deferred maintenance, and was one of the first colleges in the region to conduct a campus-wide energy audit to reduce cost.

- Designed, funded and built the 75,000 square foot, $25 million Harry R. Brooks Complex for Science, Mathematics and Technology. Earned the LEED GOLD certification for environmental excellence—unusual for a small college.

BARBARA K. MISTICK – 2011-2019

Dr. Mistick joined the Wilson community after having served with distinction as President and Director of the Carnegie Library of Pittsburgh. Prior to her position at Carnegie Library she was Distinguished Service Professor of Entrepreneurship and Public Policy at the H.J. Heinz School of Public Policy and Management at Carnegie Mellon University; and for eight years, Director of the E-Magnify Women's Business Center and Associate Professor of Entrepreneurship at Seton Hill University. A seasoned entrepreneur and advocate she has been the recipient of numerous honors and awards, including recognition from the U.S. Small Business Administration, The Girl Scouts of America and the University of Pittsburgh. Dr. Mistick has also been recognized by the Yunan Provincial Library, China, for her contributions to libraries world-wide. In addition, she is the co-author of *"Stretch: How to Future-Proof Yourself for Tomorrow's Workplace,"* among the CEO Reads top ten best sellers. During her tenure at Wilson College, she served as Board Chair of the Association of Independent Colleges and Universities of Pennsylvania, Association of Presbyterian Colleges and Universities, and on the Executive Committee of the Council of Independent Colleges. Dr. Mistick received her Doctor of Management from Case Western Reserve University; an M.B.A. from the University of Pittsburgh; and a B.S. from Carlow University.

Major Accomplishments:

- Architect of the "Wilson Today" strategic plan, transforming Wilson College from a small women's undergraduate college to a fully coeducational institution with an enrollment of almost 1,500 students, an increase of over 150%.

- Expanded and revitalized academic offerings to include many new undergraduate programs, including a division of health sciences and an expansion of animal studies, ten graduate programs, online courses, several advanced certifications, and academic partnerships with universities and educational institutions around the globe.

- Launched the "Wilson Value Equation," with a tuition reset, financial literacy programming, and the establishment of the first-in-the-nation student debt loan buyback program. Wilson is now recognized as a "tuition hero" college and has secured multi-year status with *U.S. News and World Report* as a "Best Value" college.

- Established formal dual enrollment agreements with area high schools, making it easier for 11th and 12th grade students to enroll and earn college credit; added dual admission agreements with local community colleges; added matriculation articulation agreements with Vermont Law School and Widener University Commonwealth Law; added new exchange agreement with Hannam University, Korea.

- Established the One-Stop Student Services Center, merging financial aid, billing and registration.

- Revitalized the campus, with fundraising campaigns that engaged more donors than ever before in campus improvement plans for reimagining the John Stewart Memorial Library and a new Veterinary Education Center. In addition, two residence halls were renovated and upgraded; a new student center and fitness facilities were completed; extensive campus pedestrian safety and streetscape improvements were undertaken in partnership with the Borough of Chambersburg; a new entrance now leads to a new academic quad and green space; Patterson lounge and board room have had a total renovation that includes state of the art technology; dining facilities have been upgraded; and two new bridges provide access over the Conococheague, one pedestrian and one vehicular.

- A long-term lease was established with the Borough of Chambersburg for Henninger Field, paving the way for the renovation of a historic field to serve as the home of Wilson Phoenix Baseball.

- The awarding of a highly competitive U.S. Department of Education, Title III, strengthening institutions grant has provided critical resources for technology upgrades; academic support services; and enhanced staff professionalism. A Department of Justice grant was awarded to expand Title IX services. An Andrew W. Mellon grant provided funds to assist in the establishment of a Wilson Writing Academy.

- Middle States Accreditation has been reaffirmed with commendation; Nursing programs have become accredited; and Wilson's American Veterinary Medical Association accreditation has been renewed.

- NCAA Division III athletics have been enhanced with the addition of men's sports. Wilson now offers ten sports for men and women and recently moved into the Colonial States

Athletic Conference in fulfillment of strategic plan to improve the student athletic experience. Athletic Competitiveness has been improved with some teams now participating in post-season play.

- A new College-wide identity campaign was completed.
- Wilson's Women with Children program has been rebranded as our Single Parent Scholars Program and was featured on NPR's "All Things Considered."
- The College's Sesquicentennial Anniversary has been launched, with two years of celebration planned.

THE FUTURE

Reading the history of Wilson College, there have always been challenges typical of small colleges going back to the 1890's. The two decades that seem to this author the most problematic were the 1890's and the 1970's. Enrollments were down and the financial situation precarious. The speech of the President in 1892 read almost identically to the one I gave to the faculty in 1981 as we both attempted to lay out the realities!

The Challenge

For decades, analysts of higher education have predicted many small college closings that did not take place in the numbers that were stated. However, we are now facing a time where this may become a reality. The three states with the largest number of small colleges are Massachusetts, New York, and Pennsylvania. Massachusetts is facing a sea change in higher education.

An article by Michael Damiano in the February 2019 issue of *Boston Magazine*, chronicles the financial woes of several small colleges. For example, Hampshire College will not be accepting a freshmen class in the fall 2019 and will be looking for a partner. Newbury College is closing at the end of this semester. Mount Ida College, 119 years old and with

1,000 students, is closing at the end of this semester with The University of Massachusetts purchasing the real estate of Mount Ida and assuming the $75 million debt, while guaranteeing the students acceptance at UMass Dartmouth. (*Boston Magazine*, p. 68)

> "After decades of unfettered growth, higher education, especially in New England, is tipping into a sharp decline. Enrollment is falling, skepticism about the value of a college education is soaring, and tuitions, which have been rising steadily for decades, seem to have reached the limits of what the public can pay. Over the past four years, eastern Massachusetts alone has seen eight colleges shut down or merge with larger institutions, including Wheelock College, which became a new school within Boston University. Last December, within a matter of days, news broke that Newbury College in Brookline and the College of St. Joseph in Vermont would likely shut down after the spring 2019 semester." (*Boston Magazine*, p. 67)

The 2008 recession had an effect on both incomes and birthrates. The number of high school graduates is in decline. The competition for a decreasing pool of students from the middle class and upper middle class that can pay tuition and fees is beyond fierce. As a result, the net tuition income (tuition minus institutional financial aid) is declining precipitously. Damiano notes that some colleges are recruiting students just for the price of room and board. The tuition discount is well above 50% for many.

According to Damiano, in the fall of 2018 there were 1.9 million fewer students enrolled in higher education than just seven years earlier. Some potential students did not see the point of acquiring so much debt. There are now more less expensive post-secondary option on-line or shorter term ...

There will be plenty of challenges going forward for the next President!

The Hope and The Promise

Looking back at the accomplishments of the past 40 years, the inescapable conclusion is that this college has benefited from the dedication, hard work, commitment, and plain old-fashioned love of its alumnae, trustees, faculty, students, staff, and administration. That is the hope and the promise for the future. We all stand on the shoulders of those women forty years who, driven by passion and blessed with the ability to work both hard and smart, assured that we have the College today.

On May 29, 1988, the Reverend Virginia Leopold, '63, gave the sermon during Reunion Weekend. I quote a paragraph that has stayed with me these many years. It seems like a fitting ending to this book:

> "LIFE is a pattern in which our lives weave together, touching, affecting, influencing and enmeshing, so that what we do, or say, what we produce or espouse, is NOT just our own business, but is the very woof and warp of a commonly lived existence. Like a pebble that is dropped into a pool, the ripples stretch further and further out, expanding. One small stone can disquiet the whole pond. That's influence. But this image of threads in a tapestry shows how we are all being woven together, with each thread important to a pattern. This pattern is the history of our lifetimes, but also the pattern that we affect in the history of the world. And it brings to mind that the tapestry has a designer—an artist—a master weaver who intertwines all the threads to produce a masterpiece."

We are all indebted to the women—students and alumnae—who threw those first pebbles back in 1979. They did, indeed, cause ripples and look at us now!

ABOUT THE AUTHOR

Dr. Armacost received her Ph.D. in Speech Communication from The Pennsylvania State University in 1970 and became a research associate in the College of Human Development at Penn State. In 1972, she went to Emerson College in Boston where she began her administrative career. She developed the first continuing studies program; served as vice president for administration and special assistant to the president. In 1979, she became assistant to the president (Dr. John Silber) at Boston University. She holds Honorary Degrees from Wilson College (Doctor of Laws) and Carroll College (Doctor of Humanities)

In 1981, she assumed the presidency of Wilson College and served in that capacity for ten years. During the Wilson presidency; she was president of the Association of Presbyterian Colleges and Universities and the first chairman of the Committee on Higher Education for the Presbyterian Church (USA) as well as holding leadership positions in the Women's College Coalition and the Pennsylvania Association for Colleges and University and active on a number of boards. She is President Emerita.

From 1991 to 1993, she was the president of Moore College of Art and Design in Philadelphia and again as interim president in 1998-1999. She is President Emerita of Moore College of Art and Design.

In 1993 she married Dr. Peter Armacost and spent the next nine years as a consultant, primarily in the areas of board development and strategic planning. She facilitated the Pew Higher Education Roundtables from 1994-2000 as a part of the Institute for Research in Higher Education, the University of Pennsylvania; worked with the liberal arts colleges and comprehensive universities as a part of the American Council of Education's Kellogg Grant on Transformational Change; and was a primary researcher and an author on the Teagle Foundation study of Teagle-funded college and seminary collaborations.

From 2002-2018 she served as an Adjunct Professor, Associated Faculties, Graduate School of Education, Executive Doctoral Program, University of Pennsylvania 2002-2018; part of the core graduate faculty (2013) and taught leadership and ethics in the master's program 2012-2015.

In 2003, Dr. Armacost moved to Lahore, Pakistan, where Dr. Peter Armacost was the Rector of Forman Christian College (a Chartered University). In Pakistan she served as a resource person from 2007-2010 and Senior Fellow from 2010-2012 to the Higher Education Commission; an interviewer for the Fulbright Commission (2003-2009); and as a consultant to several private and public universities in the areas of governance and academic affairs. They lived in Lahore, Pakistan from 2003-2012.

Dr. Armacost has served on the boards of Monmouth University (NJ) and Randolph-Macon Women's College and as Consultant to the Forman Christian College (a Chartered University) Board of Directors and Board of Governors in Lahore, Pakistan.

Made in the USA
Coppell, TX
20 December 2020